I0094875

The Republican Party and the War on Poverty: 1964–1981

New Perspectives on the American Presidency
Series Editors: Michael Patrick Cullinane and Sylvia Ellis,
University of Roehampton

Published titles
*Constructing Presidential Legacy: How We Remember the
American President*
Edited by Michael Patrick Cullinane and Sylvia Ellis

Presidential Privilege and the Freedom of Information Act
Kevin M. Baron

Donald Trump and American Populism
Richard S. Conley

Trump's America: Political Culture and National Identity
Edited by Liam Kennedy

Obama v. Trump: The Politics of Rollback
Clodagh Harrington and Alex Waddan

Obama's Fractured Presidency: Policies and Politics
Edited by François Vergniolle de Chantal

The Republican Party and the War on Poverty: 1964–1981
Mark McLay

Forthcoming titles
Midterms and Mandates
Patrick Andelic, Mark McLay and Robert Mason

Harry S. Truman and Higher Education
Rebecca Stone

Series website: https://edinburghuniversitypress.com/new-
perspectives-on-the-american-presidency.html

THE REPUBLICAN PARTY AND THE WAR ON POVERTY: 1964–1981

Mark McLay

EDINBURGH
University Press

Edinburgh University Press is one of the leading university presses in the UK. We publish academic books and journals in our selected subject areas across the humanities and social sciences, combining cutting-edge scholarship with high editorial and production values to produce academic works of lasting importance. For more information visit our website: edinburghuniversitypress.com

© Mark McLay, 2021, 2023

Edinburgh University Press Ltd
The Tun – Holyrood Road
12(2f) Jackson's Entry
Edinburgh EH8 8PJ

First published in hardback by Edinburgh University Press 2021

Typeset in 11/13 Adobe Sabon by
IDSUK (DataConnection) Ltd

A CIP record for this book is available from the British Library

ISBN 978 1 4744 7552 5 (hardback)
ISBN 978 1 4744 7553 2 (paperback)
ISBN 978 1 4744 7554 9 (webready PDF)
ISBN 978 1 4744 7555 6 (epub)

The right of Mark McLay to be identified as the author of this work has been asserted in accordance with the Copyright, Designs and Patents Act 1988, and the Copyright and Related Rights Regulations 2003 (SI No. 2498).

Contents

Acknowledgements

The Republican Party and the War on Poverty: 1964–1981 is the end of a long research process during which countless people have helped in their own way. In completing this manuscript, it gives me great pleasure to look back on my friends, family, students and fellow academics, who have shaped the journey to completing my first book.

This research would not have proved possible without funding assistance from a variety of institutions. I was honoured to receive the Harry Middleton Fellowship in Presidential Studies from the Lyndon Baines Johnson Foundation in Austin, Texas. Their generous support allowed me to visit numerous libraries across the United States. I was also fortunate to attend a seminar at the LBJ Library which featured former Johnson aides, Harry Middleton and Larry Temple, discussing their experience of 1968. It was a learning experience that has stayed with me as I have written this book. I also benefited greatly due to funding support from the Rockefeller Archive Center in New York, the Gerald R. Ford Presidential Foundation in Michigan, the Roosevelt Study Center in the Netherlands (twice), and the Eccles Centre at the British Library, UK.

The nature of researching abroad means that you have a very limited amount of time to find the documents that you require and therefore the whole project can be thrown off course if that time is not maximised. Thankfully, I was lucky to benefit from the expertise of excellent archivists and this book is indebted to them for their knowledge, meticulous nature and – most of all – their kindness. In particular, I want to thank Allen Fisher at the LBJ Library, Kathryn Stallard at the A. Frank Smith Jr. Library, Meghan Lee and Pamla Eisenberg at the Richard M. Nixon Library, Kary Charlebois at the Ronald W. Reagan Library, Bill McNitt and Jeremy Schmidt at the Gerald R. Ford Library, Bruce Kirby at the Library of Congress, Kirsten Nyitray at the Frank Melville, Jr. Library, and Nancy Adgent at the Rockefeller Archive Center. Furthermore, I am grateful to the staff at the Albert and Shirley Small Special Collections Library, University of Virginia and the Bentley Historical Library, University of Michigan. I was very fortunate to twice visit the charming town of Middelburg, the Netherlands while researching at the Roosevelt Study Center. The RSC staff could not have been more helpful or friendlier. Finally, thanks to Cara Rodway and Francisca Fuentes at the British Library in London.

I would also like to place on record my thanks to the donors of the Edward W. Brooke papers for allowing me access to his papers at a time when access was restricted before the former senator sadly passed away in January 2015.

I am thankful to the thriving American History community in the United Kingdom. I am grateful to the following people who took time to offer kind words or advice about my research: Patrick Andelic, Dom Barker, Nigel Bowles, Gareth Davies, Rhodri Jeffreys-Jones, Fabian Hilfrich, Fraser McCallum, Mitch Robertson, Dan Rowe, Joe Street and, of course, Joe Ryan-Hume. Most notably, I am forever indebted to Frances Houghton and Malcolm Craig, two wonderful friends and even better scholars. Finally, I am thankful to a number of historians, and their excellent scholarship, without whom this work would not have been possible.

This work has also undoubtedly been helped by the delightful colleagues I have kept at Glasgow Caledonian University and the University of Glasgow. Even more so, teaching enthusiastic and intelligent students over the past decade has often been the joy that has accompanied the long process of writing this book. Special mention is given to Sarah and Eilean who are two future academic stars in the making should they choose to pursue such a path.

ACKNOWLEDGEMENTS

I am especially grateful to my editors Michael Cullinane and Sylvia Ellis, who believed in this project and were a continual source of encouragement. Moreover, both Sarah Foyle and Caroline Richards at Edinburgh University Press have been instrumental in the delivery and presentation of this book. Of course, any mistakes that remain are mine and mine alone.

I have also had the incredible luck of having Robert Mason as my PhD supervisor and continued academic mentor. Robert is one of the kindest people I have met and his continued support (not to mention analytical rigour in proofreading chapters) is a huge part of the reason that this book ever materialised.

Thanks also to my wonderful friends and family who have kept me sane over the past few years. I mention especially my brothers, Andrew and Craig, and, of course, Fraser, the best friend anyone could ask for; and, not to forget, my beloved companion, Lyndon.

To my mum and dad, who have given me everything while letting me plot my own path, I owe special thanks.

And to Danielle. I thought completing my first book would rank as the most joyous moment in any year, but becoming your husband was easily the happiest day of my life. Thank you for your continued love and support; you bring a smile to my face every day.

Abbreviations

AFDC	Aid to Families with Dependent Children
BHO	Barack Obama
CAA	Community Action Agencies
CAP	Community Action Programs
CSA	Community Services Administration
EITC	Earned Income Tax Credit
EOA	Economic Opportunity Act
ERTA	Economic Recovery Tax Act
ESEA	Elementary and Secondary Education Act
FAP	Family Assistance Plan
FDR	Franklin D. Roosevelt
GHWB	George H. W. Bush
GOP	Grand Old Party
GRF	Gerald R. Ford
HEW	Health, Education, and Welfare, Department of
HIA	Human Investment Act
HRF	Human Renewal Fund
HUD	Department of Housing and Urban Development
IYC	Industrial Youth Corps
JFK	John F. Kennedy
LBJ	Lyndon B. Johnson
NAACP	National Association for the Advancement of Colored People
NAR	Nelson A. Rockefeller
NYC	Neighborhood Youth Corps

ABBREVIATIONS

OBRA	Omnibus Budget and Reconciliation Act
OEO	Office of Economic Opportunity
PRP	Papers of the Republican Party
RCC	Republican Coordinating Committee
Rep.	Representative
RGA	Republican Governors Association
RMN	Richard M. Nixon
RNC	Republican National Committee
RWR	Ronald W. Reagan
SFC	Senate Finance Committee
SSI	Supplemental Security Income
STA	Spiro T. Agnew
TAPP	The American Presidency Project
UAC	Urban Affairs Council
VISTA	Volunteers in Service to America

Introduction

Poverty is a partisan issue in the United States. More specifically, the battle over how to alleviate poverty is a key dividing line between America's two major parties. In the twenty-first century, most Democrats believe that the federal government has an obligation not only to keep poor people alive and well fed through temporary help, but to create a fairer society in which those in poverty are given a helping hand – a greater opportunity – to prosper. Conversely, most Republicans believe that government, while it can provide temporary minimal assistance to the poor, should play as small a role as possible to avoid encouraging dependency on government programmes.[1] For the Grand Old Party (GOP), American free enterprise remains the greatest antipoverty solution that humans have yet invented.

This divide on poverty gets to the very heart of the partisanship that has come to define American politics. It is a policy split, yes, but more importantly the poverty clash is symbolic of how partisans view themselves and how they view their opponents. 'Political parties,' journalist Clare Malone observes, 'strive to be something greater than the human beings they're comprised of; they enshrine values and ideologies for the ages.'[2] Regarding poverty, Democrats tend to prioritise compassion, believe that poor people have been dealt a rough hand in life, and they think of Republicans as rich selfish Americans, out of touch with everyday struggles.[3] On the other hand, Republican voters and politicians are more likely to blame poverty on a lack of endeavour, and as such, most GOP adherents believe their Democratic brethren are lazy, hoping for Uncle Sam to come to the rescue rather than pulling themselves up by their own bootstraps.[4] Thus, poverty is not just a political issue between partisans, it is interwoven into their moral values and identity. Moreover, for the past fifty years, the problem of poverty in the United States has become increasingly associated with urban racial minorities. The contrasting racial make-ups of Republican and Democratic voters, whereby GOP voters are roughly 90 per cent white and the Democrats are supported heavily by most racial minority groups, has thus added a further layer to antipoverty politics.[5]

It was not ever thus. Between 1964 and 1981, President Lyndon B. Johnson's War on Poverty played a decisive role in establishing the partisan divide on poverty. For the thirty years prior to Johnson's domestic war, the two parties had begun the process of sorting themselves into liberal and conservative blocs. With the Great Depression dominating political memory, Democrats were the party of Franklin D. Roosevelt's New Deal, fighting for the 'little guy' on Main Street, pitted against the mean-spirited 'country-club Republicans' of Wall Street. In such a context, Democrats dominated. During the New Deal era, the GOP were hamstrung by an image as the 'Party of Privilege'; the party that was forever saying 'no' to Democratic social welfare programmes. Nonetheless, neither party talked explicitly about poverty. It was not until 1964 – when LBJ, as Lyndon B. Johnson was widely known, unexpectedly declared his 'unconditional war on poverty' and passed the Economic Opportunity Act (EOA) – that poverty became a partisan issue.[6] Johnson himself captured the divide that would come to shape American politics, saying of Democrats, 'We are, I think, the party with a heart.'[7]

This book explores the Republican Party's successful challenge to Johnson's War on Poverty. In 1964, LBJ launched his antipoverty effort with high hopes that – in conjunction with the era's other significant social legislation in the areas of civil rights, health care and education – it would help lead the United States towards the 'Great Society' that his administration envisioned. Just seventeen years after the War on Poverty's creation, however, Republican presidents and politicians ensured that it was significantly curtailed. Following Richard Nixon's dismantling of the federal antipoverty apparatus, and Ronald Reagan's significant cuts to social welfare programmes, the federal government's will to do battle with poverty that briefly flourished during the Great Society era was definitively cast aside in favour of market-based solutions. Reagan, delivering a simple obituary for an antipoverty effort that had remained controversial and often unloved during its short history, pithily declared: 'poverty won'.[8]

In the decades since, Reagan's view of the War on Poverty has held sway among policymakers in Washington. From the 1980s onwards, even the Democratic Party has shied away from offering a renewed attack on poverty, instead choosing to focus the bulk of its energies and rhetoric on the middle class, rather than the poor. Writing in 2007, political scientist Mark Smith showed that Republican economic arguments concerning poverty have had a greater effect on government policy than any other GOP political position on social and cultural issues. Smith noted that ever since the Johnson years, government spending exclusively for the poor, such as unemployment insurance, job training and AFDC (Aid to Families with Dependent Children) payments, has decreased. Moreover, the success of Republican arguments has forced Democrats away from a strong antipoverty agenda.[9] In an era of Republican ascendancy, American politicians, on the whole, have not so much declared a ceasefire in the War on Poverty, but appear to have fled the battlefield. Fourteen years on from Smith's work, even while Democrats edge towards a full-throated embrace of the 'income inequality' agenda, little has changed.

The Republican Party and the War on Poverty shows that most elected Republicans opposed the antipoverty effort from its inception in 1964 until its ultimate demise in 1981. At first, this statement may seem unsurprising, but GOP opposition to the War on Poverty stood in contrast to their acceptance of a host of other Great Society legislation, including Medicare and the Elementary and Secondary Education Act (ESEA). Indeed, in recent years scholars have focused on these universal elements of the Great Society that survived – and often grew – during the Republican ascendance in the latter third of the twentieth century. Such works, however, have not fully grappled with why the War on Poverty was such an outlier.[10] This book therefore seeks to better understand the Republican Party's identification of the War on Poverty as the black sheep in the Great Society's legislative flock.

Republican opposition to the War on Poverty occurred in two distinct phases. The first phase lasted from early 1965 through until Nixon's re-election in 1972 and was defined by the GOP's desire to avoid appearing overly negative and further confirming the 'Party of Privilege' moniker. This opposition was often creative, rather than reflexively negative, with GOP politicians stressing their desire not to end the antipoverty impulse but instead to a fight a *better* war on poverty. Republicans even offered their own detailed alternative – the 'Opportunity Crusade'. It was not until Nixon's second term, by which point Americans were suffering during an economic downturn and were more receptive to a conservative anti-'big government' message, that Republicans moved on to the second phase of their opposition. This new phase, which took hold from the beginning of Nixon's second term in 1973 until the passage of Reagan's budget cuts in 1981, saw Republicans forsake creativity and devote their energies to curtailing the antipoverty effort rather than improving it. The Republican embrace of modern conservatism and the ebbing of the Great Society political era is thus evident through the party's evolution on the War on Poverty.

During both phases of opposition, GOP politicians achieved influence in shaping an antipoverty effort that historian Allen Matusow deems 'one of the greatest failures of twentieth-century liberalism'.[11] Nevertheless, Matusow is one among many historians who have failed to consider the Republican Party's role in the War on Poverty's life and political demise. Indeed, historians of the War on Poverty have cited myriad reasons – including racism, Johnson's overpromising rhetoric, and politically unrealistic demands from liberals – to explain the poverty war's failure and yet have ignored the Republican elephant in the room.[12] None has given extensive thought to how elected Republicans were influential in either shaping how the 'war' was fought during the 1960s or how they seized control of its destiny in the 1970s and early 1980s.[13] Given that it was Ronald Reagan's GOP, that – in conjunction with amenable southern Democrats in Congress – ultimately stymied the War on Poverty, this is a remarkable oversight. Had sufficient Republicans

4

been won over to the antipoverty effort to the same extent that they embraced other Great Society programmes, it is likely the War on Poverty would have met a very different political fate. As such, this volume offers a new perspective on the liberal reform era, which challenges previous understandings of why significant elements of that reform failed.

Overall, this book offers three clear conclusions. First, Republican presidents and politicians were a key factor in why the War on Poverty was cut short. Equally, poverty politics played a significant role in defining the GOP during its ascendant rise. During this era, Republican primary and presidential campaigns – not to mention the presidencies themselves – were all impacted by the fraught and ever-shifting political dynamics surrounding the antipoverty effort. Second, during the War on Poverty's lifespan, most Republicans were able to mute their ideological distaste for the antipoverty effort when they believed that outright opposition would hurt them politically. Certainly, they were even willing to offer government-based solutions to fighting poverty, so long as they differed from Democratic proposals. It was only when the political context shifted in the 1970s, with the ebbing of the Great Society era, that the majority of GOP politicians were in favour of abandoning the antipoverty effort. This shows that the Republican Party's rise from the nadir of the 1964 election was built not exclusively on grassroots conservative fervour or on liberal overreach on the part of their Democratic opponents, as many scholars have suggested, but on political pragmatism and savvy.[14] This study consequently finds itself in agreeance with recent scholars who have painted a more nuanced portrait of the 1960s and 1970s Republican Party, rather than the previously conservative-dominated picture.[15] Finally, from the vantage point of 2020, it is clear that Republicans have been the War on Poverty's political victors. Almost forty years on from its ending, GOP politicians still cite Johnson's antipoverty effort as the key example of big government folly, meanwhile, most Americans have agreed, remaining decidedly frosty to any renewed attempt at fighting poverty.

Before considering how leading Republicans challenged the War on Poverty, it is crucial to understand how Republicans conceptualised the antipoverty effort. Essentially, what did Republicans believe the War on Poverty included? Liberal defenders of Johnson's legacy often argue that the War on Poverty included not just the Economic Opportunity Act (EOA) and the subsequent activities of the Office of Economic Opportunity (OEO).[16] Instead, they contest that the War on Poverty included other Great Society legislation, such as Medicare and federal aid to education, which benefited all Americans – including the poor.

Whatever the apparent merits of this conception, this was not how leading Republicans – wilfully or sincerely – perceived the War on Poverty. During the first two years of the War on Poverty, Republicans focused exclusively on those initiatives created by the EOA and run by the OEO when discussing the antipoverty effort. From 1966 onwards, new programmes that tackled urban poverty, such as Model Cities, rent supplements and even a rat extermination bill, were added to the Republican perception of the War on Poverty. Such programmes were controversial due to their association with the black urban poor at a time when frequent race riots and uprisings were triggering a white backlash against further racial progress. It therefore suited Republicans to conceptualise the War on Poverty in a way that linked the whole antipoverty effort with the more controversial urban programmes. For similar reasons, conservative Republicans – led by Reagan – increasingly equated the War on Poverty with growing welfare rolls in the mid-1960s. By the 1970s, welfare was interwoven with every War on Poverty discussion, despite the fact Johnson's legislation had not created the controversial Aid to Families with Dependent Children (AFDC).[17] For the purposes of this book, the term 'War on Poverty' will relate to the narrower Republican definition, rather than the definition put forward by those who include Medicare and federal aid to education.

And who were these Republicans? The typology employed in this book to describe four different groups of Republicans is borrowed from James Reichley's *Conservatives in an Age of Change* (1981). Reichley outlines four groups (from most conservative to most liberal): fundamentalists, stalwarts, moderates and progressives. 'Ideology entered into the formation of each of these groups,' Reichley explains, 'although each also rose out of shared regional and economic interests, personal and what may be called tribal loyalties, and agreements on political strategy.'[18] How leading Republicans engaged with Johnson's War on Poverty and the wider Great Society was often a combination of the factors that Reichley outlines. To avoid confusion, this book uses 'conservatives' rather than 'fundamentalists' as the latter term has since taken on religious connotations in an American political context.

Before outlining their differences, it is worth noting that all four categories of Republicans enjoyed broad agreement on two principles which they saw as separating themselves from Democrats. First, all leading Republicans believed that the federal government was becoming too dominant over state and local governments. Second, they agreed that Democrats tended to ignore private sector solutions to social problems, in favour of more government programmes. Beyond this agreement there were many differences, however, and the following offers a guide to the four diverse groups within the GOP during the era that this book covers:

Conservatives. Conservatives had never accepted the socio-economic legislation passed during the New Deal. They advocated smaller government, particularly in Washington, DC, and longed for a return to a bygone America. Conservatives opposed almost all Great Society legislation, including the civil rights achievements of the Johnson presidency. The only federal domestic spending that conservatives advocated was in relation to law enforcement, which they wished to see strengthened. Often found in the Sunbelt (roughly, the South and Southwest), conservatives possessed great grassroots strength during the Johnson presidency but were not the leading faction in Congress or in governors' mansions. In the 1970s, their strength increased and they would become a dominant force in the GOP by the time of the Reagan Revolution.

Stalwarts. Stalwarts – the heirs of Robert Taft – were dominant in the House and also on the Republican National Committee (RNC) during the 1960s. Fiscally conservative, they still harboured disagreements with New Deal legislation but in reality showed little appetite to return to a United States that did not feature Social Security. Instead, they focused on criticising Democrats for the waste and corruption that they perceived in New Deal and Great Society legislation. Indeed, stalwarts opposed almost all major pieces of Great Society legislation, excepting the two landmark civil rights laws. Often from solid Republican districts in the Midwest and Mountain states, stalwarts were more reluctant to support measures that tackled de facto segregation in the North. Furthermore, given the choice of 'guns or butter', stalwarts would pick guns every time. They, like conservatives, also supported a focus on tougher law enforcement. By the 1980s, stalwarts retained strong influence in the party, although many had ultimately evolved into conservatives for either electoral or ideological reasons.

Moderates. Moderates were mostly likely to occupy governors' mansions – particularly in the electorally important states of the Northeast and Mid-Atlantic, but they also enjoyed decent strength in both chambers of Congress. Less averse to government intervention than stalwarts, moderates felt that many of the intentions in Democratic programmes were sound, but that Republicans could do a much better job of designing and administering them. Accordingly, many moderates had been derogatorily labelled 'me too' Republicans ever since the New Deal. Moderates had a mixed voting record with regard to the Great Society; almost all voted against the War on Poverty but most supported other socioeconomic legislation, such as Medicare and federal aid to education. They were also ardent supporters of all civil rights legislation during the Johnson presidency and feared for the GOP if the party's electoral future depended on capturing the former 'Dixiecrat' vote in the South. They had a relatively strong influence in Congress during the 1960s and early 1970s, but that influence had largely been expunged by the 1980s.

Progressives. Progressives often held positions on socioeconomic legislation that made them seem akin to liberal Democrats. The smallest faction of the four, progressives enjoyed their greatest influence in the Senate particularly after the 1966 elections. Hailing from coastal states, they had supported much of the New Deal and would also vote for most Great Society legislation – the War on Poverty included. Inheritors of Theodore Roosevelt's 1912 campaign for progressive social legislation, they differed from liberal Democrats due to their distaste for 'machine politics' and a belief that Democrats preferred to keep people on welfare so that they remained wedded to the party of FDR. By the end of the period covered by this book, Republican progressives were all but extinct.

This book is a political – rather than a policy – history of the War on Poverty. It is not an exhaustive look at every antipoverty policy between 1964 and 1981. Instead, this study prioritises those policies which were in the news, that invited the most debate among politicians, and which shaped the War on Poverty's overall image. Nor is this work an attempt to pass judgement on the merits of any poverty programme. Rather, it is more concerned with how such programmes shaped, or were shaped by, political considerations.

This study also aims to restore Congress to political narratives of this era. Existing historiography – with notable exceptions – suffers from a lack of studies that fully appreciate Congress's role in shaping policy and politics, preferring instead to focus on presidents, protestors or conservative grassroots organisers. Events beyond Capitol Hill have understandably served to avert many a historian's eye from the important developments that were influenced by the nation's legislative body. While not exclusively focused on Congress, this study will seek to provide a better understanding of congressional developments between 1964 and 1981 – particularly by adding much needed analysis of the Republican contribution. As such, the book focuses on elected Republicans, rather than grassroots activists or Republican-aligned pressure groups. After all, it was these individuals – 'in the arena', as Nixon once wrote – who often had the most direct impact on the War on Poverty's political fate.[19] Equally, while this book is about Republicans, it does not ignore Democrats. Of the Democrats during this era, it is to fair to say that many genuinely believed in the War on Poverty and a government-led endeavour to end want in America. But the party was not immune from political motivations. For electoral reasons, it very much suited Democrats that the GOP remain the Party of Privilege. As such, elected Democrats played an important role in ensuring poverty became and remained a partisan issue.

The Republican Party and the War on Poverty begins in an age of Democratic dominance; it ends in an era of Republican ascendance. It starts with the War on Poverty's launch and concludes with the antipoverty effort's curtailment. By the end, it will be clear that these two significant developments were not independent of one another.

Notes

1. 'Most See Inequality Growing, but Partisans Differ over Solutions', Pew Research Center, 23 January 2014.
2. Clare Malone, 'The End of a Republican Party', *FiveThirtyEight*, 18 July 2016.
3. Scott Clifford, 'Compassionate Democrats and Tough Republicans: How Ideology Shapes Partisan Stereotypes', *Political Behavior*, March 2019; Perry Bacon Jr, 'Democrats Are Wrong About Republicans. Republicans Are Wrong About Democrats', *FiveThirtyEight*, 26 July 2018.
4. 'Partisanship and Political Animosity in 2016', Pew Research Center, 22 June 2016; 'Trends in American Values: 1987–2012', Pew Research Center, 4 June 2012.
5. 'Party Identification Trends, 1992–2014', Pew Research Center, 7 April 2015.
6. Lyndon B. Johnson, Annual Message to the Congress on the State of the Union, 8 January 1964, The American Presidency Project [hereafter TAPP].
7. LBJ quoted in Marvin W. Watson, *Chief of Staff: Lyndon Johnson and His Presidency* (New York: Thomas Dunne Books, 2004), 303.
8. Ronald W. Reagan, State of the Union Address, 25 January 1988, TAPP.
9. Mark A. Smith, *The Right Talk: How Conservatives Transformed the Great Society into the Economic Society* (Princeton, NJ: Princeton University Press, 2007), 5–6.
10. Gareth Davies, *See Government Grow: Education Politics from Johnson to Reagan* (Lawrence, KS: University Press of Kansas, 2007);

Julian E. Zelizer, *The Fierce Urgency of Now: Lyndon Johnson, Congress and the Battle for the Great Society* (New York: Penguin, 2015).

11. Allen J. Matusow, *The Unraveling of America: A History of Liberalism in the 1960s* (New York: Harper & Row, 1984).

12. Gareth Davies, *From Opportunity to Entitlement: The Transformation and Decline of Great Society liberalism* (Lawrence, KS: University Press of Kansas, 1996); Jill Quadagno, *The Color of Welfare: How Racism Undermined the War on Poverty* (New York: Oxford University Press, 1994); Michael K. Brown, *Race, Money and the American Welfare State*, (Ithaca, NY: Cornell University Press, 1999); James T. Patterson, *America's Struggle Against Poverty, 1900–1980* (Cambridge, MA: Harvard University Press, 1994).

13. Lawrence McAndrews' book does, however, engage significantly with Republican presidents and their approaches to poverty; his focus, though, is not on the Republican Party more broadly. McAndrews, *The Presidents and the Poor* (Lawrence, KS: University Press of Kansas, 2018).

14. Mary Brennan, *Turning Right in the Sixties: The Conservative Capture of the GOP* (Chapel Hill, NC: University of North Carolina Press, 1995); Donald T. Critchlow, *The Conservative Ascendancy: How the GOP Right Made Political History* (Cambridge, MA: Harvard University Press, 2007); Nicol Rae, *The Decline and Fall of the Liberal Republicans: From 1952 to the Present* (New York: Oxford University Press, 1989); Lisa McGirr, *Suburban Warriors: The Origins of the New American Right* (Princeton, NJ: Princeton University Press, 2001); Matthew B. Lassiter, *The Silent Majority: Suburban Politics in the Sunbelt South* (Princeton, NJ: Princeton University Press, 2006); Donald T. Critchlow, *Phyllis Schlafly and Grassroots Conservatism: A Woman's Crusade* (Princeton, NJ: Princeton University Press, 2005); Thomas Byrnes Edsall with Mary D. Edsall, *Chain Reaction: The Impact of Race, Rights, and Taxes on American Politics* (New York: Norton, 1992); Dan T. Carter, *From George Wallace to Newt Gingrich: Race in the Conservative Counterrevolution, 1963–1994* (Baton Rouge, LA: Louisiana State University Press, 1996); Rick Perlstein, *Nixonland: The Rise of a President and the Fracturing of America* (New York: Scribner, 2008); John A. Andrew, *Lyndon Johnson and the Great Society* (Chicago: Ivan R. Dee, 1998).

15. Geoffrey Kabaservice, *Rule and Ruin: The Downfall of Moderation and the Destruction of the Republican Party, from Eisenhower to the Tea Party* (New York: Oxford University Press,

2012); Timothy Thurber, *Republicans and Race: the GOP's Frayed Relationship with African Americans, 1945–1974* (Lawrence, KS: University Press of Kansas, 2013); Robert Mason, *The Republican Party and American Politics from Hoover to Reagan* (New York: Cambridge University Press, 2012).

16. Mark K. Updegrove, *Indomitable Will: LBJ in the Presidency* (New York: Crown Publishers, 2012); Joseph A. Califano, *The Triumph and Tragedy of Lyndon Johnson: The White House Years* (New York: Simon & Schuster, 1991).

17. Nonetheless, AFDC grew, in part, as a result of antipoverty workers making the poor more aware of their rights.

18. A. James Reichley, *Conservatives in an Age of Change: The Nixon and Ford Administrations* (Washington, DC: Brookings Institution, 1981), 22–34.

19. Richard Nixon, *In the Arena: A Memoir of Victory, Defeat and Renewal* (New York: HarperCollins, 1990).

1

A familiar trap: the 'Party of Privilege' and the War on Poverty, 1964

Many of the new programmes with which we are to be faced are said to be part of a war on poverty. And who can be against that?[1]

Barry Goldwater, July 1964

Following the 1964 elections – disastrous in almost every conceivable way for the Republican Party – a telling dispute arose between the Grand Old Party (GOP) and the publishing company Harcourt, Brace & World Incorporated. Harcourt, much to Republican chagrin, had been distributing an IQ test for use in school classrooms which included the multiple choice query:

Q. A club that accepts only very rich members is said to be-:
A. (a) snobbish (b) exclusive (c) conservative (d) Republican (e) un-American.

Unsurprisingly, the presence of Option C, and particularly, Option D, drew complaints from Republican voters and politicians across the country, none more so than Minnesota congressman and GOP rising star Al Quie, who wrote directly to the publisher asking for them to remove the question. After a series of fraught exchanges, Harcourt's President eventually agreed to pull the controversial passage from the test, granting the Republicans a rare victory, albeit a hollow one. For while one could interpret the Harcourt row as a mildly humorous incident, it was nonetheless revealing of a serious issue with which Republicans had failed to grapple for over three decades: since the Great Depression, a large tract of voters continued to view the GOP as the Party of Privilege.[2]

Thirty years on, the Democrats remained in the public mind as the party fighting for the 'little guy' and Main Street, while Republicans were the party defending the interests of the country club and Wall Street.[3] Democrats proposed, Republicans opposed. It was a contrast in public perception that had continually frustrated GOP fortunes at the ballot box.

Consequently, Republicans had been put in an awkward position when, in January 1964, President Lyndon B. Johnson used his first State of the Union address to declare an 'unconditional war on poverty', before promptly firing his opening salvo, in the form of the Economic Opportunity Act (EOA) – an omnibus antipoverty bill – to Congress.[4] In the optimistic and hubristic early 1960s – an era when prosperity flowed through the economy and when most Americans had a residual faith in government – to oppose any war on poverty was a politically hazardous position. For a party already associated with privilege and negativism, however, such opposition held particular peril. Nevertheless, casting this undesirable contrast aside, most Republicans quickly baulked at the president's proposal. They believed that Johnson was merely posturing before the electorate, hoping to buy the votes of the poor, just as Republicans alleged the Democrats had been doing since the days of Franklin Roosevelt. Moreover, almost all Republicans were ideologically against any bill that sought to enlarge the federal government and interfere with the private sector. Even those few Republicans who were sympathetic to its goals thought the EOA an insufficient and poorly crafted attempt at fighting poverty. As such, not only did most leading Republicans oppose the War on Poverty as the bill wove its way through Congress, they did so ferociously, meaning that the EOA would ultimately be passed in a partisan atmosphere, unmatched by any other of LBJ's Great Society legislation.[5] Essentially, during the legislative battle, Republicans only confirmed their existing privileged and obstructive image.

The GOP presidential nomination duel that took place between Barry Goldwater and Nelson Rockefeller further entrenched this perception. Goldwater, the conservative who had no interest in fighting a war on poverty, triumphed over the progressive New York governor who was ready to embrace government solutions

14

to alleviate hardship in America. Having voted against the EOA in the Senate, Goldwater doubled down on his opposition to the War on Poverty come the fall campaign. Travelling to Appalachia – the symbolic heart of the antipoverty effort in 1964 – Goldwater denounced Johnson's poverty programme as a fraud, a waste of taxpayer money, and claimed that only the private sector could successfully alleviate poverty. The Arizonan's opposition to any government help for the poor, however, only helped the Johnson campaign in its strategy to portray Goldwater as an extremist. All in all, GOP opposition to the EOA in Congress, coupled with Goldwater's virulent attacks, meant that the Republicans fell into a familiar trap. The Party of Privilege attacking the War on Poverty, without offering a realistic alternative, was simply not a good look.

This chapter explores the Republican response to Johnson's announcement of the War on Poverty, the battle to pass the EOA in Congress, and Goldwater's campaign against the antipoverty effort. It analyses Republican motivations for opposition and also explains why a small minority of Republicans ended up voting for the EOA. Moreover, it reveals why themes of race and 'law and order' – which would become significant in the later years – were not key features of the Republican opposition to the War on Poverty in 1964.

Ultimately, what emerges is a picture of Republicans caught off guard by the announcement of the antipoverty effort and thus unable to offer a coherent or appealing critique of the programme that would resonate with the electorate.

'Nothing new but the barbecue sauce'

In proposing the War on Poverty, Johnson took the country – and the opposition party – largely by surprise. Despite an increased awareness of poverty that had resulted, in part, from Michael Harrington's book *The Other America*, which was published in 1962, America's poor still lacked the tools to lobby those in power and therefore to push poverty to the top of Washington's agenda.[6] President John F. Kennedy had made tentative steps to tackle hardship, but his initial legislation – the Area Redevelopment Act of 1961 – had its funding cut off in 1963 after being 'mocked mercilessly' by Republicans in Congress.[7] As such, it was an unforeseen development when LBJ made an antipoverty war the flagship announcement of his first State of the Union address.

Johnson explained that the antipoverty struggle could be fought because economic prosperity meant that it was possible, and because success in eradicating poverty translated into continued affluence for all Americans: 'The richest Nation on earth can afford to win it. One thousand dollars invested in salvaging an unemployable youth today can return 40,000 dollars or more in his lifetime.' He also drew a significant link between race and hardship that went largely unnoticed in 1964: 'Unfortunately, many Americans live on the outskirts of hope – some because of their poverty, and some because of their color, and all too many because of both. Our task is to help replace their despair with opportunity.' Finally, in a nod to conservative Democrats and Republicans, and to protect his programme from accusations of being a Washington power grab, Johnson told his audience that the attack on poverty 'must also be organized at the State and the local level and must be supported and directed by State and local efforts'.[8]

Thus, the War on Poverty, as outlined by Johnson, was a microcosm of Great Society liberalism – a policy that aimed to help every American, of every race, without taking away from anyone because the assumption of continued American prosperity meant that the size of the pie was poised to increase. FDR may have welcomed the hatred of certain types of business interests during the New Deal, but Johnson wanted everyone to bask in the Great Society's consensus. Or, as historian Allen Matusow puts it, Johnson was attempting to fight a war with no casualties.[9] According to Johnson, the War on Poverty would not just help the poor, but it would also create more wealth in America and, crucially, the President later claimed that it would reduce crime by ameliorating the social conditions in which violence flourished.[10] Furthermore, the War on Poverty as envisioned by LBJ evolved within traditional structures of government, adhering to the American principle of giving the poor opportunity over entitlement. As Gareth Davies notes, it promised a 'hand-up, not a handout'.[11] Unlike other Great Society programmes, however, the War on Poverty was not the realisation of decades of lobbying by liberal Democrats, and it is true to say, as articulated by James Sundquist, legislative aide in both the JFK and LBJ administrations, that 'Until the President's declaration on January 8, 1964, poverty had not been included in the lexicon of America's recognised public problems.'[12] While the War on Poverty was, in many ways, the nucleus of Johnson's vision, the antipoverty struggle was therefore also an outlier in the Great Society.

The ensuing Republican response to Johnson's surprise announcement must be understood within the context of the previous three decades of American politics. The War on Poverty was proposed over thirty-one years since Franklin Roosevelt had assumed the presidency and fundamentally altered the direction of American politics. Before FDR's arrival, the Republican Party had been the natural party of government since the Civil War – dominating both the presidency and Congress. Indeed, only Grover Cleveland and Woodrow Wilson proved the exceptions to well-established Republican rule in the White House. By the time of Roosevelt's death twelve years later, the pendulum had swung the other way, and the change proved enduring. The coalition inspired by FDR's New Deal ensured that LBJ was addressing a congressional audience with a substantial Democratic majority.

Continued Republican struggles, Robert Mason argues, are largely explained by the GOP's failure to deal with a Democratic agenda that advocated 'support for activist government in pursuit of economic prosperity and welfare guarantees', largely because 'the resulting Republican alternative was often reactive, oppositional, and even negative'.[13] Furthermore, the success of the 'conservative coalition' between Republicans and southern Democrats in Congress, which acted as a dam holding back liberal legislation, meant that the virtues of liberal promises rarely were exposed to public scrutiny, as widespread federal aid to education and free medical care for the aged never became reality. As a result, Democrats continued to promise and win elections, while Republicans blocked and lost at the ballot box, and in the process many in the party became overly comfortable in the minority. Massachusetts Attorney General, Edward Brooke, a GOP rising star, captured the essence of this phenomenon in reflecting on the Republican performance in 1964. Brooke bemoaned the abundance 'of Republicans who would rather lose the ball game just as long as they decide who is going to pitch' and the negative reputation attached to the GOP: 'You see, the Republican Party, in rejecting the Democratic Party's solutions to problems, often gives the impression to the people that it is rejecting the existence of the problems themselves.'[14]

It was true to form, therefore, when, before the President even submitted the EOA to Congress, leading Republicans attacked Johnson's agenda in starkly negative terms. The initial response suggested a strong distrust of the President who announced the War on Poverty and hoped to preside over a Great Society. As Geoffrey Kabaservice notes, many in the GOP indicted Johnson as an 'unprincipled political animal' who was merely overpromising voters in an election year.[15] The charge was not without foundation, as Johnson's political life prior to becoming President was epitomised by barely concealed ambition for the highest office, and he had once warned that the 'politics of principle' was the greatest danger to American stability.[16] Furthermore, questions over his accumulation of wealth during his congressional career and his role in the scandals surrounding his old protégé, Bobby Baker, left Johnson vulnerable to credibility charges.[17] Johnson's presidency was eventually to show that, having ascended to the top and achieved his ambition, he genuinely intended to use his power for liberal ends, but this was not clear to everyone during his first months in office.

Accordingly, in the immediate aftermath of Johnson's speech, many Republicans, such as House Minority Whip Les Arends (R-IL), a stalwart, seized upon this weakness in the Johnson armour and criticised the President's liberal checklist as 'Patently a 1964 political campaign document . . . he even promises to give everyone more of everything previously promised at less cost.'[18] A further personal attack on Johnson came from RNC Chair, Rep. William Miller (R-NY), a conservative:

> To put it in a nutshell, the wheeling and dealing in my judgement has started, with the most accomplished wheeler-dealer Washington has ever seen, President Lyndon B. Johnson, running the show. The New Dealers and the Fair Dealers are now only memories. Now we have the Wheeler Dealers.[19]

It was not just those on the Republican Party's right flank who accused Johnson of conjuring up political tricks. Rather than questioning the President's character, however, these Republicans challenged his highly ambitious rhetoric. Jacob Javits (R-NY), the foremost progressive voice in the Senate, caustically noted his belief 'that in his declaration of "unconditional war on poverty" the President has resorted to a superficial generality which is more of a slogan than anything else. Everyone is against poverty.'[20] Javits' Senate colleague, Hugh Scott (R-PA), a moderate, summarised his view in a speech in the Keystone State:

> The Democrats are always coming up with deals. With flourish and failure they gave us the New Deal. Then they came up with the Fair Deal. Now we are entering a new Democratic era – that of the Double Deal. Under the Double Deal, everything runs in pairs . . . We are going to practice economy and frugality within the limits of an increased debt ceiling. And that's not all, we are also going to have lower taxes and more Federally-financed programmes.[21]

New York governor Nelson Rockefeller, standard bearer for the GOP's progressive wing and presidential aspirant, summed up the sentiment of the party (a feat he rarely achieved) in his critique of Johnson's Texan-flavoured rhetoric, concluding that Republicans were still fighting the same old liberal agenda, with 'nothing new but the barbecue sauce'.[22]

Death by a thousand cuts – the Republican response to the Economic Opportunity Act

Wasting little time, in March, the President sent his EOA bill to Congress. Johnson's proposal called for a multi-pronged attack on poverty: 'What you are being asked to consider is not a simple or an easy program, but poverty is not a simple or an easy enemy. It cannot be driven from the land by a single attack on a single front.'[23] The EOA, an omnibus package, was therefore to rest on five key pillars: job training, Community Action, volunteerism, incentives for businesses to hire particularly hard-hit or stigmatised groups, and coordination of these efforts under the watchful eye of an Office of Economic Opportunity (OEO).

In its final form, the bulk of the $947.5 million appropriation provided for Title I (job training) and Title II (Community Action) – both of which proved controversial in later years. Job Corps, the headline initiative from Title I, invited poor young Americans to enrol in conservation camps and training centres for up to two years. Once there, enrolees would be provided with further education, vocational training and work experience. Under the OEO's direction, the creation of Job Corps camps could include any combination of state and local government, as well as public and private non-profit agencies. In future years, the Job Corps camps would come under widespread criticism for high dropout rates as well as a failure to secure permanent employment for those who did graduate. Title I also included an $150 million appropriation to provide assistance to state and local organisations that were offering work experience to disadvantaged youths, also known as the Neighborhood Youth Corps (NYC).[24] This part of the bill met criticism – particularly by Republicans – for giving jobs to youths who were connected in some way to local Democratic Party establishments. For Johnson, however, who fondly remembered administering the Texas branch of National Youth Administration in the 1930s, both Corps had much to recommend them.[25]

Community Action was little understood – most notably by LBJ – when it was included as a significant part of the EOA in 1964. Community Action Programs (CAP) were to form Community Action Agencies (CAA) to tackle problems in rural and urban communities. Demanding 'maximum feasible participation' from local communities, CAPs had to seek funding and approval from the OEO before beginning. As such, this aspect of the War on Poverty – despite its focus on local communities – came under strong criticism for giving too much power to the federal government at the expense of states and localities. Furthermore, the hazy nature of the phrase 'maximum feasible participation' meant that CAPs often became battlegrounds for fights between local community leaders and the local political establishment. Nevertheless, Community Action gave birth to the widely popular Head Start programme that provided pre-school education for low-income children.[26]

Another popular programme (at least in the longer term) that emerged from the EOA was the Volunteers in Service to America

(VISTA) initiative. VISTA allowed the OEO to recruit and train volunteers who would go out into the local communities across the country 'to help Indians, migratory workers . . . the mentally ill and retarded'.[27] VISTA later faced criticism in Congress when Republicans charged that some volunteers were engaged in political activities. In the 1960s, however, VISTA remained one of the least controversial aspects of the myriad of the poverty programmes spawned by Johnson's War on Poverty.

Due to its experimental nature, and also the hastiness with which the bill was thrown together, the EOA – and by extension, the War on Poverty – lacked the clarity that later Great Society programmes achieved. The sparring that unfolded in 1964 demonstrated that the War on Poverty was – somewhat uniquely – exposed to a multitude of challenges.

The multi-pronged character of the EOA was matched only by the multifaceted nature of Republican public pronouncements against it. GOP arguments ranged from the ideological to the explicitly partisan. Still, expressions of preference for the private sector over government spending and distaste for an overbearing federal government that imposed its will on state and local authorities were staple Republican beliefs that were employed against the EOA (the 'poverty bill') as it weaved its way through Congress. Furthermore, many Republican criticisms raised valid points about the overall soundness of the omnibus poverty package, such as the paltry amount being requested to fight the 'war' and the lack of jobs it would create. Most noticeable was the hostile partisan atmosphere that existed during the bill's passage, as almost all Republicans viewed the EOA as an election-year trap for the GOP, designed to aid the election of LBJ to a full term as president by portraying Republicans as being against ending poverty. Moreover, it was common knowledge on Capitol Hill that the War on Poverty was the proposal that Johnson hoped would allow him to step out of JFK's shadow before the November election.[28] Republican animosity towards the EOA therefore stemmed from a combination of pragmatic, partisan and ideological objections to the War on Poverty.

Instinctively attacking the EOA, Republicans of all stripes advocated that continued American faith in free enterprise was

21

the best way to relieve poverty. The implied accusation was that Johnson was creating more pointless or harmful government programmes that would undermine the private sector and involve inflation-inducing spending. It was a viewpoint that both united and divided the party, and in recent years had achieved more of the latter. While the GOP, from conservatives to progressives, firmly saw themselves as the party of free enterprise, the New Deal had opened up a division in the party between those who believed that government had a strong secondary role to play in socioeconomic issues and those who believed it should only be used in very well-defined areas such as education, and even then religious concerns still divided some on this issue.[29] The former had backed Thomas Dewey and Dwight Eisenhower, whereas the latter had preferred the gospel of Robert Taft.[30] Conservatives were a newer breed (or older, depending on how one looks at it) who believed government should get out of the way of the private sector in all circumstances, with Goldwater acting as the standard bearer. Thus, most progressives and moderates looked to improve the EOA, whereas the very notion of a government programme to fight poverty was distasteful to stalwarts, and anathema to conservatives.

Congressional Republicans were quick to repudiate Johnson for supposedly ignoring the virtues of the private sector in solving poverty. Rep. Robert Griffin (R-MI), a stalwart, spelled out his faith in free enterprise during a report to his constituents: 'The whole history of America has been a record of spectacular and sustained accomplishment in an age-old "war on poverty". In this struggle, our principal weapons have been a free society and a competitive economy.'[31] Senator John Tower (R-TX), a conservative with a more cerebral bent than Goldwater, stressed that poverty could only be alleviated in the long run by the creation of new jobs by the private sector.[32] For a party still associated in the public mind with government paralysis during the early years of the Great Depression, it was a response with inherent risks. Furthermore, the critiques failed to explain what Republicans planned to do to 'encourage free enterprise' and sustain a 'competitive economy'. Nevertheless, congressional Republicans all agreed that Johnson's War on Poverty was too weighted in favour of government over the private sector.

The comments of Goldwater and Rockefeller, the two front-runners for the presidential nomination when Johnson announced the War on Poverty, further demonstrate the sliver of common ground that conservatives and progressives stood on in relation to the desirable role of government. Following the State of the Union address, Goldwater had scolded Johnson, arguing that 'the private sector is the only sector that can help solve the poverty problem, and I don't think it's ever going to be completely solved'.[33] Rockefeller, commenting in less starkly ideological terms, stressed his desire to see the poverty problem tackled 'primarily upon creative free enterprise and individual initiative'.[34]

The main difference between the two men was that Rockefeller actively sought a secondary role for government in solving the problem of hardship. Essentially, he was not appalled at the idea of fighting a war on poverty, whereas Goldwater dismissed any such notion. Rockefeller's approach, despite all of his flaws as a candidate, was more in accord with the political climate of 1964. Goldwater perhaps unthinkingly admitted as much, when, later on in the primary campaign, he criticised the President's War on Poverty for seeking to 'exploit this new mood of the American people'.[35] Rockefeller was also willing to sketch out an alternative to LBJ's programme.[36] Goldwater, Rockefeller charged, simply wanted to go back to 'the good old days' of a glamourised past that never existed.[37] Thus, while the Democratic Party's supposedly relaxed approach to government interference in the private sector elicited abhorrence from all in the GOP, it also fomented dissension in Republican ranks over the extent to which differing GOP politicians were willing to tolerate any government interference at all.

Another key Republican tenet, but one that caused less division in the party, was a belief that the federal government should only do what states and localities could not do by themselves. As Republican votes for the Civil Rights Act in June revealed, members of the GOP were amenable to forgoing this theory in certain circumstances. Even conservatives, who mostly voted against civil rights, saw exceptions and called on the federal government to pass legislation to help establish 'law and order' later in the year. For most Republicans, however, antipoverty efforts did not qualify under the 'exceptional circumstances' bracket. In his attempt during the State of the Union to mute cries of federal overreach by stressing the local nature of the War on Poverty, Johnson found that his assertion fell on deaf ears. The full arrival of Great Society liberalism in 1965 and its expansion of the federal bureaucracy would only further unite Republicans in their disapproval of federal government intervention. Nevertheless, it would be the War on Poverty – born a year earlier – that remained the focus for such Republican ire.

Perhaps unsurprisingly, Republican governors were especially sensitive to any attempt by a Democratic president and Congress to intervene in state matters. In particular, statehouse worries centred on the enlargement of the grant-in-aid system – whereby the federal government (in this instance, the OEO) sent the states money, but with instructions on how to spend it. These governors tended to fall into the moderate category due to the problem-solving nature of the executive role and also because many found themselves elected in swing industrial states in the Northeast and Midwest.

One such example was the Michigan governor, George Romney, who argued that his state was already engaged in its own successful war on poverty and did not require federal interference. 'Federalism is in crisis,' Romney warned. 'It is endangered by spreading, conformist, monolithic centralism.'[38] Romney was joined in his criticism by William Scranton, Governor of Pennsylvania and the candidate who came forward in June as the moderates' last-ditch attempt at stopping Goldwater. Scranton chastised Johnson for falsely believing in 'special federal magic' to solve poverty.[39] Republican Governors Association (RGA) chair, Robert Smylie of Idaho, a moderate, was another to underscore his fear that the line between state and federal government was being 'diluted'.[40]

Congressional Republicans also pressed forward the case that the White House was paying insignificant attention to the principle of federalism enshrined in the Tenth Amendment. Rep. Peter Frelinghuysen (R-NJ), another moderate Republican and the figure who led his party's House members in opposition to the antipoverty bill, declared that the EOA's passage would show that 'The Federal–State relationship is clearly that of master and servant.'[41] He was joined by stalwart Rep. William Ayres (R-OH) in sending a letter to fellow Republicans which cautioned members of the GOP that passage of the EOA was 'dangerous and ill-conceived', arguing that there were already forty-two federal programmes fighting poverty.[42]

In the Senate, Tower – the occupant of Johnson's old Texas Senate seat – pointed to the Job Corps section of the bill, declaring that 'the first casualty of this "war" would be the principles of local control and representative government'.[43] GOP criticisms had an effect, and, with the help of southern Democrats motivated by their own racial concerns, Republicans were able to have the bill amended on a matter of federalism. Governors were thus given the right to veto the establishment of any Job Corps camp, NYC project or CAP, while the Administration only just defeated, by a margin of three votes, an amendment to give veto power to governors over all programmes set up under the Titles I and II – the core of the bill.[44]

Aside from these two familiar Republican issues, there were other signs that GOP leaders genuinely believed that the poverty bill was a poor piece of legislation, destined to fail in its goals. Responding to the antipoverty proposals, Frelinghuysen and Ayres had accentuated this point in their July letter, pleading with each member of the House to avoid approving 'scatter-gun programmes of unproved need and unknown consequences'.[45] Unsurprisingly, this sentiment was parroted by Tower: 'Many of the President's specific requests under the "poverty" umbrella are old, discredited programmes resurrected from the depression era. They have come forth in the President's proposals with a new dress, a dress that costs infinitely more than it did in the 1930s.'[46]

Tower's link to the 1930s and the New Deal was another common theme in GOP criticism of specific features contained in the bill. Given that many New Deal programmes had enjoyed broad public support, it was perhaps not the most electorally savvy approach to take. Nonetheless, the scathing Senate Minority Report, which the Texan senator co-authored with Goldwater, attempted to link the War on Poverty with perceived failures of the Roosevelt era, describing several proposals as 'almost replicas of programmes that were tried and rejected by the New Deal during the depression'.[47] Hugh Scott, who ultimately voted for the bill, saw the poverty programme as 'a "magpie's nest" of a great many old programmes, and a few new ones' and criticised the administration's proposal 'not on the basis that it goes too far . . . but because it does not go far enough'.[48]

Scott's mention of 'a few new' programmes proved one of the rare times that a Republican acknowledged that there was anything innovative included in the EOA, as most tended to focus on headline proposals like the Job Corps. That Republicans failed to pass much comment on Community Action, which was to prove a political goldmine for opponents of the War on Poverty, suggests that they understood the ramifications of this part of the bill as little as the President who proposed it.[49]

Republicans also mocked the somewhat paltry amount of money – roughly one billion dollars – that Johnson requested for an 'unconditional war on poverty' while they ridiculed remarks from Johnson's choice for OEO Director, Sargent Shriver. Many in the GOP were incredulous when Shriver suggested that the antipoverty war could be won in ten years. Appearing on ABC's *Issues and Answers* in May, Shriver was grilled by political commentator John Rolfson on GOP criticisms relating to the amount of money requested:

> Some Republicans, as you know, call this a cruel hoax, because when you consider the dimensions of poverty and consider the amount of money that we are now spending to fight poverty – perhaps 40 billion dollars, federal and state, which is one estimate – this is really just a drop in the bucket, less than a billion dollars. What real dent can it make?[50]

Shriver's response was that the money requested was only a starting point, as 'it is the size of programme that we can successfully and economically start in fiscal year 1965'.[51]

Republicans constantly referred to Shriver as a 'poverty czar', in a pointed dig at the OEO, which many in the GOP foresaw as a sprawling bureaucratic mess imbued with the power to bypass state and local legislatures.[52] Shriver also left himself open to criticism, choosing to keep his role as Peace Corps director, which earned criticism from Javits who put forth his belief that Shriver's shared responsibilities 'tend to give credence to the unfortunate charge made by some in recent weeks that this "war on poverty" is accented more by ballyhoo than substance'.[53]

Legitimate policy concerns aside, the fulcrum of the Republican critique of the EOA centred on the partisan politics of the War on Poverty. Most Republicans – even those who voted for the EOA – suspected that Johnson was engaging in election-year gimmickry when he declared his domestic war, and the antipoverty bill's substance did little to convince them otherwise. Republicans wholeheartedly echoed journalist Alistair Cooke's assessment of the proposal: 'a cunning act of largesse on the Roosevelt model, a vast Federal hand-out to milk the electorate in November and purchase the re-election of LBJ, the good provider'.[54] In both houses of Congress and in Republican-occupied governors' mansions there was a substantial effort to make sure that the public was made aware that Johnson did not care about the poor, only about their votes.

Some Republicans decided to meet Johnson's perceived political gimmickry head on by indulging in similar antics. One such effort in May was an attempt by Reps. Gene Snyder (R-KY) and David Martin (R-NE), during a visit to land owned by the Johnsons in Alabama, to out LBJ as a hypocrite on poverty:

> After flying to Autauga and Chilton counties to inspect 3,660 acres of land owned by Mrs. Johnson, [Snyder and Martin] described to a press conference the living conditions of six Negro tenants and sharecroppers living on the land. Snyder said, 'We saw people living in deplorable poverty, with little evidence of concern by their millionaire landlords.'[55]

The Republican House Minority Report also included testimony from a family, the Marlows, whom Johnson had visited in North Carolina to publicise the problem of poverty. The report quoted Mrs Marlow, who described how the family had been told to ensure that the children were barefoot upon the President's arrival, and explained, 'We didn't even feel like we were in poverty . . . And along comes the word that we're the poorest folks in the country.'[56]

Away from patent political theatre, congressional Republicans railed against the political opportunism of the EOA. In early June, when the bill was voted out of the House Education and Labor Committee by a highly partisan margin, Republicans cited their belief that the antipoverty bill was merely a Democratic attempt to buy the votes of the poor for the upcoming election. While Griffin bemoaned the exploitation of poverty for 'partisan political purposes',[57] his fellow Michigander, Gerald Ford, explained: 'All of us want to do everything we can to eliminate the evils of poverty. This does not mean that every politically-inspired programme must be fully endorsed.'[58] Unsurprisingly, Tower and Goldwater were at the forefront of similar Senate critiques. In his analysis, Tower slammed the programme as an 'election-year project . . . a hoax' and argued that 'Never in American history have catchy political slogans created jobs.'[59] Goldwater sourly, but also perceptively, observed, 'Many of the new programmes with which we are to be faced are said to be part of a war on poverty. And who can be against that?'[60] Taken together, the Republican criticism of the programme as politically motivated suggests that many in the GOP sensed that the War on Poverty was an initiative that the public found desirable in 1964.

Ultimately, pragmatic, partisan and ideological reasons combined during the initial debate over the EOA to ensure a plethora of GOP complaints across a range of issues. Unfortunately for those Republicans who opposed the bill, this 'death by a thousand cuts' approach failed to stop or significantly amend Johnson's signature legislation. Perhaps, if Republicans had rallied around a single issue, the story might have been different. An explicit focus on race, for example, remained the strategic way to persuade enough southern Democrats to maintain the conservative coalition and thus render the War on Poverty another stillborn liberal project. That this did not happen is worthy of exploration.

Still the 'Party of Lincoln'

During the debate over the EOA, Republicans rarely voiced concern that the antipoverty effort would disproportionately favour poor black Americans over poor white Americans. On the rare occasions the issue was raised, it appeared a token attempt at winning over southern Democrats to vote against the President's bill. Only Ayres, who had already used a wide variety of other ploys to try and lure southern Democrats away from voting for the poverty bill, gave voice to these concerns.[61] During questioning of the bill's sponsor, conservative-inclined Rep. Phil Landrum (D-GA), Ayres stated, 'there won't be any white people in it', but was met with the effective retort from the Georgia Democrat that 'Negroes aren't the only poor people in the world.'[62] Indeed, Shriver had already made this point quite explicit when he addressed a meeting of the National Association for the Advancement of Colored People (NAACP), and before an African American audience the future OEO director declared that 80 per cent of those in poverty were white.[63] The only other significant occasion when race intervened was when the Johnson administration attempted to persuade recalcitrant progressive and moderate Republicans to support the EOA by privately arguing that passage of the bill would help calm racial tension in the inner cities following uprisings in the summer of 1964.[64] Such arguments would come back to haunt Johnson as his presidency wore on and urban riots became a common feature of American summers. For now, however, the argument appeared compelling in light of the racial disturbances in Harlem during July.

That the Republican Party chose not to oppose the EOA on racial grounds is unsurprising. For in 1964 the Republican Party – notwithstanding its deeply flawed racial record dating back to the Civil War – could still justifiably be called the 'Party of Lincoln'. As evidence of this, one only needs to examine the Republican response to the other crucial piece of legislation that was painstakingly making its way through Congress at the same time as the poverty bill – the Civil Rights Act of 1964.

As is widely known, Republicans ultimately voted for the Civil Rights Act at a higher rate than Democrats. Some historians place GOP legislators as the reluctant heroes who preferred to pay lip service to the cause of civil rights, and who, without the arm-twisting of Johnson, would have remained on the sidelines.[65] Others see the majority of Republicans as true believers in civil rights who finally forced the hand of a hypocritical Democratic Party made up of northern liberals and pro-segregation southerners.[66] Whatever the motivation, statistics show that only thirty-five out of 173 House Republicans and seven out of thirty-four Senate Republicans voted against final passage. GOP votes thus helped secure the most sweeping civil rights legislation in almost one hundred years.[67] Nevertheless, for the American public, the role played by the GOP during the civil rights effort was largely obscured by Barry Goldwater's decision to vote against the act only a month before achieving his party's nomination.

Notwithstanding Goldwater's vote, the role of Republicans in the passage of the Civil Rights Act has been somewhat misrepresented by the focus on Senator Everett Dirksen.[68] This is not an accident. The Johnson administration and racially liberal members of the GOP, such as Sen. Thomas Kuchel (R-CA), set about wooing the Minority Leader, who was undoubtedly important to the process of securing Republican support, by ensuring that Dirksen basked in the limelight.[69] Dirksen, however, was a true pork-barrel politician and thus his aloofness during the long debate was likely a ploy to squeeze every last drop of patronage out of the Johnson administration before giving his assent to the bill. Once he had achieved this he became one of the bill's firmest advocates, denouncing Goldwater on the Senate floor for his 'extreme opinions' regarding civil rights.[70] For a partisan like Dirksen – a stalwart whose political philosophy was not too far from Goldwater's and who was to happily support the Arizonan after his nomination – the reproach carries weight. And it is Dirksen's fellow Republican stalwarts, men from the Midwest who voted against the EOA and held conservative instincts regarding federal power, that represent the most interesting case of Republican support for the Civil Rights Act. Two such examples were Reps. Thomas Curtis (R-MO) and William McCulloch (R-OH), whose districts contained few African Americans and yet both men played key roles in the fight for civil rights.[71]

It is important to consider, however, that the measures contained in the Civil Rights Act were aimed predominantly at the South, and thus precluded nominal federal government interference in the northern congressional districts to which these lawmakers belonged.

Furthermore, leading GOP politicians did achieve some small amendments to the bill that only affected enforcement of the act in the North. Republicans contested that these changes only improved the quality and practicality of the law, but the interventions also suggested that trouble lay ahead if the civil rights movement moved to the North.[72] One of the key amendments in the compromise to attract Republican votes in the Senate contained a section that strengthened House language, declaring the bill was 'not to be used to overcome "racial imbalances" not caused by official segregation policies'.[73] It was one thing to fix de jure segregation in Birmingham and Jackson, but quite another to have minorities challenging de facto segregation in the suburbs of Chicago and Los Angeles. And unlike the Civil Rights Act, which was passed to solve a southern problem, the War on Poverty was aimed at both sides of the Mason–Dixon Line.

While it is impossible to say with any certainty whether the Republican Party was destined to move in a racially liberal or conservative direction if Goldwater had not been nominated the month after voting against the Civil Rights Act, the effect of his vote on the party's racial image was immediate and dramatic. As Thomas and Mary Edsall assert, the net effect of Goldwater's 'nay' vote and his nomination in San Francisco was that, 'By 1964, the Democratic party was on its way to becoming the home of racial liberalism, and the Republican party was on its way to becoming the home of racial conservatism.'[74] Only a few months after passage, a public poll confirmed this trend with 60 per cent of respondents answering that the Democrats were more likely to support fair treatment for blacks, whereas only 33 per cent believed it was the Republicans. This represented a substantial shift from the near equal results that were given in 1962.[75]

A charitable reading of Goldwater's decision to vote against the bill would argue that it owed more to his 'states' rights' philosophy and a certain unintentional ignorance of African American issues, rather than racial prejudice. The Senator had an exemplary racial record in the Copper State having played a role in desegregation of the Phoenix school system while also being a long-time member of the NAACP's Arizona branch.[76] Such a record echoed that of Senator Tower who also voted against the bill and yet was known for his ability to court Hispanic support in his home state of Texas.[77] Still, Goldwater – notorious for his capacity to say the first thing that popped into his head while in front of a microphone – had made statements which made it easy to portray him as a race-baiter. For example, he had once instructed his party to go 'hunting where the ducks are', in reference to pursuing the support of southern whites who still voted Democratic despite the fact that the party was pursuing racially liberal politics in Washington.[78] Additionally, while Goldwater might not have been racist, Geoffrey Kabaservice correctly observes that, 'In giving aid and comfort to Southern segregationists . . . Goldwater was certainly a fellow traveler of racists.'[79]

Goldwater's candidacy helped encourage a growing segment of the party that had been evident at a 1963 RNC meeting where northern Republicans were shocked to hear new members fomenting against 'niggers' and 'nigger lovers'.[80] Furthermore, at the party's 1964 national convention black delegates were harassed to the extent that legendary baseball player and prominent Republican Jackie Robinson felt moved to compare his experience of attending the GOP convention to the Jewish experience in Nazi Germany.[81] Indeed, one Goldwater supporter and native southerner informed columnists Rowland Evans and Robert Novak, 'If I could get a half hour alone with Barry Goldwater, I'd tell him his appeal in the South never has been because he's a Republican or a conservative, but because he's been a states' rights man on the race issue who will leave it up to the states. If he changes that, he's dead.'[82] In voting against civil rights, Goldwater had tapped into something that was uglier than his own beliefs.

These concerning trends over the party's racial direction aside, in 1964 the GOP lived up to its oft-cited Lincolnian heritage by providing the votes that swept away the 'Whites only' signs from day-to-day southern life. For every Republican member who welcomed the conversion of arch-segregationist Strom Thurmond (R-SC) from a Democrat to a Republican in September, there was a Republican who worried that the chance to appeal to a new moderate South without racial appeals – coded or explicit – was being lost.[83] What is more, to moderate Republicans, Johnson's argument that a war on poverty would quell the long-festering racial tension in the nation's cities appeared logical in 1964. The 'Sunbelt', as GOP strategist Kevin Phillips coined the new racially conservative heartland from Virginia to California in 1969, had thus not yet risen to dominate GOP politics.[84] Accordingly, in 1964, the Republican Party's response to the War on Poverty was not eclipsed by matters of race.

'Anybody that votes for this bill is not a member of the Republican Party'

Following the achievement of the Civil Rights Act in June, attention turned back to the EOA. In assessing the battle ahead, the *Washington Post*'s Richard Lyons noted that 'This alone of the year's major bills is Mr. Johnson's personal creation, and it has developed into one of the fiercest partisan struggles of the session.'[85] Furthermore, during a conversation that seemed to confirm Republican partisan charges, LBJ warned Rep. George Mahon (D-TX) that the EOA 'is a party measure. This is party responsibility. If I lose this it's telegraphed around the world that, by gosh, the Republicans roll me and roll me good on the key measure, the only single Johnson measure that was sent up. Everything else was Kennedy.'[86]

With the stakes outlined, the Johnson administration applied 'unprecedented pressure' on reluctant southern Democrats and Republicans in the following months, resulting in an equally energetic backlash from GOP leaders and a hastily conceived Republican alternative.[87] Small amendments aside, the EOA was approved handily in the Senate (61–34), with ten out of thirty-two Republican senators voting for it – most of whom were progressives. The real combat took place in the House. Despite eventually winning, the EOA came at a political cost to the White House and remained a partisan bill, only passing in the House because a substantial number of southern Democrats and a small minority of eastern Republicans broke the conservative coalition to vote for the president's signature programme.

Long before August, when most of the debate took place in the lower chamber, House Republicans had already begun to indulge in arguments against the poverty bill which sounded desperate and suggested that the bill stood a good chance of passing. One such example was heard when Republicans tried to use the context of the Cold War to criticise the President's efforts to solve poverty. Griffin, stealing from a similar argument employed by advocates of civil rights, complained that 'our prestige abroad is not being enhanced when Administration spokesmen proclaim, over and over again, that one-fifth of our population lives in poverty'.[88] During the House debate, another spurious argument came from Rep. Charles Goodell (R-NY), a stalwart at this point in his career, who attempted to set alarm bells ringing for those legislators with strong views on religious issues. He charged that the bill was so loosely drafted that the funds might be used for birth control or to aid church Sunday schools.[89] Unsurprisingly, the arguments of both Griffin and Goodell gained little traction in Congress, much like the Republican substitute bill offered by Peter Frelinghuysen. At least, however, Frelinghuysen's bill showed that members of the GOP were attempting to craft legislation of their own rather than adhering to the 'Party of No' stereotype.

Frelinghuysen's alternative bill removed the Job Corps, sought to give control of funds to state and local agencies, focused more on the role of education, and – significantly – proposed half the amount of the administration's requested appropriation.[90] House Minority Leader Charles Halleck (R-IN) attempted to use the Frelinghuysen substitute to completely stall the antipoverty effort – correctly believing that the White House had no interest in passing the Republican proposal.[91] Johnson's close legislative aide, Bill Moyers, was therefore probably correct in his assessment of Frelinghuysen's submission as 'really a states' rights programme . . . [L]ike turning civil rights over to the states . . . you're for it in principle, but you don't do anything.'[92] In early August, Frelinghuysen's offering was defeated soundly by a 177–295 roll-call vote. In reality, it was not a real alternative, the type which Republicans would make serious attempts at designing in the future.

On the final day of debate, Frelinghuysen was joined in his denunciation of the poverty bill by around a dozen of his House Republican colleagues who rose to condemn the omnibus package using a collection of the reasons already outlined. Of the criticisms, perhaps two stand out as particularly significant. First, Rep. Charles Hoeven (R-IA) eloquently revealed the political quandary that Republicans perceived themselves to be in, asserting: 'Let me say that I am not in favour of poverty. Furthermore, may I suggest that the milk of human kindness does not flow alone in the veins of the sponsors of this legislation.'[93] Hoeven's defensive remarks showed that Republicans were fearful that their opposition to the War on Poverty was only further confirming the harmful Party of Privilege stereotype in an election year.

Elsewhere, Rep. Robert Taft Jr (R-OH) – in the midst of running unsuccessfully for the Senate – was alone among his colleagues in raising the (ultimately prophetic) possibility that the Community Action section of the bill could wreak havoc between local agencies:

It is the nature of health and welfare setups in many communities that there are jealousies and there is duplication between and among various agencies. The community chests and the [local] planning councils have attempted to pull these together and eliminate problems. Yet what is proposed would enable the Federal Director to come in and take sides . . . [T]hat is the primary weakness in this approach.[94]

Taft, who cited his own experience in serving on various welfare boards in Ohio, offered a rare instance of a Republican contribution that prioritised detailed and sober analysis of the EOA.

White House recordings also reveal the tug of war that existed between Johnson and Halleck for the votes of progressive and moderate Republicans. In discussing the poverty bill, Larry O'Brien, Johnson's congressional liaison aide, told the President that many observers had 'never seen Halleck so aroused'. Unambiguously, the Minority Leader was telling his members, 'by God, anybody that votes for this bill is not a member of the Republican Party'.[95] On the same day, Johnson learned that Halleck was backing his words by threatening to withhold $5,000 of campaign money from recalcitrant representatives. Rep. Silvio Conte (R-MA), a progressive, told Moyers that he had received a pleading personal phone call from Halleck, despite the fact that '[Halleck] very seldom does that. He doesn't like me.'[96] For Halleck – the epitome of the Midwestern stalwart Republican politico – opposing the War on Poverty was becoming a litmus test of party loyalty.

The President was not lacking in persuasive levers that he could pull, however, and used the United Auto Workers (UAW) leader, Walter Reuther, to apply union pressure on progressive and moderate Republicans to support the EOA. The President gave Reuther licence to both threaten their union funding and dangle White House rewards. Ultimately, the carrot-and-stick approach aided the effort and the administration won enough of what Reuther termed 'fairly liberal, 20th century Republicans' to pass the bill.[97] A combination of progressive instincts and union pressure ultimately trumped party loyalty for these Republicans.

It is also true that many of these Republicans would likely not have been especially upset with a Johnson victory in November. As early as September, Goldwater already looked destined to defeat and had especially alienated the moderate and progressive voices in the GOP during his famous acceptance speech that declared 'extremism in the defense of liberty is no vice', and perhaps importantly for moderates, that 'moderation in the pursuit of victory is no virtue'.[98] Moreover, Goldwater had once jokingly advocated cutting off the eastern seaboard from the rest of the United States – a typical off-the-cuff comment that the Johnson campaign put at the centre of a television spot.[99] As such, for eastern Republicans who would need ticket-splitting to survive in November, voting for the War on Poverty was one route to show independence from the GOP ticket by demonstrating their support for socioeconomic programmes that Goldwater deplored.

The Economic Opportunity Act of 1964 thus passed the House on 8 August by a 226–185 margin, meaning that the twenty-two Republicans who voted for the bill could have condemned the bill to defeat had they voted against passage. Nonetheless, in the less polarised era of 1960s politics, the number voting for the legislation was noticeably small. In total, 87 per cent of House Republicans had voted against the EOA, and while 69 per cent Republican opposition in the Senate was not excessively high, even those Republicans who had voted for the bill and desired some form of 'war on poverty' were not enthused by Johnson's omnibus package. Goldwater, sensing widespread Republican disapproval of the

EOA, opened a Republican 'Unity' conference in Hershey, Pennsylvania by welcoming his fellow GOP luminaries to a 'foxhole in the war against poverty'.[100] The EOA, it appeared, was poised to be a vocally partisan issue during the campaign.

On 3 September, four days before Labor Day and the traditional moment when the parties hit the campaign trail, Halleck and Dirksen devoted much of their final press conference of the 88th Congress to lambasting Johnson's War on Poverty. In characteristically cantankerous style, Halleck indicted FDR and Truman for failing to rid the United States of poverty and warned the electorate, 'It's about time the American people woke up. For 32 years Democratic candidates for President have traded on human misery each election year for political purposes.'[101] And it was left to the more colourful Senate Minority Leader to plunge the knife further:

> For three decades the Democrats every four years have issued their 'election year tranquilizers' – things are really better, but they are also bad, so elect us and they'll get better. This year we have a whole new array of election year tranquilizer pills . . . My friends, you name it and the Democrats have got it in 1964 if it sounds like it might get a vote – all for a cheap billion dollars of your money. It's called the 'War on Poverty Package'. And there's not one permanent durable job in the whole phony bundle.[102]

A clarion call had seemingly been sounded by the two Minority Leaders to take the case against Johnson's War on Poverty to the people.

Ultimately, however, it would be one of the very few times that the public heard from Republicans running for Congress or to occupy governors' mansions on the issue – the expected Republican rallying cry against the War on Poverty resembled very much a stalled crusade. Once Johnson had achieved his aim of passing legislation that stood him apart from Kennedy, the upside to criticising the War on Poverty was reduced for Republicans. The downside – that a Republican campaign against the War on Poverty only confirmed the labels of negativism and privilege – remained. Pragmatism therefore suggested that discretion would form the better part of valour for Republicans who remained opposed to the EOA. It is thus unsurprising that notable exceptions to the Republican silence on the War on Poverty were drawn from the ideologically motivated, conservative wing of the party. Indeed, the most anti-War on Poverty figures during the 1964 campaign were Goldwater and a rising star of the nascent conservative movement, Ronald Reagan.

Goldwater's Götterdämmerung

At the presidential level, the 1964 election unfolded as a clash between two differing ideas over the correct role that government – particularly the federal government – should play in American life. Throughout the campaign, Johnson implored his audiences to give him, and by extension the federal government, the liberal majorities to construct a Great Society. Goldwater, on the other hand, decried Washington expansion since the New Deal and bemoaned that 'government is becoming the master instead of the servant.'[103] The War on Poverty – the newest of all federal programmes – was, unsurprisingly, at the forefront of this ideological debate between the two candidates. For those listening to Goldwater, they would hear that the War on Poverty was a prime example of the Great Society's folly and false promises. Meanwhile, for those attuned to Johnson's campaign, Goldwater's opposition to the War on Poverty was yet more proof of the Republican candidate's extremism.

From the campaign's outset, Goldwater made clear his continued opposition to the War on Poverty. During his campaign's inaugural speech on 4 September, Goldwater attacked the 'cancerous growth of the Federal government' and strongly rebutted claims that Republicans who voted against the War on Poverty did not care about the poor:

> We, in a Republican administration, shall never abandon the needy and the aged – we shall never forsake the helpless. We understand their problems in our hearts. But we know that a true and lasting solution of those problems cannot be found in degrading, capricious, and politically motivated handouts from the White House.

Accordingly, the Arizonan argued that a solution to poverty 'must ultimately be found in a thriving and compassionate economy and in programmes principally handled by the levels of government closest to the people'.[104] For Goldwater, such rhetoric was moderate and proved the exception as the campaign wore on – his most controversial War on Poverty speech lay ahead.

On 19 September, the Republican candidate travelled to the heart of Appalachia in Charleston, West Virginia to deliver his peroration against the War on Poverty. Earlier in the year, Johnson had successfully toured the economically deprived region to rally support for the antipoverty effort. Broad public sympathy existed for Appalachians who had been hit by the effects of new technological developments, particularly in the coal mining sector. As such, Goldwater's decision to campaign against the War on Poverty in West Virginia either was a result of political naivety or suggested an acceptance that he was going to lose anyway and therefore he might as well display the courage of his convictions.[105] During the speech, the candidate condemned the EOA as 'phony' and reeled off a checklist of Republican complaints previously aired in Congress. Goldwater accused his opponent of passing the programme to 'further selfish political ambitions' and derided the notion that the $3,000 definition of poverty was accurate: 'the theorists of the much-advertised "Great Society" have redefined the luxuries of yesterday as the necessities of today'. He called the Job Corps 'a worn-out Depression gimmick' and declared that 'free enterprise, not Federal bureaucracy, licked the poverty problem in the 1930s and it can do it again today'.[106] In short, Barry Goldwater, who had bemoaned the inherent difficulty of campaigning against a 'war on poverty', did just that.

The majority of Appalachians in attendance appeared to disagree with the Arizonan. 'Audience reaction was muted,' one prominent Goldwater campaign aide remembered. 'Barry was interrupted with applause . . . but it was usually perfunctory and mild.'[107] Moreover, as he left, lines of workmen jeered him.[108] Goldwater was met with a similar response across Appalachia. While speaking in Huntingdon, Pennsylvania, where the local Republican congressman, John Saylor, had voted for the EOA, Goldwater encountered a sign, typical of those that followed his campaign in such hard-hit areas of the country, which read: 'This is Appalachia . . . Now About the Anti-Poverty Programme . . .'[109]

Ultimately, Goldwater's approach to the War on Poverty on the campaign trail owed little to political pragmatism – a quality that was also largely absent during the rest of his campaign. Running as an ideological crusader as opposed to a viable presidential candidate, Goldwater also attacked the prospect of free health care for the aged during a speech in the retirement nirvana of Florida. Perhaps the Arizonan was hoping that his honesty would reap political rewards. In attempting to justify his decision to campaign against the War on Poverty in Appalachia, the candidate explained:

> I will not attempt to buy the votes of the American people . . . I will not treat any of you as just so many special interests . . . I will not appeal to you as if you were simply pocketbooks . . . surrounded on all sides by self-serving concerns.[110]

Johnson responded to Goldwater's attacks by turning the Arizonan's opposition to the War on Poverty into another example of the Republican candidate's extremism. During an extended soliloquy that mocked the recently published book by conservative activist Phyllis Schlafly, Johnson placed himself in the modern consensus while deeming Goldwater beholden to a minority that was clinging to the past, remarking: 'The majority says . . . "yes" to a war on poverty. But the echo still says "no".'[111] Just over a month later, Johnson released a memorandum which claimed that Goldwater's ignorance of the government's role in showing 'human compassion' was, in fact, 'radical philosophy'.[112] As such, Goldwater's sharp opposition to the War on Poverty was successfully blunted by the Johnson campaign as it was lumped in with the rest of Goldwater's perceived extremism.

If Goldwater was a flawed messenger, the other high-profile Republican rebuttal of the War on Poverty was delivered by a GOP rising star with a particular talent for making conservative positions sound reasonable. Ronald Reagan arrived on the national political scene during a live television address in the final week of the campaign and tore into Johnson's signature programme.

Despite lacking experience in professional politics, Reagan was a savvier politician than Goldwater and his speech was delivered not in the hostile surroundings of Appalachia but to an audience in southern California's biggest boomtown of them all – Los Angeles. The broadcast was so popular that Goldwater staffers hurriedly turned it into a campaign ad for their less eloquent presidential candidate.

Featuring the homespun language that would become his trademark, Reagan asked his audience to do 'a little arithmetic'. Contesting that the federal government spent $45 billion on welfare, Reagan did the audience's calculations for them:

> If we divided the 45 billion dollars up equally among those 9 million poor families, we'd be able to give each family 4,600 dollars a year. And this added to their present income should eliminate poverty. Direct aid to the poor, however, is only running only about 600 dollars per family. It would seem that someplace there must be some overhead.

And the former actor, in an incredulous tone, asked his audience:

> Now do they honestly expect us to believe that if we add 1 billion dollars to the 45 billion we're spending, one more programme to the 30-odd we have – and remember, this new programme doesn't replace any, it just duplicates existing programmes – do they believe that poverty is suddenly going to disappear by magic?

Lobbing a further rhetorical grenade at Johnson, Reagan implied that the EOA was nothing but a Democratic scam: 'so now we declare "war on poverty", or "You, too, can be a Bobby Baker".'[113] Reagan's attack on the War on Poverty – one part of his wider critique of welfare – and the popular reception it received, suggested that the Johnson administration's painstaking attempts to stress the opportunity aspect of the EOA would only insulate the anti-poverty effort from anti-entitlement rhetoric for so long.

Another theme emerged during the 1964 campaign that significantly impacted the War on Poverty in the future: the politics of 'law and order'. Historian Michael Flamm's seminal study of 'law and order' argues that the phrase was a catch-all term for several phenomena and its meaning could be interpreted in several different ways. Thus, 'law and order' – and, also, Goldwater's reference to 'crime in the streets' – was linked to rising rates of violent crime, the civil disobedience employed by the civil rights movement, and urban racial uprisings. It was a racially loaded term for some, but for others it was merely a reflection of the fear stirred by rising crime rates – particularly in the later years of the Johnson presidency. In 1964, Goldwater made it a central campaign focus following the rapturous reception his condemnation of 'violence in the streets' received at the Republican National Convention in July. It was not Goldwater's extemporising on liberty that raised the crowd at the Cow Palace to fever pitch, according to Flamm, rather it was the candidate's assertion that 'security from domestic violence, no less than from foreign aggression, is the most elementary and fundamental purpose of any government'.[114]

While the debate over the War on Poverty had largely excluded racism – the same could not be said for the debate over law and order. Discussion of crime was often associated with both civil rights protestors in the south and young black men in northern cities. In 1964, Goldwater tapped into resentment of the former, while George Wallace, during his quixotic Democratic primary campaign, capitalised on fear of the latter.[115] During his opening campaign speech, Goldwater backhandedly criticised the civil rights movement, bemoaning that 'those who break the law are accorded more consideration than those who try to enforce the law'.[116] Goldwater's rhetoric resembled that of the former Dixiecrat presidential candidate, Strom Thurmond. The South Carolinian, one of Goldwater's strongest supporters, declared in October that Goldwater would salvage 'the rights of the individual, the rights of the states, and protect law-abiding citizens against riots, looting and assaults in the streets'.[117] Nevertheless, it was the fears that Wallace had briefly expatiated upon in the North that had more serious ramifications for the War on Poverty in future years.

'Law and order' politics also flipped the argument over the federal government. In this case, it was Goldwater who called for a strong federal role in American life. Drawing on polls which showed 'law and order' and 'morality' as the only issues where Johnson was vulnerable, Goldwater hammered the federal government – and by extension, Johnson – for not doing enough to prevent rising crime and disobedience, while claiming there was a lack of moral leadership emanating from the White House.[118] Importantly, he also blamed the welfare state for 'encouraging paternalism and dependence at the expense of opportunity and responsibility'.[119] This challenged the heart of the liberal argument that social welfare programmes were, in fact, helping to reduce violence by preventing poverty and unemployment – two conditions which were widely believed to increase crime.

It was this rationale that led the Johnson administration to argue that the War on Poverty was also, in fact, a War on Crime. The administration, terrified by the crime issue – especially after urban uprisings in Harlem and Rochester during July – made what Flamm correctly calls a 'fateful' decision to mute Goldwater's message in a manner that would 'haunt his administration in the years to come'.[120] In mid-October, at the swearing in of OEO Director Shriver, Johnson proclaimed that 'The war on poverty . . . is a war against crime and a war against disorder.' The President also noted that Goldwater's vote against the War on Poverty showed that he was only willing to talk about solving crime.[121]

This short-term tactic was successful, largely due to the fact that crime and urban riots, while important during 1964, were not yet issues of central importance in American politics. Nevertheless, Johnson's approach was a poor long-term strategy. It meant that not only was the War on Poverty responsible for reducing poverty in the United States, but now it was also expected to contribute to a decline in crime rates. Republicans now had more than one angle from which to attack the nucleus of LBJ's Great Society.

Away from the one-sided race for the White House, the War on Poverty featured less prominently. It appeared that most Republicans, defeated in the legislative battle in Congress, believed that Johnson's 'war' either was too popular to attack on the stump or was not an issue that stood central in voters' minds in 1964. Another explanation for Republican recalcitrance was the desire of many GOP candidates running state-wide to avoid national issues that would link their own candidacy to the unpopular Goldwater. Certainly, many Republicans – particularly moderates and progressives – refused to appear with the Arizonan.[122] Moreover, Johnson was actively pursuing moderate Republican voters who were put off by Goldwater's perceived extremism, even to the point of running commercials instructing GOP voters on how to split their tickets.[123] The *Wall Street Journal*'s Alan Otten, following Charles Percy's campaign in the Illinois gubernatorial election, observed, 'Mr. Percy has thus far carefully avoided direct attacks on President Johnson, and repeatedly declares he wants to campaign on state issues and not national ones.' Otten noted that other moderates, such as Romney, Taft and Scott, found themselves in a similar position, requiring split-ticket voting to push them to victory.[124] As such, railing against the signature LBJ programme made little political sense for Republicans hoping that Johnson's coat-tails were not going to drag their opponents to victory. The political pragmatism that defined the GOP's response to Johnson's Great Society in the years ahead was therefore already evident in 1964.

Given the heavy Republican losses, congressional Republicans who had voted for the EOA were generally successful in November. New York moderate Kenneth Keating was the only Republican to vote for the bill in the Senate to lose his seat. Even then, he ran far ahead of Goldwater's vote total in the Empire State and had to compete with the emotional factor of having Robert Kennedy as his opponent. Elsewhere, voting for the poverty bill tended to correlate with Republican success: while forty-eight House Republicans lost at the polls (or retired and Democrats won the vacant seat), only two of those defeated had voted for the EOA, and both races were decided in the Democrats' favour by razor-thin margins. Voting for the poverty bill was therefore far from a poisoned chalice for Republicans. More significantly, of the defeated Republican representatives, roughly two thirds had voted for the Civil Rights Act.[125] This development, coupled with Goldwater's electoral success in the Deep South (his only triumphs outside of his home state) and the southern Republicans he helped to elect on his coat-tails, was a harbinger of a new, more racially conservative congressional GOP. This outcome would have ramifications for the party's approach to the War on Poverty in the coming years.[126]

Goldwater's landslide defeat in November had little to do with his stance on the War on Poverty. Nevertheless, his harsh denunciations of the antipoverty effort did play into the extremist narrative that characterised the Senator's candidacy. Furthermore, Goldwater's stance on the EOA contributed to Matusow's observation that, in 1964, the voters found the Arizonan's 'conservatism merely cranky in an era of so many liberal good works'.[127] Unlike other Republicans, Goldwater did view the EOA, and Johnson's concept of a Great Society, as topics worthy of crusading against during the campaign. Goldwater's campaign also set a template for future GOP arguments against the antipoverty effort – particularly his association of the War on Poverty with welfare dependency. Finally, in pushing the crime issue, Goldwater had contributed to another strategic error by the President in 1964. Johnson's promise that a war on poverty was, in fact, a war on crime, proved the domestic equivalent of his declaration that American boys would not be sent to the jungles of Vietnam.

Conclusion

After leaving the White House in 1966, Johnson adviser Eric Goldman wrote that the 'Great Society,' in the accent of Lyndon Johnson, 'smacked of a Texas tall tale'.[128] For Republicans, the War on Poverty was the tallest tale of them all. Taken as a whole, the response of leading Republicans to the antipoverty effort was once more reactive, oppositional and negative. It demonstrated that the party was adept at drawing up a list of reasons for why something should not be done, but less successful at selling an agenda of their own. Arguments which found fault with the War on Poverty on the grounds that it would enlarge the scope of the federal government and infringe on private enterprise ultimately fell flat in 1964. Importantly, Republican opposition to an antipoverty effort only fed the narrative that they were the party of privilege and obstruction, a party not yet ready to govern.

Happily, race was not one of the cards played by GOP leaders. Indeed, the party's response to the antipoverty bill confirms the conclusion of Edward Carmines and James Stimson that 'House Republicanism of the early 1960s was conservative on fiscal issues and proud of the heritage of Lincoln on race'. Still, as the two political scientists argue, the results of the 1964 elections meant that the process of 'purging Lincolnism' from the party had begun.[129] The appearance of 'law and order' rhetoric during Goldwater's campaign was another ominous development.

Most significantly, in 1964, it was not yet clear that LBJ's War on Poverty and Great Society would prove any less of a political conundrum for the Grand Old Party than FDR's New Deal had thirty years previously. The torrent of Republican complaints that Johnson was simply playing politics in an election year implicitly suggested that many in the GOP were worried that the poverty bill enjoyed widespread popularity in the country. This was further inferred by the fact that there is scant evidence of Republicans campaigning against the poverty programme in the autumn, despite serious misgivings about the Economic Opportunity Act. Nevertheless, the partisan nature of the bill's passage did have a drawback for the Johnson administration. Leading Republicans were now waiting in the wings to criticise a poverty programme that was hastily conceived, with more hope than expectation that it would succeed, and which also required annually approved appropriations from Congress. In the first political battle over poverty, the President had emerged victorious; the war, however, was not yet won.

Notes

1. Goldwater quoted in 'Where Does He Stand on the Big Issues?', July 1964, folder 357, box 34-B, George W. Romney Papers.
2. 'Publisher is Striking Controversial Question from Classroom Test', 25 October 1965, Republican Congressional Campaign Newsletter.
3. Thomas Benham, RNC Executive Session, 22 January 1965, Papers of the Republican Party [hereafter PRP], part 1, series b, reel 4.
4. LBJ, 'Annual Message to the Congress on the State of the Union', 8 January 1964, TAPP.
5. James L. Sundquist, *Politics and Policy: The Eisenhower, Kennedy, and Johnson Years* (Washington, DC: Brookings Institution, 1968), 150.

6. Michael Harrington, *The Other America: Poverty in the United States* (New York: Macmillan, 1962).
7. Matusow, *Unraveling of America*, 101.
8. LBJ, 'State of the Union'.
9. Matusow, *Unraveling of America*, 220.
10. Michael Flamm, *Law and Order: Street Crime, Civil Unrest, and the Crisis of Liberalism in the 1960's* (New York: Columbia University Press, 2005), 46.
11. Davies, *From Opportunity to Entitlement*, 38.
12. Sundquist, *Politics and Policy*, 111
13. Mason, *From Hoover to Reagan*, 2.
14. Edward Brooke, 'A Negro Leader's Advice to Republicans', *US News & World Report*, February 1965.
15. Kabaservice, *Rule and Ruin*, 72.
16. Andrew, *Lyndon Johnson and the Great Society*, 3.
17. Robert A. Caro, *The Years of Lyndon Johnson: The Passage of Power* (New York: Knopf, 2012), 539.
18. Leslie Arends, 'Statements by Major Republican Leaders on the President's State of the Union Message', January 1964, *Political Activities of the Johnson White House* [hereafter *PAJWH*], Part 1A, Reel 18.
19. William Miller, Joint Senate–House Republican Leadership Press Release, 28 January 1964, Dirksen Congressional Center.
20. Jacob K. Javits, Statement on the State of the Union, 8 January 1964, box 31, series 1, subseries 1, Javits Collection.
21. Hugh D. Scott, Speech at Republican Dinner in Pittsburgh, PA, 29 January 1964, box 34, Papers of Hugh Scott, 1905–1994. Accession # 10200-ae, Special Collections Department, University of Virginia Library, Charlottesville, VA.
22. Nelson A. Rockefeller, Remarks at Sheraton-Park Hotel, Washington, DC, 6 February 1964, folder 89, box 16, series 17, RG 15, NAR Papers, Rockefeller Family Archives, Rockefeller Archive Center [hereafter RAC].
23. LBJ, 'Special Message to the Congress Proposing a Nationwide War on the Sources of Poverty', 16 March 1964, TAPP.
24. *CQ Almanac 1964* (Washington, DC: Congressional Quarterly, 1965).
25. 'Lyndon Johnson and Bill Moyers at the LBJ Ranch on 7 August 1964', Conversation WH6408-12-4815, 4816, 4817, 4818, Presidential Recordings of Lyndon B. Johnson Digital Edition [hereafter Johnson Tapes].

26. *CQ Almanac 1964.*
27. Ibid.
28. Zelizer, *The Fierce Urgency of Now*, 132–7.
29. Kabaservice, *Rule and Ruin*, xvii–xx.
30. Michael Bowen, *The Roots of Modern Conservatism: Dewey, Taft, and the Battle for the Soul of the Republican Party* (Chapel Hill, NC: University of North Carolina Press, 2011), 4.
31. Robert Griffin, 'Washington Report', 4 June 1964, folder 51, box b13, LF, Gerald R. Ford Presidential Library [hereafter GRF].
32. Press Release, John G. Tower, 'Washington Weekly Report: The Johnson Poverty Bill', 5 July 1964, folder 12, box 26, Series Press Office, John Tower papers, John Tower Library, Southwestern University.
33. Barry Goldwater [hereafter BMG], Remarks at press conference, 22 January 1964, folder 115, box 20, series j.2, RG 4, NAR.
34. Nelson Rockefeller [hereafter NAR], Statement at Hanover, NH, 14 February 1964, folder 89, box 16, series 17, RG 15, NAR.
35. BMG, Speech in Santa Clara, CA, May 1964, *Goldwater Freedom Special*, folder 120, box 21, series j.2, RG 4, NAR.
36. NAR, Remarks at Greeham, OR, 17 April 1964, folder 89, box 16, series 17, RG 15, NAR.
37. NAR, Remarks at Sheraton-Park Hotel, Washington, DC, 6 February 1964, NAR.
38. George W. Romney [hereafter GWR], Speech at Republican State Convention, Grand Rapids, MI, 9 May 1964, folder 357, box 34-b, George W. Romney Papers, Bentley Historical Library, Ann Arbor, MI.
39. William Scranton quoted in 'Who the Poor Are – and Ways to Help Them', *Life*, 31 July 1964.
40. Smylie quoted in ibid.
41. Peter Frelinghuysen quoted in RNC Research Division, '1964 Factbook', reel 3, PRP, part II.
42. William H. Ayres and Peter H. B. Frelinghuysen to Representatives, 29 July 1964, folder 51, box b13, Legislative File, Gerald R. Ford Congressional Papers.
43. John Tower [hereafter JGT] 'The Johnson Poverty Bill'.
44. 'President's "War on Poverty" Approved', *CQ Almanac 1964.*
45. Ayres and Frelinghuysen, 29 July 1964.
46. JGT, 'The Johnson Poverty Bill'.
47. Senate Minority Report, '1964 Factbook', PRP, part II.
48. Hugh Scott [hereafter HDS], 'The War on Poverty and the Race to the Moon', *Congressional Record*, 30 April 1964, box 39, HDS.

49. Johnson believed that Community Action would also unfold in a similar fashion to the National Youth Administration (NYA) that operated between 1935 and 1939 with the goal of providing work and education to young Americans. Johnson had administered the Texas division of the NYA in the mid-1930s; 'Lyndon Johnson and George Mahon in the Mansion on 6 August 1964', Conversation WH6408-08-4770, Johnson Tapes.
50. Sargent Shriver Interview, 'Issues and Answers', American Broadcasting Company (ABC), May 1964, folder 51, box b13, LF, GRF.
51. Ibid.
52. Ibid.
53. Jacob Javits [hereafter JKJ], 'Shriver Should Give up Peace Corps Job, Devote Full Time to "War on Poverty"', 21 March 1964, box 31, series 1, subseries 1, JKJ.
54. Alistair Cooke, 'Johnson's Strategy in War on Poverty', *Guardian*, 17 March 1964, 11.
55. 'President's "War on Poverty" Approved', *CQ Almanac 1964*.
56. House Minority Report, July 1964, '1964 Factbook'.
57. Griffin, 'Washington Report', 4 June 1964.
58. Gerald R. Ford [hereafter GRF] to S. F. Leahy, 21 May 1964, folder 51, box b13, LF, GRF.
59. JGT, 'The Johnson Poverty Bill'.
60. BMG quoted in 'Where Does He Stand on the Big Issues?'
61. Ayres quoted in *CQ Almanac 1964*.
62. Sundquist, *Politics and Policy*, 147.
63. Shriver quoted in Davies, *From Opportunity to Entitlement*, 45.
64. Lyndon Johnson, Bill Moyers and Jack Valenti on 31 July 1964, Conversation WH6407-22-4461, 4462, 4463, Johnson Tapes.
65. John L. Bullion, *LBJ and the Transformation of American Politics* (New York: Pearson Longman, 2008); Caro, *Passage of Power*.
66. Kabaservice, *Rule and Ruin*, 98.
67. Bullion, *LBJ and the Transformation of American Politics*, 80.
68. Byron Hulsey, *Everett Dirksen and His Presidents: How a Senate Giant Shaped American Politics* (Lawrence, KS: University Press of Kansas, 2000).
69. Mark Stern, *Calculating Visions: Kennedy, Johnson, and Civil Rights* (New Brunswick, NJ: Rugters University Press, 1992), 174–5.
70. Robert David Johnson, *All the Way with LBJ: The 1964 Presidential Election* (Cambridge, MA: Cambridge University Press, 2009), 127.
71. Kabaservice, *Rule and Ruin*, 98.

72. James M. Cannon, 'Gerald R. Ford: Minority Leader of the House of Representatives, 1965–1973', in *Masters of the House: Congressional Leadership over Two Centuries*, ed. Roger H. Davidson, Susan V. Hammond and Raymond Smock (Boulder, CO: Westview Press, 1998), 271.
73. 'Senate Defeats Filibuster, Passes Civil Rights Act, 73–27', *CQ Almanac 1964*, 354–67.
74. Edsall and Edsall, *Chain Reaction*, 36.
75. Ibid.
76. Mason, *From Hoover to Reagan*, 189.
77. See Sean P. Cunningham, 'John Tower, Texas, and the Rise of the Republican South', in *Seeking a New Majority: The Republican Party and American Politics, 1960–1980*, ed. Robert Mason and Iwan Morgan (Nashville, TN: Vanderbilt University Press, 2012).
78. Timothy Thurber, 'Goldwaterism Triumphant? Race and the Republican Party, 1965–1968', *Journal of the Historical Society*, vol. 7 (2007), 231.
79. Kabaservice, *Rule and Ruin*, 101.
80. Edsall and Edsall, *Chain Reaction*, 43.
81. Kabaservice, *Rule and Ruin*, 118.
82. Rowland Evans and Robert Novak, 'Inside Report: Southern GOP in Dark Mood', *The Plain Dealer*, 12 July 1964.
83. Meg Greenfield, 'Senator Goldwater and the Negro', *The Reporter*, 8 October 1964, 27–8.
84. Kevin P. Phillips, *The Emerging Republican Majority* (New Rochelle, NY: Arlington House, 1969).
85. Richard L. Lyons, 'Antipoverty Bill Due for Vote Today', *Washington Post*, 7 August 1964.
86. LBJ quoted in Zelizer, *The Fierce Urgency of Now*, 135.
87. Lyons, 'Antipoverty Bill Due for Vote Today'.
88. Griffin, 'Washington Report', 4 June 1964.
89. Lyons, 'Antipoverty Bill Due for Vote Today'.
90. 'President's "War on Poverty" Approved', *CQ Almanac 1964*.
91. Lyndon Johnson, Bill Moyers and Jack Valenti on 31 July 1964, Conversation WH6407-22-4461, 4462, 4463, Johnson Tapes.
92. Lyndon Johnson and Bill Moyers on 3 August 1964, Conversation WH6408-04-4650, 4652, 4653, Johnson Tapes.
93. Charles Hoeven, *Congressional Record*, 6 August 1964, 18314.
94. Robert Taft Jr, *Congressional Record*, 6 August 1964, 18271.
95. Larry O'Brien and Lyndon Johnson on 31 July 1964, Conversation WH6407-22-4460, Johnson Tapes.

96. Lyndon Johnson, Bill Moyers and Jack Valenti on 31 July 1964, Johnson Tapes.
97. Walter Reuther and Lyndon Johnson on 1 August 1964, Conversation WH6408-03-4624, 4625, Johnson Tapes.
98. BMG, Speech at the Republican National Convention, San Francisco, *Washington Post*, 16 July 1964.
99. Johnson Campaign, 'Eastern Seaboard', *Living Room Candidate*. Available at http://www.livingroomcandidate.org (accessed 27 October 2020).
100. 'Confidential Proceedings of Closed Session Meeting of Republican Unity Conference', 12 August 1964, reel 8, *PAJWH*, part 1, series a.
101. Charles Halleck, Joint Senate–House Leadership Press Conference, 3 September 1964, Dirksen Congressional Center.
102. Everett Dirksen [hereafter EMD] quoted in ibid.
103. BMG, Speech at Cobo Hall, Detroit, 26 September 1964, folder 121, box 21, series j.2, RG 4, NAR.
104. 'Text of Sen. Goldwater's Speech Opening His Campaign', *Washington Post*, 4 September 1964.
105. Robert Allan Goldberg, *Barry Goldwater* (New Haven, CT: Yale University Press, 1995), 223.
106. Robert E. Baker, 'War on Poverty a Fake, Goldwater Says: Old Kennedy Ground', *Washington Post*, 19 September 1964.
107. J. William Middendorf II, *A Glorious Disaster: Barry Goldwater's Presidential Campaign and the Origins of the Conservative Movement* (New York: Basic Books, 2006), 183.
108. Rick Perlstein, *Before the Storm: Barry Goldwater and the Unmaking of the American Consensus* (New York: Hill & Wang, 2001), 430.
109. Richard L. Lyons, 'Goldwater Repairs Stand for Benefits; Quiet for Poverty', *Washington Post*, 30 October 1964.
110. BMG, Transcript of Goldwater–Nixon Television Show, 9 October 1964, folder 357, box 34-B, GWR.
111. LBJ, Remarks in Harrisburg at a Dinner Sponsored by the Pennsylvania State Democratic Committee, 10 September 1964, TAPP.
112. LBJ, 'Memorandum Outlining Some of the Major Issues of the Campaign', 11 October 1964, TAPP.
113. Ronald Reagan, 'A Time for Choosing', 27 October 1964, Ronald Reagan Presidential Library.
114. BMG quoted in Flamm, *Law and Order*, 31.

115. Flamm, *Law and Order*, 31.
116. BMG, 'Text of Sen. Goldwater's Speech Opening His Campaign', *Washington Post*, 4 September 1964.
117. Thurmond quoted in Joseph Crespino, *Strom Thurmond's America* (New York: Hill & Wang, 2012), 183.
118. Flamm, *Law and Order*, 41.
119. Ibid. 33.
120. Ibid. 46.
121. LBJ quoted in ibid. 47.
122. Goldberg, *Barry Goldwater*, 222.
123. Johnson, *All the Way*, 206.
124. Alan Otten, 'Poser for Percy: How He Tries to Hold Barry's Backers While Luring Johnson Voters', *Wall Street Journal*, 17 September 1964.
125. Edward G. Carmines and James A. Stimson, *Issue Evolution: Race and the Transformation of American Politics* (Princeton, NJ: Princeton University Press, 1989), 76.
126. Ibid., 47.
127. Matusow, *Unraveling of America*, 151.
128. Eric F. Goldman, *The Tragedy of Lyndon Johnson* (London: Macdonald, 1969), 166.
129. Carmines and Stimson, *Issue Evolution*, 76.

2

A path to relevance: the Republican crusade against the War on Poverty, 1965–66

A beautiful picture was painted for the poor. Director Shriver stood upright using the long bow to shoot an arrow in the war on poverty. The arrow has begun to turn, and lo and behold, it will turn into a boomerang that will destroy those who launched it.[1]

Rep. William Ayres (R-OH), 20 July 1965

Looking out over the political landscape after the 1964 elections, Governor Robert Smylie of Idaho assessed the health of his party in near apocalyptic tones; the Chair of the Republican Governors Association (RGA) concluded, 'We are a defeated party with a defeated leadership. We have suffered a defeat as severe in quality and quantity as any that the Republican party has ever sustained.'[2] Few Republicans disagreed with Smylie's diagnosis. As such, the GOP hierarchy spent much of 1965 almost exclusively focused on how to make the party relevant again and thus position themselves for success in the 1966 midterm elections. The resulting consensus demanded that Republicans use their limited presence in the 89th Congress to replace a public image of negativity, infighting and privilege with a record of positivity – stemming from offering constructive alternatives to Lyndon Johnson's Great Society proposals – and projecting a unified image to the public.

Despite already being passed in the 88th Congress, no legislation featured more prominently in this new Republican blueprint than the Economic Opportunity Act. The EOA, which was up for renewal in both 1965 and 1966, sparked two fraught legislative battles that demonstrated Republican opposition to the War on

Poverty had only intensified since Johnson had forced it through Congress in 1964. Moreover, the antipoverty effort – which quickly began receiving negative press attention – proved the perfect vehicle for Republicans to showcase their new constructive and united image. During the EOA's second renewal in 1966, the GOP unveiled their detailed War on Poverty alternative – the 'Opportunity Crusade' – and through the amendment process they significantly shaped how the antipoverty effort would henceforth be fought. In doing so, congressional Republicans used the War on Poverty as a path back to relevance and to establish their fitness for governing.

Having shown their diplomatic side in Congress, Republicans launched a frontal assault on the War on Poverty as a key element of their strategy in securing an electoral comeback in the 1966 midterm elections. GOP candidates tugged at an important thread woven into Johnson's antipoverty tapestry – charging that the War on Poverty was nothing more than 'big government' welfare. As discussed in Chapter 1, Johnson's diligence in adhering to American beliefs in opportunity over entitlement when he launched the War on Poverty had largely blunted this traditional Republican attack.[3] By 1966, however, as the antipoverty programmes' achievements remained inconclusive and as liberal Democrats began demanding more funding, Republicans charged that the War on Poverty was indeed a handout, rather than the promised hand-up. Furthermore, many GOP candidates cited the War on Poverty as epitomising the Great Society's reckless spending which was combining with Vietnam War appropriations to drive inflation during 1966. Race, often linked to welfare, was also becoming a substantial problem for War on Poverty advocates, as uprisings and rising urban crime served to create white resentment that built to a climax as the midterm elections approached.

The 1966 campaign signalled a decisive shift to the right as many Americans grew increasingly concerned with a raft of issues which benefited conservatives: welfare dependency, rising crime and rioting, 'guns or butter', and holding back government rather than building it up. The question had moved on from asking how Americans should build a Great Society to considering how they could preserve the society that many perceived as falling apart.

The election did not constitute a backlash to the Great Society per se – only extremists advocated a repeal of Medicare, aid to education, or civil rights laws – but the nationwide vote in November did represent a backlash against the new public perception of Great Society liberalism. This perception, embodied by the War on Poverty, held that the Great Society's aims were to help the few rather than, or at the expense of, the many.

All told, by the end of 1966 Republicans had successfully moved the debate over how to solve poverty onto conservative territory. Rather than being poised to strike a new offensive in the War on Poverty, the Johnson administration would henceforth have to settle for an attritional struggle with limited resources.

Constructing an alternative party

It is difficult to overstate the perilous situation that Republicans found themselves in at the end of 1964. Defeated in seven of the last nine presidential elections and vastly outnumbered by heavy Democratic majorities in both the House and Senate, the party's future appeared bleak. Ominously, Gallup reported that only 27 per cent of Americans identified themselves as Republicans, and the party's own pollster, Thomas Benham, informed a depressed Republican National Committee (RNC) that the GOP remained hamstrung by 'the image of the Party of privilege'.[4] Moreover, as shown by the 1964 election campaign, the GOP was still a party divided. The raucous San Francisco convention and the subsequent refusal of many progressive and moderate Republicans to endorse Barry Goldwater had exposed the chasm that existed in the party. With only a touch of hyperbole, Theodore White, dean of presidential campaign chroniclers, later observed, 'Not since the Whigs had any great party seemed so completely to have lost touch with reality.'[5] As such, if Republicans were to achieve electoral success in the future, the first order of business was to clean up their own house. In this regard, Republicans were relatively successful over the next two years as hitting rock-bottom finally jolted the slumbering GOP elephant into wakefulness.

This infusion of purpose was evident from the very beginning of 1965. On 4 January, as Lyndon Johnson announced to an estimated 31 million Americans watching his second State of the Union address that the march to the Great Society would require doubling the War on Poverty budget, congressional Republicans were already preoccupied making changes of their own.[6] With emotional post-election recriminations turning to practical considerations for the future of the GOP, House Republicans completed the ousting of the ineffective and acerbic Charles Halleck from the minority leadership, replacing him with likeable team player Gerald Ford. Both stalwarts, the two differed little in ideology, but Halleck's limited television appeal and lack of dynamism in opposition cost him dearly in the wake of an election that had resulted in a net loss of thirty-six seats for an already beleaguered minority.[7] Ford, much younger than Halleck, also represented a new generation of Republicans. Three weeks later, during a high-stakes gathering in Chicago, the divisive Goldwaterite chairman of the RNC, Dean Burch, was also supplanted by the pragmatic organiser Ray Bliss.

Rather than actions of mere political bloodletting for bloodletting's sake, the two events decisively showed that senior Republicans, many of whom belonged to a generation that had known little but minority status in Congress and – excepting the eight-year Eisenhower anomaly – a Democrat in the White House, recognised the need for a shake-up. The election of sufficient numbers of northern Democrats to break the Republican comfort blanket of the conservative coalition with southern Democrats – which at least provided the minority party some influence during previous congressional sessions – 'crystallized the sentiment for change', according to Rep. Robert Griffin.[8] Griffin's House colleague, Charles Goodell, also warned his party that 'those ways of operating with southern Democrats are over . . . It's more important to spend our time communicating our program to the American people.'[9] Underscoring the GOP's dire predicament were the continuous appeals made by Republicans throughout the year stressing the necessity of maintaining the two-party system – hardly a clarion call to inspire the electorate.[10]

Upon accepting the role of party chair, Bliss told his audience that they had elected 'a man who believes that our Party should not purely be the Party of opposition but also must offer constructive alternatives to help solve the problems of our day'.[11] Such sentiment was echoed by former RNC chair and Kentucky senator Thruston Morton, who acknowledged that 'millions of voters today consider the Republican Party as absolutely negative', and his solution was for the GOP to offer 'enlightened opposition' in Congress while pleading with his party to 'achieve some degree of unity'. Importantly, Morton, aware of the GOP's ideological divisions, continued: 'we must recognize unity for what it is. Unity is not conformity.'[12] Thus, the desired unity was more akin to a truce – for the sake of public image – from the infighting that had plagued Republicans for thirty years and had been so evident during the 1964 campaign.

The formation of the Republican Coordinating Committee (RCC) in early 1965 proved a crucial element in this new strategy. The RCC, Ford explained, would 'facilitate the broadest party representation and the establishment of task forces for the study and examination of major national problems and issues'.[13] One of the tasks of the RCC – comprised of eleven members of the Joint Senate–House leadership, five ex-Republican nominees for President, and five representatives from the RGA – was to project a moderate, unified image of the Republican Party after the Goldwater election had tinged the party with extremism – a death knell for any national campaign. Change was afoot elsewhere, with Ford also announcing a new Planning and Research Committee, headed by Goodell, to lead task forces on each of the major domestic and foreign policy issues that House Republicans were poised to confront.[14] All in all, the changes showed a party grappling seriously with how to make an electoral return. With their house cleaned up, Republicans were searching for an issue upon which GOP opposition to Johnson's liberal programme could coalesce and prove popular with the electorate. The War on Poverty's first renewal provided a most timely opportunity to rejuvenate Republican fortunes.

Federalism and failures – the Economic Opportunity Act's first renewal, 1965

For electoral reasons, Republicans in 1965 may have signed up to the so-called Eleventh Commandment – 'thou shalt not speak ill of any Republican'– but it was continued reverence for the Tenth Amendment that helped bind the party together.[15] While it was easy enough to preach unity in the wake of a heavy election defeat, as time wore on an issue was needed to provide a common purpose. It was crucial to the rebuilding process that Republicans perceived Johnson's Great Society programmes to be redefining the federal structure of the United States. As a result, Republicans ensured that the White House's request that Congress remove state governors' veto power over proposed Job Corps, Community Action, work training, adult basic education, and VISTA programmes in their states proved the most controversial and headline-grabbing issue surrounding EOA's first renewal – even more so than the requested doubling of funds. Despite the fact that other Great Society measures, such as those related to health care and education, drove a greater expansion of the federal government, it was the antipoverty effort that was used as the poster-child policy for brewing discontent with federal expansion.

Federalism remained an issue that united Republicans from all factions of the party; most of whom were already concerned with the War on Poverty for what they perceived as federal encroachment on the rights of states to govern themselves. The unity engendered by the distaste of federal control was on display when every single House Republican (excepting John Lindsay, who was bucking the GOP trend and on his way to victory in New York City's Mayoralty contest) successfully voted to recommit the Senate's bill with the intention of reinstating the governor veto.[16] As well as Republicans, southern Democrats were needed to achieve the successful 209–180 vote to send the bill to conference where the limited veto was reinstated. In a year when the conservative coalition was largely impotent, the veto victory was a timely reminder that the informal alliance was dormant rather than extinct.

The other main GOP criticism of the War on Poverty in 1965 was less ideological. Instead, when the EOA's renewal came up for debate in July, Republicans simply argued that War on Poverty did not work and should therefore be scrapped. Indeed, Republicans may have desired to project a new and positive image to the country, but it was a trick that they struggled to pull off entirely convincingly during the EOA's first renewal. To combat the GOP's stodgy image, the party leadership attempted to put some fresh paint on old criticisms by letting younger Republicans take the lead in criticising the War on Poverty. This was particularly true in the House where Al Quie, along with fellow 'Young Turks' Goodell and Ayres, replaced Peter Frelinghuysen as the bill's opponent-in-chief. Promoted following roles in Ford's elevation and with temperaments more in line with the new Minority Leader's welcoming appeal, Quie and Goodell especially were savvy politicians and careful to stress sympathy with the plight of the poor while harshly criticising the Johnson programmes. Moreover, these Republicans shunned fighting against popular aspects of the War on Poverty, notably Head Start, which had far exceeded the administration's expectations with over 400,000 more enrolments in the pre-school programme than had been anticipated in its first summer.[17]

Quie, a young and quite charismatic politician, used the War on Poverty's controversies to position himself, and thus the Republican Party, on the side of the poor who – according to Quie – were being failed by the administration's offering.[18] As with Ford's political philosophy being scarcely less conservative than Halleck's, Quie differed little from Frelinghuysen in substance. Rather, the change was one of image and willingness to explore alternatives to Democratic programmes. For instance, Quie was never heard uttering similar public opinions to those of Tower, who picked up Goldwater's torch in the conservative struggle and voiced his view that the War on Poverty was un-American and that there were always going to be people at the bottom of society.[19] Instead, Quie took aim at CAPs (Community Action Programs), which were already generating negative headlines, as power struggles emerged at state and local levels between elected officeholders and 'representatives' of the poor. The vague nature of the phrase 'maximum feasible participation', which the EOA had prescribed for community involvement in CAPs, was providing headaches to all involved in the antipoverty endeavour.

In a letter to fellow Republicans in late April asking colleagues to notify him of any specific examples of these struggles, the Minnesota congressman slated the OEO for not achieving the 'maximum feasible participation' of the poor. Citing testimony from various clergymen in Chicago, where Democratic Mayor Richard Daley had quickly snatched control of any nascent local CAPs, Quie was careful to couch his appeal in the manner of a concerned friend of the War on Poverty rather than a partisan enemy.[20] For example, Quie quoted community organiser Reverend Lynward Stevenson: 'In Chicago there is no War on Poverty; there is only more of the ancient galling war against the poor. It is a war against the poor when the great ideas of two presidents and Congress are twisted into cheap slogans to benefit local politicians.'[21]

Indeed, Chicago – and urban America more generally – quickly became the epicentre of Republican criticism of the War on Poverty. Rep. Glenn Andrews (R-AL), a conservative who was swept in on the mini Goldwater wave in Alabama, summed up the growing centrality of the city to the War on Poverty's image. Andrews, somewhat disingenuously, declared that he would love to support the poverty effort, but stressed that if it 'is an instrument for perfecting the United Cook Counties of America for the political exploitation of the poor, then I am against it'.[22] While Andrews was revisiting an old GOP trope about Democratic urban corruption, his comments also hinted that the perception of the War on Poverty was moving away from the mountains of Appalachia and into the maelstrom of urban America.

Republicans were able to call upon many examples of political corruption, which suggested that the War on Poverty was a heavily stuffed piñata that was too tempting for local politicians not to whack. In calling the programme a 'political pork barrel by big city machines whose only interest in the poor is to exploit them', the House Minority Report was drawing on various press accounts, including criticism from individuals on the left such as the Chicago-based activist Saul Alinsky.[23] Even the programme's foremost Republican friend, Senator Jacob Javits, felt the need to call for an enquiry into political corruption affecting New York CAPs.[24]

Republicans derided the OEO for administrative grandeur and incompetence, complaining bitterly that it had a superior number of employees on 'supergrade' salaries compared with any other federal department, and yet the OEO was being led by a part-time director who, as a result, was unable to coordinate operations effectively.[25] Regarding the salaries, Sen. John Williams (R-DE) mocked the expense accounts of poverty employees who, according to Williams, were charging the taxpayers for tuxedos hired during research trips.[26] On Shriver's position, Javits introduced an amendment in the Senate – which narrowly failed – calling for the role of OEO director to be enshrined in statute as requiring a full-time occupant. Javits's amendment seemed perfectly reasonable. Given the centrality of the War on Poverty to Johnson's Great Society, it is surprising that the President continued to allow Shriver to divide his responsibilities between the Peace Corps and the OEO. Shriver's lack of full-time control only served to lend credibility to criticisms that the War on Poverty was, in the words of Goodell, 'the worst administered program that I have seen in Washington'.[27]

It played into Republican hands that beyond a vague and distant target of 'ending poverty', there was little awareness of what results a successfully implemented programme would show. Besides the political cover afforded the Johnson administration by a slowly declining poverty rate, Republican criticisms could not be met with hard evidence of progress.[28] Conversely, Republicans were able to point to specific figures and evidence, such as dropout rates at Job Corps camps, high salaries for OEO staff and stories of political corruption, as proof of the War on Poverty's failings.[29] Attempting to paint the GOP as the same old 'Party of No', Rep. Charles Joelson (D-NJ) counterattacked:

> [Republicans] are trying to have it both ways. On the one hand, they do not want to pay professionals the way professionals should be paid; and, on the other hand, they do not want what they call 'political hacks'. I believe they just do not want the program but are not willing to say so.[30]

Other Democrats in the House rose to demand the GOP's alternative, and it was here that Republicans were found wanting during the EOA's first renewal.[31] When the time came to vote, the majority of Republicans baulked at doubling appropriations and opposed the Economic Opportunity amendments in greater numbers than they opposed other contentious Great Society initiatives. In the House, twenty-four out of 132 Republicans voted for renewal, while in the Senate, only progressives held firm, giving the programme nine out of the twenty-nine GOP votes cast.

All told, the War on Poverty's controversies represented a helpful tool in the Republican rebuilding process. Federalism may have provided a theoretical concept around which the party could rally, but the obvious flaws of the EOA's application – executed by a federal agency (OEO) – allowed for practical examples of failure at which Republicans could point. Had the War on Poverty enjoyed a seamless beginning, alarm bells raised by Republicans over federal control would have rung hollow and sounded as if the GOP was still the 'Party of No'. Nevertheless, to finally shed the burden of negativism under which the GOP elephant had so long laboured, Republicans still had work to do in proving that they had a feasible alternative to the War on Poverty. The EOA's beauty – as far as Republicans were concerned – was that it would once again need renewing; right in the middle of an election year. This presented a golden opportunity for a Republican crusade into Democrat territory.

The Opportunity Crusade

At the beginning of 1966, congressional Republicans, spearheaded by Reps. Goodell and Quie, took aim at the failings of the War on Poverty and launched their alternative – a GOP 'Opportunity Crusade'.[32] The Republican 'Crusade' was, in one sense, a serious effort to offer a constructive alternative to the War on Poverty – the type of alternative to Johnson's Great Society that Republicans had promised throughout 1965. This was demonstrated when one of the key proposals contained within the Crusade represented the most significant change to the EOA in 1966. It is also true, however, that the Opportunity Crusade was a proposal that would have reduced the budget of the anti-poverty effort while neutering the main innovation of the EOA: the OEO. If the so-called War on Poverty was, in fact, more of a 'skirmish', as Javits claimed, the Opportunity Crusade arguably resembled a minor squabble with poverty.[33] This, of course, is not surprising given that most Republicans had never desired a 'war' on poverty in the first place. Moreover, the War on Poverty's early struggles had not given GOP politicians much cause to change their mind. Ultimately, in offering their alternative, Republicans were pragmatically targeting the most vulnerable Great Society programme and their solution – with its focus on federalism and private enterprise – conveniently played into ideological concepts that united the GOP.

The Republican strategy in presenting the Opportunity Crusade was twofold. On the one hand, Quie and Goodell, having spent much of 1965 criticising the War on Poverty, redoubled their efforts to discredit the OEO's record. At the same time, they sought to present the Republican Party as the saviours of the antipoverty effort – as without significant changes, Quie argued, the War on Poverty would be abandoned.[34] While the Opportunity Crusade was an extensive and multifaceted opposition proposal (the draft of the bill ran to over 100 pages), boiled down, it essentially called for five key changes. These included fewer responsibilities for the OEO, more participation by the poor in their own struggle against poverty, more permanent jobs for the poor, an increase in the private sector's role, and reduced federal authority over states and localities. Quie and Goodell supported these proposals with thirty-eight 'poverty memos' that were released between March and April, and that served as a way of reciting the problems with the poverty programme and laying the ground for a Republican alternative.[35]

Primarily, the Opportunity Crusade proposed stripping the OEO of all responsibilities, excepting Community Action and VISTA. As such, the GOP proposal advocated shifting job training initiatives, such as the Job Corps and Neighborhood Youth Corps, to the Department of Labor, while all education programmes, such as the popular Head Start (which would enjoy an increased budget), to the Office of Education. This negative approach to the OEO is unsurprising as it is an understatement to say that Republicans never warmed to it. Goodell referred to Shriver's newly created agency as the 'fuddle factory' and vowed that the Opportunity Crusade would 'eliminate the waste and scandal and abuses' that the New Yorker believed characterised the OEO.[36]

Republican criticisms also suggested that many in the GOP saw the OEO as a tool of the Democratic Party. Quie and Goodell's poverty memos often drew upon examples of the OEO's excessive patronage to city politicians – most of whom belonged to Director Shriver's own party.[37] In March, Quie cited the OEO's funding of a hotel renovation in West Virginia under the pretence of setting up a Job Corps centre where the State Commerce Commissioner, a Democrat, was president of the corporation that owned the hotel. Linking the poverty programme to a frequent Republican charge levelled at Lyndon Johnson primarily over his conduct of the Vietnam War, Quie suggested that there existed a 'Credibility Gap at [the] OEO'.[38] As such, the OEO – founded as a coordination agency – would have had little left to coordinate under Republican plans.

Community Action – the one major programme that would have remained in OEO hands under the Republican proposal – was earmarked for significant alteration. First, and perhaps surprisingly, the Opportunity Crusade budget set federal funding for CAPs at $700 million – a vast increase on the $475 million requested by the Johnson administration.[39] Second, Quie and Goodell proposed that the poor be guaranteed one-third representation on poverty boards. Their rationale for the guaranteed representation was that the War on Poverty had failed to achieve the 'maximum feasible participation' on behalf of the poor for which the EOA had legislated. The two Republicans cited events in Watts, Los Angeles, where widespread rioting had broken out in a poor, predominantly black neighbourhood in August 1965 as proof of the OEO's failure to include the poor.[40]

While Quie and Goodell's proposed doubling of federal funds for Community Action may have been in good faith, it is also possible that they saw a further opportunity to divide Democrats. By 1966, there were over 1,000 CAAs in existence, largely based in urban areas, and many of them were causing headaches for big-city mayors – of whom most belonged to the Democratic Party.[41] Chicago was the prime example, with Mayor Daley maintaining an iron grip on the programme despite criticism from local neighbourhood groups about the lack of participation by the poor.[42] Meanwhile, Rep. Adam Clayton Powell (D-NY), the controversial chairman of the House Education and Labor Committee through which the EOA was reported, was so furious with the politics surrounding the antipoverty effort that he threatened to 'wash this war on poverty right down the drain and forget it'.[43] The flamboyant Powell, who saw CAAs as a means to provide services for his constituents, was in conflict with New York City residents who saw Community Action as a vehicle for social action and protest.[44] Thus, Community Action stirred many layers of division in Democrat-controlled cities.

Furthermore, while many CAAs undoubtedly did important and successful work, there were also stories emerging from Community Action that embarrassed the Johnson administration.[45] For example, the Harlem CAA in New York City – HARYOU-ACT – indulged in poor financial practices that left it over-budget while paying high salaries to its employees. Later in the year, it stood accused of funding revolutionary black nationalist LeRoi Jones.[46] At the other end of the ideological spectrum, Goodell pointed to a CAA in San Jose, California where only three elected representatives turned up to a poverty board meeting, and one of them was member of the far-right John Birch Society.[47] For Republicans looking to discredit the War on Poverty and drive divisions in the Democratic Party, inflating the importance of Community Action made great sense. Republicans also mainly represented rural and suburban districts, and therefore difficult changes to the predominantly urban Community Action would have little effect on the GOP.[48]

The main job training programmes – the Job Corps and the Neighborhood Youth Corps – were different in this regard as they also operated in rural, small-town and suburban America. Here, Quie and Goodell assured Congress that the Opportunity Crusade would provide 'productive and dignified' jobs while also interacting with the private sector more effectively than the OEO had achieved.[49] On the first point, Republicans often derided the War on Poverty's job training initiatives as placing poor youngsters in dead-end jobs, such as 'leaf raking and make-work in public employment'.[50] Therefore, the Opportunity Crusade included an Industrial Youth Corps (IYC) that would provide incentives for private companies to train unskilled youths and, in exchange, the youths would be paid only one third of the minimum wage for their labour.[51] Youth unemployment, Quie and Goodell argued, had stubbornly remained at 12 per cent over the previous five years because the minimum wage was pricing young people out of the market.[52] This was, of course, a convenient argument for Republicans who, more often than not, opposed minimum wage laws.

The IYC proposal was coupled with another overt appeal to the private sector – the Human Investment Act (HIA). This Act called for a 7 per cent tax credit to employers if they engaged in certain types of employee training. The HIA would act as an incentive for employers to engage in training of the poor and unemployed that would offset other proposed reductions in federal spending. Indeed, the Opportunity Crusade proposed that private companies would pay two thirds of the trainees' wages rather than the 10 per cent the companies currently contributed under Johnson's War on Poverty. This meant a reduction in federal spending on job training, and allowed Quie and Goodell to claim that the Opportunity Crusade would help more poor people while spending $200 million less than Johnson's War on Poverty.[53]

The Opportunity Crusade was irrefutably a thorough opposition proposal that stood in contrast to the GOP's record of negativism. Quie and Goodell, leading the charge against the War on Poverty for the GOP, had presented a clear Republican alternative. The Crusade drew heavily upon the War on Poverty's failures but was also spearheaded by Republican ideological principles. When the EOA's renewal reached Congress in September, House Republicans were now armed with their own proposal and were ready for a fight.

Shaping the War on Poverty – the Economic Opportunity Act's second renewal

The 1966 debate over renewing the EOA was more acrimonious than the previous year's deliberations. With an election nearing, the stakes were high and Republicans duly arrived with a long list of grievances but also a great number of alternatives. Ohio's Ayres set the tone during the first day of debate in September when he told the lower chamber that 'I am of the opinion . . . that there are very few Members of this body who really believe in their hearts

66

that this is good legislation.'[54] While many Democrats robustly defended the antipoverty initiatives, Republicans echoed Ayres' sentiments. Over the next four days, the War on Poverty was subjected to harsh Republican rancour, the type of which few other Great Society ventures were to endure. Most importantly, Republicans had their first notable successes in shaping how the War on Poverty would be fought.

Emblematic of the caustic atmosphere that surrounded EOA's second renewal was Rep. Alphonso Bell's (R-CA) contribution to the debate. The moderate Californian rose on 27 September to lead a long monologue of 'I told you so' to those who had initially voted for the War on Poverty. Bell, who voted for other significant Great Society legislation but against the EOA, believed that Congress had been 'naïve' as 'none of us realized in 1964, when we enacted the EOA, just how formidable a task we had taken on'. His specific complaints related to the 'impossible task' facing the OEO, which was expected to juggle five programmes. While he conceded the popularity of Head Start, Bell warned that if responsibility for the programme was not shifted from the OEO to the Office of Education, Head Start would be stifled by OEO confusion. Bell concluded his anti-EOA soliloquy by quoting an Iowa school superintendent who had been waiting months for OEO funds and had said of the War on Poverty's help: 'We're getting to the point where we don't know if it's worth it.'[55]

Bell's testimony was damning of the OEO, but it paled in comparison to that of his fellow moderate Republican, Paul Fino (R-NY). Fino, a New Yorker who had voted for the EOA on both previous occasions, had a moderate voting record but would, as the Johnson presidency progressed, emerge as one of the GOP's loudest proponents of racial conservatism. The Bronx congressman denounced his previous votes and told his fellow representatives:

I have become completely disenchanted with the whole concept for rooting poverty out of the American soil. I might go further and admit that I am disgusted with these glamorous-sounding programmes that have and will continue to produce confusion, hate, bitterness and misuse of our taxpayers' money.

Calling the War on Poverty a 'shabby, disgraceful thing [that] has let American down', Fino's criticisms were a mix of traditional GOP arguments over OEO waste and corruption, but they were also products of the white backlash stirred by Watts and Goldwaterite fears over the decline of morality in the United States. Speaking of the Job Corps, Fino asked, 'Why spend $370,000 getting [the poor] special blazers? I know another type of outfit they could wear. It has brass buttons too. I firmly believe we ought to draft out the Nation's punks and hoods instead of coddling and paying them in the Job Corps.' Mocking OEO employees as 'poverty beatniks and troublemakers', the congressman defiantly argued that Congress should 'say "no" in definite terms to care and feeding of punks, rioters and black nationalists'.[56]

Fino's key example of OEO folly was the black nationalist, LeRoi Jones, and the federal funds that Jones's Black Arts Repertory Theater in Harlem received from the OEO. Quoting Jones as saying 'I don't see anything wrong with hating white people', Fino noted that police had raided the theatre to find a 'secret black nationalist arsenal full of rifles, shotguns, cross bows, and meat cleavers'. Fino concluded his story with an intentionally alarming thought: 'I still wonder if any of these lethal weapons were bought with poverty funds?'[57]

Rallying to the EOA's support, liberal Democrats sought to discredit Republican criticisms and alternatives. Before addressing the detail of Republican proposals, numerous Democrats situated GOP criticisms within a long history of Republican negativism towards Democratic social welfare programmes.[58] Affirming the 'Party of No' narrative, Rep. James O'Hara (D-MI) described Republican charges as 'familiar old friends to all of us, polished by the frequency of their use . . . like an old slipper, almost comfortable from age alone'.[59] New Jersey's Charles Joelson backed up O'Hara, asserting that 'the minority report, in the typical minority fashion, was negative'. Of the GOP's alternative, Joelson mocked, 'the Republican substitute is not an opportunity crusade: it is just opportunity delayed, opportunity mislaid, and opportunity dismayed'.[60]

Despite the strong riposte from Democrats favourable to the War on Poverty, there were also reminders that a strengthened conservative coalition after the 1966 midterms could endanger the EOA. Many southern Democrats – some of whom had voted against the EOA in 1964 – agreed with their GOP colleagues on the War on Poverty's failures. One such example was Rep. Charles Bennett (D-FL), who blamed the poor execution of poverty programmes for the increase in urban uprisings. Bennett charged that the War on Poverty 'has contributed more than any other single factor to the riots and unrest among the underprivileged of our country. It is impossible to legislate self-respect.'[61] For the time being, however, both Bennett and the majority of Republicans found themselves on the wrong side of the voting tally. The Opportunity Crusade – which Bennett supported – was defeated handily (228–117 against, with all but six Republicans voting in favour) as enough Democrats remained loyal to the President's signature legislation.

Rather than accept defeat, House Republicans moved onto Plan B – offering a total of thirty-three amendments to the EOA before final passage – and it was during this process that Quie and Goodell's work bore fruit.[62] The most substantial change to the EOA as it made its way through the House was Quie's amendment that the poor's representatives must make up one third of every poverty board. The OEO attempted to stave off the one-third proposal by releasing statistics that showed 29 per cent of CAAs were already made up of representatives of the poor. Ultimately, the attempted rebuff was to no avail as the Quie amendment was adopted, suggesting that the effort invested in proposing constructive Republican alternatives was not entirely in vain. Indeed, the *New York Times* editorialised that 'One of the interesting developments of the [EOA] debate was a Democratic concession that let the Republicans become the champions of "maximum feasible participation" by the poor.'[63] Such an image was no bad thing for a party attempting to prove to the public that it was longer in hock to privilege and negativism.

Republicans also exercised influence when the EOA arrived in the Senate in early October. The GOP provided the votes to ensure acceptance of a 'law and order' amendment requiring that the EOA barred assistance to anyone who incited or carried on a riot or was a member of a subversive organisation.[64] Elsewhere,

California's George Murphy, a conservative, successfully had the Hatch Act applied to the EOA – prohibiting OEO employees from engaging in political activity. This development lent credence to Republican claims that antipoverty workers were verging into partisan territory while doing their work.[65] Meanwhile, Winston Prouty's (R-VT) accepted amendment that earmarked 36 per cent of Community Action funds for Head Start confirmed the bipartisan support for that programme.[66]

Most significantly, Minority Leader Dirksen's proposal to reduce the appropriation from the $2.5 billion requested by the President to the $1.75 billion approved by the House was passed with GOP votes. On the Republican side, only progressives Clifford Case and Jacob Javits voted against the proposal. Javits went so far as to refute his party's own election themes, arguing that, 'War and inflation notwithstanding, morality dictates that we do what is required to relieve the unbelievably shocking incidence of unemployment.'[67] Once more confirming his status as an outlier in the GOP, Javits was the only Republican to address a Poor People's March that arrived in Washington to influence debate over the EOA.[68]

The EOA's second renewal demonstrated that the War on Poverty was the primary target for Republicans looking for a weakness in the Great Society's armour. The GOP's Opportunity Crusade had taken aim at both the theory behind the War on Poverty and also the experience of the OEO's first two years in operation. Importantly, the Opportunity Crusade showed that the GOP were offering affirmative solutions rather than indulging in all-out negativism. When Republicans railed against the War on Poverty on the campaign trail during 1966, they could – and many did – point to a constructive alternative that the party had offered. At the same time, influential new criticisms of the antipoverty effort emerged during an election season that saw the GOP make a strong comeback from the depths of 1964.

Dawn of the 'creative' Republican – poverty politics and the 1966 midterms

Republicans could be forgiven for beginning the election year with uncertainty and trepidation. With a popular Democratic president in the White House, the GOP faced the daunting task of restoring some balance to the two-party system. Such fears subsided, however, as events unfolded creating a more favourable political climate for Republicans come November. While John Lennon outraged religious groups in March by sardonically claiming that The Beatles were more popular than Jesus Christ, Lyndon Johnson – known for his own grandiloquent statements – was indulging in no such declarations about his presidency or his War on Poverty. For LBJ, the loss of public approval proved to be swift.

Gathering in January, the RNC Executive Committee had been informed by in-house pollster Benham that the antipoverty effort still enjoyed two-thirds approval with voters, while Johnson's presidency remained popular thanks to abnormally high ratings on 'employment' and 'prosperity'. Attempting to put a positive spin on the news to his employers, Benham indulged his audience with a prophetic prediction:

> This war on poverty, since it hasn't proved to be a complete fiasco yet, has gained some acceptance among the voters. . . . If scandals are developed this opinion might change. Should there be any sort of downturn in the business cycle its effects will be rapidly felt by the Johnson administration and the level of support they have so that this is about as high as you can go on a rating of this type . . . [Prosperity] and [employment] make everything else seem alright.[69]

Five months later, Benham returned to inform an ebullient RNC that the support for the War on Poverty had fallen to 57 per cent, while Johnson's approval had sunk to 46 per cent. Moreover, aside from Johnson's obvious travails in Vietnam, inflation was beginning to bite, leading to 61 per cent saying they favoured a cut in federal spending. Respondents, asked which programmes should be cut, cited 'Aid to Cities', 'Farm Subsidies' and the 'War on Poverty' as three of the top four. Out of the most common responses, only the 'Space Program' did not directly affect the nation's poor.[70] Throughout the year, Republicans had done their level best to precipitate the War on Poverty's decline in popularity. This was done by highlighting the flaws of the antipoverty effort and by tying it to voter concerns surrounding welfare, race and inflation.

One of the biggest shifts in Republican rhetoric during 1966 was a renewed emphasis on a staple GOP argument that Democratic welfare programmes encouraged a morally corrupting dependency in their beneficiaries. Such an assertion had been repeated on countless occasions by Republicans since Roosevelt's New Deal put the federal government in the business of helping less fortunate Americans. FDR, however, as well as being happy to assail big business and economic privilege, had also been quick to warn against the scourge of welfare dependency and stressed the extraordinary circumstances of the Great Depression.[71] In essence, both Roosevelt and the Republicans demonstrated an awareness that most Americans distinguished between a deserving and an undeserving poor, viewing the latter as unworthy of the average worker's tax dollars. Even at the height of the War on Poverty's popularity, a Gallup survey showed an 'even split in popular attribution of poverty causation between individual responsibility and forces beyond one's control'.[72] As such, at least half of Americans – believing that poverty was a matter of one's own personal responsibility – were not likely to offer support to welfare programmes that transferred taxpayer money from the middle class to the poor, unless fully convinced of the virtues of such programmes.

Johnson, without the political cover of the Great Depression, had made it clear in 1964 that the War on Poverty was not a welfare initiative. Meanwhile, other Great Society programmes, such as Medicare and education spending, clearly offered benefits to all Americans and therefore were less likely to cause resentment. Furthermore, the EOA's appropriation when it was first passed in 1964 was a mere $947.5 million – roughly one per cent of the federal budget. Nevertheless, the doubling of EOA appropriations in 1965, and the subsequent calls from liberals in the Democratic Party to vastly increase funding – including Shriver's request for $9 billion to add a public jobs programme to the War on Poverty – harmed LBJ's argument that the anti-poverty effort remained focused on opportunity rather than entitlement.[73] Republican candidates sensed an opportunity to attack the heart of Johnson's Great Society. Emblematic of these attempts to tie the War on Poverty to welfare during 1966 were the widely differing campaigns of Ronald Reagan and Edward Brooke.

Reagan's gubernatorial campaign in California was the star turn in 1966. The former Hollywood actor emerged from the elections as the new occupant of California's governor's mansion and with a national profile that was the envy of many a battle-hardened politician. Historian Matthew Dallek highlights the dual role of university protests and the Watts riots in Reagan's victory over Democratic incumbent Pat Brown, but it was the former actor's 'Creative Society' vision that lay at his campaign's core.[74] The Creative Society, in Reagan's mind, focused on inserting the private sector into areas that the public sector dominated, while it would also root out welfare dependency from Californian life.

As the name 'Creative Society' suggests, in 1966 Reagan was very much the anti-Great Society candidate. Significantly, however, in advocating his Creative Society vision, Reagan weakened the usual Democratic riposte that he was just another member of the 'Party of No' club. Reagan's main talent was in casting his anti-government policies as populist and positive, contrasting his ideas with Democratic welfare programmes that he claimed were working against the interests of most Americans. Arguing that 'today's conservative is actually the radical of revolutionary day', Reagan labelled the modern liberal as the 'tory of yesteryear' owing to liberal support of centralised power.[75]

Regarding the War on Poverty, Reagan was loath to concede any virtue in Johnson's programmes and he framed antipoverty initiatives as Democrats doling out welfare to undeserving Americans. While Reagan accepted that 'human compassion and simple brotherhood demand that where there is need we should do our utmost to provide some of the comforts that make life worthwhile', he cautioned that 'this should be in response to need, and where the need is temporary, the help should be temporary, aimed at restoring self-sufficiency'.[76] He also contested that if less were spent on welfare cheats then more money would be available for pensioners and those with physical incapacities – a clever position that helped to moderate the candidate's image.[77] Reagan's implication that he would shift money from the perceived undeserving poor to the deserving poor conveyed an image of compassion not often associated with conservative Republicans.

Moreover, Reagan was keenly aware of the popularity of his position. By September, the GOP candidate noted that one of the first questions he was regularly asked was: 'If elected Governor, what will you do about welfare?'[78] Reagan was therefore aware of the political damage that he could cause by tying the War on Poverty to voter concerns surrounding welfare and dependency. Furthermore, in running against Pat Brown, Reagan was in competition with one of the nation's state executives most in step with Great Society liberalism. The stakes for the War on Poverty in the nation's most populous state were clear.

Reagan, however, was not the only GOP headline act of 1966. Massachusetts Republican Ed Brooke shared centre stage, becoming the first black senator since Reconstruction when he defeated Democrat Endicott Peabody in the Bay State. Brooke was unabashedly a progressive Republican, and was comfortable with such a label. He did, however, venture 'Creative Republican' as his preference, a designation not too dissimilar from Reagan's Creative Society vision. Brooke believed that Democrats conceived of good ideas but were unable to convert those ideas into workable policy due to the party's attachment to city machines and the patronage demanded by such a system. Harking back to moderate and progressive arguments since the New Deal, Brooke reasoned that Republicans could run current programmes better and also offer smarter initiatives if elected.[79]

In particular, Brooke described Democratic programmes as having a 'very serious flaw and that is that the Democratic Party seems to give temporary relief to problems. It doesn't cure the problems'.[80] During one of his many appearances on national television, Brooke identified the War on Poverty as the key programme where the GOP could make a difference. Despite widely varying political philosophies, Brooke agreed with Reagan's assertion that the current antipoverty effort was increasing welfare dependency.[81] Rather than stoke anger with welfare or sound the klaxon for private enterprise to come to the rescue, Brooke – mirroring the Quie amendment in Congress – instead called for increased participation by the poor in the War on Poverty.

Criticising the War on Poverty's supposed drift to welfare was a key theme in Brooke's campaign. The Massachusetts Attorney General believed that Democrats were happy to keep people on welfare programmes indeterminately because the agencies behind the War on Poverty had a 'vested interest in maintaining a status quo that thrives on the poor man's dependence and submissiveness'. The only route forward, Brooke preached, was to treat the 'poor as individuals' and then 'we would be on our way to eliminating the feelings of dependency and inadequacy that keep the poverty cycle going'.[82] On his way to victory in a state where LBJ's popularity remained disproportionately high, Brooke criticised Johnson directly for raising expectations for political gain and then failing to enforce the 'fresh approach to combating poverty' that the President had promised.[83]

Away from coastal battles, in America's Midwestern heartland, Governor George Romney was also battling with the concept of welfare dependency during his successful re-election effort in Michigan. Romney, on a visit to Los Angeles in late 1965, had remarked: 'Handouts, although sometimes necessary and always well-intentioned, are degrading to the human spirit.'[84] Despite his own record of government intervention and utilisation of EOA funds in Lansing, Romney focused his rhetoric on volunteerism – a distinctive element of his philosophy. In May, Romney explained to his fellow Republicans that 'Our Republican opportunity in 1966 is to present superior candidates and superior programmes that will turn loose America's vast, as-yet-untapped potential of voluntary people-power to solve the people's problems.' In particular, the former American Motors chairman cited the need for government 'to develop independence, not dependence' in those less fortunate.[85] Romney's dual critique was characteristic of Republican governors in Midwestern and Northeastern states who had decided to try to use the EOA as much as possible, but still felt that Republicans could do a better job of drawing up the legislation in Washington.

Elsewhere, Senator Tower – cruising to re-election in 1966 – condemned the War on Poverty as a failure because it focused 'too closely to hand-outs rather than to self-help projects'.[86] Tower was joined in his critique by Richard Nixon – the 1966 election's most active non-candidate. Nixon, an often reliable weathervane in pointing to where the majority of his party stood on any given issue, jumped on the dependency bandwagon, telling a Chicago audience, 'When the time comes when the government makes it more profitable not to work than to work, then it is time to change that administration.'[87] Gerald Ford summed up the Republican distinction between the undeserving and deserving poor, asserting that 'the compelling need in this nation today is to build a good society for the employed-but-poor. They have been shut out from Lyndon Johnson's Great Society.'[88]

The insertion of welfare into the debate over the War on Poverty marked a key change. In 1964, Goldwater and Reagan had been isolated Republican voices in linking the War on Poverty to welfare dependency; by 1966, a deafening GOP cacophony preached this line of attack. If Republicans could convince voters that Johnson and the Democrats were offering entitlement over opportunity then they would be on the popular side of American political culture that condemned giving money to those perceived as unwilling to work. At the forefront of this change in rhetoric was Reagan, whose views were amplified during frequent national television appearances during 1966.[89] A favourite part of Reagan's repertoire was to treat his audience to a lesson from the Jewish Talmud. Citing the book, Reagan noted that the Talmud had several steps for helping people and that 'the least desirable, the last resort, is the handout, the dole'. Rather, according to Reagan, the sacred text counselled that 'the most desirable, and the most effective is to help people to help themselves and that, I think, probably typifies the Republican approach'.[90] Attempting to line up on the right side of Jewish scripture would prove to be just one of the War on Poverty's many challenges during 1966.

Decrying welfare and dependency was by no means a new Republican tactic in assailing Democratic social programmes. The GOP had condemned Roosevelt's and Truman's policies in a similar vein as Democrats continued to win elections. Race therefore played a key role in making dependency arguments more electorally appealing for Republicans in 1966. As white sympathy for African Americans eroded in the wake of perceived rising crime, rioting, challenges to northern racism and 'Black Power', politicians who played on old inaccurate stereotypes of black Americans, such as a poor work ethic and questionable morals, were more likely to reap rewards.[91] This was particularly true of politicians appealing to the largely urban and ethnic white working class – a loyal component of the Democratic coalition and the group most fearful of black advancement. The meshing of welfare dependency, race and the War on Poverty was captured by bumper stickers that began appearing in white working-class areas across the United States that read simply: 'JOIN THE GREAT SOCIETY – GO ON WELFARE; I FIGHT POVERTY. I WORK.'[92]

Undoubtedly, the key development in making these arguments resonate was the spate of uprisings that took place in a largely African American neighbourhood in Watts, Los Angeles in August 1965. In retrospect, the Watts riots – which lasted six days, resulted in 34 deaths, and caused an estimated damage of $40 million – proved an inflexion point from which the War on Poverty never recovered. The uprising provoked a white backlash among millions of Americans who turned decisively against programmes that were perceived to be disproportionately helping African Americans.[93] This trend was then compounded by the many violent confrontations that erupted across the country in 1966, as the summer saw racial disorder in the Midwestern cities of Chicago, Cleveland and Lansing. According to James Sundquist, 'the image of the Negro in 1966 was no longer that of the praying, long-suffering nonviolent victim of southern sheriffs; it was a defiant young hoodlum shouting "black power" and hurling "Molotov cocktails" in an urban slum'.[94] The War on Poverty, given its growing perception among the public as a minority-orientated programme, was in the cross hairs of politicians who chose to ride the backlash wave into office. Republicans approached this development in varying ways: some chose to openly stoke this sentiment while others were troubled by its emergence.

Given his standing as the highest-profile African American running for elected office, Ed Brooke was afforded a significant media platform to voice his views on race and the War on Poverty. Brooke was explicit in tying the dependency problems he outlined in his War on Poverty critique to the black community, perhaps giving voice to an opinion that many white politicians subscribed to but could not voice. Raised near a town so segregated that a black person needed a note from a white resident before they could pass through, Brooke offered a perspective that set him apart from most elected Republicans (and Democrats).[95] Rather than fudge the issue of race, Brooke chose to meet it head on:

> Let us admit that the great majority of people who are classified as on the borderline of poverty in this country are Negroes, and people who live in the ghettoes. These people are not only interested in civil rights . . . they are interested in good education, they are interested in good housing, interested in good food and improving the conditions of their own family and their children.[96]

Of course, in one sense, Brooke was incorrect. While poverty disproportionately affected the black population, a greater number of impoverished Americans in the country were white and belonged to rural communities.[97] Brooke, clearly hoping to improve rather than kill the antipoverty effort, was conceivably helping to undermine it by moving the War on Poverty further and further away from the image of the struggling, down-on-his-luck, white Appalachian.

Other Republicans, such as Reagan, were less concerned than Brooke about undermining the War on Poverty, yet they could not indulge in such outright statements on race. Reagan, however, did not dodge the subject entirely. At his gubernatorial campaign launch, only six months after the Watts riots, Reagan was asked by one reporter to give his views on the events. Stressing that only 2 per cent of the local population was involved in the riots, Reagan mused:

> You have a number of people who were recent immigrants here from states in the Deep South, and they came here like the immigrants of a hundred years ago . . . with an idea that the streets were paved with gold and I think also there were promises made in connection with some of the poverty programmes – promises that couldn't materialise for a long time.[98]

It was not hard to decipher to whom Reagan was referring when he spoke of 'immigrants'. Asked more directly if the blame lay with his opponent, Governor Brown, Reagan chose to attack Brown's 'entire philosophy of government' which viewed poverty programmes as an answer to the problems of the poor.[99] As an alternative, Reagan highlighted the role of private industry and praised the Chamber of Commerce for funding 'fine responsible Negro businessmen who are providing the people' with job training opportunities. Specifically, Reagan pointed to Operation Bootstrap (OB), a burgeoning training programme established by two members of the Congress of Racial Equality (CORE) following Watts. OB's motto of 'Learn Baby Learn' (as opposed to 'Burn Baby Burn'), and its appeal for private rather than government funds, meant that such initiatives stood a greater chance of appealing to many white Americans who feared more racial violence and perceived their tax dollars as being spent on ungrateful minority groups.[100]

Republicans were also quick to criticise Vice President Hubert Humphrey for continuing to equate the war against poverty with a war against crime. Addressing a Temple University audience on the subject of the War on Poverty in June, Humphrey told students: 'We have ample reason today to heed Aristotle's grim warning that poverty is the parent of revolution and crime.' Ford, however, strongly rebuked Humphrey's statement that 'things may get worse, not better, unless we win our war against poverty'.[101] The House Minority Leader asked:

> How long are we going to abdicate law and order – the backbone of any civilization – in favor of a soft social theory that the man who heaves a brick through your window or tosses a firebomb into your car is simply the misunderstood and underprivileged product of a broken home?[102]

Ford's out-of-character remark – the Michigander was not known for strident statements – reflected a worrying trend for those engaged in the antipoverty effort.

In a rebuke to the direction in which his party was heading, Clarence Townes Jr, the RNC's head of minority outreach, scorned the GOP for taking his race for granted and warned that Republicans could no longer ride on Lincoln's coat-tails without offering policies to benefit black Americans. In counselling the RNC on how to win black votes, Townes – an African American – offered a simple goal for the party: to win the War on Poverty.[103] Stressing the mismanagement of Johnson's War on Poverty, Townes believed Republicans could do a much better job of running the antipoverty effort and thus appeal to the black poor. By the mid-1960s, however, black Republican voices were increasingly ignored.[104] Townes's plea fell on deaf ears in a conservative-orientated RNC.

Most Republicans fell between the rhetoric of Ford and Townes. All told, Republicans did not need to speak frequently about race and the War on Poverty; events were unfolding in such a way as to harm the Democratic Party – now seen as the home of racial liberalism – by default. Besides, many Republicans believed that they had other winning cards against Johnson's poverty effort, and the economic conditions in 1966 only helped to strengthen the GOP's hand.

During 1966, the United States experienced a 'long-delayed but painfully-experienced' period of inflation.[105] Such was the concern that President Johnson requested that housewives buy cheaper cuts of meat. The feel-good factor associated with the economy was evidently on the wane, symbolised by the US stock market's nine-month decline, from February to October, that wiped 22 per cent from its value.[106] Many Republicans, who had decided early in the year that inflation would be the party's key theme in 1966, were ready to pounce on the Great Society's spending, hoping to force a choice between 'guns or butter' – between the war in Vietnam and the War on Poverty. Liberal Democrats, now requesting more money for the antipoverty effort, only served to help Republicans make the inflation argument to the electorate. Two corresponding events in June served to illustrate this point.

Sargent Shriver, testifying during Senate hearings on the War on Poverty's progress in June, confidently predicted that, 'By 1976, the 200th anniversary of the Declaration of Independence, we can finish the job [of ending poverty in the US].' *Newsweek* theorised that to fulfil Shriver's promise, appropriations for the

War on Poverty would have to rise to $10 billion each year, with the magazine noting that even the OEO Director's allies 'left the hearing shaking their heads in quiet embarrassment'.[107] Meanwhile, Thomas Benham, having informed the RNC Committee of both Johnson's and the War on Poverty's weak polling figures, had further good news for the gathering. In 1958, the most recent period of substantial inflation, voters had overwhelmingly blamed business rather than government, but now, eight years later, the pollster observed that the public were turning their ire from Wall Street to Pennsylvania Avenue and Capitol Hill.[108] Taken together, Shriver's testimony and Benham's polling data offer a glimpse into the War on Poverty's vulnerability to shifts in the economy.

Nobody was more pleased with these developments than Gerald Ford. An All-American footballer in his youth, Ford spent the year as an All-American politician, travelling the length and breadth of the continental United States to fire up Republican audiences for November. Running in a safe Republican district, Ford's real test was to prove that Republicans could make substantial House gains under his leadership. His main strategy was to attack the White House for the rise in the cost of living and continue to stress the perception that the President was suffering from a 'Credibility Gap'.[109] Throughout the election year, Ford frequently peppered his speeches with linked attacks on the War on Poverty's spending, the Johnson administration's failure to hold down inflation, and the President's refusal – dishonest in Ford's view – to acknowledge that there needed to be a choice between guns and butter.[110]

Ford, however, was reticent to come out full-bore for cuts in the War on Poverty without having an alternative in mind. The Minority Leader's speeches revealed his keen awareness of the need to avoid both the 'Party of Privilege' stereotype and the typical charge of GOP negativism. Accordingly, he spent the year as the main booster for the Opportunity Crusade as an alternative to Great Society extravagance.[111] By stressing a GOP alternative that pledged more money (albeit partly drawn from the private sector), Ford hoped to avoid walking into a political trap set by the White House. At the forefront of his thinking was likely Johnson's 1966 State of the Union address, when, according to Ford, LBJ had 'turned and looked directly at the Republican side of the Chamber,

81

and with somewhat of a hard, snarling look said in effect to the Republicans, whom will they sacrifice – the poor?'[112] The Minority Leader's indignant response was a full-throated 'no'.

Ford's Senate counterpart, Dirksen, was less prone to finessing his argument. Responding to a question on cost-of-living rises in August, the Illinoisan left little to the imagination in advocating that Congress 'put the axe at some of these "Great Society" programmes. Look at the waste there has been in the anti-poverty program.'[113] Furthermore, Tower drew an unflattering comparison between the spending on the War on Poverty and the spending on the Vietnam War: 'Right now there are 1,557 federal poverty-crats making more than $10,000 a year – 25 of them making more than General Westmoreland in Vietnam.' Tying this in with the rise in the cost-of-living index, Tower opined that 'the lesson of history is that every major modern inflation has been aggravated by excessive government spending. It is a matter of grave concern to me that continual federal deficit spending and continual federal fiscal irresponsibility have operated to drive the cost-of-living ever upward.'[114]

Others in the GOP resisted this rhetoric. Brooke, for example, argued that, despite its failings, the War on Poverty was the one piece of social legislation that should be ring-fenced, and other unspecified areas of the budget should be targeted. While Brooke, similarly to other Republicans, saw space for private enterprise to be involved in the War on Poverty, he argued, 'I don't think we can afford to cut back when we have 25 percent of the nation living either in poverty or on the borderline of poverty.'[115] Hugh Scott agreed with Brooke and also resisted the 'guns or butter' angle. 'It would be an empty victory,' the Pennsylvanian declared, 'if we won the war against Communism overseas and lost the War on Poverty here at home.'[116] Such disagreements in the GOP aside, most Republicans found a common attack in bashing both inflationary spending and the War on Poverty.

This standard GOP argument charged that a depreciating dollar – created by Great Society spending – hurt the poor more than other Americans. By such logic, it made little sense for the government to be spending more money to alleviate poverty when government spending inherently hurt the poor. While this argument had rarely brought Republicans success in the past, the context of Johnson's Great Society and the increase in federal spending on social programmes that it entailed helped the GOP's case in 1966 as Republicans could argue that government spending was driving inflation.

Inflation thus allowed Republicans to find the sweet spot between criticising government spending without appearing overly negative or cruel. Ford could therefore sound compassionate while criticising the War on Poverty in Fort Wayne, Indiana, in October: 'some of these billions [of dollars] are being fed into the economy in the name of the poor. And yet the poor [are] hit hardest by rising prices.'[117] Nixon simply charged that to continue the Democrats' inflationary spending would in fact 'wage war on the poor'.[118] Not only did this Republican position offer a critique of spending levels in 1966, it also made Shriver's requests for massive appropriations seem counterproductive. Conversely, the modest increases proposed by the Opportunity Crusade – drawn heavily from private sector sources – were made to appear eminently reasonable. Republicans, perhaps heartened by Benham's figures and a Louis Harris poll in August that showed 85 per cent of Americans were upset with the cost of living, continued to hammer away at the administration.

Johnson took note, defending his achievements in typically bombastic style. In July, the President told an audience in Des Moines, Iowa:

> On the inflation front, if you are distraught, if you are worried about high prices, if you have a stomach ulcer because of high wages, if you are concerned about hogs bringing too much, calves bringing too much, or wages getting too high, and you are really worked up about inflation, it may be that you ought to vote Republican, because there is one guarantee I can give you from my 35 years' experience: If you vote Republican and by chance you should win, you won't have to worry very long about high prices – or high wages.[119]

Although LBJ conceded to fellow Democrats in September that 'Inflation is one of our problems,' he ridiculed Republican attacks on programmes such as the War on Poverty, noting the late Sam Rayburn's observation that 'Any jackass can kick down a barn, but it takes a good carpenter to build one.'[120] For Johnson, reminding the electorate of Republican negativism was an important point for Democrats to stress.

For all of the President's bluster, no longer were Johnson's political enemies merely charging him with inflated rhetoric. Nor were Republicans solely 'kicking down the barn' without paying heed – at least rhetorically – to helping the poor. What is more, GOP arguments appeared to enjoy some success with voters. A September poll showed Johnson's handling of the poverty war as down to 41 per cent, a point lower than his handling of the war in Southeast Asia, and two points lower than his handling of civil rights.[121] If one considers the incredibly difficult racial climate, Johnson's lesser mark for the War on Poverty represented a dramatic fall from grace for the antipoverty effort. Taken together, the details of the poll also suggested that Johnson's increasing unpopularity dictated that Republicans stood to make significant gains in November.

Republican revival

Election Day 1966 was a momentous day for the War on Poverty. As voters were delivering their verdict at the ballot box, Johnson signed the EOA's renewal. Following a successful conference between the House and Senate, the EOA had received an appropriation of $138 million less than the administration had requested, while Job Corps and Community Action were gutted in favour of less controversial initiatives such as Head Start and the Neighborhood Youth Corps. Furthermore, Quie's amendment to Community Action remained the greatest change to how the War on Poverty would be fought. This represented a significant achievement for minority members who had enjoyed little influence in the 89th Congress. In his signing statement, Johnson chose to ignore such political challenges and instead stressed that 'the majority of Americans [now] recognize the problem of poverty in our Nation and are determined to defeat it'.[122] Whether this assertion was true is open to debate, but by the time Johnson had gone to bed that night, many Americans had repudiated the President's agenda at the polls. As voters sent 47 additional Republicans to the House and three to the Senate, LBJ's War on Poverty was more politically vulnerable than ever.

Election Night made happy viewing for Republicans. Colour returned to the cheeks of those in the GOP who, watching the news two years previously, had felt the blood drain from their faces. The *New York Daily News* declared that 'the Republican Party put on a performance like ... that of Mark Twain when he remarked that reports of his death had been greatly exaggerated'.[123] Even foreign observers took notice: British Pathé accurately described the election as the 'biggest shot in the arm' for the Republican Party and focused its newsreel footage heavily on the victories of Ronald Reagan – already described as a potential presidential candidate – and Ed Brooke.[124]

Reagan aside, the high-profile victories that grabbed the most media attention belonged to moderates and progressives. In addition to Brooke's triumph, Romney and Nelson Rockefeller retained their governorships. Meanwhile, Winthrop Rockefeller in Arkansas and Spiro T. Agnew in Maryland ran successfully as moderate gubernatorial candidates, while moderates Charles Percy (R-IL) and Mark Hatfield (R-OR) were elected to the Senate. The latter two successes, combined with the re-elections of John Sherman Cooper (R-KY), Clifford Case (R-NJ) and Margaret Chase Smith (R-ME), meant that the Senate would become a bastion of Republican progressivism for the foreseeable future. Few of these moderate and progressive Republicans viewed rolling back the War on Poverty as their chief aim.

Away from the immediate limelight, however, Republican stalwarts and conservatives strengthened their position in the party and in Congress. Of the Democrats brought in on Johnson's coattails in 1964, only four of the twenty-one in the Midwest and Mountain states survived, replaced by mostly stalwart Republicans. Moderates and progressives, meanwhile, largely failed to reclaim seats in the Northeast and Far West that had been relinquished two years previously. As a result, the House Republican caucus shifted to an ever more conservative position.[125] In addition to the capture of the California governor's mansion, there were other successes for conservatives in statehouse races: Claude Kirk Jr was elected to the Florida governorship, and Don Samuelson bested the moderate Smylie in the Idaho GOP primary. Samuelson went on to secure victory in November.[126] The Idaho primary was one part of a larger phenomenon in 1966 that saw a resurgence in fortunes for those conservatives who had been associated with Goldwater in 1964.[127] An increase in this wing of the party obviously spelt trouble for the War on Poverty – particularly if Republicans opposed to the programme revived the conservative coalition with southern Democrats.

Conclusion

The results on 8 November completed the GOP's path back to political relevance, built on a tentative unity conceived in the wake of the 1964 debacle. On Capitol Hill, congressional Republicans – despite their lopsided minority status – significantly influenced the EOA's second renewal. While Quie and Goodell failed to pass their Opportunity Crusade – always the likeliest outcome – the very existence of such a detailed proposal suggested that the Republican Party was grappling seriously with how best to use their role as the opposition party to propel the GOP into the majority. Gone, it seemed, were the days when – in the words of Ed Brooke – Republicans 'would rather lose the ball game just as long as they decide who is going to pitch'. Moreover, in 1966, Republican amendments represented the most significant changes to the EOA. The War on Poverty thus proved the perfect vehicle for Republicans looking to shift away from the 'Party of No' image to being seen as the party with constructive and creative alternatives.

The 1966 midterm elections also witnessed a turning of the tide against the War on Poverty. While it is wrong to claim that the War on Poverty was the key issue on Election Day, it was the single piece of Great Society legislation that heavily overlapped with hotly contended issues such as race, welfare, inflation and even Vietnam. Moreover, if one judges solely by how voters responded to the War on Poverty then the evidence suggests that 1966 represented, as historians have theorised, a victory for conservatism, or, at the very least, a broad disillusionment with liberalism that was gaining traction in the United States. Yet, the picture is far more complicated than that. Quite clearly, the election did not constitute a backlash against every constituent part of Johnson's Great Society. No Republicans, not even Reagan or Tower, felt able to denounce Medicare, aid to education or the two landmark civil rights acts with the frequency or passion that was directed against antipoverty efforts. Rather, then, the 1966 election must be interpreted as evidence of a swelling perception in the American public consciousness (carefully nurtured by the GOP) that the increasingly contentious War on Poverty was synonymous with Johnson's Great Society. As Johnson aide Henry Wilson bitterly remarked to his boss in December, 'the Great Society has become associated in the public mind with eliminating ghettos and generally pouring vast sums into the renovation of the poor and the Negro. The average American is tired of it.'[128] The War on Poverty was moving onto a new battleground – urban America – which would decidedly favour a rejuvenated Republican Party with increased influence to wield. Nevertheless, the results of this increased Republican power were often surprising.

Notes

1. William Ayres, *Congressional Record*, 20 July 1965.
2. Quoted in Stephen Hess and David Broder, *The Republican Establishment: The Present and Future of the G.O.P.* (New York: Harper & Row, 1967), 1.
3. Davies, *From Opportunity to Entitlement*, 147.
4. Fred Panzer to LBJ, 28 August 1968, reel 8, *PAJWH*, part 1, series a; Thomas Benham, RNC Executive Session, 22 January 1965, reel 4, *PRP*, part 1, series b.
5. Theodore White, *The Making of the President, 1968* (New York: Atheneum Books, 1969), 31.
6. LBJ, 'Annual Message to the Congress on the State of the Union', 4 January 1965, TAPP.
7. John Lindsay, Interview with Robert Peabody, 14 January 1965, Robert L. Peabody [hereafter RLP] Research Interview Notes, 1964-67, box 1, GRF.
8. Robert Griffin, Interview with RLP, 6 January 1965, RLP Research Interview Notes, 1964–67, box 1, GRF.
9. Charles Goodell [hereafter CG], Interview with RLP, 6 January 1965, RLP interviews, box 1, GRF.
10. Richard Nixon and Ray Bliss, Meeting of the RNC in Chicago, 22 January 1965, Meetings of the Republican National Committee 1911–1980, reel 4, PRP, part i, series b: 1960–80.
11. Ibid.

12. Thruston Morton, Speech to RNC in Chicago, 22 January 1965, PRP.
13. William Ayres, *Congressional Record,* 20 July 1965.
14. Ibid.
15. 'The 11th Commandment' was supposedly coined by California's Republican State Chairman, Gaylord Parkinson, when Ronald Reagan's gubernatorial candidacy threatened to divide the party during the 1966 GOP primary. Thereafter, Parkinson's term grew in popularity in Republican circles beyond California.
16. Ibid.
17. 'Antipoverty Program Funds Doubled', *CQ Almanac 1965.*
18. Davies, *See Government Grow*, 63.
19. JGT, Speech at Indiana State College, PA, 25 March 1965, folder 12, box 26, Series Press Office, JGT.
20. Quadagno, *The Color of Welfare*, 54.
21. Albert H. Quie [hereafter AQ] to GRF, 26 April 1965, folder 14, box b28, Correspondence File, GRF.
22. Glenn Andrews, *Congressional Record*, 20 July 1965.
23. House Minority Report, 27 May 1965, 'Antipoverty Program Funds Doubled', in *CQ Almanac*; Saul Alinsky quoted by Peter Frelinghuysen, *Congressional Record*, 20 July 1965.
24. JKJ, 6 May 1965, *CQ Almanac 1965.*
25. Rep. Harold Gross (R-IA), *Congressional Record*, 20 July 1965; Gordon Allot, *Congressional Record*, 18 August 1965.
26. Harry McPherson, *A Political Education: A Washington Memoir* (Austin, TX: University of Texas Press, 1995), 80; John Williams, *Congressional Record*, 18 August 1965.
27. CG, *Congressional Record*, 20 July 1965.
28. James T. Patterson, *The Eve of Destruction: How 1965 Transformed America* (New York: Basic Books, 2012), 205.
29. AQ, *Congressional Record*, 20 July 1965.
30. Charles Joelson, *Congressional Record*, 20 July 1965.
31. Carl Perkins, *Congressional Record*, 20 July 1965.
32. Mark McLay, 'A High-Wire Crusade: Republicans and the War on Poverty, 1966', *Journal of Policy History*, vol. 31, no. 3 (2019), 382–405.
33. JKJ, Keynote Speech for 1964 Republican Mock Convention in Ohio, 1 May 1964, box 31, series 286, subseries 1.1, JKJ.
34. AQ, Poverty Memo, *Congressional Record*, 16 March 1966.
35. CG, Poverty Memo, *Congressional Record*, 17 March 1966.

36. AQ, 'Launch of Opportunity Crusade Act of 1966', *Congressional Record*, 7 March 1966.
37. CG, Poverty Memo, 17 March 1966, 6165; AQ, Poverty Memo, *Congressional Record*, 7 March 1966.
38. AQ, Poverty Memo 14 inserted into record, *Congressional Record*, 27 September 1966.
39. 'Launch of Opportunity Crusade Act of 1966', *Congressional Record*, 7 March 1966.
40. AQ and CG, Poverty Memo, *Congressional Record*, 18 March 1966.
41. Matusow, *Unraveling of America*, 245–70.
42. Quadagno, *The Color of Welfare*, 54.
43. Powell quoted in AQ and CG, Poverty Memo, *Congressional Record*, 29 March 1966.
44. Daniel E. Crowe, 'HARYOU', in *Organizing Black America: An Encyclopaedia of African American Associations*, ed. Nina Mjagkij (New York: Garland, 2001), 259–60.
45. See Quadagno, *The Color of Welfare*.
46. RNC Research Division, 'Improving the War on Poverty', PRP, 2 June 1966, reel 4; Crowe, 'HARYOU'.
47. CG, 'Alice in Blunderland', *Congressional Record*, 6 April 1966.
48. Zelizer, *The Fierce Urgency of Now*, 13.
49. CG, 'Launch of Opportunity Crusade Act of 1966', *Congressional Record*, 7 March 1966.
50. AQ and CG, ibid.
51. AQ, ibid.
52. AQ and CG, ibid.
53. AQ and CG, 'Launch of Opportunity Crusade Act of 1966', *Congressional Record*, 7 March 1966, 5030.
54. William Ayres, *Congressional Record*, 26 September 1966.
55. Alphonso Bell, *Congressional Record*, 27 September 1966.
56. Paul Fino, *Congressional Record*, 27 September 1966.
57. Fino's story was largely correct as confirmed in Michael Stern, 'Arms Cache Laid to Small Group', *New York Times*, 19 March 1966. Stern, however, states that the grant was $40,000 whereas Fino asserted that it was $115,000.
58. Sam Gibbons, James O'Hara and Charles Joelson, *Congressional Record*, 27 September 1966.
59. O'Hara, ibid.
60. Joelson, ibid.

61. Charles Bennett, *Congressional Record*, 27 September 1966.
62. Joseph A. Loftus, 'House Rejects Republican Plan to Revise Anti-poverty Program', *New York Times*, 29 September 1966, 82.
63. Editorial, 'The Nation: Everybody's in the Poverty Act', *New York Times*, 2 October 1966, 204.
64. 'Antipoverty Funds Reduced and Earmarked', *CQ Almanac 1966*, 22nd edition (Washington, DC: Congressional Quarterly, 1967), 250–65.
65. Murphy, *Congressional Record*, 4 October 1966.
66. 'Antipoverty Funds', *CQ Almanac 1966*.
67. JKJ quoted in Loftus, 'Senate Takes Up Antipoverty Bill', *New York Times*, 1 October 1966, 14.
68. Don Robinson, 'Powell's Fiery Talk Inspires Antipoverty March', *Washington Post*, 28 September 1966, B1.
69. Thomas Benham, RNC Executive Session, 31 January 1966, reel 6, PRP, part 1, series b.
70. Benham, RNC Executive Session, 20 June 1966, ibid.
71. Davies, *From Opportunity to Entitlement*, 1.
72. Edward R. Schmitt, 'The War on Poverty', in *A Companion to Lyndon B. Johnson*, ed. Mitchell B. Lerner (Malden, MA: Wiley Blackwell, 2012), 94.
73. Patterson, *The Eve of Destruction*, 203.
74. Matthew Dallek, *The Right Moment: Ronald Reagan's First Victory and the Decisive Turning Point in American Politics* (New York: Simon & Schuster, 2000); Lou Cannon, *Governor Reagan: His Rise to Power* (New York: Perseus, 2003).
75. Remarks, Ronald Reagan [hereafter RWR], Occidental College, LA, 8 March 1966, box c30, 1966 Campaign, Ronald Reagan Governor's Papers, Ronald Reagan Library.
76. Speech, RWR, 'A Plan for Action', 4 January 1966, box c30, 1966 Campaign, RWR.
77. RWR on ABC's *Issues and Answers*, 5 May 1966, box 30c, 1966 Campaign, RWR.
78. Remarks, RWR in Hayward, CA, 27 September 1966, box c30, 1966 Campaign, RWR.
79. Edward W. Brooke [hereafter EWB], remarks on NBC's *Meet the Press*, 13 February 1966, box 562, Edward William Brooke Papers, Manuscript Division, Library of Congress, Washington, DC.
80. Ibid.
81. Ibid.
82. Ibid.

83. Opinion Research Corporation (ORC) did Brooke's polling and found in June that LBJ's approval rating was 67 per cent in Massachusetts, compared with 51 per cent nationally; ORC, 'The Massachusetts Public Appraises EWB', September 1966, box 624, EWB papers; quote from EWB, 'The War on Poverty and the Realities of Community Action', May 1966.
84. AP, 'Romney Lambasts Intrusion of "Great Society"', *The State Journal*, 24 November 1965.
85. GWR remarks at Republican Appreciation Dinner, Lincoln, NE, 19 May 1966, folder 410, box 18, RG4 P-Whitman, RAC.
86. Press Release, 'Poverty', 4 September 1966, box 716, 1966 Tower Senatorial Campaign, JGT.
87. Richard M. Nixon [hereafter RMN], quoted in 'Nixon Bids Doctors to Fight Curbs', *Chicago Tribune*, 27 June 1966.
88. GRF speech at Republican Rally, Philadelphia, PA, 9 May 1966, box 59, Robert T. Hartmann Papers, GRF.
89. RWR appeared on CBS, NBC and ABC programming throughout 1966. See files in 1966 Campaign, RWR.
90. RWR remarks at Press Conference, 4 January 1966, box c30, 1966 Campaign, RWR.
91. Thurber, *Republicans and Race*, 260.
92. Perlstein, *Nixonland*, 113.
93. Philip E. Converse, *The Dynamics of Party Support* (Los Angeles: SAGE, 1976), 72–110.
94. Sundquist, *Politics and Policy*, 281.
95. Remarks, Barack Obama awarding Congressional Gold Medal to Edward Brooke, 28 October 2009, http://www.whitehouse.gov.
96. EWB remarks on NBC's *Meet the Press*, 13 February 1966.
97. Race figures by Carmen DeNavas-Walt, Bernadette D. Proctor and Jessica C. Smith, US Census Bureau, Current Population Reports, *Income, Poverty, and Health Insurance Coverage in the United States: 2012*, http://www.census.gov/; rural figures by Institute for Research on Poverty, 'Who Is Poor', University of Wisconsin-Madison, http://www.irp.wisc.edu/.
98. RWR, Press Conference remarks, 4 January 1966, box c30, 1966 Campaign, RWR.
99. Ibid.
100. RWR speech at Occidental College, Los Angeles, CA, 8 March 1966, box c30, 1966 Campaign, RWR.
101. Hubert Humphrey, Address at Temple University, Philadelphia, PA, 16 June 1966, box 364 (17), Office Files of Frederick Panzer, LBJ.

102. GRF, 20 September 1966, quoted in Edsall and Edsall, *Chain Reaction*, 51.
103. Clarence Townes Jr, RNC Meeting, 20 June 1966, PRP, part 1, series b, reel 5.
104. Leah Wright Rigueur, *The Loneliness of the Black Republican: Pragmatic Politics and the Pursuit of Power* (Princeton, NJ: Princeton University Press, 2014); Joshua D. Farrington, *Black Republicans and the Transformation of the GOP* (Philadelphia, PA: University of Pennsylvania Press, 2016).
105. Hess and Broder, *The Republican Establishment*, 9.
106. 'Dow Jones 100 Year Historical Chart', *Macrotrends*, http://www.macrotrends.net.
107. 'War on Poverty – Spirit of '76', *Newsweek*, 4 July 1966.
108. Benham, RNC Executive Session, 20 June 1966, PRP, part 1, series b, reel 5.
109. GRF on 'the Issues of '66' at RNC event, 19 April 1966, box 57, RTH Papers, GRF.
110. GRF remarks at Republican Rally, Philadelphia, PA, 9 May 1966, box 59, RTH Papers, GRF.
111. GRF remarks at Wisconsin GOP Finance Committee Dinner, Milwaukee, WI, 18 June 1966, box 59, RTH Papers, GRF.
112. GRF remarks at Republican Women's Conference, Washington, DC, 18 June 1966, box 59, RTH Papers, GRF.
113. EMD remarks on NBC's *Meet the Press*, 7 August 1966, Releases, and Interviews, Remarks and Releases File, EMD Papers, TDCC.
114. JGT, 'Reports from Washington', May 1966, box 715, folder 8, 1966 Tower Senatorial Campaign, JGT.
115. EWB remarks on ABC's *Issues and Answers*, 4 September 1966, box 562, EWB; Press Release, 'Fighting for a Future: The Poor in America', box 568, EWB.
116. HDS, 'Sen. Scott Proposes 4-Point Poverty Legislation', 11 January 1966, box 40, HDS.
117. GRF remarks at GOP dinner, Fort Wayne, IN, 28 October 1966, box 59, RTH Papers, GRF.
118. RMN quoted in *Washington Post*, 5 June 1966, folder 66, box 8, series j.3, RG4, NAR.
119. LBJ quoted in Memo, RTH to GRF, 11 July 1966, box 56, RTH Papers, GRF.
120. LBJ remarks to Democratic Congressional Candidates, White House, 22 September 1966, box 6, Papers of Ceil Bellinger, LBJ.
121. William Ayres, *Congressional Record*, 20 July 1965.

122. LBJ, 'Statement by the President Upon Signing Bill to Provide for Continued Progress in the Nation's War on Poverty', 8 November 1966, TAPP.

123. *New York Daily News* quoted in RNC, 'Party Clinches Comeback With 4 Million Vote Margin', *The Republican*, vol. 2, no. 11, 30 November 1966.

124. 'Election Shocks 1966', British Pathé, 17 November 1966, http://www.britishpathe.com/.

125. William Ayres, *Congressional Record*, 20 July 1965.

126. Ibid.

127. Ibid.

128. Henry Wilson to LBJ, 10 December 1966, *PAJWH*, reel 19.

3

Order or justice? Republicans and the 'urban crisis', 1966–67

Administration leaders no longer talk about 'the Great Society.'
Perhaps this is because our society is more and more that of a
nation in agony.[1]

Gerald Ford, 30 October 1967

Just over one year before the 1966 elections, the Watts uprising
that took place in August 1965 triggered a transition that would
focus politicians' minds on the 'urban crisis' more than any other
domestic issue in the latter half of the Johnson presidency. No
longer were the White House or Congress contemplating which
road to take to the Great Society; rather, both were now searching
for the escape route from the tension and violence that plagued
the nation's cities. This change, which was confirmed by reaction
to the Newark and Detroit uprisings in July 1967, affected the
way Republicans spoke about and approached the whole Johnson poverty programme. New initiatives beyond the Economic
Opportunity Act's scope, such as Model Cities, rent supplements
and even a rat extermination bill, became part of the wider War
on Poverty discussion. Using these new initiatives as examples,
House Republicans played a key role in making sure that the
urban crisis cemented the perception of Johnson's poverty agenda
as focusing wholly, or at least disproportionately, on the black
urban community at the expense of the white population. Playing to white backlash sentiment, many in the House GOP caucus
either openly discussed racial preference or chose the more subtle
language of 'law and order'. These Republicans, however, made
up only one element of the Republican response.

The urban crisis divided Republicans into two distinct camps: those who favoured restoring order through punishment of the rioters and those who preferred to focus on achieving social justice for the peaceful majority in the nation's ghettos. To be sure, there was some significant overlap. For instance, those who focused on justice prefaced their arguments with a warning that law and order must be observed at all times, insisting that they were not rewarding rioters. Still, their focus was clearly on aiding the urban areas. Conversely, those Republicans whose sights were trained primarily on achieving order were sometimes quick to note that they were aware of the challenges faced in urban areas. Largely, this GOP dichotomy emerged in the two chambers of Congress: senators were more likely to pursue the 'justice' approach, while their counterparts in the House proclaimed the need for 'order'. Republicans in the nation's statehouses were split, although the more high profile members of the Republican Governors' Association (RGA) – with the exception of a prominent outlier, Ronald Reagan – tended to be in step with the Senate approach.

While this cleavage existed, however, Republicans did not let the split lead the party down the GOP's oft-trodden path to internecine warfare. With the party increasingly sensing electoral victory as the urban crisis worsened, Republicans disagreed with – rather than fought – each other on how to soothe the nation's cities. As different members of the Democratic Party's coalition accused each other of all manner of sins, the Republican Eleventh Commandment held firm. By the end of 1967, this Republican unity, combined with a strong appeal to white backlash sentiment that rejected Johnson's urban poverty programmes, made the possibility of Republican victory in 1968 appear far more possible than any observer could have imagined only four years previously.

'It is the urban crisis . . . that is the real testing ground of the Great Society'[2]

Historians are largely in agreement that the 1960s saw the cities supplant the suburbs in the American consciousness. Transformed from exciting modern spaces, cities quickly became seen through the lens of racial tension, poverty, violence and decay. At

95

the same time, cities became the front line in the War on Poverty, with the President warning in January 1966 that the United States was in danger of becoming 'two people – the suburban affluent and the urban poor'.[3] If the Dust Bowl farmer in Oklahoma symbolised the New Deal, the Great Society was increasingly embodied by the black ghetto dweller in any one of the nation's large cities. Certainly, more than any other development, the urban crisis ensured that the Great Society became pigeonholed as helping the few rather than the many. Ultimately, this pushed the Johnson administration's poverty efforts to the forefront and, coupled with the civil rights measures that Great Society liberalism pursued, bestowed a racial hue upon the whole endeavour.

The urban crisis began in earnest with the Watts uprising in August 1965 and reached its zenith in the summer of 1967, during which two huge riots erupted in Newark and Detroit.[4] In 1967 alone, there were 164 disorders and uprisings, while between the years 1964 and 1968 there were 329 significant outbreaks of violence in 257 cities.[5] At the same time, while such statistics have since been challenged by historian Elizabeth Hinton, reported rates of violent crime continued to soar, with instances of murder, robbery, rape and aggravated assault doubling between 1960 and 1969.[6] The net effect of the urban crisis was a 'white backlash' against further black progress, despite the fact that black Americans were the most likely to be killed during a riot or become the victims of violent crime.[7] At the peak of the urban crisis, in July 1967, pollster Louis Harris warned that 'Whites and Negroes appear to be at an impasse on civil rights progress. Moreover, the impatience of the Negro and the resistance of the White are forming a tinder for potential racial flare-ups in the summer.'[8] In addition to rioting and crime, city governments struggled to cope with the combination of increased demands and withdrawal of resources precipitated by the influx of residents – many from the Great Migration of black southerners to the North – and an eroding tax base that resulted from 'white flight' to the suburbs.[9] The urban crisis played a great role, perhaps only second to Vietnam, in shaping the Johnson presidency and American politics thereafter. By 1968, the nation's problems in the cities made the term 'Great

Society' already seem to many like a fanciful utopian vision dreamt up in a distant age. In short, it presented an opening for a Republican alternative.

Given that the cities had long been bastions of Democratic rule, the Democrats, of the two parties, were most implicated in this crisis.[10] Most worryingly for Democrats, riots and tension in the cities threatened to – and did – divide the New Deal coalition and left many Democratic politicians questioning the rationale behind Great Society programmes. The urban crisis pushed many white, ethnic working-class voters,[11] who perceived the existence of preferential treatment towards black Americans, away from the national Democratic Party. Increasingly, Democrats were at loggerheads over whether to punish rioters or reward those rebelling against racial injustice in the cities. This was a tension laid bare for the public to see during televised hearings conducted by Senator Abraham Ribicoff (D-CT) between August and December 1966 on the subject of urban blight.[12] Tellingly, it was Sam Yorty, the confrontational Los Angeles mayor made famous by his hard-line response to Watts, whose anger at liberal Democrats dramatised the split in the Democratic Party.[13] Liberal Democrats also faced anger from their own constituents. Following Newark and Detroit, Rep. Jonathan B. Bingham (D-NY) lamented that 'folks back home' were demanding deep budget cuts and laws to punish rioters – 'alas, no suggestion that we also do something about the slums, ignorance and discrimination and poverty that breeds riots and crime'.[14]

Republicans were not the natural party to tackle the problems of the cities. Most GOP congressmen belonged to districts that represented rural and suburban areas, and the party routinely lost big cities in presidential elections.[15] Such Democratic supremacy meant that many Republicans were largely opposed to city governments, seeing them as at best wasteful or, at worst, wholly corrupt. During the urban crisis, Gerald Ford repeated this GOP trope, claiming that 'many of the evils of our cities are products of unbroken Democratic machine rule for many decades'.[16] It was a view that progressive Republicans shared with their more conservative colleagues: John Lindsay's choice of political party was largely because of the presence of Tammany Hall in New York

City – the most famously corrupt of all Democratic machines.[17] Even before the urban crisis, many Republicans had attacked the War on Poverty because it gave funds to city politicians who in some cases used the money for corrupt ends.

The realities of electoral arithmetic forced Republicans to wrestle with their urban shortcomings during the 1960s. In the wake of the 1960 election, when many blamed Nixon's loss on his poor showing in the cities (on top of some dubious ballot counting in Illinois and Texas), the Republican National Committee (RNC) commissioned a Committee on Big City Politics under the stewardship of future RNC chair Ray Bliss, which reported its findings in 1962. The RNC report demonstrated that the GOP's traditionally poor showing in urban areas was beginning to stretch into the suburbs surrounding eastern cities and thus providing a new dimension to an old electoral problem.[18] It recommended focusing on organisational steps that could be taken to improve the party in urban America, and therefore shied away from contentious policy disputes. In any case, the report was left to gather cobwebs as William Miller's chairmanship of the RNC and Barry Goldwater's nomination as the GOP's presidential candidate in 1964 meant that the choice between the Big City report and Operation Dixie was a foregone conclusion. Goldwater's candidacy actually saw the party regress in the urban and suburban South where the GOP had been gaining a foothold in the post-Second World War era.[19] Jacob Javits, a rare Republican in his ability to win urban pluralities, continued to advocate an appeal to voters that he termed 'metropolitan man', but such appeals were drowned out until the crushing 1964 electoral defeat and the arrival of Bliss as chairman in 1965.[20]

Bliss's approach to party leadership rested on one specific principle: Republican victory. Happily for Bliss, the majority of the GOP was ready for such pragmatism following elections which guaranteed a minimum of eight years without the presidency and twelve years in the minority in both chambers of Congress. Similarly to the Republican push for relevance in 1965, the prospect of victory would help bind the party together as differences in how to respond to the urban crisis widened in 1967. In early 1965, however, with electoral success seemingly far away, Bliss began implementing parts of the Big City strategy. Under Bliss's leadership, efforts were made to appeal to black voters and union voters, while his pursuit of strong candidates for that year's city elections resulted in Lindsay's high-profile capture of the New York mayoralty.[21] Republicans also took encouragement from Arlen Specter's victory in the District Attorney race in Philadelphia, as well as gains in Louisville, Kentucky and St. Louis, Missouri.[22]

Nevertheless, a real challenge remained for Republicans as the country edged over the brink of the urban crisis. The simple truth that most House GOP representatives were from rural or conservative-orientated suburban districts meant that they were unlikely to feel pressure to rush to the aid of the cities should the need arise. Julian Zelizer notes that House Republicans – most of whom were happy to join with southern Democrats to block liberal initiatives – represented 'rural interests, fiscally conservative small-town voters, and small- and midsize-business leaders'.[23] Such GOP representatives were catering to constituents who, segregationist southerners aside, felt the most enmity towards black progress and feared what the riots they were witnessing on television meant for the country. Another Louis Harris poll found, in mid-1967, that white tensions over black progress were keenest among 'rural people who do their shopping in the smaller towns and cities'.[24] In contrast to their House colleagues, most GOP senators and governors had to please their city-dwelling constituents, among others, and were therefore subjected to differing constituent pressures. These constituency pressures, in combination with differing ideological principles, explain why two very different Republican responses to the urban crisis emerged in the wake of Watts and over the remainder of the Johnson presidency.

Republican response during the 89th Congress

After Watts, the Johnson administration broadened the scope of its poverty efforts – as contained in the EOA – to include an assault on the urban crisis. Arguably, the overall effect of this addition was to shift the perception of the War on Poverty, and even the entire Great Society, further away from its roots in white Appalachia and place it into minority-dominated, inner-city America.

Two proposals during the 89th Congress – rent supplements and Model Cities – attracted Republican objections similar to those to which the Economic Opportunity Act had been subjected: too much federal government intrusion and too much needless spending. Unlike the EOA, however, which Johnson had presented in 1964 as largely Appalachian – and therefore white – initiatives, rent supplements and Model Cities were undeniably linked to the urban black population. Backlash-inclined House Republicans therefore added race as a reason to oppose urban antipoverty legislation, and it was these Republicans who were most outspoken. It was not until after the 1966 election and the subsequent arrival of more high-profile Republican senators, who were largely progressive in their approach to the cities, that the dichotomy in the GOP between the House and Senate approaches would become more evident. In the aftermath of Watts, therefore, those who favoured 'order' possessed the biggest microphone.

It is significant that such House Republican opposition to urban Great Society proposals was aimed specifically at urban antipoverty legislation. Rent supplements, Model Cities, and later urban antipoverty proposals that emerged during the 90th Congress gained a maximum of 20–35 GOP votes. Contrastingly, the same Republicans backed other urban-orientated Great Society programmes with little opposition or controversy. For example, House Republicans offered minimal resistance to the Clean Water Act (1965), the Urban Mass Transit Act (1966) and the Air Quality Act (1967), even though such legislation disproportionately affected the city, appropriated substantial federal dollars, and increased the size and scope of the federal government. This seemingly contradictory voting is explained by the fact that House Republicans had both pragmatic and ideological reasons for supporting such measures: Clean water, mass transit and clean air offered more-tangible benefits to suburban residents while not encouraging, in Republican eyes, any individual to become dependent on government money. Under such circumstances, most Republicans were willing to forgo their usual objections to federal spending and Washington overreach to deal with the urban crisis. Urban antipoverty proposals, beginning with rent supplements in 1965, did not enjoy a similar exception.

The Johnson administration's rent supplements initiative faced firm Republican opposition from its very inception. Rent supplements provided government assistance for poorer Americans to live in properties that they would normally not be able to afford. The initiative proved the most controversial aspect of a broader bill that created the Department of Housing and Urban Development (HUD), and only twenty-six House Republicans voted for final passage of the sweeping legislation, with many citing the rent supplements section as a key reason for their opposition.[25]

Republican opposition to rent supplements often echoed that which had been heard against the War on Poverty. For instance, House Republicans returned to the familiar GOP trope that there were shades of socialism in the rent supplements proposal. Senator Tower trotted out the dependency argument, contesting that the measure represented a 'powerful incentive for a person to discontinue being a homeowner and become a renter on a public dole'.[26] The rhetoric of some House Republicans was stiffer still, with Ohio Representative Jackson E. Betts decrying rent supplements as 'one of the most far-reaching and dangerous plans to come before the House in a generation'. Specifically, Betts saw the initiative as 'foreign to American concepts' and – in his view – the programme offered yet another route to dependency by 'killing the incentive of the American family to improve its living accommodations by its own efforts'.[27] Others, such as Minority Leader Ford, pointed to the spending and increased federal control that would result from the legislation.[28]

While it seemed that congressional Republicans were motivated to oppose rent supplements for the same reasons as they had opposed the War on Poverty, there was another force at work. Race significantly influenced the debate over rent supplements, helping to reveal the growing white backlash sentiment that was on the rise after Watts. Rent supplements acquired a racial context as opponents commonly viewed the initiative as a way to force housing integration, because, unlike public housing schemes (of which Republicans were largely supportive in the 1960s), rent supplements could be used in any neighbourhood.[29] It was one of the first signs that the federal government's civil rights agenda, which had been restricted to tackling southern de jure segregation thus far, was travelling northwards to challenge the de facto seg-regation evident in the white-only suburbs that surrounded cities such as New York, Detroit and Chicago.

In the post-Civil Rights Act era, Republicans who viewed this shift negatively had to exercise caution in how they phrased their opposition so as to not appear overtly racist. Such rhetorical tight-rope-walking was in evidence during the initial rent supplements debate in July when Senator Tower criticised the initiative as an attempt 'to create socio-economic integration' which he said, with alarm, would 'get low-income, middle-income and high-income groups all living together'.[30] Tower was forced by media pressure to deny that his statement had any racial meaning, but the message – contained largely in the word 'integration' – had been sent, and the Texan employed similar rhetoric as part of the successful opposi-tion to the Civil Rights Act of 1966.[31] In the House, Rep. Paul Fino, whom historian John Andrew describes as 'the point man for those who raised the issue of race', criticised rent supplements as a proposal to 'subsidize forced economic integration' and argued that the legislation was a civil rights bill in disguise.[32]

Unsurprisingly, therefore, rent supplements became the first Johnson administration initiative targeted in the Watts aftermath. The change in political climate precipitated by the uprising offered the previously dormant conservative coalition in the House a rare opportunity to reunite effectively, and, in mid-October, the lower chamber refused to fund rent supplements, with only two Republi-cans voting against withholding appropriations. During the House debate, Fino urged his fellow representatives to 'Vote against this bill if you believe in localities having the right to draw up their own civil rights ordinances.' Fino, a Republican rarity in his will-ingness to discuss his opposition in racial terms so openly, further counselled the chamber to 'Vote against this bill if you think that the time has come to draw the line and stand up to black power.'[33] Such a framing had clear appeal to the majority of the white popu-lation who feared the nascent black power movement – a fear that was exacerbated by Stokely Carmichael's explicit call for 'black power' in June 1966. A Harris poll during that year showed that only 2 per cent of white Americans believed that Carmichael was helping the cause of civil rights.[34]

In temporarily defunding rent supplements in late 1965, Republicans achieved a rare success in blocking the Johnson administration's wishes during the 89th Congress – suggesting that the party stood to benefit from any Watts effect. On 14 October, the day on which the rent supplements policy was successfully defunded, Rep. Melvin Laird (R-WI) captured the newly confident mood of the GOP House caucus, telling the crowd at a Republican dinner in Asheville, North Carolina, 'let's talk about the breakdown in respect for law and order which could have been and still could be substantially halted by enlightened leadership in our federal government'.[35] Laird, a strategic thinker who revelled in the cut and thrust of politics, noted a potential opportunity for Republicans to take advantage of the Democrats' split on how to deal with urban crisis:

> The Democrats are divided . . . because half of their party doesn't agree with the other half on basic principles of government. [T]he sooner this country realizes the hopeless division in the Democratic Party on crucial issues of our time, the sooner we will have our President back in the White House and the sooner we'll regain control of the Congress.

Laird believed that, in contrast to the Democrats, Republicans were '90 percent united on principles and policies'.[36]

As Watts receded further into memory, the political shockwaves it had created continued to reverberate.[37] In December, the McCone Commission – a group, led by former CIA director John McCone, who had been appointed by California governor Pat Brown to study the events in Watts – published their findings. The report cited a multitude of reasons for the Watts riots, but it specifically chastised politicians for raising expectations for what antipoverty programmes could achieve, while also condemning the inept administration that plagued existing initiatives. Such analysis supported consistent Republican claims that the War on Poverty was mired in politics and poorly administered. Furthermore, the McCone Commission supported an increased focus on finding employment for poor minorities rather than funding additional antipoverty programmes – a position with which the majority of Republicans agreed.[38]

When Congress returned to rent supplements in March 1966, Republicans and southern Democrats in the House attempted to permanently kill the programme by recommitting an appropriation bill with specific instructions to delete rent supplements' $12 million funding. In the same week, the Republican Coordinating Committee (RCC), normally a moderating influence on GOP domestic policy, issued a 'unanimous declaration' calling for sharp cuts in non-defence spending, emboldening rank-and-file Republicans ahead of a key showdown with the Johnson administration.[39] The cost of the Vietnam War and rising inflation was creating a context in which this traditional GOP message might have achieved more resonance. The motion, however, ultimately failed by a margin of 190–198, with a mere six progressive Republicans voting against deleting the funds, thereby providing the Administration with a razor-thin victory.

House Republicans continued to apply pressure when the cities once again flared in the summer of 1966. Fino cried 'reverse racism' in accusing HUD of hiring only minorities to fill rent supplements positions. Sensing Republicans were in step with the majority of Americans, Ford inflated the importance of programme, declaring rent supplements 'the major 1966 issue', and pronouncing in October that 'Republicans welcome the opportunity to debate this issue in every precinct of the nation'.[40]

A minority of Republicans did offer support to urban poverty initiatives during 1966 – preferring to seek social justice for the slums rather than tapping into any backlash sentiment. In the wake of the rent supplements controversy, Javits once again appealed for the GOP to give immediate attention to the urban crisis and 'metropolitan man'.[41] In late May, he first publicly mooted the idea of a 'Marshall Plan for Deprived Americans', and later bemoaned the response of those who preferred to punish the rioters rather than help slum conditions. In warning both the President and Congress to 'stop watching the budget as if the anti-poverty programs were endlessly negotiable', Javits cautioned his fellow senators that 'It may be that the problems caused by big-city ghettos will overshadow everything else in our national life in the decade to come.'[42]

Senator Hugh Scott, a politician who was becoming increasingly progressive during the Johnson presidency, justified his support for rent supplements on the grounds that they furthered 'independent, free enterprise', as the government's subsidies would go to private companies and were therefore consistent with Republican beliefs.[43] Nevertheless, the Senator from Pennsylvania, who had to consider the importance of Philadelphia and Pittsburgh in any state-wide election, and his colleague from New York were ignored by the vast majority of House Republicans and represented, at most, a third of their own Senate caucus. On 15 August, the announced closure of the *New York Herald Tribune* – mouthpiece of progressive Republicanism – symbolically portrayed the declining political influence of such senators in 1966.[44]

Urban poverty legislation may have had little traction with House Republicans, but the Watts effect did not kill all GOP support for civil rights progress in the lower chamber. During the summer, Republican actions on the failed Civil Rights Act of 1966 demonstrated that legislation focusing solely on civil rights could still attract GOP support, as House Republicans voted by a margin of 76–61 to pass the Civil Rights Act. Conversely, the amendment process highlighted that racial conservatism continued to rise in the 'Party of Lincoln', with every voting GOP House representative backing Rep. William Cramer's (R-FL) successful amendment to make it a federal crime to travel interstate with the intention of inciting a riot. Significantly, House Republicans also voted 86–50 in favour of deleting Title IV – the heart of the bill that aimed to outlaw both de facto and de jure housing segregation. With the exception of committed civil rights advocates in the GOP, most Republicans were less keen to insert the federal government into civil rights disputes that affected the North. Republicans often claimed that neighbourhood agreements that excluded minorities were a private matter.

Nevertheless, it was stalwart Senate Republicans who, along with the evergreen opponents of racial progress, southern Democrats, killed the civil rights bill. Everett Dirksen, so crucial to the passage of earlier civil rights legislation, strongly opposed Title IV on the grounds that it was a restriction of a private homeowner's freedom. Dirksen's opposition freed other Republican senators to vote against both attempts at cloture and, when asked by reporters if his opposition to civil rights legislation would doom Republican chances of gaining votes in the urban centres, the Senate Minority Leader bristled in response: 'Why do you tie this to politics and throw principle overboard? With me there is a basic principle involved here, and I don't know that anybody would expect me to throw that overboard with an eye on the ballot box.'[45] Undeniably, however, Fair Housing was very unpopular with the white suburban voters on which the GOP relied and was a convenient dimension of Dirksen's position.[46] For the time being, the GOP's actions on the failed civil rights legislation showed that those who belonged to the party's 'order' camp were in the ascendancy.

The increased confidence of the stalwart-dominated House Republican caucus was confirmed during debate over the final piece of significant legislation to go through the 89th Congress in October – the Demonstration Cities and Metropolitan Development Act of 1966. The controversial part of the Act, which became known as 'Model Cities', was a three-year-long, $1.2 billion plan to coordinate a wide array of existing federal and local programmes which, together with some new initiatives, would attack the problems of impoverished slums in chosen American cities. Those cities whose applications were successful then received federal grants to cover up to 80 per cent of the financial burden that the city governments normally would have to shoulder as their share of all federally assisted programmes.[47] On the face of it, Model Cities – with its focus on improving coordination – seemed to endorse the oft-repeated Republican argument that federal aid programmes were a sprawling, confusing mess. Model Cities, however, attracted great criticism from House Republicans with only sixteen voting for final passage and the GOP side of the debate unfolding to a similar script as the rent supplements fight.[48]

The repetition of arguments was so clear that one might as well have recorded the Republican objections to rent supplements in March, taken a tape recorder into Congress for the Model Cities debate in October, and pressed 'Play'. Employing his favourite expression, Dirksen charged that Model Cities was a great 'boondoggle' and that the programme would be 'shot through with waste and corruption and goodness knows what all before we get through'.[49] Gerald Ford rolled out the federalism argument, claiming that the legislation would require cities to jump through more bureaucratic hoops to receive funding and thus it represented 'a rather unimaginative federal tail wagging a very restless urban dog'.[50] Once more, Paul Fino raised the spectre of race in opposing Model Cities, claiming that it was a 'tool of black power'.[51] Fino, who also charged that the legislation would force the busing of children in northern cities, was reprimanded by Rep. Donald Fraser (D-MN) for such a blatant 'appeal to the white backlash'.[52] In the end, the famous 'Rubber-Stamp Congress' cobbled together enough ink to approve Model Cities, but as with the other Johnson antipoverty legislation, it was destined to remain a bone of contention throughout the latter half of his presidency.

The Model Cities debate, which unfolded in the midst of the 1966 election campaign, once again confirmed that the dominant voice emerging from congressional Republicans in response to Johnson's urban antipoverty initiatives remained one of sustained and virulent opposition. Many in the House GOP, especially, were yelling 'order!' at the ghettoes rather than offering solutions to the challenges faced by urban residents. As public faith in Johnson's Great Society ebbed with each uprising, and as racial conservatism took hold in the population, House Republicans' opposition to an urban War on Poverty made sense from both a pragmatic and an ideological point of view.[53] Furthermore, Republican gains in the November elections only seemed to confirm the popularity of the 'order' approach – the *Christian Science Monitor* noted that, 'In many areas where civil-rights riots occurred, the Democratic vote sank significantly. Analysis indicates the greatest racist influence is on blue-collar, second-generation immigrants, fearful of Negro encroachment.'[54] Such analysis suggested that a key group of the coalition that FDR's New Deal constructed was now abandoning Great Society liberalism, believing that Johnson's programmes focused on helping an unruly minority rather than the majority. The press thus expected Republicans to use their increased legislative muscle to strong-arm the Johnson administration into cutting back – or abolishing altogether – the War on Poverty, Model Cities and rent supplements.[55] That the party eventually ended up offering very different, competing visions for urban America during the final two years of Johnson's presidency emerged as a surprise.

A choice and an echo

The 89th Congress may have borne witness to the initial attempts to deal with problems of the cities, but it was during the 90th Congress that the urban crisis overwhelmed all other domestic issues. Arguably, the crisis's apogee came during the tempestuous summer of 1967 when uprisings befell many of the nation's cities, most notably Newark and Detroit in July. If it had not already done so beforehand, the whole War on Poverty now became inextricably linked to the urban crisis; a point further proved by the fact that, according to *Congressional Quarterly*, congressional debate over EOA's renewal in 1967 was delayed to allow for a 'cooling-off period' in the aftermath of Newark and Detroit.[56] Meanwhile, all urban poverty measures faced stiff opposition from the conservative coalition in the House, re-energised by the 1966 election results, the 'guns or butter' debate and the continuing backlash to race riots.

Two clear visions emerged from the Republican Party as the crisis worsened. In the House, the vast majority of Republican representatives offered a sharp diversion from Great Society liberalism by rejecting new urban poverty measures out of hand while simultaneously attempting to defund previous initiatives passed in the 89th Congress. These Republicans, often heard calling for the restoration of 'law and order', preferred to introduce crime control legislation as a deterrent to rioting. Such a proactive approach, however, at least helped House Republicans to protest that they were not merely engaged in negativism. In contrast, a majority of Senate Republicans supported Johnson's urban poverty bills and offered their own grand plans to improve the nation's cities.

Progressive Republicans, previously a largely ignorable minority in Congress, were bolstered by the arrival of media darlings Charles Percy, Edward Brooke and Mark Hatfield, all of whom took a progressive approach to the cities. Furthermore, their increased voting strength now meant that they held the balance of power in the upper chamber.[57] Their influence was also enhanced by the support of high-profile, activist Republican governors such as Nelson Rockefeller, George Romney and Pennsylvania's new statehouse occupant, Ray Shafer. Carefully prefacing their arguments with warnings that they were not rewarding rioters, these Republicans looked both to the federal government and to the private sector to solve the problems of the ghetto. In essence, many were quasi-Johnson Republicans, offering echoes of what the President – who had already heavily included the private sector in the War on Poverty – was promising. The support and votes of high-profile progressive Republicans, much like LBJ's reliance on hawkish Republicans to continue the Vietnam War during his final two years in office, helped sustain many of the President's urban poverty programmes.[58]

Despite this contrasting approach to tackling the urban crisis, Republicans were successful in not letting such differences divide the party as they had in the past. One reason for this accomplishment was that the GOP was once again optimistic of winning the presidency and even taking Congress. The bright afterglow of the 1966 elections meant optimism abounded in the GOP ahead of the 1968 contest, and the pull of victory was enough to supersede any ideological differences. In early 1967, Romney giddily declared that 'it's fun to be a Republican', while Ford confidently told an Ohio audience: 'I start from what I consider to be an undebatable premise – Republicans want to win in 1968. Let us go on from there.'[59] The Minority Leader further contested that, rather than debating policy, 'The mission of the minority party is to become a majority.'[60] Even Javits, who normally preferred to scold his party for its lack of progressivism, believed that there was 'a new spirit of hope and excitement in the Republican Party today'. Speaking to young Texas Republicans in January, Javits asserted that the American people were becoming aware that the GOP was now 'capable of pointing the way toward positive, practical solutions to the Nation's problems'. Javits believed that the GOP, in contrast to the Democrats, was not beholden to the 'stale dogmas of the past' and 'not bound at all to the dogma of so-called "New Deal thinking"'.[61] Javits's final comment echoed other Republicans who believed that, in the urban crisis, they were witnessing the unravelling of New Deal liberalism and the coalition that had sustained the Democrats for over thirty years.

The urban crisis fundamentally divided the Democratic Party on the part that the federal government should play in achieving social and economic progress for black Americans. Johnson, whose Great Society liberalism was now seen by many in his own party as either offering too much or too little, came under fire from all angles. Most southern Democrats, for instance, remained sour on the President due to his racial liberalism and showed little inclination to pass programmes to help northern inner cities. Meanwhile, many white working-class voters resented what they perceived as preferential treatment for African Americans in the poverty programmes, and these largely ethnic voters had already helped elect Republicans in November.[62] In contrast, civil rights leaders and liberals grew colder as Johnson refused to propose the 'Freedom Budget', put forward in October 1966, which would have appropriated $185 billion over ten years for a variety of social and economic programmes, and included a guaranteed minimum income.[63] Such was the dissatisfaction that one human rights organisation took to poetry to express its members' disgust with the Great Society's direction:

> Lyndon Johnson took an ax
> To make inflation bygone.
> He gave the budget forty whacks
> And sent the chips to Saigon.
> While war and space go on apace,
> Both funded in entirety,
> The needs of poverty and of race
> Are of the chopped variety.
> For each man kills the things he loves:
> Farewell, Oh Great Society.[64]

As it had clear implications for the GOP's chances in the 1968 election, witnessing this Democratic division over the urban crisis helped to maintain Republican unity through the latter half of Johnson's presidency.

Forging a renewed conservative coalition with disaffected southern Democrats, however, presented a dilemma to House Republicans. Party leaders wanted Republicans to fashion their own identity separate from southern Democrats – a process viewed as crucial if the GOP were to make the South competitive in congressional elections. Ford had announced after the 1966 elections that there would be no 'Republican–Dixiecrat hookup', and the following May he outlined his views on the matter: 'I say if you're a Democrat, be a Democrat. My aim is to direct these [southern] Democrats into the bosom of President Johnson's Great Society with all it implies, politically, socially and economically. If they can't live there, we welcome all converts to Republicanism.'[65] Ford's words rang hollow, however, as he was speaking the day after the conservative coalition had reunited to pass a Model Cities bill which funded the programme at half the rate the Johnson administration had requested. At one stage, it looked as if Model Cities was going to lose all funding – a fate that did befall the rent supplements section of the bill.[66]

The problem for Ford, who publicly denied engaging in any dialogue with Dixiecrats, was that legislation triggered in response to the urban crisis – which dwarfed all other domestic legislation in importance during the 90th Congress – offered a context in which the majority of House Republicans and southern Democrats resolutely agreed.[67] Neither held any enthusiasm for funding urban poverty measures, while both were keen to pass crime and anti-riot legislation. Ford's rhetoric aside, the 90th Congress showed that – for all the upheavals of the 1960s – the bond between House Republicans and southern Democrats proved enduring.

Long, hot summer

From July 1967 onwards, Republicans clearly split into two camps on how to respond to the intensifying urban crisis, with each side choosing to prioritise either order or justice.[68] The vast majority of House Republicans and conservative-inclined GOP governors took a three-pronged approach to the frequent urban riots and uprisings occurring over the summer. These Republicans ascribed blame to the Johnson administration and poverty workers for raising expectations in the ghetto; they denounced any new urban poverty programmes, often employing the language of white backlash; and finally, they called for punitive crime bills to discourage rioters and agitators while making vague noises about providing more jobs to quell the urban unrest. A majority of Senate Republicans and progressive-leaning GOP governors also attributed blame to the Johnson administration – sometimes for not doing enough

111

for urban dwellers – but these Republicans called for Congress to pass Johnson's urban poverty initiatives, and to strengthen civil rights legislation, and some even offered programmes for the ghetto that went beyond the President's request. Essentially, the summer's events forced Republicans off the fence on how to best tackle urban crisis.

The events that triggered this change were the frequent racial uprisings and disorders that transpired in the United States from June through to August. During the Johnson presidency, urban rebellion had started to seem almost inevitable during the summer months, but previous outbreaks did not match the size and scale of those that erupted in Newark (12–17 July) and Detroit (23–27 July). The latter was the worst urban riot since angry New Yorkers had protested the draft during the Civil War, and Michigan governor George Romney remarked during a flyover of Detroit that 'it looked like the city had been bombed'.[69] The Detroit riots in particular shook politicians who had previously seen the Motor City as an African American success story. Daniel Patrick Moynihan, a liberal now questioning his own faith in Great Society liberalism, reflected in 1968 that 'Detroit had everything the Great Society could wish for in a municipality; a splendid mayor and a fine governor. A high-paying, and thanks to the fiscal policies of the national government, a booming industry, civilized by and associated with the hands-down leading liberal trade union of the world.'[70] The mayor, Jerome Cavanagh, had been an especially prominent War on Poverty supporter.[71] In the longer run, the summer of 1967 further shattered Great Society liberalism, and in the short run it made Lyndon Johnson, in the words of his political adviser Frederick Panzer, the 'lightning rod' for public discontent.[72]

It was hardly new for LBJ to attract the discontent of GOP conservatives and stalwarts, but the summer's events allowed these Republicans to renew their attacks on the President with gusto. Ford slammed the raised expectations that Johnson and poverty war officials had created in the ghetto, and, as a first step to prevent further disorder, called immediately for 'A total re-vamping and re-direction of the Poverty War – where waste has been astronomical and administration ineffective.'[73] Maryland governor Spiro Agnew, for whom the riots had the effect of moving his political philosophy in a more conservative direction, backed the Minority Leader in bemoaning the fact that federal programmes were 'overpublicized and under-funded'.[74] California House Republican James Utt, blinkered to the numerous challenges facing ghetto dwellers, saw the money spent on the programmes as a waste. Utt blamed the ghetto conditions on a lack of initiative among the black population, claiming that it 'takes only effort to clean weeds and remove trash'.[75] In the midst of the Detroit riot, the Republican Coordinating Committee endorsed the drive to blame Johnson, releasing a statement in July which accused the President and poverty workers of having stirred up the ghettos.

Over in Congress, a rat extermination bill met the whirlwind of anger emanating from conservative voices. The proposed leg-islation, which called for a modest appropriation of $40 million to rid inner-city neighbourhoods of rats, attracted much oppro-brium from House GOP members during debate and Republicans successfully voted 148–24 against consideration of the measure (Democrats supported it by 154–59). *Congressional Quarterly* noted that the bill's defeat was 'widely interpreted as being anti-President Johnson's "Great Society" and anti-poor people'.[76]

The debate over the rat extermination bill often focused on issues of race, with opponents mocking the measure as a 'civil rats' bill.[77] Iowa Republican Harold Gross derided the proposal of another federal programme, telling the House that the measure would lead to the establishment of a 'rat corps' and the appoint-ment of a 'high commissioner of rats'.[78] James Latta (R-OH) belittled the problem that the bill intended to solve, claiming that 'The matter of putting out a little bit of rat poison should not be requested of the Federal Government', and Virginia Republican Joel T. Broyhill made House Republican feelings clear, intoning in a southern accent, 'I think the rat smart thing for us to do is vote down this rat bill rat now.'[79] Thomas and Mary Edsall con-vincingly conclude that the distasteful debate over the rat exter-mination bill showed that 'The full force of white backlash had reached the House of Representatives.'[80]

Johnson attempted to shame House Republicans into action, releasing a statement on the same day of the debate that portrayed the GOP as caring more about animals than about children: 'We are spending Federal funds to protect our livestock from rodents and predatory animals. The least we can do is give our children the same protection we give our livestock.'[81] In a further attempt to quell the rising storm of criticism aimed at the administration, Johnson employed the age-old tactic of appointing a commission to study the reasons behind the summer uprisings, with the National Advisory Commission on Civil Disorders (later known as the Kerner Commission) including three Republicans: Rep. William McCulloch (R-OH), Brooke and Lindsay. House Republicans, for the time being at least, were not placated, choosing to focus on their own solution to the riots.

The day before the rat extermination debate, House Republicans made clear that their priority was to re-establish order in the United States. Significantly, one of the very few pieces of noteworthy legislation bearing a Republican name which passed either congressional chamber during the Johnson presidency was a crime bill, on 20 July. Similar to the amendment that was part of the failed Civil Rights Act of 1966, the bill made it a crime to travel across state boundaries to incite a riot. Many perceived the bill, proposed again by Florida Republican William Cramer, as a direct attack on militant 'black power' advocates Stokely Carmichael and H. Rap Brown.[82] House Republicans approved the legislation by a margin of 179–4 as even progressive Republicans largely acquiesced to the new political mood of the country. Rising backlash sentiment was evident across the United States as national polls revealed that whites had a lower regard for black Americans than before the urban uprisings and, consequently, white opposition to any civil rights legislation had hardened. Furthermore, when asked by Gallup what their solution to the riots would be, whites most regularly favoured strong, repressive measures against the rioters.[83] Accordingly, the House Republican alternative to Johnson's urban poverty initiatives clearly enjoyed majority support in the country.

This rising 'law and order' sentiment also provided a context that allowed conservatives to regain more credibility in the GOP following Goldwater's 1964 defeat. In August, Ford went as far as describing the Arizonan as an 'oracle', noting that during the 1964 election the crime issue 'didn't have the ferment' it enjoyed in 1967.[84] Meanwhile, Ronald Reagan's popularity continued to soar, not just in California but throughout the nation. Reagan – who referred to rioters as 'mad dogs' – had been ahead of the 'law and order' curve, essentially declaring his own war on crime in his January inaugural address.[85] During a June speech in Indianapolis, entitled 'Little Minds and Timid Men Do Not Build Great Societies', Reagan had told the crowd that, on the crime issue, 'It is time to get angry.'[86] Reagan went on to score liberals for social programmes that discouraged personal discipline and instead wrought 'Permissiveness from cradle to crime', which was embodied, according to the him, by the 'right to adjust any grievance by the nearest means at hand, be it rock, club or firebomb'.[87] A Harris poll in September revealed that 86 per cent of Americans knew who Reagan was, 82 per cent agreed that he was right in wanting to 'put a firm hand to race riots', and that, by an impressive 4–1 margin, respondents believed that he was doing a good job as governor.[88] Unsurprisingly, Reagan's name was mentioned with increasing frequency as a potential Republican candidate for the 1968 presidential race.

In this atmosphere, the House delivered its official response to the summer of urban rebellion by passing the Republican-backed omnibus crime bill on 8 August and by continuing to refuse to fund urban poverty programmes. *Washington Post* journalist George Lardner Jr correctly noted that the 'crime issue ties in perfectly, as [Republicans] see it, with their calls for a cutback in the maze of often narrowly tailored federal aid programs'.[89] As such, it was unsurprising that Ford and the House leadership continued to be obdurate in the face of increasing media pressure for the House to reverse course and support Johnson's urban poverty programmes. Ford remained defiant that the GOP would not provide votes to increase funds for Model Cities or to provide any appropriations at all for rent supplements and rat control.[90] Instead, House Republicans told reporters that, with crime legislation passed, the second solution to increased rioting was to provide more jobs.

Republicans who were convinced – genuinely or expediently – that programmes such as the War on Poverty had played a key part in triggering riots, would increasingly return to the need for jobs as a solution. To keep the appeal broad, Republicans often did not specify if they meant more jobs for everyone or specifically for those living in ghettoes. Melvin Laird, chairman of the House

Republican Conference, wrote to the President on 31 August that 'We are all sick at heart over the turmoil and disruption that has marked many of the cities in our nation during these past three summers.' Laird, who published the letter in the middle of election year 1968, told LBJ that what the nation needed was 'decisive leadership' to provide jobs for those who were rioting. The Wisconsinite urged Johnson to adopt the Republican-sponsored Human Investment Act that would give private industry a 10 per cent tax credit for training workers.[91] Given that the United States was enjoying an unemployment rate of 3.8 per cent – the lowest since 1953 and almost unfathomable in the post-1960s era – the jobs argument remained fraught with difficulty.[92] Black unemployment, while clearly worse, was also in decline – standing at just over 6 per cent.[93] Six years of JFK and LBJ in the White House had seen unemployment halve and, at this stage, the GOP's call for increased focus on jobs appeared a token effort on behalf of House Republicans hoping to soften the blow of the stick by offering a little carrot to black ghetto residents.

At a Republican Leadership press conference on 30 August, Ford reaffirmed the House Republican stance on the uprisings and in doing so summed up his caucus's order-focused response to Newark and Detroit: 'When a Rap Brown and a Stokely Carmichael are allowed to run loose to threaten law-abiding Americans with injury and death, it's time to slam the door on them – and slam it hard.'[94] In a strange way, this approach offered House Republicans a route to actively pursue legislation rather than just saying 'no' to everything. Offering stricter crime legislation was, after all, proactive rather than negative. Furthermore, in advocating such legislation that prioritised order, House Republicans knew that they enjoyed broad public support.

Senate Republicans chose a markedly different path when the riots took centre stage in July, and a short walk across Capitol Hill revealed a big difference in Republican thinking. Together with progressive governors, the majority of GOP senators offered support for Johnson's urban poverty initiatives at a crucial juncture for the War on Poverty. In a swipe at the House, a group of ten ideologically diverse Senate Republicans issued a statement, on

27 July, warning that 'Our cities and metropolitan areas, where most Americans live, face a grave crisis unless Congress lives up to its commitment made over the past two years.' The statement, whose signatories included stalwarts such as Senators Frank Carlson and James Pearson of Kansas, as well as Iowa's Jack Miller, urged the House to quickly fund Model Cities and rent supplements at appropriate levels. The group also noted that the problems of the cities affected the suburbs and as such should be treated as metropolitan problems, thus including a key Republican voting base.[95] Because of this approach, Senate Republicans – with the odd exception – rose above the mounting white backlash in diagnosing the reasons behind the uprisings. Kentucky's Thruston Morton summed up the sense of responsibility on display, declaring on 27 July: 'Blame is on us all.'[96]

Approaching the riots in stark contrast to the House GOP, some Senate Republicans came very close to breaking the GOP's hallowed Eleventh Commandment. On 7 August, Hugh Scott released a statement in response to the farcical rat control debate, sarcastically describing the performance of the House as 'amazing'. Recounting the 'bad humor and poor jokes' during the debate, Scott scolded House members that 'Rats are hardly a topic for levity.' The Pennsylvanian, who would later tour rat-infested areas of Pittsburgh, announced that he had already introduced an identical rat control bill for consideration by the Senate.[97] Maverick Senator Thomas Kuchel (R-CA) also backed the Johnson administration's legislation. Speaking to the *Los Angeles Times*, the Californian regretted that the Detroit riots put a 'considerable damper' on efforts to pass bills that benefited the black community.[98] Predictably, Javits led the chorus of criticism against the House's behaviour, testifying in the Senate that 'There seems to be little perceptiveness that while there may be some outside agitators, they are only riding the storm – not making it – and that the real agitators are slum landlords unmindful of their responsibilities, irresponsible public officials, bigots of all kinds – and rats.'[99] Overall, Senate Republicans chose to sympathise with ghetto residents, noting that only a small minority of residents ever participated in actual rioting. There was an acceptance that 'law and order' legislation was going to pass and even Javits admitted that he would begrudgingly vote for a

117

crime bill, but the GOP senate caucus emphasised programmes that focused on social justice.[100]

Some Republican senators even offered legislation that was more progressive than that which the Johnson administration was prepared to endorse. Thruston Morton, for example, called for a one billion dollar 'crash' programme to aid the cities in the imme- diate aftermath of the Detroit riots.[101] Soon after, Javits repeated his advocacy of a 'Marshall Plan for Deprived Americans'. On 10 August, the Empire State Senator advocated that the federal government set aside one third of the surtax – currently being proposed to help fund the Vietnam War – to launch a ten-year anti-slum effort. Explaining the proposal, Javits noted that this would earmark the $50 billion envisioned by the aforementioned Freedom Budget.[102] Charles Percy also drew on the 'guns or but- ter' theme, telling his fellow senators: 'If we continue to spend 66 million dollars a day trying to save sixteen million people of South Vietnam while leaving twenty million poor in our own country unresolved then I think we have our priorities terribly confused.'[103] Clearly, no one could accuse Senate Republicans of adhering to the 'Party of No' moniker in response to the summer's events.

The Senate approach found favour with important Republi- can governors. Following a hastily called governors' meeting in August, eleven Republican state executives, led by New York's Rockefeller, demanded a 'sweeping program to eradicate the root causes of rioting'.[104] In Rockefeller, who had already announced a $4.5 million state rat control programme for New York, John- son found a firm Republican ally. Indeed, ahead of the governors' meeting the White House had provided Rockefeller with a list of stalled urban poverty legislation that he could persuade other GOP executives to endorse.[105] Under Rockefeller's leadership the governors released a 60-point plan which criticised the rigidity of existing federal urban programmes and also made clear that a firm hand was needed in response to rioting. Nevertheless, the overwhelming tone of the message was progressive. The eleven governors prioritised sympathy for ghetto residents, blaming the 'misery and frustration' which inner-city residents had to endure, and urged Congress to supply funds that were currently being withheld from programmes such as Model Cities and rent supplements.[106] Following the meeting, Ray Shafer, impatient with House intransigence, went home and initiated Pennsylvania's own Model Cities programme.[107]

While Rockefeller's role was important, the most prominent Republican governor in the summer of 1967 was undoubtedly George Romney. When the Detroit riots struck in Romney's own backyard, he was a leading contender for the Republican nomination and was enjoying favourable poll ratings when matched against Johnson.[108] Romney was acutely aware of the political challenge presented by urban America, having noted earlier in the year that 'It's an urban age, genuine urban renewal is of particular concern to the new generation – because that's where most of them will spend their lives.'[109] Romney, despite being one of the eleven signatories to the governors' message, was no fan of the Great Society's urban initiatives, referring to the President's agenda as the 'Great Façade'. But he also had no time for the House Republican approach which focused solely on punishment.[110] The Michigander hoped to find a middle way that would provide him with a path to 1600 Pennsylvania Avenue. Romney's interest in attracting black voters to the GOP, his faith in volunteerism, and also his compassionate zeal to see the underdog succeed as he had done while in charge of American Motors, led the Michigander to set up the Detroit Action Center in 1967 as a means of inner-city outreach.[111] The Center largely focused on providing advice to urban residents looking for jobs, chiming with Romney's previous appeals to self-help as a remedy to poverty.

In the wake of the riots, Romney redoubled his efforts to appeal to urban America, embarking on a tour of seventeen American cities over three weeks in September. After meeting with public officials, community leaders and city residents throughout his tour, Romney concluded that while private initiatives were the most effective at tackling urban unrest, government had to do more to aid city residents.[112] Employing dramatic rhetoric, Romney declared in late September: 'I am more convinced than ever before that unless we reverse course, [and] build a new America, the old America will be destroyed.'[113] Unfortunately for those who agreed with the Michigan governor, by the time he made this declaration, Romney's star

119

was already fading. While it is unclear if conservative and stalwart Republicans could ever have rallied behind a Mormon moderate who had failed to endorse Goldwater in 1964, Romney's comments on 30 August that he had been 'brainwashed' by officials following a trip to Vietnam proved the death knell of his candidacy. Geoffrey Kabaservice argues that this represented a significant moment for the GOP's intraparty struggle, concluding that Romney's candidacy was the final chance for GOP moderates and progressives to leave a lasting imprint on the party.[114] While Kabaservice's conclusion goes a step too far – Romney would be part of a Nixon administration that briefly pursued progressive domestic legislation – it is certainly true that Romney's fall from grace meant that those advocating social justice in response to the problems of the ghetto had lost a significant spokesperson for their cause.

Despite Romney's decline, Republicans who had advocated a progressive response to the summer's rioting saw legislative success emerge after tempers had cooled. While the long-term effects of riots would harm Great Society liberalism (and, indeed, Republican progressivism), in the short term, the 1967 summer uprisings actually had the effect of generating a sufficient sense of crisis to pass Johnson's urban poverty measures. Rat control, rent supplements, Model Cities and the Economic Opportunity Act all received funding to an extent that had seemed unlikely before the summer. The Senate approach of pursuing social justice gradually asserted itself over September and October, acting as a check on the knee-jerk, populist white backlash embodied by the conservative coalition in the House.

This process began in late September when over forty House Republicans changed their votes on rat control, bowing to pressure from the media and the White House. The new bill was proposed in a bipartisan spirit, with progressive House Republican Charles Mathias (R-MD) co-sponsoring the legislation. The next day, backed by a majority of GOP votes, the Senate passed a Model Cities appropriation of $537 million – double what the House had passed in May – and the increased funding also included $40 million for rent supplements. The appropriation was ultimately whittled down after the House, backed by the overwhelming majority of Republicans, rejected the original conference report which had agreed to the Senate's spending levels. Still, $312 million for Model Cities and $10 million for rent supplements appropriations that passed in October represented a success for supporters of urban poverty initiatives.[115]

After having its debate delayed to allow for a period of post-riot reflection by legislators, the EOA was the final piece of legislation to profit from change of heart. Since the 1966 elections, the Johnson administration had feared that the renewed conservative coalition in the House would kill the legislation that was up for renewal in October. The OEO was still dogged by GOP claims of wastefulness and corruption. Moreover, Republicans and southern Democrats amplified these concerns during 1967, arguing that Shriver's agency was an expensive luxury that the nation could ill afford during wartime. In a March message to Congress, Johnson had attempted to placate other prominent GOP criticisms by stressing a renewed focus on giving more power to the states to run OEO programmes and also further involvement from private enterprise. By 1967, however, Great Society liberalism – of which the OEO remained the symbol – was firmly perceived as an exercise in big government by the GOP and House Republicans were not in the mood for compromise. Moreover, some observers saw the summer riots as throwing further doubt on the legislation to which Congress eventually returned in late September.[116]

Senate and House Republicans divided along similar lines as they had done in response to other urban poverty legislation. This is unsurprising as the EOA was now, according to *Congressional Quarterly*, 'considered a plan for Northern cities and their large Negro populations'.[117] Brooke, an adopted northerner whose Massachusetts electorate included Boston's substantial black population, delivered a passionate appeal to his fellow Republicans to embrace the War on Poverty and recognise the 'realities of the twentieth century'. Brooke, symbolically speaking in Detroit, called on House Republicans to seize their own 'Disraeli moment'[118] by fully meeting the challenge of urban poverty:

> It is a sound tenet of the Republican Party that government should do for the people only what they cannot do for themselves. But what the people cannot do for themselves has, in many instances, increased. In

121

the days when our country was young, a man could go West without money or education. . . . These days are gone. Today's uneducated man lives in a slum.

To speak of free enterprise and equality of opportunity is to mock this young man and the multitudes who share his failure and frustration. Yet many Republicans share a fear that big, centralized government will undermine the freedom of the individual.[119]

Other Senate Republicans who, along with liberal Democrats, attempted to attach an Emergency Employment bill to the EOA's renewal accepted Brooke's challenge. The bill – which bore resemblance to the Works Progress Administration of the 1930s – would have authorised over $2 billion to help public and private agencies, during 1968 and 1969, provide jobs for poor residents of slum ghettos and economically distressed rural areas.[120] Despite the mention of rural areas, it was commonly accepted that the bill was in response to urban rioting; Hugh Scott justified his support of the measure by noting that the unemployment rate in the slums was three times the national average. Scott, who claimed the bill would create 500,000 jobs, also cited an appeal from Philadelphia's Republican District Attorney Arlen Specter. Specter draped his call for the Emergency Employment bill with traditional Republican rhetoric: 'It is not possible for our urban centers to pull themselves up by their bootstraps without the assistance of the Federal Government.'[121] Self-help rhetoric aside, the bill was a remarkably New Deal-like response to the riots.

Ultimately, the Emergency Employment section was removed, as the Johnson administration feared that its presence would sink the EOA in the House. Both Javits and Scott tore into the President for failing to stand by a progressive response to the urban crisis.[122] Scott was especially scathing, skewering the President for ignoring the 'plight of the hard-core unemployed'. 'The contrast between promise and performance has been one of the hallmarks of the Great Society, Mr. President,' Scott charged, 'but it was never as evident as it is now.'[123] Despite the failure of the Emergency Employment bill, Senate Republicans did help pass a two-year renewal of the EOA which left the controversial OEO largely untouched and delivered an appropriation of $198 million more than Johnson had requested.

The bill even attracted some support from GOP stalwarts with Republicans, including Dirksen and Karl Mundt (R-ND), voting in favour of EOA's renewal.

After much wrangling between the House and the Senate over funding levels, the EOA's two-year renewal was eventually signed by LBJ two days before Christmas with an appropriation only slightly less than that which the administration had requested. Historian Gareth Davies, reflecting on the political environment in which the renewal took place, concludes that 'The survival of the War on Poverty in these circumstances represented the administration's greatest legislative achievement in 1967.'[124] Taken together with the successful passage of other legislation such as rat control, rent supplements and Model Cities, it is clear that the summer uprisings had the short-term effect of spurring Congress – and especially the House – to acquiesce to funding urban poverty proposals that otherwise seemed doomed before the summer. With specific reference to the Republican Party, the urban antipoverty triumphs represented a short-term boost in status for Senate Republicans who had led the way in calling for such legislation, but the overwhelming trend of white backlash sentiment, which rejected social welfare programmes for inner-city residents, suggested that those favouring social justice for the ghetto were not likely to remain in the ascendancy for long.

Big tent party

Notwithstanding the divided response that Republicans had offered, the GOP proved itself capable of being a 'big tent' party as the differing approaches did not lead to a breakdown in party unity. In the midst of the summer crisis, thirty-five House Republicans and ten Senate Republicans of varying political ideologies had released a statement entitled 'Preventative Medicine in the Cities' which perfectly balanced appeals to both order and justice:

> All responsible men know that stern measures must be taken to assure that law and order will prevail. But we should not make the mistake of weakening or abandoning the Nation's commitment to equal opportunity and equal justice for all.[125]

Much like the Democrats, who had spoken with two distinct voices on the issue of racial segregation since the 1930s, Republicans were applying a similar response to the urban crisis. Senate Republicans could argue that they had salvaged urban poverty measures while not ignoring – at least rhetorically – the need to restore order to the cities. House Republicans, on the other hand, could justifiably claim that they had put a check on the big spending of Great Society liberalism and firmly advocated a restoration of order. While journalists often tried to tempt Republicans into denouncing these contrasting points of view, GOP politicians, mindful of the Eleventh Commandment, were careful to avoid any divisive comments.[126]

Undoubtedly such unity was helped by the fact that the riots further eroded the credibility of Johnson and the Democratic Party to such an extent that Republican victory in 1968 seemed increasingly likely. An RNC meeting held in September – at which point the President's approval rating had fallen to 37 per cent – showcased the increased confidence in Republican ranks.[127] Lee Nunn, Director of the National Republican Senatorial Campaign Committee, observed that 'The Press and commentators across the Nation are, as usual, having a field day as to what political philosophy we Republicans should embrace to ensure victory next year.' Nunn, who reminded the gathering that the membership comprised ideologically diverse figures ranging from Jacob Javits to Strom Thurmond, confidently asserted that 'Fortunately, we do not have a philosophical problem with our committee. . . . We are all going to be running against the Johnson administration – unity of purpose should present no difficulty.'[128]

Nunn was likely drawing strength from the GOP's pollster Thomas Benham, who told the meeting that such was the public anxiety over the summer riots and the prolonged Vietnam War that the GOP could win in 1968 even if LBJ somehow managed soon to bring the conflict in Southeast Asia to a successful conclusion.[129] Sen. Margaret Chase Smith (R-ME), who possessed a voting record that was largely progressive, believed that people were yearning for a return to Eisenhower's America when people 'could walk the streets of our cities and towns without such great fear of being attacked'.[130]

Republicans, after many years in the political wilderness, were now exuding a confidence beyond even that of Ike's heyday and the urban crisis had played a key role in this transition. If the War on Poverty had provided the Republican Party with a path to relevance in 1965, by the autumn of 1967 the urban crisis was providing the GOP with a path to victory.

Conclusion

By 1967, the War on Poverty was now seen by almost everyone as favouring urban and black Americans. The House Republican response to the urban crisis – which included inflammatory rhetoric that linked urban poverty programmes to the growing white backlash – had helped promote this perception. From Paul Fino's provocative remarks after Watts to House Republicans joking about a 'civil rats' bill in the midst of Newark and Detroit, the House GOP had played a significant role in racialising the nucleus of the Great Society. The politically adept Johnson administration had managed to fend off Republican attacks but the War on Poverty remained imperilled if the white population continued to view it as targeting the few, instead of the many.

In responding to the urban crisis, House Republicans had been afforded the chance to offer their own alternative to an assault on urban poverty; disavowing social programmes, they chose instead to either accept or stoke 'law and order' sentiment which was afraid of rising crime and urban disorder. Such a response, while capable of drawing some support from the traditionally Democratic white, ethnic working class, did not suggest that House Republicans were overly concerned with going down the path that the party's Big City report had suggested. Offering a short-term, reactive response, House Republicans believed that if the United States was indeed a 'nation in agony' as Gerald Ford claimed, then a sharp dose of painkillers was all that was required.

Senate Republicans, retaining a faith in preventative medicine, offered critical support to Johnson's poverty programmes during the urban crisis. Without GOP support – from both senators and governors – it is hard to see how rent supplements, Model Cities, rat control and even the Economic Opportunity Act would have survived the fallout from the summer upheavals in 1967. Progressives in the upper chamber also pushed hard for their own urban poverty measures; Javits's 'Marshall Plan for Deprived Americans' and the Emergency Employment bill championed by GOP senators were all examples of Republicans living up to their 1965 promise to offer constructive alternatives to Johnson's poverty programmes. Moderate and progressive governors were also taking the lead in their home states. Nevertheless, it was not always entirely clear how these Republican constructive alternatives differed greatly from those offered by Johnson's Great Society.

In its response to the urban crisis, then, the Republican Party fashioned two different paths down which it could travel in the coming years, and in its 1968 presidential candidate it would find a politician who was happy to ride both lanes to victory. In his journey to the White House, Richard Nixon would loudly embrace 'order' while also issuing a quieter appeal for 'justice', and, in doing so, he would offer the electorate both a choice and an echo.

Notes

1. GRF, Address at the 70th annual convention of Ohio Association of Insurance Agents, Cleveland, OH, 30 October 1967, box 59, RTH, GRF.
2. Editorial, 'The Nation – The Dimming of the Dream', *Time Magazine*, 9 December 1966.
3. LBJ, 'Special Message to the Congress Recommending a Program for Cities and Metropolitan Areas', 26 January 1966, TAPP, https://www.presidency.ucsb.edu/.
4. The 1968 elections arguably represented the end of the urban crisis. While many other events could be pointed to both before and after these bookends, the period outlined represents the time during which the problems of the American city were most prominent in the political sphere.
5. Edsall and Edsall, *Chain Reaction*, 51.
6. For statistics, see Flamm, *Law and Order*, 125. For a challenge to the statistics, see Elizabeth Hinton, *From the War on Poverty to the War on Crime: The Making of Mass Incarceration in America* (Cambridge, MA: Harvard University Press, 2016).

7. James T. Patterson, *Grand Expectations: The United States, 1945–1974* (New York: Oxford University Press, 1996), 675.
8. Louis Harris, 'Most OK Great Society', *The Philadelphia Inquirer*, 3 April 1967.
9. EWB, Speech to B'nai B'rith Humanitarian Award Dinner, New York City, NY, 10 April 1968, box 557, EWB.
10. In 1959, Democrats held 61.7 per cent of urban districts – a percentage that had likely increased by 1967. Julius Turner, *Party and Constituency: Pressures on Congress*, rev. Edward V. Schneier Jr (Baltimore, MD: Johns Hopkins University Press, 1970), 110.
11. 'White ethnic voters', in US political parlance during this era, referred mostly to the descendants of immigrants from central and eastern European countries, who were often located around the big cities of the Midwest and more likely to be Catholic: Polish-Americans, Italian-Americans etc.
12. *CQ Almanac 1966*, 231–44.
13. Sam Yorty testimony in ibid.
14. Jonathan Bingham quoted in John Herbers, 'House Liberals Waver', *New York Times*, 30 October1967.
15. Zelizer, *The Fierce Urgency of Now*, 13.
16. GRF speech before the Annual Business Banquet, University of California, Los Angeles, 18 May 1967, box 59, RTH, GRF.
17. Vincent J. Cannato, *The Ungovernable City: John Lindsay and His Struggle to Save New York* (New York: Basic Books, 2001), 26.
18. Mason, *From Hoover to Reagan*, 183.
19. Meg Greenfield, 'Senator Goldwater and the Negro', *The Reporter*, 18 October 1964.
20. Jacob K. Javits, *Order of Battle* (New York: Atheneum Books, 1964).
21. Philip Klinkner, *The Losing Parties: Out-Party National Committees, 1956–1993* (New Haven, CT: Yale University Press, 1994), 82–3.
22. Hugh D. Scott, *Come to the Party* (Englewood Cliffs, NJ: Prentice Hall, 1968), 229.
23. Zelizer, *The Fierce Urgency of Now*, 13.
24. Louis Harris, 'White Fears, Negro Militancy Continue to Show Steady Rise', *Washington Post*, 6 June 1967.
25. *CQ Almanac 1965*.
26. JGT, ibid.
27. Betts, ibid.
28. GRF, 'Your Washington Review', 30 March 1966, box 56, RTH, GRF.

29. Andrew, *Lyndon Johnson and the Great Society*, 133; Edsall and Edsall, *Chain Reaction*, 62.
30. JGT, 'Major Housing Legislation Enacted', *CQ Almanac 1965*.
31. Sean P. Cunningham, 'John Tower, Texas, and the Rise of the Republican South', in *Seeking a New Majority*, ed. Mason and Morgan, 106.
32. Andrew, *Lyndon Johnson and the Great Society*, 142; 'Major Housing Legislation Enacted', *CQ Almanac 1965*.
33. Fino quoted in Andrew, *Lyndon Johnson and the Great Society*, 142.
34. Hazel Erskine, 'The Polls: Demonstrations and Race Riots', *Public Opinion Quarterly*, vol. 31, no. 4 (1967–68), 662.
35. Melvin R. Laird remarks at Eisenhower Dinner, Asheville, NC, 14 October 1965, box a16, Baroody Subject File, Melvin R. Laird Congressional Papers, GRF.
36. Ibid.
37. A Harris poll in mid-1967 also recorded that 82 per cent of whites were 'Unfavorable to negro demonstrations' – a statistic that was up from an already high 66 per cent in mid-1966. Erskine, 'The Polls', 659.
38. The Governor's Commission on the Los Angeles Riots, 'Violence in the City – An End or a Beginning?' 2 December 1965, http://www.usc.edu.
39. David S. Broder, 'G.O.P. Chiefs Urge a Cut in Spending', *New York Times*, 29 March 1966, 17.
40. GRF quoted in 'Major Housing', *CQ Almanac 1965*.
41. JKJ, 'Republican Comeback from 1964 Still Very Much in Doubt', 3 July 1966, box 36, subseries 1.1., series 285, JKJ.
42. JKJ speech, 'Long and Short-Term Action Need Against Slums', 22 July 1966, box 36, subseries 1.1, series 285, JKJ.
43. HDS, 'Statement on Rent Supplemental Appropriation', 5 May 1966, box 40, HDS.
44. Rae, *Decline and Fall of the Liberal Republicans*, 87.
45. Dirksen quoted on NBC's 'Meet the Press', 8 August 1966, The Dirksen Congressional Center, http://www.dirksencenter.org.
46. In California, for example, the electorate had voted overwhelmingly in 1964 to repeal the Rumford Act – the Golden State's own Fair Housing legislation – by a greater margin than LBJ carried the state.
47. 'Housing, Demonstration Cities Bill Enacted', *CQ Almanac 1966*, 210–30.
48. Ibid.
49. EMD quoted in Marjorie Hunter, 'Senate Approves Johnson Slum Aid', 20 August 1966, *New York Times*, 1.

50. GRF remarks before the Virginia Municipal League Convention, 18 September 1966, box 59, RTH, GRF.
51. Fino quoted in Hunter, 'Senate Approves Johnson Slum Aid'.
52. Fraser quoted in ibid.
53. LBJ had told an FBI liaison officer during the 1964 elections that 'One of my political analysts tells me that every time one [riot] occurs, it costs me 90,000 votes.' Quoted in Flamm, *Law and Order*, 37.
54. Richard Strout, 'U.S. Impact of GOP Victories', *Christian Science Monitor*, 13 November 1966.
55. Lyn Shepard, 'U.S. Legislative Logjam Seen', *Christian Science Monitor*, 12 November 1966, 6; John H. Averill, 'Urban GOP Worried by Economy Ax', *Los Angeles Times*, November 1966; Edmond Lebreton, 'Reinforced Hill Republicans Pick Targets from President's Programs', *Washington Post*, 12 November 1966.
56. 'Antipoverty Program Survives Assault, Gets $1.8 Billion', *CQ Almanac 1967*.
57. Reichley, *Conservatives in an Age of Change*, 32.
58. Andrew L. Johns, *Vietnam's Second Front: Domestic Politics, the Republican Party, and the War* (Lexington, KY: University Press of Kentucky, 2010).
59. GWR remarks at Michigan Federation of Republican Women, 5 May 1967, box 12, Robert Hardesty papers, LBJ.
60. GRF address at Bowling Green University, Bowling Green, OH, 11 May 1967, box 59, RTH, GRF.
61. JKJ remarks at Texas University Young Republican Club, Austin, TX, 23 January 1967, box 37, subseries 1.1, series 285, JKJ.
62. Richard Strout, 'U.S. Impact of GOP Victories', *Christian Science Monitor*, 13 November 1966.
63. Patterson, *The Eve of Destruction*, 224–5.
64. Robert E. Baker, 'Promise and Fulfillment-II: Rights Coalition – Fractious, Fragmented', *Washington Post*, 16 January 1967.
65. Godfrey Sperling, 'Republicans Hoist Civil-Rights Banner', *Christian Science Monitor*, 23 November 1966; GRF speech before the Annual Business Banquet, University of California, LA, 18 May 1967, box 57, RTH, GRF.
66. 'Congress 1967 – the Year in Review', *CQ Almanac 1967*.
67. Don Oberdorfer, 'Where Are You Going Jerry Ford?', *Detroit Free Press*, 27 August 1967.
68. Mark McLay, 'The Republican Party and the Long, Hot Summer of 1967 in the United States', *Historical Journal*, vol. 61, no. 4 (2018), 1089–111.

69. GWR quoted in Kabaservice, *Rule and Ruin*, 214.
70. Daniel Patrick Moynihan, 'Where Liberals Went Wrong', in *Republican Papers*, ed. Melvin Laird (Garden City, NY: Anchor Books, 1968), 132.
71. Jerome P. Cavanagh to GRF, 28 June 1965, folder 15, box b28, Congressional Correspondence, GRF.
72. Memo, FP to LBJ, 10 August 1968, box 398, FP, LBJ.
73. GRF quoted from Joint Leadership Press Conference, 3 August 1967, box 21, Research Unit, Governor's Papers, RWR.
74. Agnew quoted in Senate Republican Policy Committee memorandum, 3 August 1967, *PAJWH*, reel 19.
75. Utt quoted in Thurber, *Republicans and Race*, 240.
76. 'Antipoverty Program Survives Assault', *CQ Almanac 1967*.
77. 'Congress 1967', *CQ Almanac 1967*.
78. Harold Gross, *Congressional Record*, 20 July 1967.
79. James Latta and Joel Broyhill in ibid.
80. Edsall and Edsall, *Chain Reaction*, 65.
81. LBJ quoted in DNC Press Release, 'Reactionaries in Congress Kill Rat Bill, President Johnson Asks Reconsideration', 21 July 1967, box 408, FP, LBJ.
82. Thurber, *Republicans and Race*, 240.
83. FP to LBJ, 15 August 1967, box 398, FP, LBJ.
84. GRF quoted in George Lardner Jr, 'GOP Blasts LBJ: Rising Crime Stirs Politics', *Denver Post*, 20 August 1967.
85. RWR, 'Inaugural Address', 5 January 1967, box 21, Research Unit, Governor's Papers, RWR.
86. RWR speech, 'Little Minds and Timid Men Do Not Build Great Societies',' Indianapolis, IN, 13 June 1967, box 127, RU, GP, RWR.
87. Ibid.
88. Louis Harris, *Harris Survey*, 11 September 1967, box 407, FP, LBJ.
89. George Lardner Jr, 'GOP Blasts LBJ', *Denver Post*, 20 August 1967.
90. Robert C. Albright, 'Dirksen, Ford Claim LBJ Losing Crime War', *Washington Post*, 30 August 1967.
91. Laird, Letter to LBJ, *Republican Papers*, 221–5.
92. 'Unemployment Rate', Bureau of Labor Statistics, http://data.bls.gov.
93. Robert W. Fairlie and William A. Sundstrom, 'The Racial Unemployment Gap in Long-Run Perspective', *American Economic Review*, 87 (1997), 307.
94. GRF quoted in Albright, 'Dirksen, Ford Claim LBJ Losing Crime War', *Washington Post*, 30 August 1967.

95. Press Release, 'Senator Scott and Republican Colleagues Urge Funds for Urban Programs', 27 July 1967, box 39, JKJ.
96. Morton quoted in Thurber, *Republicans and Race*, 241.
97. HDS statement on rat control, 7 August 1967, box 41, HDS; HDS, 'Senator Scott to Tour Rat Infested Areas of Pittsburgh', 16 September 1967, box 41, HDS.
98. Richard Bergholz, 'Kuchel Backs President's Racial Programs: Doubts GOP Alternatives Are Needed', *Los Angeles Times*, 1 August 1967.
99. JKJ testimony to Housing Subcommittee, Senate Banking and Currency Committee, 25 July 1967, box 39, JKJ.
100. JKJ remarks during Senate News Conference, 23 July 1967, box 39, JKJ.
101. William C. Selover and Lyn Shepard, 'Opposition to Great Society, Hardens', *Christian Science Monitor*, 5 August 1967.
102. JKJ, 'Senator Javits Offers Plan to Implement Domestic Marshall Plan Idea', 10 August 1967, box 39, JKJ.
103. Percy quoted in Thurber, *Republicans and Race*, 241.
104. Nathan Miller, 'GOP Urged to Support Race Bills', *The Baltimore Sun*, 12 August 1967.
105. Joe Califano to NAR, 9 August 1967, *PAJWH*, reel 19.
106. Homer Bigart, '8 Governors Give Antiriot Program', *New York Times*, 11 August 1967.
107. Republican Congressional Committee, 'Speech of the Week', 11 October 1967, box 34, series 1925, HDS.
108. Kabaservice, *Rule and Ruin*, 223.
109. GWR address at Lincoln Club Banquet, Louisville, KY, 11 February 1967, folder 410, box 18, series P-Whitman, RG4, NAR.
110. Ibid.
111. Kabaservice, *Rule and Ruin*, 214.
112. Ibid. 217.
113. GWR quoted in ibid. 217.
114. Kabaservice, *Rule and Ruin*, 223.
115. *CQ Almanac 1967*.
116. Ibid.
117. Ibid.
118. The reference is to nineteenth-century UK Conservative Prime Minister Benjamin Disraeli. Disraeli attempted to recast his party – often seen as the party of privilege – as the party of the rich and poor alike by embracing social and electoral reform to which the Conservative Party had been traditionally opposed.

119. EWB, Speech to Republican Party Dinner, Detroit, MI, 9 October 1967, box 570, EWB.
120. HDS, 'Statement in Support of the Emergency Employment Act', 26 September 1967, box 41, HDS.
121. Arlen Specter quoted in ibid.
122. JKJ remarks during Senate News Conference, 3 September 1967, box 39, JKJ.
123. HDS, 'Statement in Support of the Emergency Employment Act', 26 September 1967.
124. Gareth Davies, *From Opportunity to Entitlement*, 196.
125. 35 House Republicans and Five Senate Republicans, 'Preventative Medicine in the Cities', 3 August 1967, box 41, HDS.
126. John Herbers, 'House Liberals Waver', *New York Times*, 30 October 1967.
127. Presidential Job Approval, 'Lyndon B. Johnson', Gallup data compiled by Gerhard Peters, TAPP.
128. Lee Nunn remarks during RNC Meeting, 8 September 1967, reel 6, PRP.
129. James G. Wieghart, 'War, Riots "Could Help Unseat LBJ"', *Milwaukee Sentinel*, 9 September 1967.
130. Margaret Chase Smith remarks during RNC Meeting, 8 September 1967.

4

The choice and the echo: poverty politics and the 1968 campaign

---

If the conviction rate were double in this country, it would do more to eliminate crime in the future, than a quadrupling of the funds for any governmental war on poverty.[1]

Richard Nixon, 'Toward Freedom from Fear',
8 May 1968

It's no longer enough that white-owned enterprises employ greater numbers of Negroes ... This is needed, yes – but it has to be accompanied by an expansion of black ownership, of black capitalism.[2]

Richard Nixon, 'Bridges to Human Dignity',
25 April 1968

Richard Nixon presided over an election campaign in 1968 that accurately reflected how the Republican Party had challenged Lyndon Johnson's War on Poverty over the four years since its inception in 1964. Taking heed from conservative Republicans, Nixon disparaged the President's four-year-long antipoverty efforts for perpetuating welfare dependency, especially in the black urban community. Borrowing from stalwarts, the former Vice President charged that poverty spending was generating inflation which was disproportionately hurting the poor, while he also shared moderate Republicans' concerns that the administration's antipoverty efforts had been shot through with waste and corruption that was undermining an otherwise laudable initiative. Finally, in his espousal of 'black capitalism', Nixon offered a progressive private enterprise alternative that resembled a quieter echo of Johnson's

133

scheme. And through it all, Nixon's campaign in 1968 argued that the growing crime and continued rioting in the United States could be solved not by poverty programmes, but by a Republican administration that would prioritise the restoration of 'law and order'. Essentially, Nixon offered a strong Republican choice for order, and a quieter echo for justice. In 1964, the War on Poverty had been central to Lyndon Johnson's vision of a Great Society, but in 1968 Richard Nixon made clear that it would be an after-thought in his appeal to the 'forgotten Americans'.

The broader campaign in 1968 represented both a triumph and a failure of the Republican response to the antipoverty nucleus of Johnson's Great Society. On the plus side for the GOP, the War on Poverty – with all of its flaws and obscurities – was increas-ingly fertile campaign fodder for the opposition party. Established Republican tropes about a failed antipoverty effort were taking hold among more voters. Nevertheless, the election that resulted in Nixon becoming the first twentieth-century president elected with-out his party winning either chamber of Congress demonstrated the New Deal coalition's enduring strength. Democrats had once again revived – with varying success – the oft-repeated 'Party of No' argument in 1968 that had contributed to Republican electoral failure for the majority of the past three decades. This argument was helped by Nixon's insipid autumn campaign in which the GOP candidate, fearful of losing votes to George Wallace, stopped talk-ing about black capitalism in favour of devoting more time to law and order. Ultimately, the narrowness of Nixon's victory afforded no mandate to scrap antipoverty efforts in the short term. At the same time, however, continued Republican opposition to such programmes during the entire Johnson presidency had ensured by 1968 that the War on Poverty was unlikely to become part of the American consensus in the same sense that civil rights legislation, Medicare and federal aid to education most definitely had.

Primary choice

The controversial Kerner Commission report, released on 29 February 1968, served to return the two competing impulses of order and justice to the American political scene just as the spring primary season was getting under way. The Kerner report, most remembered for its conclusion that the United States was 'moving towards two societies, one black, one white – separate and unequal', marked the beginning of a series of turbulent events over the next six months. Politicians were provided ample opportunity either to place emphasis on restoring law and order or to advocate social justice in response to Kerner. The turbulence continued with Martin Luther King Jr's assassination and subsequent uprisings; the Poor People's Campaign; Robert Kennedy's assassination; and finally, the chaotic Democratic National Convention in August. GOP leaders continued to disagree over this choice but not to the extent that party harmony was shattered. Indeed, one of the main achievements of Nixon's successful primary campaign was the candidate's ability to straddle his party's divide on the issue. In offering both a 'militant crusade against crime' and 'black capitalism', the former Vice President advocated both order *and* justice – although undoubtedly Nixon put more emphasis on the former.[3] His challengers for the nomination – Nelson Rockefeller and, eventually, Ronald Reagan – offered starker choices and, as a result, a narrower appeal to the majority of convention delegates. What united all candidates was their firm denunciation of Johnson's War on Poverty as a solution to the urban crisis.

The Kerner report was an avowedly racially liberal document released in the context of a trend towards racial conservatism among whites. The Commission's majority largely ignored calls for tougher law enforcement and instead focused on social justice for black Americans:

> Segregation and poverty have created in the racial ghetto a destructive environment totally unknown to most white Americans.
> What white Americans have never fully understood – but what the Negro can never forget – is that white society is deeply implicated in the ghetto. White institutions created it, white institutions maintain it, and white society condones it.[4]

It was not just Kerner's rhetoric of white guilt that ran counter to the public mood, but also the report's recommendations, which included proposals for a guaranteed minimum income and a call for the government to create two million jobs in three years for the hard-core unemployed. In essence, it was an appeal for an all-out war on poverty. Historian Gareth Davies, who calls the recommendations 'unrealistic' and 'dramatic', concludes that 'The commission clearly saw its main function as being to stir the nation's conscience and anxiety to the point [the recommendations] would become suddenly feasible.'[5]

The nation's conscience, however, was proving ever harder to stir. The Kerner Commission reported at a time when white Americans appeared far more concerned with crime rather than further advancements for black Americans. Indeed, a common refrain in 1968 posited that 'A conservative . . . was a liberal who had been mugged; a liberal was a conservative who hadn't been mugged – yet.'[6] Johnson, who refused to act, or even comment, on Kerner's politically unrealistic recommendations, received advice from White House adviser Frederick Panzer that there was a cantankerous mood among the majority of white Americans with regard to helping urban blacks. In February, Panzer informed the President that a Gallup poll suggested that Americans, who previously viewed law enforcement as a local issue, now wanted action from the federal government on crime. Thirty-one per cent of Americans had told Gallup they were afraid to walk alone at night, and Panzer told Johnson that the poll results had a 'strong tie with fear of Negroes', and that they 'show the racial overtones to the crime problem'.[7] Gallup's poll was also the first recorded that showed 'crime and lawlessness' as the foremost domestic problem.[8] Such a context was not favourable for the War on Poverty.

While racial fears alienated white working-class voters from the War on Poverty, long-time columnist Doris Fleeson, writing in the *Washington Star*, cited another group – the 'discontented haves' – as the voters whom the Republican Party could conceivably win over. The 'discontented haves', according to Fleeson, were affluent Americans who 'have fled the cities and find them uncomfortable, occasionally even dangerous' and whose socioeconomic views did not align with unions, black Americans or other minorities.[9] Unlike the disillusioned white working classes, who were fiscally liberal, Fleeson's discontented haves were fiscally conservative and were opposed to spending taxpayer money on programmes that did not directly benefit them. In essence, Medicare, for example, was desirable as it offered clear benefits to all Americans, but the War on Poverty and the Kerner Commission's spending recommendations, viewed as helping indolent ghetto residents, were not.

Unsurprisingly, conservative House Republicans were at the forefront of the backlash to Kerner. In March, Rep. Durward Hall (R-MO) surmised that the lesson of the Kerner report was that 'If the only way to avoid new racial outbreaks and violence in our cities is to spend money we do not have, for programs which do not work, then we are indeed a nation in crisis.'[10] Fellow Rep. John Ashbrook (R-OH), a conservative, made clear what side of the order/justice divide he stood on, arguing that 'remedies recommended by the Commission centered on massive Federal aid programs, and woefully absent was reference to the individual's responsibility for maintaining law and order'.[11] The *Chicago Tribune*, mouthpiece of Midwestern conservatism, denounced the 'blind demagogs [sic]' on the Kerner Commission who, the newspaper claimed, were 'awash with tears for the poor oppressed rioters'.[12]

Some House Republicans used the Kerner report as an opportunity to blame the War on Poverty for the urban uprisings. At the forefront in employing such arguments was Indiana's Richard Roudebush, who accused War on Poverty workers of taking part in riots, before claiming that the Johnson administration had deliberately incited the poor to riot. During the March debate, Roudebush outlined his objections to Kerner's findings:

> We are told that the 99.9% of taxpaying, law-abiding, church-going Americans who did not participate in the riots are just as guilty as the snipers, looters, murderers, thugs and hoodlums who burned American cities to the ground the past several summers.
>
> Congress is not only concerned with the organization factors of the riots, but possible out-and-out subsidization based on reports of activity by Federal 'poverty' workers.[13]

Roudebush also criticised the report's contention that '$29 billion annual spending on welfare is not enough'. Making an ideological point, James Utt (R-CA) claimed that the report's authors 'could not have prepared a better blueprint for socialism'. 'In seeking economic equality, you must be willing to accept a society in its lowest common denominator,' Utt thundered. 'This I will not accept.'[14] The House Republican response to Kerner was further proof that the War on Poverty was exceptionally vulnerable to politics of white backlash.

Nixon added his voice to this substantial attack on Kerner's findings. Nixon's solution to the urban uprisings had already been outlined in an article for *Reader's Digest* in October, when Nixon – in an article ghosted by conservative aide Pat Buchanan – cited the need to reverse the decline in respect for public authority and the rule of law in America.[15] Jules Witcover, a journalist covering Nixon's revival in national politics, noted that the *Reader's Digest* article 'projected the domestic Nixon as more conservative. Although when taken as a whole, the article recognized the need to attack social problems in the black slums, the bulk of it was a hard pitch for repressive police measures.'[16] As such, Nixon was quick to make a high-profile response to Kerner's findings, and during a televised speech on 7 March, Nixon – who was five days away from his first primary contest in New Hampshire – firmly criticised the report for blaming American society for the riots rather than the rioters themselves.

Nixon also added his voice to the chorus of Republicans upbraiding the War on Poverty's overpromising rhetoric. The Republican front-runner noted that the Kerner Commission had cited as a cause for riots the 'frustrated hopes' resulting from the 'residue of the unfulfilled expectations aroused by the great judicial and legislative victories of the civil rights in the South'. Nixon, however, felt that the report 'might also have included the inflated rhetoric of the War on Poverty, which added to the dangerous expectation that the evils of centuries could be overcome overnight'. Finally, he saw fault in logic that suggested that all the federal government had to do was wave its magic wand and all of the urban problems would go away, arguing that it was a 'disservice to suggest to the dwellers in those slums that they need only wait for Federal housing, Federal jobs, a Federally guaranteed income'.[17] At this stage in the campaign, without anyone to push Nixon further on remedies for urban America's complex problems, it appeared that Nixon was happy to run solely as the 'order' candidate.

There were some in the GOP who offered more progressive proposals in the wake of Kerner. Most notable of these Republicans was New York mayor John Lindsay who had essentially directed the Kerner Commission's findings while serving as vice chair. Prior to the report's release, the Johnson administration and others had become aware that Lindsay, a progressive who would switch parties and become a Democrat in 1971, had effectively taken control of the Commission and that the majority were agreeing with Lindsay's thesis that 'the cities are in a state of war, a $40 to $50 billion program is essential, [and] the cities' expenditures should be compared with outlays for Space and Viet Nam'.[18] Fearing such a situation, New York Republican congressman Paul Fino, a leading exponent of white backlash arguments, had appealed to the White House to kick Lindsay off the Commission before the group reached its findings.[19] Following the report, Lindsay went on CBS's *Face the Nation* and told the television audience that he did not believe the Kerner report should have a price tag. The former congressman argued that as much as possible should be spent on restoring the nation's cities.[20]

Lindsay was not the lone Republican seeking to offer constructive words and legislation following Kerner. In the House, Rep. Charles Goodell led a group of moderate Republicans in working on a proposal entitled the 'Human Renewal Fund' (HRF). The HRF proposed to set aside over $2 billion in its first year, essentially to implement many GOP alternatives to the War on Poverty but also to expand popular initiatives such as Head Start. It also sought a $6 billion cut in federal non-essential spending as a way for these House members to stress the Republican commitment to fiscal prudence.[21] While the details of the HRF were not made clear until September, it attracted significant attention in March when the Republicans lined up black Washington Redskins star Bobby Mitchell to endorse the proposal.[22] The White House was worried enough by the potential public relations boost Republicans would receive if the HRF passed that the President refused a meeting with Goodell to discuss the proposal in April; Joe Califano warned his boss that 'the Human Renewal Fund is a massive Republican proposal' in an election year.[23] The HRF proponents finally presented full details in September, but its momentum had fizzled as events overtook the best-laid plans of many a politician.

One such event was the assassination of Dr Martin Luther King Jr on 4 April. The assassination sparked uprisings in over 100 American cities, including the nation's capital, and kept the urban crisis at the forefront of the domestic agenda. The chaotic scenes across the United States had the dual effect of helping to pass the Civil Rights Act of 1968 while simultaneously further stoking the fires of white backlash. In the wake of the uprisings, progressives such as Edward Brooke and Rockefeller deemed the present poverty efforts inadequate and demanded further action. In contrast, Strom Thurmond and the increasingly conservative Maryland governor, Spiro Agnew, launched attacks on antipoverty efforts for encouraging ghetto dwellers to believe rioting would reap rewards. The main beneficiary, however, was Nixon, who offered a solution that earned him praise from advocates on both sides of the Republican debate. Over late April and early May, Nixon established himself as a figure offering both a choice and an echo to the Johnson administration's approach and thus adroitly positioned himself as the unifying candidate for the GOP nomination.

While progressives remained a minority in the Republican Party, they also continued to exercise a disproportionate share of the GOP voice on the urban crisis due to the high profile and influential status of many GOP progressives. One such Republican, Brooke, had assumed a crucial role in the Republican senatorial caucus. He was credited with convincing many conservative GOP colleagues to vote for the Civil Rights Act that passed on 11 April.[24] Four days previously, and with the Washington, DC riots ongoing, Brooke had turned his ire on the entire Congress for behaving 'punitively' in response to the uprisings of the previous year – implicitly warning the legislature not to do the same again. During an April appearance on *Face the Nation*, Brooke criticised the President for not endorsing the Kerner recommendations, but he also leapt to Johnson's defence: 'I think we ought to recognize, in this whole field, that no President in the history of this country has done more for civil rights than has Lyndon Baines Johnson. And I say this as a Republican.'[25]

Brooke viewed entrenched urban poverty as the foremost problem facing Americans, telling a New York City audience in April that, 'if our country's central priority can be summarized in a single statement it is this: The United States must re-open the traditional paths out of the ghetto.'[26] To pay for an increased focus on healing urban blight, Brooke had already advocated postponing the government's space programme.[27] While Brooke's endorsement of the Kerner recommendations showed that he was not afraid of government intervention in the cities, when he spoke of solutions he continued to advocate the Republican 'bootstrap' ideology – espousing his belief that ghetto dwellers achieved self-respect through jobs. During a radio appearance with Hugh Scott, Brooke also made sure to stress the need for the restoration of order, demanding that the United States must 'return to a society of law and order' as it could not 'survive as a lawless society'.[28] Still, Brooke's stress was on social justice and finding jobs for the urban poor, not on hiring more police officers. Having previously warned Martin Luther King not to lead the Poor People's March for fear it would set off violence, Brooke about-turned; he endorsed the march's goals, expressing the hope that it would stand as a memorial to its fallen leader.[29]

Rockefeller, who announced his presidential candidacy on 30 April, was another Republican who largely agreed with Brooke's stress on social justice. 'Rocky' mocked the notion that restoring 'law and order' would solve the crisis in the nation's cities. Instead, he proposed an extensive urban programme for New York that he claimed would educate and train those trapped in the ghetto; transform slums into decent communities; generate job opportunities; attract private investment; and control the rat population. Having already appealed to their better angels, Rockefeller cautioned the Empire State legislators: 'History will not judge kindly an affluent people indifferently tolerating the poverty and injustice that can tear their society asunder.'[30] Following his announcement for the nomination, newspaper advertisements appeared that championed Rockefeller as the politician 'who knew urban problems and how to harness big government to cope with them'.[31] Despite continually implying that the current administration's poverty efforts were not sufficient to meet the current crisis, it is clear that Rockefeller was essentially offering a response that embraced Great Society liberalism. Rockefeller's support of such programmes meant he was always a long shot for the GOP nomination.

If anything, the post-King assassination uprisings solidified white backlash sentiment amongst the white voters the GOP needed to win in November. Witcover cited specifically 'that white, middle-class segment' of the population for whom 'the spectacle of the Capital City under siege, finally was too much'.[32] This sentiment was given a voice by the *Chicago Tribune*, which railed against the notion that white society was implicated in ghetto poverty, in the riots, or in King's assassination. On 9 April the *Tribune* editorialised:

> If you are black, so goes the contention, you are right, and you must be indulged in every wish. Why, sure, break the window and make off with the color TV set, the case of liquor, the beer, the dress, the coat, and the shoes. We won't shoot you. That would be 'police brutality'.
>
> If you are white, you are wrong. Feel guilty about it. Assume the collective guilt of your progenitors, even if neither you or anyone you know is a descendant of slave owners. Yield the sidewalk to the migrants from the South who have descended on your cities. Honor their every want, because the 'liberals' tell you that it is your fault they have not educated themselves, developed responsibility, trained themselves to hold jobs, or are shiftless and dependent on your taxes.[33]

With such backlash sentiment hardening, prospects for further antipoverty measures, or even the continuation of existing programmes, seemed bleak. Emerging from this backlash cauldron were two very different Republicans: Spiro Agnew and Strom Thurmond.

Agnew – a little-known moderate governor who had championed a Rockefeller candidacy – made national news in April with his upbraiding of local Maryland civil rights leaders for not doing enough to quell rioting. Agnew's televised remarks, delivered in an uncomfortably paternalistic fashion, featured numerous patronising comments – 'I bet you expected an endorsement of Kerner' – before the black community leaders walked out en masse. In the midst of his lecture, Agnew scolded the raised expectations of the black community: 'Somewhere the goal of equal opportunity has been replaced by the goal of instantaneous economic equality.' Agnew sounded a strikingly different note to the New York governor whom he had supported only a few weeks previously, telling his audience that included leaders who represented the poorest parts of Baltimore, 'I did not request your presence to bid for peace with the public dollar.'[34] Despite accusations that Agnew's actions were 'more in keeping with the slave system of a bygone era', the response to his surprise peroration was emphatically positive – Agnew received mail that was over 100 to one in favour of his message.[35] 'Backlash-minded whites,' explains Geoffrey Kabaservice, 'were gratified by the symbolism of a white leader putting down blacks and standing up to their supposed demands for what Agnew termed "instantaneous economic equality".'[36]

It was less surprising that Strom Thurmond – a key player in the 1968 GOP nominating process – told his constituents that the riots were the result of the 'whirlwind sowed years ago when some preachers and teachers began telling people that each man could be his own judge in his own case'.[37] The Palmetto State senator mocked the Poor People's Campaign, which planned to begin its pilgrimage to the capital in May. In April, Thurmond wrote to Nixon to ask him to support a proposal Thurmond had made on the Senate floor to force the antipoverty marchers to 'channel their energies toward cleaning up the rubble in their nation's capital'. Playing to the dependency narrative, Thurmond continued: 'Let the marchers come to town to work, and not to depend on charity. Let them come to rebuild, not to tear down.'[38] As had been seen in the House Republican response to the Kerner report, Thurmond's sentiment was not out of place in the Republican Party. Any successful presidential candidate looking to unite the GOP and ultimately win the White House was therefore required to appeal to the overt backlash sentiment espoused by Agnew and Thurmond, while also not shutting the door on remedies to solve urban poverty that had been championed by Rockefeller and

Brooke. Beginning on 25 April, Richard Nixon began to thread this particularly tricky political needle.

Nixon undoubtedly gave more weight to 'order', and a regular feature of his stump speeches included the assertion that 'the right to be free from domestic violence has become the forgotten civil right'.[39] Nevertheless, it was Nixon's proposals to achieve social justice that attracted the most attention during April and May. On 25 April, Nixon took a calculated gamble with a national radio broadcast entitled 'Bridges to Human Dignity'. In a move that must have horrified the *Chicago Tribune*'s editorial board, Nixon accepted the white population's responsibility for the ghetto – although he made sure that he emphasised that liberal Democrats were the most guilty of all: 'For too long, white America has sought to buy off the Negro – and to buy off its own sense of guilt – with ever more programs of welfare, of public housing, of payments to the poor . . . payments that perpetuated poverty, and that kept the endless, dismal cycle of dependency spinning from generation to generation.'[40] Nixon's solutions – or 'bridges' as he called them – to black urban poverty were rooted in private enterprise and volunteer effort, and it was his proposal of 'black capitalism' that garnered the most media attention.

'Black capitalism' was not a particularly new or inventive concept – but the slogan made it sound as if it was. During his speech, Nixon had declared that 'It's no longer enough that white-owned enterprises employ greater numbers of Negroes. . . . This is needed, yes – but it has to be accompanied by an expansion of black ownership, of black capitalism.'[41] The problem was most definitely real as blacks and Hispanics accounted for 17 per cent of the population but held 4 per cent of the nation's businesses, and one per cent of business assets.[42] The detail behind Nixon's slogan was for a combination of the federal government and private enterprise to provide aspiring and current minority entrepreneurs with technical assistance, loan guarantees and new sources of capital.

Such proposals echoed similar measures that the Johnson administration had already established. In 1967, the EOA had been amended to increase the Small Business Administration's (SBA) budget with a clause that required at least half of the department's loans to go to ghetto areas, and, by 1968, this was packaged by the SBA under the slogan 'Project OWN'. Historian Dean Kotlowski convincingly argues that these belated Johnson administration efforts were seen as election year gimmicks and therefore Nixon's political masterstroke was in outselling Democrats on a programme that enjoyed popularity. With less ambiguity than the War on Poverty, black capitalism appealed directly to Americans' faith in opportunity rather than entitlement. Moreover, as Kotlowski correctly points out, ideals such as 'Aiding small entrepreneurs advance opportunity, social mobility, and economic independence' were associated with moderate Republicans.[43] Accordingly, black capitalism helped Nixon – who had heartily embraced 'law and order' – maintain an appeal beyond the Agnews and Thurmonds of the GOP.

The media response to Nixon's advocacy of black capitalism was overwhelmingly positive. Friendly outlets such as *Time*, the *Wall Street Journal* and the *New York Daily News* heaped praise on Nixon for achieving the political equivalent of reinventing the wheel in American race relations. *Time* saw particular virtue in a 'philosophy that combined pragmatism, compassion and faith in the black American's will to achieve his aims within the framework of society'.[44] And while the more sober *Wall Street Journal* was pleased with 'a turning away from the old, proven failures, a starting afresh with the people themselves',[45] the *New York Daily News* compared Nixon to Abraham Lincoln. The newspaper unconvincingly declared it had not yet committed to endorsing a candidate, 'But this Nixon speech rather reminded this reporter of Lincoln's Gettysburg Address. President Abraham Lincoln befriended Negroes of his time, but never kidded or cajoled them.'[46] The Republican front-runner even received praise from liberal Tom Wicker in the *New York Times* who noted that Nixon 'is saying some remarkably interesting things in this campaign'. Wicker believed that Nixon's 'radio speech on the need for the development of black capitalism and ownership in the ghetto could prove to be more constructive than anything yet said by the other Presidential candidates on the crisis of the cities'.[47]

Not only did 'black capitalism' achieve a warm reception from the national press, it also caused great consternation in Camp

Rockefeller. By presenting himself as the politician with practical ideas to solve the urban crisis beyond tougher law enforcement, Nixon had moved into Rockefeller territory before the latter had even officially entered the race. Howard Gilette, a Rockefeller adviser, later confessed that 'Nixon was triangulating Rockefeller by appropriating some of [Rockefeller's] language . . . even while [Nixon] was already beginning to talk law and order.' For Gilette, Nixon's choice of black enterprise was savvy as it 'wasn't going to alienate his business base and could also appeal to moderates'.[48] Graham Molitor, a veteran of previous Rockefeller campaigns, put it more bluntly; Molitor saw black capitalism as a 'stroke of political genius'.[49] Awkwardly, Rockefeller found himself in the position of having to agree with Nixon's proposals.[50]

While Nixon continued to promote black capitalism on the campaign trail, he moved adroitly to remind Americans that his main focus if elected remained the restoration of law and order. The Nixon campaign released a position paper in May that justified his rhetorical war on crime by tearing at the logic of Johnson's War on Poverty. Nixon quoted LBJ's 1964 remarks that 'The war on poverty which I started is a war against crime and a war against disorder.' The candidate then skewered the President: 'If the President genuinely accepted that proposition, the near 50 percent increase in crime rate since 1964 would be adequate proof of the utter failure of the government's war on poverty.' Continuing to pull at one of the War on Poverty's premises, Nixon charged the administration with having 'grossly exaggerated' the link between poverty and crime. He went so far as to predict that 'we would not rid ourselves of the crime problem even if we succeeded overnight in lifting everyone above the poverty level'. Nixon's solution sounded very simple: 'If the conviction rate were double in this country, it would do more to eliminate crime in the future, than a quadrupling of the funds for any governmental war on poverty.'[51]

Appropriating FDR's rhetoric – the paper was entitled 'Toward Freedom From Fear' – Nixon also positioned himself on the side of the urban poor. He noted that ghetto dwellers were 'the silent victims' of most crime.[52] Yet this was a document whose primary audience was not the urban poor – it was to appeal to the same white Americans who had told Gallup in February that crime was the most pressing domestic problem. Moreover, it was a timely reminder to conservative-inclined Republicans, who might be tempted to go with a new shining hope in the Golden State, that Nixon had not gone soft on the crime issue following his advocacy of black capitalism.

By 1968, Reagan – who continued to avoid ruling himself out of consideration for the GOP nomination – had fully inherited the Goldwater mantle as the conservative, anti-federal government hero in the Republican Party.[53] Such continued popularity was impressive given that Reagan had begun his pursuit of California's 'Creative Society' by passing the biggest one-off tax rise in the Golden State's history – a measure that he claimed was needed to balance the state's budget.[54] Despite the tax rise, his appeal to the growing number of conservative Republicans in the South and West had only heightened during his two years in office. Part of Reagan's appeal was that his popularity in the swing state of California remained high while he continued to push an agenda that was centred on reducing welfare benefits, vetoing antipoverty projects, and calling for stricter law enforcement.[55] An impressive orator – no one was better at selling conservatism with a smile than Reagan – he had even managed to make a tax rise seem a positive for conservatives, remarking that 'taxes should hurt so that the people will be aware of what government is costing them and will make it clear to their legislators how big a tax burden they are willing to bear'.[56]

The 'Gipper' was, moreover, inheriting Barry Goldwater's ideological mantle during a presidential election cycle that was poised to occur in a much more favourable context for Goldwater's message. The Arizonan had been an outspoken advocate for a federal government that, regarding domestic policy, focused almost solely on order before that position was fashionable. Thus, Reagan's continued unofficial campaign meant that Nixon had to always be aware of his right flank. In reality, however, there was little to choose between Reagan's and Nixon's approaches to the problems of crime and poverty in 1968. Similarly to Nixon, Reagan pursued a small carrot and large stick approach to the problems inherent to the urban crisis – speaking strongly on the issue of law and order while offering a self-help approach to poverty.

147

Reagan's rhetoric was given ideological cohesion by the theme of self-reliance. He portrayed those who participated in crime or were poverty programme recipients as lacking this virtue. As such, Reagan wholeheartedly rejected Kerner's conclusions. In May, Reagan commented that 'We must reject the idea that every time a law is broken, society is guilty rather than the law-breaker.' Aping order Republicans, Reagan argued that 'it is too simple to trace all crime to poverty. Our time of affluence is also a time of increasing lawlessness.'[57] In an article for the *Sacramento Union* in June, Reagan made clear that the way to restore self-reliance in relation to crime and poverty was to remove government from American lives:

> We [Reagan's Administration] have set out to prove that the old concept of a highly centralized, highly paternalistic government, rejected by our forefathers in 1776 and resurrected by the New Deal in 1933, cannot serve the people half as well as the people can serve themselves, if they are given a chance.[58]

For Reagan, without government tying the hands of poor Americans, those same hands would be freed to pull on the nearest set of bootstraps.

Reagan coupled this strident individualist rhetoric with a slick public relations outfit that carefully presented Reagan's anti-government message in a positive light. One such endeavour, the Governor's Awards for Creative Citizenship, involved a celebration of successful individuals who helped others discover self-reliance. The first winners of the award, announced in June, were the personification of Reagan's philosophy of self-help. One of the awards went to Lee Toller, who had set up a group in Seaside, California, to improve the socioeconomic conditions of young adults with a criminal past 'by private means'. Toller's group also viewed itself as a means to prevent riots breaking out. Another winner was a Fresno group that had created 'Dropouts, Anonymous' which put would-be school dropouts in contact with men and women who had faced the same problems.[59]

Reagan presented his agenda not as Republican nay-saying, but as a proactive and compassionate approach: 'A lot of effort has been put forth by well-meaning people who would have us be our brother's keeper. It is time we became our brother's brother. He needs a hand up – not a handout.' Furthermore, in words that Lyndon Johnson could have spoken in 1964, Reagan admitted that, 'We cannot guarantee every citizen success, but we must guarantee every citizen an equal place at the starting line and his right to try to succeed.'[60] This was not rhetoric aimed at a right-wing Republican audience; this was the rhetoric of the centre ground – the same consensus position that commentators in the 1964 election had hailed Johnson as occupying. There were two differences, however. First, Reagan's programmes were state initiatives and therefore fitted into the preferred GOP framework for delivering antipoverty programmes. The second variation on Johnson was that Reagan's message on economic opportunity included a warning. 'Mobs do not generate progress; they retard it,' Reagan said. 'Mobs do not establish rights; they trample them. No mob will ever build a better California, or a better world.' As Nixon, Rockefeller, and now Reagan had shown, every discussion of poverty in 1968 required a discussion of crime.

'And this brings me to the clearest choice among the great issues of this campaign'

Having positioned himself as a figure who held at least some appeal to all factions of the Republican Party, Nixon won the nomination battle comfortably. On 8 August, in Miami Beach, Nixon became the standard bearer of a party that was undoubtedly more unified than its Democratic opponent – a fact that was laid bare to a national audience when Hubert Humphrey was nominated, to little acclaim and much chaos, in Chicago three weeks later. Nonetheless, Nixon began the campaign with a huge lead in the polls that steadily dwindled to almost nothing by Election Day as Johnson's pursuit of peace with the North Vietnamese loomed large over proceedings. The Republican candidate also struggled to articulate a domestic vision for the country, running what historian Rick Perlstein calls an 'antiseptic' campaign that dealt in rhetorical banalities designed not to alienate the majority of voters.[61] George Reedy, LBJ's former press secretary, quipped to Humphrey that, in both the domestic and foreign sphere, 'One of the most interesting aspects of Richard Nixon's campaign is that he is presenting himself to the voters as a man who will bring about a change – but he is keeping the nature of that change a deep, dark secret.'[62]

Nixon – with Rockefeller unpopular and Reagan undeclared – the presumptive nominee, arrived at Miami Beach to offer a clear message to the RNC's Platform Committee. *New York Times* journalist John W. Finney noted that, together with Reagan, Nixon 'attempted to push the Republican party to the right on the issue of law and order'.[63] By mid-1968, this task was arguably as strenuous as pushing open an automatically assisted door. Contrastingly, John Lindsay told the committee that 'the root cause of the most crime and civil disorder is the poverty that grips over 30 million of our citizens, black and white'. The New York mayor proffered his view that such problems would not be solved by 'simplistic cries for law and order'.[64] Nixon rejected the suggestion that his call was simplistic or, for the avoidance of any doubt, racist. Indeed, Nixon argued that 'It is the poor, black and white alike, that bear the brunt of crime and violence.' Nixon also reiterated his choice and echo approach, contesting that 'A militant national crusade to protect society from criminals does not preclude a continuing national crusade to eliminate the social conditions from which so many of today's criminals have emerged and tomorrow's criminals are certain to emerge.'[65] For all the Republican charges during the Johnson presidency that the Democrats used inflated rhetoric when they declared 'war' on poverty, the GOP's alternatives often called for a 'crusade'.

Ultimately the committee followed the Nixon approach and offered a strong law and order plank, accompanied by a somewhat progressive social welfare pledge – both with the blessing of the former Vice President.[66] Finney observed that 'the urban and crime planks reflected the ideological split developing within the Republican ranks over the direction the party should move on domestic issues'.[67] Despite this division, party unity remained largely intact. On social welfare, southern conservatives could be happy that they had beaten back an attempt by progressives to pass an amendment that would have criticised LBJ for ignoring the recommendations of the Kerner Commission.[68] Alternatively, progressives – while irked at the strong crime plank – could take satisfaction that social justice had been paid appropriate heed in the platform. All things considered, it was another reflection that the GOP was behaving like a big tent party. In this case, it was the tent that Nixon had help construct.

Having won the nomination easily on the first ballot, Nixon took to the stage in Miami Beach to offer a stirring convention speech to position himself as a uniting figure for both party and country. In stark contrast to Goldwater's ode to extremism four years earlier, Nixon told Americans that 'We are going to win because at a time that America cries out for the unity that this Administration has destroyed, the Republican Party ... stands united before the nation tonight.' Then, moving on to what Nixon called the 'clearest choice among the great issues of this campaign', the candidate declared that he would offer a different path to the one trodden by Johnson's War on Poverty.[69]

Taking into account almost every charge that Republicans had levelled against the antipoverty effort for four years, Nixon offered his alternative:

> For the past five years we have been deluged by government programs for the unemployed; programs for the cities; programs for the poor. And we have reaped from these programs an ugly harvest of frustration, violence and failure across the land.
>
> And now our opponents will be offering more of the same – more billions for government jobs, government housing, government welfare.
>
> I say it is time to quit pouring billions of dollars into programs that have failed in the United States of America ...
>
> The war on poverty didn't begin five years ago in this country. It began when this country began. It's been the most successful war on poverty in the history of nations. There is more wealth in America today, more broadly shared, than in any nation in the world.

Having firmly established the reasons why the War on Poverty was a disastrous, government-led failure, Nixon then sounded a racially moderate note and returned to his call for black capitalism:

> Black Americans, no more than white Americans, they do not want more government programs which perpetuate dependency.

151

They don't want to be a colony in a nation.

They want the pride, and the self-respect, and the dignity that can only come if they have an equal chance to own their own homes, to own their own businesses, to be managers and executives as well as workers, to have a piece of the action in the exciting ventures of private enterprise.[70]

Nixon also skilfully took aim at welfare in a way that Republicans had struggled to since the establishment of the New Deal. Telling the story of two different children – one who grew up on welfare and the other who got by thanks to the help of the people around him – Nixon portrayed the first as a boy for whom 'the American system is one that feeds his stomach and starves his soul. It breaks his heart.' The other boy, who comes from little but is helped through life by the generosity of others, achieves his dreams – 'And tonight he stands before you – nominated for President of the United States of America.'[71] Although Nixon was prone to exaggerating the poverty he came from, it is undeniable that he was able to talk about poverty and welfare without being tarred effectively as just another member of the 'Party of Privilege'.

While the Republican nominee had called the difference between the Democratic and Republican approach to poverty 'the clearest choice among the great issues in this campaign', he demurred from drawing similar distinctions with other significant Great Society achievements. Indeed, he approvingly mentioned civil rights and education spending once each, while not even referring to Medicare. Wittingly or unwittingly, Nixon and the majority of the GOP were displaying – to a nationwide audience – their acceptance of the Great Society programmes that had entailed the biggest increases in government spending during the Johnson presidency. The War on Poverty, with its relatively small budget in comparison to ESEA (Elementary and Secondary Education Act) and Medicare, remained, in Republican eyes, an outlier.

Nixon's speech, together with a convention that was largely uncontroversial, ensured that Republicans left the Sunshine State more united and positive than they had been for over a decade. The one threat to this harmony was Nixon's selection of Agnew as his running mate. Agnew, who was only known to a wider audience for his outburst at Maryland's black community leaders, was selected to help deliver the Upper South for Nixon and also because he was a choice that would not offend South Carolina's Thurmond – the figure who had a hold on many southern delegations.[72] Given that Nixon had courted Rockefeller in 1960, it was a sign of how the GOP had shifted in a conservative and southern direction over the previous eight years.

Progressives, such as Javits and Lindsay, initially withheld their endorsement of the ticket because of Agnew's nomination.[73] The Maryland governor's approach to social welfare could hardly have provided much solace for these progressives; asked why he was not campaigning in poor communities, Agnew told reporters that 'If you've seen one city slum, you've seen them all.'[74] He also diverged from the position that Quie and Goodell had staked out in 1966, arguing that the poor should not be involved in the decision-making process for urban poverty programmes. Instead, Agnew reasoned, they should only be consulted in the 'diagnosis' stage.[75]

Aside from delivering the Border States, Agnew's role involved appealing to working-class whites who had abandoned the Democratic Party once in 1966 to elect Republicans and who might be willing to do so again. Historian Dan Carter notes that, by 1968, 'a combination of accelerating price increases and sharp hikes in payroll and income taxes led to a near stagnation in real wages for the average blue-collar and salaried white-collar worker'.[76] Michael Flamm outlines how this phenomenon encouraged white backlash sentiment: 'Anxious about the economic competition blacks seemed to pose at work and the physical threat they seemed to pose at home, many whites felt besieged.'[77] Agnew's previous upbraiding of black leaders over welfare and his rejection of Kerner's conclusions, coupled with his comments about the slum, were just the formula for appealing to whites who now felt that the federal government had been disproportionately paying attention to black Americans for too long. Many such voters saw the War on Poverty as providing help to the very people they feared.

George Wallace's candidacy was the 1968 campaign's great unknown, in the sense that no one knew precisely from which candidate he was likely to take more votes. His appeal was most effective in the poor rural Deep South (voters Goldwater had won, but a voting bloc that had been traditionally Democratic) and in the ethnic white working-class areas of the North (voters LBJ had won, but a bloc that Republicans had had some success in wooing in 1966). According to the *Washington Post*'s Laurence Stern, 'Wallace's strength is his ability to articulate the dark fears that flutter through suburbia and the white city neighborhoods standing in the path of the black urban glaciers. He is the political diagnostician of the Nation's viscera, not its brain.'[78] Put simply, for Stern, Wallace was the tribune of the white backlash.

Aside from the obvious racial element to the Wallace campaign, the former Alabama governor also embraced the old economic populism of bygone southern Democrats, such as Huey Long. Indeed, as Donald Critchlow notes, Republicans viewed Wallace as just a typical New Dealer – and with good reason.[79] During the campaign, Wallace promised that, if elected, he would increase Social Security by 60 per cent and expand Medicare. Wallace, however, was no supporter of the War on Poverty – likely due to the perception that the antipoverty effort was aimed at black and minority Americans. Wallace instead returned to the solution of the New Deal, declaring that he would fight poverty by instituting a large increase in public works spending.[80] Wallace's promises were never likely to be put into practice – he never stood any real chance of winning – but he did have a strong influence on the presidential race. Thanks to Wallace's presence the two major party candidates whom the Alabaman christened 'Tweedledum' and 'Tweedledee' had to devise different ways of appealing to those rural southerners and ethnic northerners.[81]

Humphrey, the 'Tweedledum' to Nixon's 'Tweedledee', chose to appeal to those voters' economic interests. The liberal 'Happy Warrior' knew little other way. In the South, he appealed to the material interests of traditional Democrats.[82] The Humphrey campaign ran a television advert to remind Americans that Democrats had delivered a minimum wage, Social Security and Medicare – implying that the Republicans had never done anything to help the average American. Revealingly, the television spot never boasted about the War on Poverty, aside from an oblique reference to the Democrats helping American children get 'good summer jobs'.[83] Regarding urban voters in the North, Humphrey promised a 'Marshall Plan for the Cities'.[84]

Humphrey did not run away from the politically flagging War on Poverty. He promised to expand programmes such as Head Start, the Job Corps, the Neighborhood Youth Corps and Upward Bound. Furthermore, he proposed going further and making the federal government 'the employer of the last resort' for the hard-core unemployed.[85] The Humphrey campaign's desire to draw a stark contrast with Nixon on the issue of alleviating poverty was further revealed when it created a campaign ad named 'Law and Order'. Rather than embracing the Nixonian message as the title suggested, the television spot featured a Humphrey press conference where the Happy Warrior angrily questioned his Republican opponent's values:

> When a man says that he thinks that the most important thing is to double the rate of convictions, but he doesn't believe and then he condemns the Vice President, myself, for wanting to double the War on Poverty, I think that man has lost his sense of values.[86]

It was a telling sign of the times that Humphrey, having drawn this contrast, released another advert in which he stressed that 'rioting, burning, sniping, mugging, traffic in narcotics and disregard for law are the advanced guard of anarchy and they must and they will be stopped'.[87] Furthermore, he announced an ambitious programme that would have provided one billion dollars per year to fighting crime.[88]

Republicans, rebutting Humphrey, relentlessly reminded Americans that the Vice President had told a New Orleans audience in 1966 that if he had lived in a slum 'you would have had a little more trouble than you have already, because I have enough spark left in me to lead a mighty good revolt under those conditions'.[89] During one speech in Pennsylvania, Gerald Ford informed his audience that the United States had experienced 225 riots since Humphrey had made those remarks.[90] In the climate of the 1968 election, Humphrey's vulnerability on order was irrefutable, but he was the justice candidate anyway. Humphrey's attack on Nixon suggested that the Minnesotan still believed that a government-led war on poverty continued to be the most effective war on crime.

By contrast, Nixon's autumn campaign focused almost exclusively on restoring law and order at home, and 'peace with honor' in Vietnam. Despite warnings from fellow Republicans that his uninspiring campaign threatened to render him the next Thomas Dewey, Nixon's campaign never returned to the innovative rhetoric on social justice that it had employed during the primary season.[91] Witcover summarised Nixon's campaign as one in which the candidate was 'wrapped in cellophane' and where his key domestic messages were a promise to control inflation and a 'velvet-glove version of the mailed fist with which Wallace saluted the white backlash'.[92] Nixon only visited two black communities and spoke little of black capitalism, while his campaign ads on domestic policy failed to go beyond promises to tackle crime and a vague, if appealing, notion of uniting the country.[93]

Nixon had come to believe that if the election was a referendum on domestic issues he would not win regardless of his positions. He told Theodore White that his likely route to victory was if the Vietnam War was the most prominent issue in voters' minds on Election Day.[94] Whether Nixon's observation was correct is another matter. After all, the growing disillusionment of the American people with 'big government' and the rising racial conservatism threatened the Democratic advantage on domestic issues that had endured since the New Deal. It is, however, almost certainly true that Nixon stood to gain from continuing problems in Southeast Asia.

Nixon, however, could not ignore domestic issues entirely. His choice of Agnew and his consistent focus on law and order meant that the Nixon campaign faced accusations of stoking white backlash sentiment – even from within his own party. One of Nixon's first challenges after the convention was to woo Brooke who had balked at Nixon's law and order rhetoric. Brooke had warned the delegates at the Republican convention that the GOP must put the phrase 'a hand-up, not a hand-out' into practice and thus help to break the 'endless cycle of poverty' experienced by many Americans.[95] In response to Brooke's disenchantment, Nixon aides – including his secretary Rose Mary Woods who wrote to Brooke telling him 'we miss you' – penned pleading correspondence to the Massachusetts senator to return to the campaign trail.[96] Furthermore, Nixon went on television in early September to reiterate that 'law and order' was not a 'code word for, basically, racism'. Speaking vaguely, Nixon affirmed his belief that 'To me law and order must be combined with justice. I have often said that you cannot have order unless you have justice.'[97] Nevertheless, most black Americans remained unconvinced by Nixon's explanation of law and order.[98]

Ultimately, Nixon's charm offensive worked on Brooke as the senator returned to the fold in October – stumping strongly for the Republican nominee. Appearing on ABC's *Issues and Answers* in the final month of the campaign, Brooke declared himself satisfied by Nixon's explanation of law and order. 'I think [Nixon] understands the problems of the ghettos,' Brooke explained, 'and when he talks about law and order and justice, I think he means it.' Brooke also gave his blessing to Agnew while laughing off comparisons between Nixon and Wallace. The Senator believed that 'if [Wallace] were elected he would bring about revolution in the country'.[99] Brooke's return to the fold spoke volumes about the Nixon campaign's ability to maintain party unity.

Despite such outward unity, Republicans in down-ticket races offered varying positions on issues such as poverty, race and crime – reflecting the continued order and justice split within the party. Rep. Joel Broyhill (R-VA) described federal welfare and anti-poverty programmes as 'pouring money down a rathole'. Instead, Broyhill preferred the federal government to focus on a more 'effective deterrent' to crime and violence.[100] Florida senatorial candidate Ed Gurney, who had opposed most of the Great Society legislation while in the House – with the notable exception of Medicare – also ran a campaign focused on law and order. His billboards read simply: 'It's time to treat criminals like criminals'; 'It's time to stop riots'; 'It's time to halt reckless spending'.[101] Most drastically, the GOP's Lieutenant Governor candidate in Delaware went as far as proposing 'sterilization' of mothers with two 'illegitimate children who had to be supported by the state' so as to avoid 'perpetuating poverty and problems as well as entrapping a large group of our citizens in a degrading and self-defeating system'.[102] All three candidates were successfully elected in November.

Not all Republicans ran on such platforms – Senate candidates running in states in the more liberal Northeastern corridor tended to speak more positively about using government to fight poverty. In Maryland, Charles Mathias eschewed strong rhetoric on crime and instead stressed the need for government to solve ghetto unemployment and housing for the poor. This stood in contrast to his Democratic opponent's strong use of law and order rhetoric.[103] In neighbouring Pennsylvania, the GOP candidate Rep. Richard Schweiker, a moderate, was running against the liberal Democratic Senator Joseph Clark. Schweiker – on his way to victory in the Keystone State – emphasised his support of the Republican Human Investment Act as a way to tackle ghetto poverty.[104] Elsewhere, Goodell – who had been appointed by Rockefeller to fill Bobby Kennedy's Senate seat – was moving in a more progressive direction as he began to cater to constituents beyond his old upstate district. Executing a shift from his position as one of the War on Poverty's chief critics, Goodell – who would not face the voters until 1970 – declared that 'Poverty workers generally have helped defuse riots.'[105] Such a position stood in contrast to many of Goodell's former colleagues in the House who had accused poverty workers of stirring up trouble.

Brooke's *Issues and Answers* appearance suggested that Nixon had provided assurances to the Senator on how a Nixon administration would approach poverty. The Bay State senator told the television audience that Nixon would 'conserve the best programs of the past, such as Head Start and Upward Bound, and education and model cities'. Most interestingly, Brooke – who had often stressed poverty in a black context – accentuated the benefits of poverty programmes to white Americans:

> I understand that when the protest is made many white Americans don't want to be paying taxes where they think some black Americans are on relief. The fact is that the great majority of poor people in the country are not black, but they are white.[106]

Brooke's point was reminiscent of that made by the Johnson administration when the War on Poverty was launched in 1964.

During a rare appearance on the campaign trail, the outgoing president echoed Brooke's sentiment. On 26 October, Lyndon

Johnson returned to largely white Appalachia to deliver a speech in Pikeville, Kentucky – a town that LBJ noted had been 'a symbol of the entire Appalachian problem'. 'Today,' Johnson triumphantly declared, 'it is a symbol of the entire Appalachian progress.' He refuted Republican claims that the War on Poverty 'only stirs up the poor' and held up Pikeville as an example of what poverty pro-grammes could achieve.[107] The same day, he travelled to Morgan-town, West Virginia, and reminded his audience that 'Four years ago when we passed the first poverty bill there were 33 million human beings below the poverty level. We have taken 7 million up above it and there are 26 million left to do something for.'[108] Johnson's appearance in Appalachia was a reminder that the region – which remained an economically depressed area of the country – had once been viewed as the front line in the war against poverty, but that was no longer the case.

The 1968 campaign had confirmed that it was the cities that were the new frontier in the struggle against poverty. The War on Poverty may have been born in Appalachia but it was now perceived by most Americans as living in the urban centres of the United States. This shift during the Texan's presidency had undoubtedly changed the racial dynamics of the politics of pov-erty. No matter what Brooke said about the racial orientation of poverty programmes, or where Johnson chose to speak about them, such programmes were now largely viewed by the public, and by politicians, through a racial lens. *New York Times* journal-ist E. W. Kenworthy captured this change in his assessment of the election in late October: 'If a campaign issue is to be defined as something that really agitates the ordinary voter on a nationwide scale, then the domestic issues of this campaign can generally be grouped under the heading "the cities".' To Kenworthy, the prob-lems of 'the cities' were 'poverty, jobs, housing, schooling, health and "law and order"', and 'At their core lies race – blackness.'[109]

Victory's lessons

The 1968 election unfolded against a backdrop of unease in the United States, the riots and assassinations of the year still promi-nent in voters' minds. The Vietnam War loomed large over the 1968 campaign but it was by no means the only issue at play as the urban crisis also attracted a great amount of column inches. Four years of racial uprisings and the failure of Johnson's War on Poverty to prevent such disorder meant that many Americans were ready for a change. Minority Leader Ford captured the sense of despair that the GOP hoped to exploit to propel the party back into the majority when he told an audience in October: 'The saddest song a band can play today is "Happy Days Are Here Again".'[110]

Nixon's razor-thin victory, coupled with modest Republican success (five net gains in both the House and Senate) led many different commentators to varying conclusions on the role of domestic issues in the campaign. The added complication of the conflict in Southeast Asia meant that this was not an election that provided clear answers for those looking to map out an appealing domestic policy – although some did try. Kevin Phillips – a Republican analyst who had once worked for prominent backlash tribune Paul Fino, and who was also part of the Nixon campaign – wrote in 1969 that Nixon's triumph signalled the beginning of an 'emerging Republican majority' if the party successfully took advantage of the resentments associated with the white backlash.[111] Phillips challenged the new focus on urban ills and argued that the GOP should refocus government spending on 'sharecroppers, Appalachian mountaineers, fishing villages' and other traditional groups who, in the American political culture, belonged to the deserving poor. He also advocated New Deal-style programmes for such deserving groups to replace the 'gimmickry' of Johnson's poverty programmes, but also to avoid the laissez faire economics to which some in the GOP, much to Phillips's chagrin, still subscribed. Phillips believed that the Democrats' association with the 'Negro socioeconomic revolution' was likely to dictate voting patterns – to the GOP's advantage – for the next era of American politics.[112] The War on Poverty, of course, had been crucial to the association of Democrats with black socioeconomic advancement. Phillips's analysis also helps explain why most Republicans were happier to oppose the War on Poverty than to oppose Medicare or education spending. After all, the deserving poor stood to benefit directly from the latter rather than the former.

Challenging Phillips's analysis, Democrats Richard Scammon and Ben Wattenberg warned their party that the American electorate was 'unyoung, unpoor and unblack', the opposite of the three groups that were viewed as the War on Poverty's prime beneficiaries.[113] To capture the centre again, Scammon and Wattenberg believed Democrats had to speak less about poverty programmes and more about crime. They noted that 'most of the War on Poverty programs of the Office of Economic Opportunity are generally approved', but that it was also true that 'when angry blacks, funded under the Community Action Program, led disruptions, the American public drew a line'.[114] Scammon and Wattenberg, in advising Democrats to capture the 'real majority', believed that the Democratic Party had to neutralise the GOP's strength on social issues such as crime, race riots and the perceived immorality of the 1960s.[115] The analysts concluded that the Democrats retained an advantage on economic issues but that they should be wary of expanding welfare and antipoverty programmes to those perceived to be undeserving of such aid.[116] They also reminded Democrats that the poor did not vote as a bloc and that they only made up one fifth of the nation's population.[117] Evidently, if both parties took heed of either Phillips's or Scammon and Wattenberg's analysis, a continuation of the War on Poverty seemed highly unlikely – especially with a Republican now in residence at the White House. Other significant Great Society programmes, however, were clearly less endangered.

Conclusion

And what of the Republican challenge to the War on Poverty during the 1968 election? Nixon's campaign had confirmed a trend that began during the 1966 elections: Republicans were not going to allow Johnson's War on Poverty to achieve the same acceptance as the rest of the Great Society's marquee programmes. Reflecting the majority of Republican sentiment, Nixon had avoided criticising civil rights legislation, Medicare and federal aid to education, but he had named his opposition to the War on Poverty and the Johnson administration's solutions to the urban crisis as the 'clearest choice among the great issues of this campaign'.

161

Certainly, Nixon was not an anti-Great Society candidate but he was, in fact, an anti-War on Poverty candidate. Whether he would behave as such in the presidency remained an open question.

Notes

1. RMN, 'Toward Freedom from Fear', 8 May 1968, box 4, Marje and Phil Acker collection, series iii, Richard M. Nixon Library, Yorba Linda, CA.
2. RMN, 'Bridges to Human Dignity', CBS Radio Network, 25 April 1968, box 4, M&PA collection, series iii, RMN.
3. John W. Finney, 'Nixon and Reagan Ask War on Crime', *New York Times*, 1 August 1968.
4. Kerner Commission, *Report of the National Advisory Commission on Civil Disorders* (Washington, DC: US Government Printing Office, 1968).
5. Davies, *From Opportunity to Entitlement*, 204.
6. Patterson, *Grand Expectations*, 677.
7. Memo, FP to LBJ, 27 February 1968, box 407, Panzer, LBJ.
8. Perlstein, *Nixonland*, 238.
9. Doris Fleeson, 'What Choice Will GOP Offer?', *Washington Star*, 29 February 1968.
10. Durward Hall quoted in Press Release, Richard L. Roudebush, 'Blame for Riots Misplaced by LBJ Commission', 14 March 1968, box 407, Panzer, LBJ.
11. Ashbrook quoted in ibid.
12. *Chicago Tribune* quotation from Perlstein, *Nixonland*, 240.
13. Roudebush, 14 March 1968.
14. Utt in ibid.
15. RMN, 'What Has Happened to America?', *Reader's Digest*, October 1967.
16. Jules Witcover, *The Resurrection of Richard Nixon* (New York: G.P. Putnam's Sons, 1970), 218.
17. RMN speech on Riot Commission Reports, 7 March 1968, folder 30, box 5, series g, RG4, NAR.
18. Correspondence, Irv Sprague to Barefoot Sanders, 15 January 1968, box 214, WHCF Lindsay, LBJ.
19. Correspondence, Barefoot Sanders to Paul Fino, 13 May 1968, box 214, WHCF Lindsay, LBJ.
20. Memo, Bob Fleming to LBJ, 4 March 1968, box 214, WHCF Lindsay, LBJ.

21. Republican Congressional Committee, 'GOP Builds Strong Record of Major Proposals', *Republican Congressional Committee Newsletter*, 8 April 1968, 4.
22. Press Release, House Republican Conference Task Force on Urban Affairs, 29 March 1968, box 407, Panzer, LBJ.
23. Memo, Jim Jones to LBJ, 11 April 1968, *PAJWH*, reel 20.
24. Press Release, EWB, 28 February 1968, box 557, EWB.
25. EWB appearance on CBS's *Face the Nation*, 7 April 1968, box 563, EWB.
26. EWB speech to B'nai B'rith Humanitarian Award Dinner, NYC, 10 April 1968, box 557, EWB.
27. EWB, *Face the Nation*, 7 April 1968.
28. EWB and HDS, 'Your Senator's Report', 15 April 1968, box 41, HDS.
29. EWB, *Face the Nation*.
30. NAR, 'Special Message to the Legislature following Martin Luther King's death', 11 April 1968, folder 11, box 4, series j.3, RG4, NAR.
31. Witcover, *The Resurrection of Richard Nixon*, 308.
32. Ibid., 286.
33. Editorial, 'Day of Mourning', *Chicago Tribune*, 9 April 1968.
34. Agnew, 'Opening Statement at Conference with Civil Rights and Community Leaders, Baltimore, MD', 11 April 1968, box 640, EWB.
35. Richard Homan, 'Agnew Defends Negro Lecture', *Washington Post*, 13 April 1968, A6; Perlstein, *Nixonland*, 258.
36. Kabaservice, *Rule and Ruin*, 244.
37. Strom Thurmond quoted in ibid., 257.
38. Correspondence, ST to RMN, 23 April 1968, box 45, subseries A, series I, Wilderness Years Collection, RMN.
39. Perlstein, *Nixonland*, 203.
40. RMN address, 'Bridges to Human Dignity', CBS Radio Network, 25 April 1968, box 4, series iii, M&P, RMN.
41. Ibid.
42. Dean Kotlowski, *Nixon's Civil Rights: Politics, Principle, and Policy* (Cambridge, MA: Harvard University Press, 2001), 129.
43. Ibid. 130.
44. *Time*, 3 May 1968 (newspaper clippings from box 4, M&P, RMN).
45. *Wall Street Journal*, 21 May 1968.
46. *New York Daily News*, 27 April 1968.
47. Tom Wicker, 'In the Nation: A Coalition for What?' *New York Times*, 19 May 1968.

48. Gilette quoted in Kabaservice, *Rule and Ruin*, 236.
49. Molitor quoted in Kotlowski, *Nixon's Civil Rights*, 132.
50. Ibid.; NAR, Speech to Economic Club of Detroit, MI, 22 May 1968, folder 7, box 1, series j.3, RG4, NAR.
51. RMN position paper, 'Toward Freedom From Fear', 8 May 1968, box 4, M&P, RMN.
52. Ibid.
53. This is despite the fact that Goldwater gave his support to Nixon during the nomination contest.
54. RWR, Report to the People on Taxes, 31 March 1968, box 127, RU, RWR.
55. Kabaservice, *Rule and Ruin*, 239–40; RWR, 'Creative Paper' on Law and Order, 10 May 1968, box 127, RU, RWR; '"Creative Society" at a Crossroads', *San Jose Mercury*, 11 November 1968.
56. RWR on Taxes, 31 March 1968.
57. RWR on Law and Order, 10 May 1968.
58. RWR quoted in Victor Riesel, 'Reagan's Creative Society', *Sacramento Union*, 29 June 1968.
59. RWR Press Release on first annual Governor's Awards for Creative Citizenship, 17 June 1968, box 127, RU, RWR.
60. RWR on Equal Opportunity, 14 July 1968.
61. Perlstein, *Nixonland*, 329.
62. Correspondence, George E. Reedy to HHH, 18 September 1968, box 120, WHCF Nixon, LBJ.
63. John W. Finney, 'Nixon and Reagan Ask War on Crime', *New York Times*, 1 August 1968, 1.
64. JVL quoted in ibid.
65. Nixon quoted in ibid.
66. John W. Finney, 'G.O.P. Urban Plank Asks Industry Aid in 'Crisis' of Slums', *New York Times*, 3 August 1968, 1.
67. Ibid.
68. Ibid.
69. RMN, 'Address Accepting the Presidential Nomination at the Republican National Convention in Miami Beach, Florida', 8 August 1968, TAPP.
70. Ibid.
71. Ibid.
72. JKJ on STA role during television appearance on *Newsmakers*, WCBS-TV, 11 April 1968, box 41, JKJ.
73. Ibid.; JVL said he would not consider endorsing Nixon 'unless someone strangled Agnew'. Quoted in Perlstein, *Nixonland*, 244.

74. STA quoted in Peter A. Jay, 'Agnew Declares Poor Can't Control Anti-Poverty War', *Washington Post*, 19 October 1968, A4.
75. Ibid.
76. Carter, *From George Wallace to Newt Gingrich*, 28.
77. Flamm, *Law and Order*, 7.
78. Laurence Stern, 'Wallace Is Appealing to Viscera, Not Brain', *Washington Post*, 20 October 1968, B1.
79. Critchlow, *The Conservative Ascendancy*, 85.
80. Stern, 'Wallace Is Appealing . . .'.
81. Wallace quoted in ibid.
82. Perlstein, *Nixonland*, 342.
83. 'Voting Booth' (1968), *Living Room Candidate*, Museum of the Moving Image.
84. Wolf Van Eckardt, 'The Candidates Serve Up Solutions for the Cities', *Washington Post*, 21 July 1968.
85. Editorial, *New York Times*, 18 September 1968.
86. 'Law and Order' (1968), *Living Room Candidate*, Museum of the Moving Image.
87. 'Every American' (1968), *Living Room Candidate*, Museum of the Moving Image.
88. Robert Mason, *Richard Nixon and the Quest for a New Majority* (Chapel Hill, NC: University of North Carolina Press, 2004), 33.
89. HHH quoted by GRF, Speech to Republican dinner in Lancaster, PA, 2 October 1968, box 59, RTH, GRF.
90. GRF quoted in ibid.
91. Witcover, *The Resurrection of Richard Nixon*, 383.
92. Ibid. 364.
93. Ibid. 397.
94. Perlstein, *Nixonland*, 352.
95. EWB speech, 'To Forge a New Unity', Miami, FL, 5 August 1968, box 573, EWB.
96. Correspondence, Rose Mary Woods to EWB, 24 September 1968, box 640, EWB; correspondence, Bob Ellsworth to EWB, 8 September 1968, box 640, EWB.
97. RMN appearance on an Illinois Statewide TV Program, 4 September 1968, box 640, EWB.
98. John Herbers, 'Republican Efforts to Gain Support Among Negroes Appear to Have Failed', *New York Times*, 6 October 1968, 78.
99. EWB appearance on ABC's *Issues and Answers*, 13 October 1968, box 563, EWB.

100. Broyhill quoted in Richard Corrigan, 'Broyhill Expects to Win His 9th Straight Election', *Washington Post*, 2 September 1968.
101. Eve Edstrom, 'Collins in Tight Senate Race', *Washington Post*, 24 October 1968.
102. AP, 'Sterilization Proposed on Welfare Mothers', *Washington Post*, 17 September 1968.
103. Peter Jay, 'Brewster's Woes Tied to 3-Way Race', *Washington Post*, 22 September 1968.
104. Robert G. Kaiser and Eve Edstrom, 'Thirteen Newcomers and Goldwater to be Seated in Senate', *Washington Post*, 7 November 1968, A7.
105. CG quoted in James Clarity, 'Top G.O.P. Leaders Pleased with Goodell Choice', *New York Times*, 9 September 1968.
106. EWB, *Issues and Answers*, 13 October 1968.
107. LBJ, 'Remarks at the Dedication of Fishtrap Dam Near Pikeville, Kentucky', 26 October 1968, TAPP.
108. LBJ, 'Remarks in Morgantown at a Dinner Honoring Representative Harley O. Staggers of West Virginia', 26 October 1968, TAPP.
109. E. W. Kenworthy, 'Urban Issues Dominate Candidates' Domestic Views', *New York Times*, 25 October 1968.
110. GRF, Speech at dinner honoring Rep. Barber Conable, Batavia, NY, 3 October 1968, box 59, RTH, GRF.
111. Phillips, *The Emerging Republican Majority*.
112. Phillips quoted in James Boyd, 'Nixon's Southern Strategy', *New York Times*, 17 May 1970.
113. Richard M. Scammon and Ben J. Wattenberg, *The Real Majority* (New York: Coward-McCann, 1970), 57.
114. Ibid. 296.
115. Ibid. 40.
116. Ibid. 296.
117. Ibid. 54.

5

The crossroads: Nixon's early years, 1969–70

Years from now, when historians look back on our times, I believe they will say that this welfare reform is the most important piece of social legislation in almost four decades. There is no proposal I have sent to the Congress more central to my own philosophy of fairness and progress for all the American people.[1]

Richard Nixon, 16 April 1970

Richard Nixon's first two years in office were the crossroad in the Republican challenge to the War on Poverty. Prior to 1969, the GOP's response to Lyndon Johnson's antipoverty effort – save for the odd instance of support from progressives and a few moderate Republicans – was oppositional. While congressional Republicans had offered constructive alternatives to avoid falling into the familiar trap of negativity and privilege, these alternatives were almost always watered-down versions of Johnson's antipoverty war. Given the choice, most Republicans would have taken the option that Johnson had refused in Vietnam: declared victory and withdrawn from battle. For the GOP, American private enterprise guaranteed overall triumph against the poverty foe, not government programmes. Yet, Nixon's early moves in office saw the Republican president save Johnson's antipoverty war and then attempt to launch his own, in the form of the Family Assistance Plan (FAP). Had Nixon been successful in passing FAP – which included a guaranteed government income for millions of poor Americans – the War on Poverty would have finally (and surprisingly) become a bipartisan effort.

Nixon, in attempting to migrate the Republican response to the War on Poverty from opposition to embrace, did so for a variety of push and pull factors. Regarding the former, the White House was worried that if they scrapped Johnson's antipoverty effort, then they would invite yet another summer of racial uprisings in America's cities. In proposing FAP, Nixon was also attempting to placate rising public anger at spiralling welfare claims, a sentiment which had grown – often nurtured by Republican politicians – during the 1960s. Lastly, Nixon was pushed away from the oppositional Republican message because he was aware of the GOP's negative image. As has been noted in previous chapters, Republicans had remained in the minority for much of the previous thirty years because they had been unable to craft an appealing alternative to New Deal liberalism. In 1964, Barry Goldwater's disastrous campaign – a painstaking howl in the night against the changes the New Deal had wrought – further cemented the electorate's image of the Republicans as the 'Party of No'. Nixon, who had borne witness to Goldwater's defeat having loyally campaigned for the Arizonan, was not about to fall into the familiar trap. For electoral reasons, he had long believed that the GOP had to accept the popular elements of the New Deal, and his initial presidential actions suggested that he felt no different about Johnson's Great Society programmes.

The enticements for Nixon's embrace of an activist antipoverty agenda were even clearer. In taking office, Nixon believed he had ascended to the presidency at a uniquely opportune moment in American political history. As various historians have noted, Nixon and his advisers saw an opportunity to realign the electorate to the GOP banner.[2] In particular, the Nixon White House saw the northern white working class (and some lower middle class) – previously the bedrock of the Democratic Party's New Deal coalition – as ripe for Republican picking.[3] In plotting to capture this vote, Nixon cast himself as an American Disraeli, once remarking that it was 'Tory men with liberal policies who have enlarged democracy'.[4] Scrapping the War on Poverty simply would not have fitted with this Disraelian image. In addition to this electoral ambition, Nixon – a person who worked his way up from semi-impoverished beginnings and shared an affinity with the fabled 'little guy' on Main Street – genuinely wanted to do something for the poor, or at least, those 'deserving poor' who worked and still found themselves in poverty. And, of course, in passing FAP, Nixon had his eye on being remembered as one of America's great presidents.

Nixon's problem, as events revealed, was that the President proved inept in his role as party leader. If leadership is defined as the ability to inspire others to follow your direction, then – on poverty policy – Nixon failed. The tail, ultimately, wagged the dog, as most elected Republicans refused to rally behind their president's most significant policy proposal. While a few leading Republicans heartily endorsed FAP, and many others swallowed their own feelings out of loyalty to their president, it was not enough. In the end, it was Republicans who ensured that Nixon's new War on Poverty never became a reality. Partly, this was because the Nixon administration proved inept at congressional relations. But mostly, it was because the majority of elected Republicans had primarily opposed Johnson's War on Poverty not because it was poorly executed, but because they simply did not want any War on Poverty. Nixon was attempting to lead them somewhere they were unwilling to go. While historians have effectively documented the role played by liberal Democrats – unhappy at a $1,600 guaranteed income threshold they perceived as inept and a work requirement they saw as draconian – in ensuring FAP never became a reality, the role played by members of Nixon's own party was arguably more significant.[5] This is partly because it saw Republicans defying their own president. More importantly, however, their firm opposition was also a harbinger for how the GOP – whose future lay in the type of conservativism espoused by most Republican FAP detractors – would react to antipoverty proposals over the next fifty years. Given this period witnessed the party ascend to power, it also had significant ramifications in the following decades for poor Americans.

Transitioning to power

From the moment that Nixon squeaked over the line to victory in the 1968 presidential election, his actions foretold an administration that would not make a clean break from the domestic policies of its predecessor. Indeed, the election results simply did not offer the President-Elect a clear mandate to take the country in a new direction. Not only had Nixon's once vast polling lead almost entirely evaporated by Election Day, but the Republican Party's limited gains (an impressive five-seat swing in the Senate, a lacklustre five-seat gain in the House) and continued minority status did not offer a ringing endorsement of GOP policies. Moreover, Nixon's myopic focus on 'law and order' during the autumn – despite Congress having already passed an omnibus crime bill in the summer – meant that the President himself had not sold the electorate a fully developed governing agenda. With the Economic Opportunity Act (EOA) up for renewal in early 1970, Nixon's will to offer a Republican alternative to LBJ's War on Poverty was quickly tested.

The American people offered the new president mixed guidance. Extensive polling conducted near the end of the 1968 campaign in battleground states revealed that all-important swing state voters still supported antipoverty programmes.[6] A Harris poll the following year also showed 83 per cent of respondents in favour of using federal funds to wipe out city slums, at a time when urban America was seen as the front line of the War on Poverty. On the other hand, voters were apprehensive about the growth of government in Washington. Gallup showed that 46 per cent of Americans thought that 'big government' represented a greater threat to the country's future, compared with 26 per cent for 'big labor' and 12 per cent for 'big business'.[7] Such numbers represented promise for the more business-orientated Republicans who could allow their hopes to grow that memories of the Great Depression, which had occurred on the Republicans' watch, were finally beginning to recede. Perhaps, at long last, it was liberalism's failures that now held sway with the electorate. Still, the fear of 'big government' remained somewhat abstract. The nation, despite its respective foreign and domestic challenges in Southeast Asia and in unruly American cities, was still prosperous; the post-Second World War economic juggernaut continued to thunder. It made sense that the American people were still happy to fund poverty programmes as there was as yet no feeling that the middle class needed to make any sacrifice to do so.

Had Nixon desired to make sweeping changes to the War on Poverty, his next challenge was the Congress.[8] While Nixon's arrival in office took place a few decades before the feverish partisanship that would latterly grip the United States, this did not mean that Democrats – with comfortable majorities in both congressional chambers – were keen to acquiesce to scrapping Democratic achievements at the request of a Republican president. Moreover, the War on Poverty's uniquely partisan beginnings, coupled with Nixon's own image as a distinctively partisan Republican, made it even less likely that Democrats would stand aside as the new President dismembered the antipoverty effort. There were also, of course, many Democrats who simply still believed that, despite its travails, the War on Poverty was sound and desirable policy.

Nixon's own Republican congressional delegation was split on the future of the poverty war. While most were ideologically opposed to the current incarnation, they differed on the path forward. Conservatives would happily have seen the back of anti-poverty programmes but they were still, in some senses, a coming force. While individually they had greater numbers than each of the other three Republican factions in Congress, they were only able to affect legislation when sufficient numbers of stalwart Republicans and conservative southern Democrats joined their cause. Moreover, the 1968 election had further swelled the Senate ranks of progressive and moderate Republicans, with the high-profile additions of Richard Schweiker (R-PA), Robert Packwood (R-OR), William Saxbe (R-OH) and Charles Mathias (R-MD). In the House, among the few Republican gains, was Lowell Wiecker (R-CT), who became one of the most consistently progressive voices in the lower chamber. Indeed, as Geoffrey Kabaservice notes, the early years of Nixon's presidency were the height of moderate Republicanism.[9] This was confirmed when moderate Hugh Scott became the successor to Everett Dirksen. Scott was preferred over stalwart Howard Baker (R-TN), when the long-serving Senate Minority Leader lost his battle with ill health in September 1969. As already discussed, many moderate and progressive Republicans had voted for the EOA in at least one of its iterations. Rather than scrap the War on Poverty, they wanted to improve it by making its initiatives more efficient, with more

171

involvement from the private sector, and by moving away from the image of corruption and partisanship that dogged the Office of Economic Opportunity (OEO). As such, the antipoverty effort retained enough congressional support to make reform much more likely than repeal.

Nixon, the avowed centrist, sought to satisfy everyone. The presidential candidate who had shown his ideological dexterity – embracing both order and justice in capturing the Republican nomination in 1968 – reappeared during the transition period. Nixon assembled a cabinet and White House staff that offered something to everyone. For the premiere 'order' post, he appointed an order Republican, his campaign manager John Mitchell, as Attorney General. For the high-profile social justice positions, he appointed social justice advocates, such as his protégé Robert Finch, at the Department of Health, Education, and Welfare (HEW) and George Romney at the Department of Housing and Urban Development (HUD). This ideological diversity was reflected throughout his White House staff, from assistants to speechwriters. Even his two closest advisers, Chief of Staff H. R. Haldeman and Counsel John D. Ehrlichman, offered conservative and moderate views respectively. Most importantly for the administration's approach to poverty during his first year in office, Nixon appointed duelling advisers in the conservative economist Arthur F. Burns, and the Harvard professor – not to mention former member of both Kennedy and Johnson administrations – Daniel Patrick Moynihan. As 1969 unfolded, the two counsellors would engage in their own tale of ice and fire, as the buttoned-up Burns and the colourful Moynihan sought the president's ear on poverty policy.

Overall, while congressional Republicans and even high-profile Republican governors continued to play a role in shaping the War on Poverty during Nixon's tenure, the new President was the only Republican with the power, not to mention the bully pulpit, to direct such efforts. His early successful effort to force the impressive Ray Bliss out as RNC chairman, as the result of an unforgotten petty grievance, showcased that the Republican Party would – at least initially – be somewhat bent to Nixon's will.[10] Nixon – who loved American football almost as much as politics – viewed congressional leaders as mere players in a team he coached and he expected them to follow his plays. For the most part, Minority Leaders Ford and Scott loyally fulfilled this role.[11] Rank-and-file members, however, proved more independent as time wore on. Nevertheless, this was Richard Nixon's Republican Party, and his moves on poverty policy held the potential to redirect the GOP's challenge to the War on Poverty.

A stay of execution for Johnson's war

Nixon's first War on Poverty decision was whether to renew the antipoverty effort's foundational legislation – the EOA. Would the new President retain the War on Poverty's most visible programmes, such as the Job Corps, Head Start and Community Action? OEO staff were not optimistic. In the days before Nixon's inauguration, anyone riding the elevators at the OEO building would have encountered a sign which read: 'This building will self destruct on January 20'.[12] The resort to gallows humour is revealing of how the OEO viewed its chances under a Republican administration. To some extent, their pessimism was justified, for the OEO itself was allowed to survive, but not thrive. As for the War on Poverty overall, however, Nixon's first year represented a pleasant surprise for liberals who feared the worst.

One of Nixon's first actions as president was to create, by executive order, the Urban Affairs Council (UAC). This group – like the wider administration itself – featured an ideologically eclectic mix of cabinet officials and presidential advisers, albeit with the liberal Moynihan at its symbolic head as the UAC's Executive Secretary. Nixon was also personally involved. By June, the UAC had already met on twelve occasions, with the President presiding over ten meetings.[13] During its two-year existence, the UAC played a key role in shaping Nixon's approach to poverty issues, while its name served as yet another symbol that politicians viewed urban America as the hub of nation's socioeconomic struggles. The UAC's creation also helped Nixon signal to voters that he was not neglecting the slum conditions that had birthed the urban crisis; that this was not a Republican administration that deserved the 'Party of No' moniker. Nixon's administration would continue to fight poverty and with new, better, more efficient – more Republican – ideas.

Before the UAC could craft a new Republican War on Poverty, however, the White House needed to signal how it felt about the old one. The EOA's impending congressional renewal meant that the new administration had an opportunity to advocate either continuing, reshaping or completely scrapping the existing antipoverty effort. In the end, it chose the centrist option. Nixon, much like the vast majority of Republicans, disdained the OEO. He regarded the recently created agency as troublemaking rather than problem solving – an incubator for left-wing radicals and black nationalists, who had contributed to the violent upheavals in the nation's cities.[14] In deciding to save the OEO therefore, Nixon instructed that people with 'our views' must be installed in the nation's poverty hub.[15]

Most pertinent to this was appointing a new permanent OEO director. Nixon failed to convince moderate former Pennsylvania governor William Scranton to take the post, and was initially unsuccessful in luring his next target, moderate congressman Donald Rumsfeld (R-IL). A rising star in Congress, Rumsfeld did not want the job as he believed that all he would be presiding over was the end of the OEO and 'the liquidation of the Johnson poverty approach'. Aside from feeling that such a role would not be the most glamorous task, Rumsfeld sensed that deploying an Ivy League-educated, suburban Republican from the wealthiest congressional district in the nation to dismantle the antipoverty agency was not the ideal image for the administration. If they wanted a hatchet man who could provide political cover, Rumsfeld advised Nixon to appoint a liberal.[16] The President had to wait a while longer until he successfully convinced Rumsfeld – peeved at having lost a leadership race in Congress – to give up his safe seat for the unenviable task of running the OEO.[17]

Nixon had other reasons for wanting to see Johnson's War on Poverty ended. He was wholly unconvinced by the policy merits of the main initiatives that the EOA had birthed – especially Job Corps, Community Action, VISTA, and even the popular Head Start. Nixon also believed that his presidential campaign had vowed a clear shift away from LBJ's creations, and he needed to deliver on his campaign promise. In early February, he informed his cabinet that the conservative Burns was conducting a full study of the OEO's effectiveness. Finally, he made it clear that there was to be no extra funding for any poverty programme until Burns's assessment – unlikely to be favourable – was complete.[18]

Yet, Nixon was reluctant to completely revoke his predecessor's antipoverty approach. In mid-February, his special message to Congress on the nation's antipoverty programmes revealed his thinking. Stressing in his message that 'the blight of poverty requires priority attention' and that it 'engages our hearts and challenges our intelligence', Nixon sought to cast the first Republican administration in eight years as compassionate. In addition to warm words, there was hard policy to back it up. The President, surprisingly, advised Congress that he wanted the legislature to extend the EOA for another year at present funding levels. The message was clear: Nixon – and by extension the Republican Party – would not take a swinging axe to the antipoverty budget.

The OEO, however, did not escape unscathed. In the revised legislation which was sent to Congress in March, the GOP's bête noire was stripped of the Job Corps, which was moved to Labor, while the popular Head Start, as well as other smaller initiatives, such as Foster Grandparents, were moved to HEW. Formed as a coordinating agency in 1964, the OEO would now evolve into an 'incubator' agency for experimental measures. While it retained the controversial Community Action, the OEO's main function was to test and trial new poverty initiatives – to be the innovative arm of US antipoverty policy. Nixon, striking a consistent Republican theme, also highlighted the need for better, more efficient, less bureaucratic management of the antipoverty effort.[19] Overall, Nixon's pronouncements amounted to a stay of execution for the OEO and the War on Poverty as a whole.

In the month after Nixon's announcement it quickly became clear that poverty policy – much like it did for Johnson – was to prove a tricky minefield for the new administration. Head Start, seemingly the least controversial of all the poverty initiatives, and certainly the most politically popular, created an unwanted headache. Despite its popularity, Head Start had one significant problem: it did not work. Or, more precisely, social scientists showed that while early education for disadvantaged youngsters had an immediate positive impact on child learning, this effect quickly wore off once the Head Start summer sessions ended and the child grew older. These findings were laid bare by an OEO-commissioned independent report in March by Westinghouse, which caused a stir in Washington.

Despite the report's fallow findings, the reaction it generated made clear that Head Start was already a sacred cow for many politicians. Such was the controversy and wilful denial of the report's conclusions that the independent consultant had his name removed from the Westinghouse study to avoid damaging his professional status. Moreover, the OEO sent the report back to Westinghouse and told them to look again. The Westinghouse findings also led to fevered media speculation that the Nixon administration would use the report as justification for scrapping Head Start. Many journalists remained unconvinced that Nixon truly wanted to continue the government's fight against poverty.[20] For instance, columnist Joseph Alsop speculated that Nixon's maintenance of the OEO was purely out of fear of urban riots rather than genuine concern for the poor.[21]

At least with regard to Head Start, journalists were right to regard Nixon's continuation of the programme as a purely political calculation. Nixon privately harboured serious doubts about its effectiveness. Yet, he was also a political pragmatist. In March, he regretfully told Ehrlichman that it was too late to scrap Head Start.[22] Meanwhile, Nixon's aide, Bob Patricelli, laid bare to the President that Head Start was the single most popular OEO programme, both in Congress and among the American people. It was a tool of racial integration and was seen as the most beneficial programme by community leaders and residents themselves. 'Head Start cutbacks,' Patricelli speculated, 'would further alienate a group [urban African Americans] which is already highly suspicious of the Administration.' While Nixon accepted this political reality, he ruefully (and revealingly) noted that such African Americans were a group 'who have never voted and will never vote for me'.[23]

As such, the administration did not incite anti-Head Start sentiment among conservative Democrats and Republicans on the House Education and Labor Committee that was considering Head Start's fate. Nixon had Finch draw up recommendations with the intention of making Head Start more effective. Finch's recommendations included a shift from summer only to full year sessions, and an increase in funding for Follow Through, an initiative that was aimed at making Head Start benefits more long-lasting for participants. Finally, in true Republican fashion, Finch recommended greater inclusion of private enterprise as well as an experimental initiative that would allow parents to pick to which Head Start institution they sent their child.[24]

Ultimately, these changes would make it into the final legislation. The result was a mixed bag for Head Start, which received the same amount of money, while being expected to open full year, rather than summer only, centres. While the education received was therefore more thorough, the number of enrolees benefiting fell. Head Start, as historian Elizabeth Rose notes, henceforth continued its policy life as an 'orphan' of the War on Poverty, an initiative which enjoyed more affection than its beleaguered parent.[25] Elsewhere, the Job Corps was also downsized, with over sixty centres shuttered, replaced with thirty new venues closer to urban areas – and closer to where politicians perceived the real problem of poverty. Thus, Nixon went some way to keeping his campaign promise on Job Corps.[26]

One idea that did clearly bleed over from the 1968 campaign was 'black capitalism'. Nixon was keen to use his much-vaunted idea to demonstrate that he had compassion for the black poor, while the White House was also worried that a sixth straight summer of uprisings lay ahead in the cities.[27] In March, Nixon established the Office of Minority Business Enterprise (OMBE) by Executive Order. Yet, while the cities did not go up in flames in 1969, this proved a largely symbolic rather than substantive move. While black capitalism had played a major role in allowing Nixon to reach out to moderate and progressive Republicans during the nomination battle, it was a minor factor in his administration. Placed in the hands of conservative cabinet members Maurice Stans (Commerce) and Hilary Sandoval (Small Business Administration), the OMBE helped few African Americans and served to annoy progressive Republicans in Congress who complained of its failure.[28]

Nixon's early moves on antipoverty policy were also revealing of how he would handle Republican congressional opinion: namely, he was not particularly interested, and he was not very good at pretending he was either. When Robert Taft Jr (R-OH), freshly elected to the Senate and someone who had engaged seriously in the initial 1964 House debate over the original EOA, proposed to fund an initiative to get more unemployed poor Americans ready for work in the industrial sector under the EOA, the White House responded coolly. They advised Taft that they were doing a thorough review of the War on Poverty and would not welcome any changes.[29] Such a response was also delivered to the progressive congressman Pete McCloskey (R-CA) when he proposed a White House-sponsored Inner-City Ghetto Program. McCloskey, who had toured a variety of inner cities to help inform his proposals, advocated for more recreation areas for children, by developing unused and barren areas of the landscape.[30] The White House also drew the ire of another GOP congressmen when they failed to reveal their antipoverty plans before a key congressional debate on the issue.[31] While congressional Republicans had felt empowered to be creative in offering GOP-led alternatives to the War on Poverty during the Johnson years, that time appeared over. As far as the White House was concerned, poverty policy was to be driven by the President alone.

All in all, Nixon's initial steps with regard to the War on Poverty showed an administration keen to make dramatic change, but unwilling to take political heat for doing so. Furthermore, underneath it all lay an unspoken fear that, if the antipoverty effort was dramatically scrapped by the new Republican president, 1969 would become the sixth straight summer of urban upheavals. Such calculations led the Nixon White House to resort to some bureaucratic reshuffling, while advocating the EOA's renewal. Nevertheless, while this may have allayed the worst liberal fears of Nixon's domestic agenda, the White House's fraught relationship with congressional Republicans represented either teething problems of a new administration or a sign that the Nixon domestic agenda would face continued intra-party challenges in implementing its antipoverty agenda.

Conceiving the Family Assistance Plan

Arguably, Nixon's greatest domestic policy legacy was a proposal that never became reality. The 37th President, sometimes dubbed – with varying degrees of seriousness – the 'last liberal President', signed into law sweeping environmental legislation; a bold upsurge in food stamps; Social Security amendments that increased benefits for all recipients and expanded coverage to the disabled and blind; while also quietly implementing school desegregation at a pace far surpassing that of his predecessor.[32] Yet, it is Nixon's proposal of the Family Assistance Plan (FAP) that was truly radical. FAP would have guaranteed every family in the United States a minimum income of $1,600, so long as the parents (if able-bodied) fulfilled a working requirement. Had FAP become a reality, the antipoverty policy landscape in the United States would have shifted dramatically. While Nixon eschewed the militarist terminology deployed by Johnson, FAP – whatever its policy merits – arguably represented a true war on poverty. Indeed, Moynihan (FAP's key administration cheerleader) perhaps undersold family assistance when he deemed it the 'second stage in the War on Poverty'.[33]

Upon arriving in the presidency, Nixon was determined to halt the skyrocketing rates of welfare claimants. By early 1969, the media was consistently running stories that an explosion in welfare recipients was a national crisis, and one which was stirring resentment among working Americans. Nixon was personally convinced that many of those seeking welfare were fit to work but choosing a life of government largesse. Indeed, prior to his inauguration he told key members of his administration that he did not want welfare scandals swept aside purely to have an 'era of good feeling with bureaucrats'. 'The whole thing [welfare],' Nixon declared, 'stinks to high heaven and we should get charging on it immediately.' Tellingly, he observed, 'the American people are outraged and in my view they should be.'[34] One such American was the influential reverend, Billy Graham, who wrote in the *Washington Post* of his disgust at welfare dependency, and noted favourably that he had seen a sign recently which read: 'I Fight Poverty, I Work'.[35] Graham, who had a mass following, had initially been supportive of Lyndon Johnson's Great Society, but became more disillusioned and conservative as the 1960s wore on.[36] For Nixon, such sentiment only reinforced his desire to take dramatic action on welfare.

In conceiving FAP, Nixon relied heavily on Moynihan and Burns. While all relevant cabinet members and advisers were consulted, Moynihan was the figure relentlessly urging, cajoling and flattering the President into announcing a strikingly bold policy for tackling poverty. During this time, the Nixon White House was a hub of activity on antipoverty policy, with Moynihan using his intellect, energy and charisma to propel innovation for helping poor Americans.

Moynihan arrived in his unexpected post in Nixon's administration convinced that LBJ's War on Poverty had been a tragic mistake, both politically and as a matter of public policy. Rather than binding the nation in an effort to fight poverty, Moynihan believed that liberals – of which he was one, albeit of the heterodox variety – had mistakenly divided the American people. He advised Nixon that the War on Poverty 'defined a large portion of the population as somehow living apart from the rest'. That large portion, Moynihan knew, existed in the mind of white Americans as the urban black poor. Instead, Moynihan counselled Nixon to 'seek programs that stress problems and circumstances which working people share with the poor. Too frequently of late the liberal upper middle class has proposed to solve problems of those at the bottom at the expense, or seeming expense, of those in between.'[37] Such an analysis played to Nixon's own oft-espoused disdain of the liberal elite.[38] Moreover, for a White House that never forgot the need to target those white working-class voters whom Wallace had captured in 1968, or who had reluctantly remained Democratic out of party loyalty, the need to make the Nixon antipoverty approach more universal (rather than appearing to prioritise African Americans) was desirable.

For Moynihan, even those poverty programmes that had achieved popularity were poor policy. He viewed Head Start as essentially the OEO paying the middle class to provide services to poor people. In his opinion, this 'service' approach was misguided, which meant that the government's antipoverty money was flowing, not to the poor, but to affluent America. These beliefs laid the ground for FAP – an 'income' based approach to tackling poverty. Appealing unapologetically to his boss's desire for presidential greatness, Moynihan advised that FAP 'will enable you to begin cutting back sharply on these costly and questionable services, and yet to assert with full ability that it was under your Presidency that poverty was abolished in America'.[39] Essentially, Moynihan was telling Nixon that to win the antipoverty war, the President must rip up the previous general's battle plans and start anew.

To counteract this influence, Nixon had installed the conservative Burns. According to Ehrlichman, Nixon enjoyed playing the two off against each other, in what amounted to a 'fair, equal, and brutal battle'.[40] Burns, the conservative voice, was fervently opposed to progressive Republicanism, Moynihan and FAP from the outset. In February, Burns despaired that, 'as I watch our Cabinet in action, I wonder more and more whether or how they differ from the LBJ people . . . if this continues, people all over the country will be asking what promises for change we are fulfilling'.[41] Meanwhile, he and the conservative Haldeman were quickly exchanging memos regarding the 'Moynihan problem'.[42] When Burns realised that Nixon was being lured into a high-stakes gambit that threatened to blow a hole in the federal budget, the former economist worked assiduously to ensure that a strong working requirement was attached to the guaranteed income that was being promoted by Moynihan.[43]

As the White House was busy working out the details of FAP, it studiously avoided revealing its plans to congressional Republicans. Bryce Harlow, Nixon's experienced congressional liaison who had been Eisenhower's key contact with Congress during the 1950s, implored the White House to reverse its silence. In July, Harlow advised Ehrlichman that, 'if the President hopes for the maximum favorable response from the Republican Party, and if he desires to enact [FAP] rather than merely propose it, then I consider present plans inadequate'. He then provided a list of influential congressional Republicans who should be wooed by the White House. Harlow, however, was ignored. On that list was Sen. John Williams (R-DE), who would prove an intractable and powerful foe of FAP.[44]

What made the White House's refusal to include their own congressional party in discussions surprising was the fact that they were happy to consult with pretty much anybody else. As early as April, Moynihan was sent on a mission to confer with the great and the good of the American business world, as well as other figures deemed 'influential'. FAP's number one salesperson gleefully informed Nixon that his pitch worked: 'without exception [the businessmen] were enthusiastic, and stated they would unhesitatingly support'.[45]

Meanwhile, the Nixon administration did deem it correct to confer with influential Republican governors. In July, Nelson Rockefeller was brought firmly into the loop. The New York governor was not keen on FAP, as the funding formula meant that the Empire State would be one of only two states that would lose welfare money from the federal government. He thus informed Nixon directly that he would have to oppose the measure.[46] Nixon, who harboured a fear that Republican governors might run against him in 1972, was quick to take action. Ehrlichman advised Moynihan to arrange a full briefing on FAP for Republican governors who presided over electorally rich states, such as Rockefeller, Ronald Reagan (California), Ray Shafer (Pennsylvania), Jim Rhodes (Ohio) and Richard Ogilvie (Illinois). Moreover, the funding formula was eventually reworked to bring Rockefeller on board.[47] Congressional Republicans, however, remained in the dark and had no opportunity to vet the plan.[48]

Nixon's FAP announcement on 8 August struck upon one consistent theme that had belonged to the Democrats since the New Deal: fairness. Appearing before a national television audience, Nixon outlined the shortcomings of the present welfare system, declaring it 'unfair to the welfare recipient, unfair to the working poor, and unfair to the taxpayer'. For the welfare recipient, Nixon hit upon the widely varying rates of welfare payments dependent upon which state the recipient resided. Noting that for a mother with three children, benefits ranged from a high of $263 per month in one state, down to a low of $39 in another state. With all the solemnity he could muster, Nixon told Americans that no American child was worth more than another. For the working poor, Nixon signalled his sympathy with their resentment at earning less than some families on welfare. For taxpayers, the system simply cost too much and rising welfare rolls meant there was a possibility of even higher taxes.[49]

Surprisingly, Nixon candidly acknowledged that FAP would initially cost more than the present welfare system. Nevertheless, he stressed that the nation would be saved untold sums as welfare recipients became self-reliant workers. Moreover, Nixon was adamant that FAP was not a guaranteed income – that the strong work requirements and job training initiatives meant that there was no guarantee, only an opportunity for the poor to receive this income. It is unsurprising that Nixon made this claim; even Rockefeller's progressive advisers had counselled him that a guaranteed income was grossly unpopular with the electorate and to ignore the idea in his 1968 primary campaign.[50] Nevertheless, it was never clear how the work requirement would function without a massive bureaucracy – one of the goals of scrapping the existing welfare system – to monitor every FAP applicant.

Finally, FAP's unveiling was accompanied by Nixon's announcement of his wider domestic agenda: New Federalism. While the slogan was lacking in appeal – anything with the word 'Federalism' was unlikely to stir the public's imagination – Nixon sought to frame New Federalism as a significant break from New Deal/Great Society liberalism. 'After a third of a century of power flowing from the people and the States to Washington,' Nixon implored, 'it is time for a New Federalism in which power, funds, and responsibility will flow from Washington to the States and to the people.'[51] To achieve this change Nixon made four proposals: FAP, an expanded job training programme, OEO reorganisation and revenue sharing with states and localities. Combined, these proposals essentially outlined Nixon's complete vision of a new War on Poverty. Only FAP, however, emerged as a significant proposal.[52]

In the immediate aftermath, Nixon was lauded by the press. Moynihan's assistant reported back that, of 400 editorials on Nixon's address, only 30 were negative on FAP. Most newspapers responded favourably to Nixon's carrot and stick approach, lauding the combination of the work requirement with the income floor for poor Americans. Even conservative outlets, such as the *Chicago Tribune* and the *National Review*, initially responded positively to FAP. Moreover, the Nixon White House was inundated with favourable correspondence from the public. Over 2,300 examples of such correspondence were received in the first fortnight, with 83 per cent expressing unqualified approval, and only 7 per cent expressing outright opposition to the President's plan. Many correspondents also indicated they were contacting their representative to support the plan in Congress.[53]

Yet, while Nixon was ebullient at his favourable reviews, he encountered a quick reminder that FAP and his goal of a New Federalism had a long way to travel to become reality. Having flown to the Western White House in San Clemente, California in the wake of his much-lauded speech, Nixon met Ronald Reagan and attempted to convince the governor that FAP was sound, fundamentally conservative, policy. Despite Nixon's extensive preparation for Reagan's visit and devoting much of the meeting to emphasising the work requirement, Reagan came away unconvinced and the pair parted without coming to an agreement.[54] Conservative apprehension, which had been articulated internally by Burns for months, was already a clear issue.

The congressional outlook was only slightly better as Republican leadership offered mixed reviews of Nixon's speech. Minority Leader Ford loyally came out fully behind FAP, only for his Senate counterpart Dirksen – who passed away the following month – to offer a non-committal comment. Elsewhere, Republican progressives, and even moderates, thoroughly endorsed the general idea of FAP, but many were already taking issue with the funding formula. Nixon's plan provided far more federal help to less generous welfare states (often in the South) as opposed to the northern industrial states that already offered higher benefits.[55] Republican progressives and moderates almost always represented such northern states. Predictably, Democrats did not respond enthusiastically to the Republican President's proposal. Liberals quickly denounced the $1,600 income floor as too small, while conservative southern Democrats – for a variety of reasons discussed below – were unimpressed by the President's offer.[56] All in all, FAP's outlook was far from certain when it arrived in the legislative branch in November.

Even with congressional challenges on the horizon, Richard Nixon's first six months in the office represented a quite remarkable response to the War on Poverty. Arguably, in proposing FAP, Nixon was offering a more serious approach to fighting poverty than was found in LBJ's EOA. Despite campaign promises otherwise, Nixon had not abolished his predecessor's initiatives and had requested an extension at the same funding levels. Moreover, he had refocused the OEO – long loathed by Republicans – as a research and development hub to come up with new ideas for continuing the fight against poverty. In an August statement, an optimistic Nixon, basking in the glow of the Apollo 11 mission having landed man on the moon only a fortnight before, sought to harness the pride permeating American society at the nation's achievement. 'Abolishing poverty, putting an end to dependency – like reaching the moon a generation ago – may seem to be impossible,' Nixon declared, 'but in the spirit of Apollo, we can lift our sights and marshal our best efforts.'[57] Unfortunately for Nixon – and for the prospects of a new War on Poverty – the President's Republican team did not offer him the same unity and support in his mission as that enjoyed by Neil Armstrong.

A brewing intraparty war

Looking back more than a decade after he had departed his job as OEO director, Donald Rumsfeld reflected on the uniquely challenging nature of his post in the Nixon administration. He recalled coming home from the OEO one night:

> . . . reaching in the ice box for a beer, and there was a note that my wife, Joyce, always supportive and helpful, had taped up on the door of the icebox, It said: 'He tackled a job that couldn't be done. With a smile, he went right to it. He tackled a job that couldn't be done, and couldn't do it.'[58]

Rumsfeld – and his wife – were likely referring to the fact that the former congressman was heading an agency that his own party did not like, that he had voted against as a congressman, and yet, as an ambitious politician, he was determined to succeed and make the OEO work. As if such a task were not daunting enough, Rumsfeld encountered a media that thoroughly distrusted him, and a leaky agency, where staff opposed to him were happy to brief against Nixon's man at the OEO. Indeed, barely months into the job, the *Washington Post*'s Jack Anderson, in an article riddled with insider gossip, scathingly wrote that Rumsfeld had gutted the OEO's budget, targeted Washington, DC initiatives due to the capital's predominantly black population, all whilst sprucing up former OEO director Sargent Shriver's previously spartan office décor with lavish interiors.[59] Despite Rumsfeld convincingly refuting each accusation and his ongoing efforts to defend the OEO from its political enemies, the media and liberals remained suspicious of Rumsfeld's intentions throughout his twenty-month OEO tenure.

Yet, Rumsfeld's real foe was not the media or liberal Democrats, but his old congressional Republican colleagues. Three days after Nixon announced his New Federalism agenda to the nation, the President asked Congress to renew the EOA for two further years (rather than the one he had requested in March) at existing funding levels, while reiterating his desire for the OEO to focus on innovation. Following this announcement, Nixon quickly received word from Rep. Carl Perkins (D-KY), now the Democrats' key custodian of the War on Poverty. Perkins expressed his pleasure at Nixon's commitment to the antipoverty effort, but warned the President that congressional Republicans were threatening to derail the proposed extension. Nixon followed Perkins's advice, hastily arranging a meeting with key Republicans in hopes that White House pressure would convince them to pass a clean renewal of the EOA. Even after this presidential intervention, Perkins reported back to Nixon that 'your message still appears not to have been communicated to the rank and file members of the Republican Party in the House'. He warned the president that these were not small differences: 'many, if not most [Republicans], appear to be inclined to revise substantially the entire thrust of the Economic Opportunity Act'. If Nixon could guarantee just a third of House Republicans, then Perkins assured the president there was enough Democratic support to pass the bill.[60] For Nixon, such a show of disunity was not what he had envisaged so early in his presidency. Moreover, it is striking that he required a Democrat to inform him of such issues.

With Perkins looking to renew EOA before Congress broke for Christmas, the intraparty fight between Republicans broke out into the open in early December. On one side stood Rumsfeld, who wanted the clean renewal, with no amendments, to give him and the administration the time to properly assess the OEO's current initiatives and to avoid charges that Republicans were gutting the War on Poverty. Yet, House Republicans, led by Al Quie and William Ayres, who had been the main Republican challengers to the antipoverty effort during LBJ's tenure, were unwilling to toe the administration's line. Nixon found himself caught between both sides of the dispute.[61]

The main area of contention was over a typically Republican gripe – federal control. In October, the Senate had comfortably passed EOA's renewal with a bipartisan vote (79–3). During the debate, however, the upper chamber narrowly approved an amendment from conservative Republican George Murphy (R-CA) that granted governors the right to veto any Legal Services initiative in their state. The successful vote was the result of a coalition of conservative and stalwart Republicans, teaming up with conservative southern Democrats. While the amendment appeared benign and limited in scope, Rumsfeld believed that it would ultimately 'eviscerate the poverty program'. He advised the White House that he would vigorously campaign against it.[62] Ayres, who co-sponsored the amendment in the House, appeared to acknowledge the significance of its ramifications, mocking that, with regard to Rumsfeld, 'We are only taking away his canoe. He's still got his paddle.'[63] Minority Leader Ford was keen to keep loyal lieutenants like Ayres happy, and personally asked the White House not to undermine his authority by going over his head with a presidential plea to vote against the amendment.[64] Nixon was thus left in a situation where he either backed his OEO director or he supported the rebellious Republicans and risked losing Rumsfeld and much of the goodwill built up among the media and progressives over his antipoverty agenda. In the end, Nixon sided with Ford and quietly backed those supporting the amendment.

To the shock of many, however, the amendment failed in the House. Some Republicans backed Rumsfeld out of loyalty to an old colleague, but more important were the many Democrats who hailed from states with Republican governors and believed that the amendment spelled the end of the War on Poverty in their state. When the bill went to conference, it emerged with no state control amendment, and ultimately passed both chambers, albeit without the bipartisan Senate vote that had initially been achieved. The final bill received minimal support from conservative or stalwart Republicans and southern Democrats.[65]

Something larger than a mere amendment had been at stake. Sharp GOP observers Rowland Evans and Robert Novak discerned in their column that the whole incident was merely a proxy battle that signalled a brewing intraparty war. The two columnists wrote that the state control squabble 'symbolizes deepening polarization in the Republican Party', and was about two different directions for the GOP. On the one hand, Rumsfeld and moderate/progressive Republicans believed they could capture a greater share of the poor and the black vote if they pursued an agenda that appeared supportive to the War on Poverty. Conservatives, however, had their eyes on the Wallace vote in 1968 and, with it, an end to the antipoverty effort that Wallace voters believed only helped black Americans.[66] Nixon's hesitancy, before siding with the eventual losers, showed that the White House lacked the deft touch to manoeuvre around such intraparty squabbling. The President, rather than doing a victory lap for having managed to have a bill he called for approved, was perceived by the media as a loser in the EOA renewal – a captive of the lost conservative effort for state control. The amendment fight sent a further signal: Republican opposition to the War on Poverty persisted. This opposition's power base, for the time being, was in Congress rather than the White House.

Gunning for FAP

Nixon attempted to regain control of the narrative with his first State of the Union address on 22 January 1970. During the speech, Nixon sought to turn the page on 'the sixties', while still clearly being a captive of the decade's political milieu. In observing the tumultuous decade as one in which 'never has a nation seemed to have had more and enjoyed it less', Nixon blamed government for raising expectations, noting that 'we had too many visions – and too little vision'. And yet, unlike a future Republican president who signalled a turn away from government as a solution, Nixon's own solution was rooted in the 1960s Great Society ethos. Nixon boasted – in a sentence that would have made Lyndon Johnson proud – that to tackle the nation's problems, 'I will offer at least a dozen more major programs in the course of this session.'[67]

This contradiction in message spoke to Nixon's dilemma as he sought to craft a new electoral coalition: a desire to offer a clear Republican alternative to the Great Society agenda, while still appealing to many of those voters who had voted for the Democrats for the previous thirty years. Nixon had won support from many disaffected white working-class Democrats during his 'Silent Majority' address the previous November, in which he had divided the nation between the 'non-shouters' who supported the American mission in Vietnam and those anti-war protestors the President deemed unpatriotic.[68] Culturally, these Silent Majority voters were within his grasp, but economically they were unlikely to embrace a conservative Republican Party which harked back to the anti-government, pro-business economic policies which preceded the Great Depression.

During the State of the Union, Nixon listed the nation's number one domestic priority as welfare reform and he implored Congress to enact FAP in 1970. If he hoped to achieve this goal, however, he needed to prove that he was sincere and invested in his own proposal. 'The poor and the blacks don't believe Richard Nixon is nice,' Mary McGrory noted, 'and the Democrats and liberals never thought he was that bold, so a massive skepticism has engulfed the President's Family Assistance Plan.'[69] Even Republicans were not convinced that their President fully understood his own proposal, let alone that he was willing to throw his political weight behind it.[70] It also did not help Nixon in selling his initiative that Moynihan and Burns – the two chief protagonists who had conceived FAP's income and work requirement balancing act – were no longer guiding domestic policy in the White House. Moynihan was promoted to Counsellor to the President, which, ironically, saw him lose influence with the President; meanwhile, Nixon appointed Burns Chair of the Federal Reserve. The moderate Ehrlichman was now the key adviser directing the President's domestic agenda.

In response to Nixon's bold appeal, liberal Democrats began to outbid the President. Most notably, Sen. George McGovern

(D-SD), not wanting to be outdone by a Republican, proposed his Human Security Plan. McGovern's blueprint featured vast increases in its payments for poor families in comparison with Nixon's offer; moreover, he proposed a guaranteed government job for all able-bodied adults. As time went on, liberals – egged on by the National Welfare Rights Organization (NWRO), whose lobbyists referred to FAP as 'Fuck America's Poor' – sought to outdo each other over who could provide the most generous guaranteed income.[71] By February, the Nixon administration believed that congressional liberals would coalesce around a $3,600 income floor. As such, Nixon directed the White House machine to launch a concerted attack on the 'irresponsibility of the Democrats for more than doubling the offer which we made'. Nixon wanted all Republicans, from his vice president to backbenchers in Congress, parroting the line 'that this plan would require a tax increase of $40 billion which would cost every working family $2,500 a year'.[72] As such, while dealing with liberal alternatives made FAP's congressional passage trickier, it also offered Nixon the opportunity to occupy the political centre ground – in favour of helping the poor, but in a fiscally responsible manner.

Unfortunately for Nixon, Republicans were not sufficiently unified on FAP to successfully implement such a strategy. Partly, this was because many stalwart and conservative Republicans were being told by their key supporters not to support their President on his number one domestic priority. By January, the White House was being asked to help provide political cover for Gerald Ford, whose support for FAP was causing him to take flak from influential leaders in his conservative constituency.[73] In February, the US Chamber of Commerce announced its intention to launch a strong publicity and lobbying campaign against the proposal. Despite polls showing business leaders across the country in favour of a FAP-like measure, the Chamber began buying full-page anti-FAP advertisements in national newspapers.[74] Meanwhile, by March, the *National Review* – the mouthpiece of conservative Republicanism – reversed its previous support of FAP and advised its readers to oppose the measure.[75]

Sensing that this momentum shift was affecting congressional Republicans, Rep. John Byrnes (R-WI), a stalwart loyally shepherding FAP on behalf of the White House, begged the Nixon administration to start emphasising the conservative aspects of the proposal. Byrnes believed that 'the Congress is beginning to believe [FAP's] all welfare and very little work-fare'.[76] The White House responded by sending Vice President Spiro Agnew, a politician trusted by conservatives, out to campaign for FAP. Agnew himself harboured misgivings about FAP but was a loyal team player. In a March speech, he told his audience that the current welfare system was a 'scandal . . . binding successive generations in a lifetime of despair'. While he acknowledged that FAP was an initially expensive solution, he placed this in the language of the country-club Republican: 'Every businessman knows what "start-up costs" are.'[77]

Despite this change in White House tone, Republican support continued to be lukewarm with a House vote looming. At a February meeting of Republican members of the powerful Ways and Means Committee, the tenor ranged from uncertainty to hostility regarding FAP. Those who agreed to support the proposal, according to one Nixon aide, were doing so 'because they realize something must be done and the Administration plan is the only one that has been put forth'.[78] There was, however, a fear that FAP could become a 'political liability' for Republicans in future elections. Not all Republicans in attendance agreed to support it, either. Conservative Rep. James Utt (R-CA), warned he would write a thundering minority opinion to rally other conservatives against Nixon's key proposal. While Utt never got to write the opinion (he died the following week), the sentiment he expressed lived on among conservative Republicans.[79]

Progressive Republicans were also causing trouble. Charles Goodell – in the process of pirouetting from stalwart congress-man to progressive New York senator – opposed FAP as having an inadequate payment structure and deemed the workfare requirement as 'offensive' and 'demeaning' to poor Americans. He subsequently proposed a plan with a floor of $3,800 – even more generous than the liberal Democratic alternative. Goodell, an outspoken dove on the Vietnam War, said his proposal could be paid for if the administration withdrew troops from Southeast Asia. The country could then use funds accrued

191

from the Vietnam War surtax to fight poverty in a radical and effective fashion.[80] His fellow New York senator, Jacob Javits, also took issue with the need for a work requirement.[81] Such dissent from progressives, coupled with conservative concerns, meant that coalescing Republicans behind FAP, let alone gaining support from the Democrats, was not an easy task for the White House. Prophetically, Don Webster, the Nixon aide who had attended the dispiriting February meeting, mused that 'I can visualise a situation where misgivings arising from both the left and the right could combine in such a way to cause the bill to be defeated.'[82]

It was therefore a considerable victory when the White House did manage to successfully move FAP through the House. Partly, this was a result of time Nixon personally spent wooing the powerful Democratic Chairman of Ways and Means, Wilbur Mills (D-AK). Having initially opposed FAP, the conservative Mills became a staunch advocate, and worked hard in tandem with his Republican counterpart, Byrnes, to report the bill out of committee.[83] In April, before the final vote, the House Republican Policy Committee (HRPC) endorsed the bill in a statement that was more of a damning indictment of the present welfare system than a hearty FAP endorsement.[84] Ford's leadership and stature as a solid stalwart Republican helped bring along every other GOP representative, with the exception of conservatives. The final vote tally was a comfortable 243–155 in FAP's favour.

In this moment of triumph for Nixon, however, his White House showed an unwillingness to put in the hard yards with Congress that was required to see the bill become law. Responding to an internal memo urging Nixon to call Byrnes, Ford and Mills to thank them for their efforts, an angry Haldeman scrawled in response: 'calls not made. [The President] will not keep calling the same people over and over to thank them for doing what it is their job to do'.[85] Sensing the need for Nixon's leadership to secure FAP, Moynihan implored his boss to take 'personal charge of the effort to get Family Assistance through the Senate'.[86] Moynihan, clearly desperate to see FAP enacted, told Nixon that the entire legacy of his first term in office hung in the balance as the Senate began considering FAP in May.

Hitting the buffers

In 1970, Republican Senator John J. Williams, known simply as 'Honest John', was in his twenty-fourth and final year representing Delaware in the upper chamber. Williams's voting record resembled a typical stalwart Republican: steadfastly opposed to federal government expansion but willing to tolerate it when necessary, such as in the case of the Civil Right Act. What stood Williams – a respected and feared senator – apart was his dual reputation for rooting out government corruption coupled with a fierce fiscal conservatism. If the federal government was spending a dollar, Williams wanted to know who was receiving it, and he was willing to devote time and energy to finding out. He was a principled politician, to the extent that when he pressed unsuccessfully for a law that would have forced elected officials to retire at the age of 65, he still announced his own impending retirement when he turned 65 in 1969. Williams had also, since 1964, been a fierce foe of the War on Poverty. He viewed the OEO as a corrupt organisation doling out patronage to Democratic supporters. Most notably, he had embarrassed the OEO during Sargent Shriver's tenure over its footing the bill for staff tuxedos.[87] Yet, while Williams's antipathy for LBJ's War on Poverty might have led him to support Nixon's new Republican antipoverty effort, he was equally unimpressed with FAP. With his career nearing an end, defeating FAP proved Williams's last battle.

Crucially, Williams sat on the Senate Finance Committee (SFC), which among its many powers was the ability to decide FAP's fate. Without a majority of the seventeen committee members, FAP would not reach the Senate floor, a larger arena in which commentators speculated that the bill had a decent chance of passage.[88] The liberal columnist Tom Wicker observed of the SFC's make-up that it was 'dominated by a bipartisan conservative majority just to the right of Genghis Khan'.[89] Moreover, of the Republican members, Wicker deemed them (not entirely unfairly), 'a collection of conservatives that would make [former Republican President] Rutherford B. Hayes turn pale'.[90] The seven Republicans hailed respectively from Arizona, Delaware, Idaho, Iowa, Nebraska, Utah and Wyoming. While these states had on occasion elected a populist Democrat, they were mostly bastions of conservative Republicanism, and among the most sceptical states of federal social welfare policies. With regard to FAP, these Republican members were particularly concerned that Nixon's proposal, in contrast to the administration's own sales pitch, would disincentivise work and lead to more, not fewer, Americans existing on welfare alone.[91]

Meanwhile, the Democratic make-up of the committee was also unfavourable to FAP. Half of the ten Democrats – including Chairman Russell Long – were from the South, a region famous for its welfare parsimony. As Republican strategist Kevin Phillips observed, the southern elite were concerned that FAP would play havoc with their socioeconomic future. By placing more money in the hands of the millions of poor workers who laboured for a small wage, southern senators feared FAP would hit the region with a double economic whammy – triggering sharp inflation and bankrupting local businesses unable to prosper in a higher-wage economy. Moreover, while it went unsaid, conservative southerners were likely unenthused by the prospect of millions of poor black southerners suddenly receiving a substantial income boost. Of the other Democrats, some were fervent liberals, such as Abraham Ribicoff (D-CT) and Eugene McCarthy (D-MN), who were loath to help the President and wanted a much higher income floor than £1,600 for a family of four. Summing up the bipartisan challenge facing FAP, Long told reporters, after the Nixon programme's first SFC hearing in May, 'Why don't we just junk the whole thing and start all over again?' The ranking Republican, Clifford Hansen (R-WY), replied: 'Mr Chairman, I'd like to offer my bipartisan support.'[92] The SFC, in the space of one day, sent the bill back to the White House for a rethink.

Facing such opposition meant that passing FAP required a White House at the top of its legislative game. There were arms that needed twisting, promises of White House help at election time forthcoming, and appeals to party loyalty proffered with the right amount of implicit threat. The Nixon administration, however, was entirely unprepared for FAP's frosty reception. In a remarkably candid and revealing memo to Nixon, Moynihan admitted that no one involved in managing FAP's passage 'really knows the Senate'.[93] Such naivety revealed itself in committee hearings, where one SFC member called the administration's FAP testimony as 'the most ill-prepared presentation I've heard since I've been in Congress'. The White House was also blindsided by Williams's damaging revelation that, under FAP, a family in New York could receive $7,615 without a single member of the family working. Devastatingly, Williams asked how the government could pay a non-working family such an amount and then 'ask a postman to go out and deliver the mail for $7,000 or $8,000?'[94] Moynihan confessed that – while such an example was rare – the White House could not entirely refute Williams's charges. '[FAP's opponents] are right,' Moynihan grumbled to Nixon, 'welfare is crazy. If you can manage to get on all the right programs, there is a tremendous disincentive to work.'[95]

Belatedly, Nixon sought to recapture lost FAP momentum. In response to the SFC's actions, a White House group was formed to revise the proposal, and then in a June announcement he sought to please both conservatives and liberals. Acknowledging conservative concerns, the President announced that FAP had been revised to strengthen the work requirement, while the White House had removed a special dispensation for single fathers about which the SFC senators had expressed concern. For liberals, he announced a wider agenda to supplement FAP, including reforms to expand and strengthen health care for the poor under Medicaid, as well as more generous access to food stamps and housing.[96] Also, by reorganising how these programmes were administered, the White House hoped to minimise the type of embarrassing examples that Williams had raised in committee.[97] Having said his piece, Nixon once again dispatched Agnew to do some 'missionary work' with conservatives. Nixon wanted his VP to convince recalcitrant Republicans, who were sceptical of Nixon's own commitment to the bill, that FAP was the administration's most important domestic initiative. The President confided that he had been advised that a sufficient number of Democrats on the SFC would support FAP, if only enough Republicans were won over and could thus provide bipartisan political cover.[98]

Agnew's efforts proved futile. When in July the SFC began reconsidering FAP, it quickly became clear that the Republican members remained the 'major obstacle' to White House success. Elliot Richardson, the new HEW Secretary, briefed the President that only Utah's Wallace Bennett – whom one journalist deemed a 'benevolent Mormon just slightly to the left of [ruthless Gilded Age financier] Jay Gould' – was supportive. Richardson believed that Williams especially was immovable in his opposition and was using every trick to stymie FAP.[99] With the midterm elections fast approaching, time was not on the administration's side if it hoped to trumpet welfare reform during the campaign. In a last-ditch effort to extricate FAP from the SFC, Nixon invited the rebellious Republicans to the White House for some presidential wooing. By stressing the strong work incentives within the trappings of 1600 Pennsylvania Avenue, the administration believed the President had successfully converted a few wavering Republicans into firm supporters.[100]

Such hopes proved wildly naive when, in October, FAP was defeated resoundingly by a 14–1 SFC margin. Every Republican present, including the previously supportive Bennett, voted against their own president's new war on poverty. In the *New York Times*, Warren Weaver credited Williams with having 'managed to hold all his fellow Republicans in line against the Republican Administration bill'.[101] Moreover, the Nixon White House had not been helped by high-profile scepticism emanating from Republican governors. Most notably, despite Nixon's personal appeal the previous year, Reagan publicly condemned FAP as 'costly and unworkable'. Reagan claimed that it would result in almost 3 million more Golden State welfare recipients, at an exorbitant cost to the taxpayer.[102] It was not just Reagan, however; several Republican governors of mixed ideological and geographical backgrounds expressed hostility to FAP, some of whom shared their concerns in SFC testimony.[103] On FAP, on his new antipoverty effort, the President increasingly resembled a lone figure without a party.

Midterm stalemate

Despite congressional failure, Nixon was not shy of advocating for welfare reform when he toured the country endorsing Republicans before the November elections. At various campaign stops, including for Minority Leader Hugh Scott, he trumpeted the Republican candidate's help in trying to pass FAP. In the *New York Times*, Weaver observed that 'President Nixon is campaigning more strenuously for his welfare reform program now than he did when it stood a chance of Congressional approval before the election.'[104] While this observation is a touch harsh given Nixon's noted interventions during FAP's struggles, it is hard to entirely dismiss Weaver's assertion that the President was happier to have the welfare issue rather than the new welfare bill on the campaign trail.

Interestingly, Nixon's use of FAP as a campaign issue was part of his strategy to make the election a cultural, rather than economic, clash between the two parties. In attempting to assemble his Silent Majority voters to speak loudly at the ballot box, Nixon riled up audiences with an appeal to stay the course in Vietnam, to oppose Democrats for being soft on law and order, and finally, he made consistent pleas for welfare reform. His calls for FAP were always wrapped in language that implicitly condemned welfare recipients and stressed the workfare element of his proposal. Gone, it seemed, was the Richard Nixon of 1969, who wanted acclaim as the innovator who boldly tackled poverty more effectively than Democrats. Nixon now appealed directly to the resentment that many Americans harboured for welfare recipients. The *US News & World Report* observed that in his tour of the country endorsing Republican candidates, 'Mr. Nixon can always count on a tremendous response when . . . he denounces "a system that makes it more advantageous for a man not to work than to work".' The line worked well with 'working-class people [who] show resentment of welfare, Medicaid, and poverty programs'.[105] If the campaign held any signs for the future, the portents were not encouraging for the retention of the antipoverty impulse in the White House.

The midterm results resembled a stalemate. A solitary Republican net gain in the Senate was offset by an overall loss of twelve House seats and the Democrats emerging with eleven more gubernatorial mansions. The results reaffirmed the Republican Party's standing as the minority in Congress for the foreseeable future. One might argue, however, that the results were more impressive when put into context. Nixon avoided the drastic midterm losses that many Presidents suffer in their first term. Particularly impressive, when one considers that the Republicans had picked up fifty-two House seats and eight Senate seats in the previous two cycles, and thus, by the laws of political science, were exposed to some districts swinging back to the Democrats. The only route to Republican gains would have been through the South, but that region's voters – for reasons ranging from tradition to congressional power – were unwilling to abandon incumbent Democrats, even if they would happily vote for a Republican president. Moreover, Nixon achieved this limited success without having any landmark domestic achievements, without peace or imminent victory in Vietnam, and with the signs of a worsening economic environment becoming more apparent as the year wore on.[106] His strategy – to make sure the Silent Majority voter turned up and ticked their box 'Republican' – perhaps helped stave off more dramatic losses.

Nevertheless, Nixon was irate at the results. Rather than Democrats, it was his own Republican Party at which he aimed most opprobrium. In a six-hour debrief with senior staff at his holiday home in Key Biscayne, Nixon raged at targets extending from the RNC, to poor Republican candidates, to underperforming cabinet members in the administration. Perhaps unburdening himself of pent-up annoyance for their FAP opposition, Nixon also declared 'we should stop playing to the Governors. They are our enemies.' Revealing of his continued worries regarding GOP vulnerabilities since the Great Depression, he believed that the worsening economy had been especially tricky for a Republican administration, noting that 'the mythology of the Republican Party handling the unemployment issue is tough to overcome'. He believed that by personally campaigning on cultural issues – what Nixon called 'the social issue' – he had stemmed the tide of Republican defeats.

Looking ahead, Nixon told his lieutenants that it was time to 'start playing rougher with Congress'. He envisioned that the Democrats would push more new spending proposals and new programmes, and that he was happy to draw a contrast by appealing to fiscal sanity. Moreover, predicting the Vietnam War's imminent conclusion, he believed the economic issue would be key in the upcoming presidential election.[107] As such, while the Nixon administration would continue to try and pass FAP over the following year, it is hard to convincingly argue that the President's heart was truly in the issue. From the 1970 midterms onwards, the Republican challenge to the War on Poverty – which had undergone a surprising twist during the first two years of Nixon's tenure – was returning to a more predictable course. In December, Moynihan left the White House, and with him he took the administration's focus on the issue of poverty.

Conclusion

In April 1970, with FAP having passed the House and appearing to stand a good chance in the Senate, Nixon was exultant at a widely syndicated column, written by Roscoe Drummond, which appeared under the title 'Nixon and the Poor'. In the article, Drummond lavished praised on the President and warned readers, 'Don't try to pin a cliché-label on Richard Nixon. It won't stick.' Observing that both the extreme left and the far right were unhappy with Nixon's approach, Drummond purred that 'the first activist Republican president since Teddy Roosevelt is saying less and doing more to remove the blight of poverty in the US than his predecessors'. Predicting that FAP would become Nixon's capstone accomplishment, the columnist concluded, 'There is no thundering rhetoric from the White House on a "war against poverty", but it is already evident that action is exceeding promises.'[108] Nixon was so pleased with the column that he personally wrote to Drummond expressing his appreciation.[109] More importantly, he had both Republican Congressional and Senate Campaign Committees send the article to all Republican candidates and state chairmen for use in their upcoming midterm campaigns.[110] Despite such enthusiasm on the President's part, it is likely that most of those mailings – save for those that were sent to progressive and moderate Republican candidates – ended up in the nearest waste disposal. In the end, it was primarily conservative and stalwart Republican senators, egged on by scepticism among Republican governors and House members, that ensured that FAP never became a reality. One might suggest that Nixon was unlucky in the SFC's ideological make-up, but in truth, the majority Republican sentiment won out. Moreover, the White House's inept strategy for cajoling congressional Republicans had hardly helped. Overall, FAP's defeat is unsurprising if put in the context of Republican opposition to the original War on Poverty, which was always the majority sentiment in the GOP since 1964.

It makes perfect sense that Nixon got out ahead of his party; he was acutely aware that he – the first twentieth-century president to arrive in the White House without his party in control of either congressional chamber – was more popular than the wider GOP. In offering FAP, Nixon was attempting to win voters that he believed were within his reach if he avoided the anti-Republican stereotypes of negativism and privilege. Part of this gambit was to bring the traditionally Democratic white working class into the War on Poverty, through the inclusion of a government income for the working poor. His failure to convince conservative Republicans to toe this line suggested that any chance Nixon had of realigning such voters to the GOP banner more permanently was diminished – at least in the short term.

As it happened, FAP's failure was not disastrous for Republicans. Nixon's initial approach to the War on Poverty showed that while Lyndon Johnson may have left the White House, the Great Society's spirit lived on for at least another two years. Whether through political calculation or out of a genuine desire to help the poor, Nixon's two main decisions stood in contrast to his previous War on Poverty opposition: he saved the OEO and proposed FAP. Had FAP passed the Senate in 1970, the federal government would have been in charge of not one War on Poverty, but two. Nevertheless, with worsening economic news on the horizon, the era of Great Society liberalism – of belief in government social programmes as solutions to problems, fuelled by the funds of American prosperity – was about to ebb. And with it, Republican opposition to the War on Poverty was on the cusp of being accelerated. As FAP faded into the rear-view mirror, Nixon – spurred on by conservative Republicans – was the politician with his foot on the pedal.

Notes

1. Richard M. Nixon, 'Statement about House Approval of the Family Assistance Act of 1970', 16 April 1970, TAPP.
2. Garry Wills, *Nixon Agonistes: The Crisis of the Self-Made Man* (Boston, MA: Mariner, 2002); Iwan Morgan, *Nixon* (New York: Arnold, 2002); Mason, *Richard Nixon and the Quest.*
3. Scott J. Spitzer, 'Nixon's New Deal: Welfare Reform for the Silent Majority', *Presidential Studies Quarterly*, vol. 42, no. 3 (2012); Thurber, *Republicans and Race*, 341.
4. RMN quoted in Morgan, *Nixon*, 67.
5. Davies, *From Opportunity to Entitlement*; Alex Waddan, 'A Liberal in Wolf's Clothing: Nixon's Family Assistance Plan in the Light of 1990s Welfare Reform', *Journal of American Studies*, vol. 32, no. 2 (August 1998), 203–18.
6. Gerald Hursh to Orville Freeman, 'Accomplishments and Failures of the Johnson Administration', 12 October 1968, Polls, Box 148.B.15.9B, Papers of Hubert H. Humphrey, Minnesota Historical Society.
7. Both polls in Reichley, *Conservatives in an Age of Change*, 171–2.
8. Many historians have cited the Democratic majority as a key explanation for Nixon's activist presidency. This is not entirely convincing; the 91st Congress was barely different in its composition from the 90th Congress that had become decidedly prickly towards any further advancements in Johnson's Great Society.
9. Kabaservice, *Rule and Ruin*, 272.
10. Ibid. 253.
11. Nixon was more wary of high-profile governors, such as Ronald Reagan and Nelson Rockefeller, and therefore allowed small changes to his antipoverty policies in an effort to keep such figures from launching a future primary challenge.
12. Daniel P. Moynihan [hereafter DPM] to RMN, 15 December 1969, box 52, WHCF Welfare, RMN.
13. DPM to RMN, 1969, box 46, WHSF, SMOF, HRH Alpha Name Files, HRH Cabinet Notes, RMN.
14. Arthur Burns, *Inside the Nixon Administration: The Secret Diary of Arthur Burns* (Lawrence, KS: University Press of Kansas, 2010), 12.
15. H. R. Haldeman to DPM, 17 February 1969, box 46, WHSF, SMOF, HRH Alpha Name Files, HRH Cabinet Notes.
16. Donald H. Rumsfeld [hereafter DHR] to RMN, 4 April 1969, OEO, Donald H. Rumsfeld Papers.

17. Kabaservice, *Rule and Ruin*, 253.
18. RMN to George P. Shultz and Robert H. Finch, 1 February 1969, box 52, WHCF Welfare, RMN.
19. RMN, Special Message to the Congress on the Nation's Antipoverty Programs, 19 February 1969, TAPP.
20. M. A. Farber, 'Head Start Report Held "Full of Holes",' *New York Times*, 17 April 1969.
21. Joseph Alsop, 'Reprisals Fear Spared OEO', *Washington Post*, 24 February 1969.
22. John D. Ehrlichman [hereafter JDE], Notes of Meetings with the President, March 1969, box 3, WHSF, SMOF, RMN.
23. Robert E. Patricelli to JDE, 27 March 1969, box 58, WHCF Welfare, RMN.
24. Edward Morgan to JDE, 19 March 1969, box 59, WHCF Welfare, RMN.
25. Elizabeth Rose, 'Head Start: Growing Beyond the War on Poverty', in *LBJ's Neglected Legacy: How Lyndon Johnson Reshaped Domestic Policy and Government*, ed. Robert Wilson, Norman Glickman and Laurence Lynn Jr (Austin, TX: University of Texas Press, 2015), 153–86.
26. Cabinet Meeting, 19 December 1969, reel 7, folder 198, Papers of the Nixon White House, Roosevelt Study Center.
27. James W. Button, *Black Violence: Political Impact of the 1960s Riots* (Princeton, NJ: Princeton University Press, 1978), 48–9.
28. Rowland Evans and Robert D. Novak, 'Administration is Losing Interest in Nixon's Black Capitalism idea', *Washington Post*, 14 August 1969; '"Black Capitalism" Now: Success or Failure?' *US News & World Report*, 23 November 1970; Kotlowski, *Nixon's Civil Rights*; Mehrsa Baradaran, 'A Bad Check for Black America', *Boston Review*, 9 November 2017.
29. Robert Taft Jr to Robert P. Mayo, 30 June 1969, box 52, WHCF Welfare, RMN.
30. WH Internal Correspondence regarding Pete McCloskey Inner-City Ghetto Program, 5 June 1969, box 52, WHCF Welfare, RMN.
31. Alexander P. Butterfield to DPM, 27 March 1969, box 52, WHCF Welfare, RMN.
32. Morgan, *Nixon*, 67–94.
33. Daniel P. Moynihan, *The Politics of a Guaranteed Income: The Nixon Administration and the Family Assistance Plan* (New York: Vintage, 1973), 190.

34. RMN to Senior Staff, 15 January 1969, box 46, WHSF, SMOF, HRH Alpha Name Files, HRH Cabinet Notes, RMN.
35. Graham quoted in AFB to RMN, 23 June 1969, box 59, WE; DPM to RMN, 17 May 1969, box 46, WHSF, SMOF, HRH Alpha Name Files, HRH Cabinet Notes, RMN.
36. Daniel K. Williams, *God's Own Party: The Making of the Christian Right* (New York: Oxford University Press, 2010).
37. DPM quoted in Steven R. Weisman, *Daniel Patrick Moynihan: A Portrait in Letters of An American Visionary* (New York: Perseus, 2010), 168.
38. Perlstein, *Nixonland*.
39. DPM to RMN, 26 March 1969, box 52, WE, RMN.
40. John D. Ehrlichman, *Witness to Power: The Nixon Years* (New York: Simon & Schuster, 1982), 219.
41. Burns, *Secret Diary*, 7.
42. AFB to HRH, 22 February 1969, box 52, WE, RMN.
43. Burns, *Secret Diary*, 19–21; Ehrlichman, *Witness to Power*, 219.
44. Bryce Harlow to JDE, 28 July 1969, box 60, WHCF WE, RMN.
45. DPM to RMN, 23 April 1969, box 59, WHCF WE, RMN.
46. NAR to RMN, 14 July 1969, box 60, WHCF WE, RMN.
47. John Price to DPM, 29 July 1969, box 60, WHCF WE, RMN.
48. Scott Kaufman, *Ambition, Pragmatism, and Party: A Political Biography of Gerald R. Ford* (Lawrence, KS: University Press of Kansas, 2017), 141.
49. RMN, Address to the Nation on Domestic Programs, 8 August 1969, TAPP.
50. NAR, Staff Memo on Negative Income Tax, 24 May 1968, box 1, series j.3, RG 4, NAR.
51. RMN, 8 Aug 1969.
52. While Nixon was successful in passing Revenue Sharing, its effects were minimal and it was not the panacea for transforming power from the federal government to the states that many Republicans in the 1960s had hoped.
53. John R. Brown to HRH, 23 August 1969; Art Klebanoff to DPM, 5 September 1969, box 60, WHFC WE, RMN; Anon., 'The Family Assistance Plan: A Chronology', *Social Service Review*, vol. 46, no. 4 (1972), 604.
54. William Crafton, 'The Incremental Revolution: Ronald Reagan and Welfare Reform in the 1970s', *Journal of Policy History*, vol. 26, no. 1 (2014), 32.

55. Marjorie Hunter, 'Parties' Leaders Support Program: But Some Reservations are Expressed in Congress', *New York Times*, 9 August 1969; Sylvan Fox, 'Rockefeller Calls Nixon's Proposal Unfair to State', *New York Times*, 11 August 1969.
56. For more on liberal Democrats and FAP, see Davies, *From Opportunity to Entitlement*.
57. RMN, Statement on the Office of Economic Opportunity, 11 August 1969, TAPP.
58. DHR, Speech in Receiving the George Catlett Marshall Medal, 17 October 1984, Rumsfeld Papers.
59. Jack Anderson, 'Anti-Poverty Czar Embellishes Office', *Washington Post*, 22 September 1969.
60. Carl Perkins to RMN, 9 June and 14 June 1969; RMN to Perkins, 22 September 1969; Perkins to RMN, 8 October 1969, box 52, WHCF WE, RMN.
61. Harlow to Bill Timmons, 28 November 1969, box 52, WHCF WE, RMN; Richard Lyons, 'Poverty Act Extended by House', *Washington Post*, 13 December 1969.
62. Rumsfeld to Moynihan, 4 November 1969, box 36, WHCF SMOF, John Price, RMN.
63. Lyons, 'Poverty Act Extended'.
64. Rowland Evans and Robert D. Novak, 'Nixon's Treatment of Rumsfeld a Symbol of Party Polarization', *Washington Post*, 15 December 1969.
65. Lyons, 'Poverty Act Extended'.
66. Evans and Novak, 'Nixon's Treatment'.
67. RMN, 'Annual Message to the Congress on the State of the Union', 22 January 1970, TAPP.
68. RMN, 'Address to the Nation on the War in Vietnam', 3 November 1969, TAPP.
69. Mary McGrory, 'Nixon and Family Assistance', *Sunday Star*, 25 January 1970.
70. RMN to Spiro T. Agnew, 22 July 1970, box 61, WHCF Welfare, RMN.
71. Evan Thomas, *Being Nixon: A Man Divided* (New York: Random House, 2015), 250.
72. John R. Brown to Ehrlichman, 5 February 1970, box 61, WHCF Welfare, RMN.
73. Bill Timmons to Moynihan, 12 January 1970, WHCF Welfare, RMN.
74. Ed Morgan to Don Webster, 20 February 1970, WHCF Welfare, RMN.

75. Ibid., 21 February 1970.
76. Harlow to Staff Secretary, 26 January 1970, WHCF Welfare, RMN.
77. Agnew, 19th National Congressional Banquet, Order of Ahepa, Sheraton Park Hotel, DC, 9 March 1968, box 61, WHCF Welfare, RMN.
78. Don Webster to Ed Morgan, 27 February 1970, box 61, WHCF Welfare, RMN.
79. Utt quoted in ibid.
80. 'Goodell Hits Nixon on Welfare', *Washington Post*, 30 March 1970.
81. Davies, *From Opportunity to Entitlement*, 237.
82. Don Webster to Ed Morgan, 27 February 1970.
83. Ed Morgan to Don Webster, 26 March 1970.
84. House Republican Policy Committee Statement on H.R. 16311, 7 April 1970, box 61, WHCF Welfare, RMN.
85. Dwight Chapin to Haldeman, May 1970, box 61, WHCF Welfare, RMN.
86. Moynihan to RMN, 11 May 1970, box 61, WHCF Welfare, RMN.
87. John Williams, Senate Debate on the Economic Opportunity Act, *Congressional Record*, 18 August 1965.
88. Worth Bateman and Alice M. Rivlin, 'Mr Nixon's Welfare Plan', *Washington Post*, 16 August 1970.
89. Tom Wicker, 'The Welfare Crunch', *New York Times*, 6 December 1970.
90. Tom Wicker, 'In the Nation: Family Assistance in Need of Help', *New York Times*, 9 July 1970.
91. Elliot Richardson to RMN, 8 August 1970, box 61, WHCF Welfare, RMN.
92. Frank Porter, 'Rewrite Welfare Bill', *Washington Post*, 1 May 1970.
93. Moynihan to RMN, 11 May 1970.
94. Porter, 'Rewrite Welfare Bill'.
95. Moynihan to RMN, 11 May 1970.
96. For more on various Nixon antipoverty initiatives, see McAndrews, *The Presidents and the Poor*, 33–58.
97. RMN, Statement by the President on Welfare Reform, 10 June 1970, TAPP.
98. RMN to Agnew, 22 July 1970.
99. Elliot Richardson to RMN, 8 August 1970.
100. Alexander P. Butterfield to RMN, 10 August 1970, box 61 WHCF Welfare, RMN.

101. Warren Weaver Jr, 'Welfare Not Dead But It's Breathing Hard', *New York Times*, 18 October 1970.
102. Warren Weaver Jr, 'Moynihan Says Nixon Limits Welfare Bill Revision', *New York Times*, 6 May 1970.
103. Ken Ringle, 'Governors Wary of Nixon Welfare Bill', *Washington Post*, 11 September 1970.
104. Warren Weaver Jr, 'Nixon Campaigns on Welfare Issue', *Washington Post*, 21 October 1970.
105. 'Nixon's Last-Minute Push for a Republican Victory' and 'Campaign Wind-Up', *US News & World Report*, 2 November 1970.
106. Kevin P. Phillips, 'Deficit and Family Aid', *Washington Post*, 14 August 1970.
107. Confidential Memo, Key Biscayne Meeting, 7 November 1970, Rumsfeld Papers.
108. Roscoe Drummond, 'Nixon and the Poor', *Christian Science Monitor*, April 1970.
109. RMN to Drummond, 20 April 1970, box 52, WHCF Welfare.
110. Harry Dent to John Brown, 9 April 1970, box 52.

6

The conservative turn: Nixon, Ford and the beginning of the end, 1971–76

We don't even call it a War on Poverty any more. The antipoverty campaign has never recovered from Nixon.[1]

John Macomber, Community Services Administration
spokesperson, 1980

During his first two years in office, Richard Nixon had saved one War on Poverty and attempted to launch another of his own. In the final three and a half years of his abortive presidency, he abandoned both. By August 1974, when a disgraced Nixon turned to onlookers and defiantly staged one last 'V for Victory' pose as he boarded the helicopter that would usher him out of national political life, antipoverty workers at the Office of Economic Opportunity (OEO) were all but defeated. Meanwhile, advocates of the departing president's Family Assistance Plan (FAP) were left wondering whether Nixon had ever truly believed in his own signature policy in domestic affairs, such was the haste and contempt with which he abandoned it. The reforming President who had attempted to drag his recalcitrant Republican Party to a position of advocating a government-led gambit to end poverty, began, in 1971, to evolve into a typical conservative Republican opponent of such an effort. By the end, he was a full-blown cheerleader in the war on the War on Poverty.

If analysed through the prism of poverty politics, Nixon's presidency experienced an early and decisive conservative turn that is misunderstood in historiographical reassessments that position Nixon as a liberal, reformist president in domestic policy. Since 1995, when historian Joan Hoff began a needed reconsideration of

Nixon's presidency, which had too long been shrouded by historians' loathing for a president who wantonly violated the rule of law
to the point that he had to resign to avoid impeachment, an emphasis has been placed on Nixon's embrace of government activism. If
a conservative turn away from this activism is acknowledged, then
most historians place the shift in 1973, following Nixon's landslide victory over Democratic candidate George McGovern.[2] Yet,
regarding the War on Poverty, it is clear that Nixon's conservative
shift began as early as 1971.

During this time, Nixon still espoused activist rhetoric – most
notably with his advocacy for a 'New American Revolution' – but
in private he was already voicing his reluctance to fund Johnson's
War on Poverty or to continue to fight for the passage of his own.
In August 1971, he publicly called a halt to FAP – essentially ending its chances of congressional success – and by the end of the
year he had delivered the first ever veto of the Economic Opportunity Act (EOA). To be sure, Nixon's conservatism with regard
to poverty programmes accelerated after his re-election, when he
actively sought stories to discredit the OEO in a successful effort
to scrap the agency. Meanwhile, he grew irate with anyone in his
administration who clung to hopes that FAP might one day be
realised. Nevertheless, this behaviour merely continued a trend
that had manifested during the final years of his first term.

Nixon's conservative turn was just one of the many challenges
that the War on Poverty faced during the 1970s. His successor,
Gerald Ford – who had voted against and campaigned in opposition to the War on Poverty during the 1960s – showed little interest
in resuscitating the OEO or in launching any new antipoverty ventures. Beyond presidential politics, the Republican Party's increasing
capture by conservatism as the decade wore on intensified opposition to the antipoverty effort from the GOP congressional caucus.
A new breed of congressional Democrats, bemused by the Great
Society's failings, were also less willing to go to the mat for the War
on Poverty in the face of Republican attacks. Finally, the socioeconomic context of the 1970s further hamstrung antipoverty efforts,
as concerns over inflation, unemployment and taxation increased,
at the same time as the threat of urban uprisings that had spurred
action in the late 1960s receded. This shift in context meant that

ending the War on Poverty became a less politically toxic position for Republicans to hold. For the first time since Johnson launched the antipoverty effort, most Republicans found that their pragmatic and ideological motivations were finally aligned.

Abandoning the Family Assistance Plan

Richard Nixon began the year 1971 with soaring activist rhetoric that hid the reality of his conservative shift. During his State of the Union address, Nixon challenged Congress to join him in enacting six 'great goals' that, if achieved, would lead to a 'new American revolution'. Priority number one, Nixon told both chambers, was to enact his FAP. Part of his domestic plan and another 'great goal' was for Congress to pass revenue sharing legislation and thus provide state and local governments with more funding to provide services, including antipoverty measures, for their own populations as they saw fit.[3] All in all, Nixon proscribed an aggressively activist governing agenda that belied his Republican label.

Nixon's oration was so convincing that many in Congress believed that the President's reaction to the disappointment of the 1970 elections was to move decisively to the left on domestic issues. Conservative Republicans, in particular, listened in horror as their own president outlined an activist agenda that would – in their view – drain the federal coffers, while simultaneously adding millions to the welfare rolls. To them, the President was abandoning the conservative GOP base that provided the money and activism that had helped him over the line in 1968. Nixon only confirmed such fears when he met with congressional Republicans in early 1971 and, in a bid to boost morale after the midterm disappointment, urged them to embrace an activist agenda. Reaching far back in GOP history, Nixon told the Republican gathering that – for the first time since Teddy Roosevelt's progressive heyday – 'it is we who stand for sweeping change, we who stand for restoring power to the people'.[4] While Nixon tried to emphasise the state and local government focus of his reforms, his choice of former president was a misstep: Roosevelt, who remained a hero to progressive Republicans, was not the best figure to rally conservative Republicans who were more likely to long for the days of Calvin Coolidge.

209

Such was the concern among elected conservatives about Nixon's apparent move to the left that they began to organise themselves to fight it. In the Senate, Carl Curtis – a key foe of FAP – formed the Steering Committee, with the goal of growing conservative influence in Senate business. The move followed on from similar steps among conservative House Republicans who had watched askance as their GOP brethren – stalwarts included – voted for FAP in 1970. Following on from that vote, key conservatives such as Phil Crane (R-IL), Edward Derwinski (R-IL) and John Ashbrook (R-OH) founded the Republican Study Committee with the goals of coordinating votes and legislation, reaching out to conservative academics, and getting directly involved in elections.[5] The latter goal was quickly evident when Ashbrook emerged in 1971 to challenge Nixon from the right in the upcoming GOP primaries. While Ashbrook offered a wide-ranging critique of Nixon, he guaranteed he would pull out of the race if Nixon dropped FAP.[6] Ashbrook's challenge, which also stemmed from foreign policy concerns, was weak – he would barely break 10 per cent in the New Hampshire primary – but his presence on the ballot was a reminder to Nixon that he could not ignore a Republican Party that was shifting ever rightward.

Nixon's move to the left, however, was a facade. In 1969 and early 1970, Nixon had genuinely toyed with bold reforms – none more so than FAP. Nonetheless, as the economic conditions began to worsen throughout 1970, in private the President began to sound an increasingly conservative note when in the presence of fellow conservatives. In July, Chief of Staff H. R. Haldeman confided in his diary that his boss hoped that the Democrats would kill FAP as it was no longer affordable.[7] Moreover, following the 1970 elections, Nixon delighted his former adviser – and chief FAP opponent internally – Arthur Burns when he told the now Federal Reserve chair that the administration planned to scrap all federal grant-in-aid programmes. Such a move would have effectively ended Johnson's War on Poverty.[8] Nixon also had no belief that revenue sharing would help improve state and local governments deliver services. In December, prior to declaring it one of his six 'great goals', the President told his advisers, 'Let's not kid ourselves into thinking [revenue sharing's] a bold domestic program.'[9] In retrospect, it is fair to suggest that the last hope that progressive Republicans might have had for Nixon's administration was extinguished when Daniel Patrick Moynihan departed the White House at the end of 1970. Indeed, Abraham Ribicoff – a key liberal on the Senate committee that held FAP's fate in its hands – continued to believe years later that Nixon fully withdrew from the FAP battle following Moynihan's exit.[10]

Despite the President's shifting views, his administration publicly maintained its FAP pursuit throughout the first half of 1971. In the House, FAP was given first priority, apparent in the bill's name: H.R.1. Following negotiations between Republicans and Democrats, this new version of FAP had a higher minimum income floor of $2,400, although food stamps were factored into this floor unlike the prior version. Moreover, included in H.R.1 was a less controversial – but far reaching – proposal, the Supplemental Security Income (SSI), which would provide a guaranteed income to the aged, blind and disabled.[11] Such recipients were firmly in the 'deserving' category for Americans and thus aiding them was more acceptable for most politicians.

By June, the bill emerged from the House with an impressively increased majority (288–132) from the previous year's FAP vote. Minority Leader Gerald Ford continued to loyally follow (what he believed were) Nixon's wishes, and corralled Republican votes effectively in support of the measure. Nonetheless, even Ford's efforts almost came unstuck when an amendment to strike FAP from H.R.1 was defeated by a narrower margin (234–187). On this vote, Republicans only voted 93–83 in favour of FAP, as opposed to the two thirds who would go on to vote for the whole H.R.1 package.[12] In justifying their FAP support, House Republicans essentially argued that Nixon's proposal could not be any worse than the existing welfare system.[13] As such, Republican enthusiasm was lukewarm at best, as doubts about FAP's cost and implications for work persisted.

With momentum accrued from an increased House majority, FAP was sent to the Senate Finance Committee (SFC) that had ensured FAP's abrupt curtailment in the previous Congress. The bill's advocates could find optimism in the development that FAP's most implacable foe, Delaware's Republican senator, John Williams, had departed Congress. Still, Republicans who remained on the committee remained largely opposed and Democratic chair Russell Long (D-LA) was a continued sceptic of guaranteed income. Nonetheless, it is feasible that a united White House in pursuit of FAP could have built on momentum from the bill's success in the House and applied pressure to Republicans that their president – soon to be up for re-election – needed a key legislative success to stymie Democratic charges that the GOP remained a do-nothing party of big business. Passing FAP, in theory, could have prevented such a narrative re-emerging in 1972.

Some high-profile Republicans sought to aid Nixon's effort to reorient GOP messaging by boosting this line of argument. In July, new Republican National Committee (RNC) chair, Sen. Bob Dole (R-KS), boasted of the 'progressive, positive' welfare reforms being offered by Nixon. While Dole was ideologically a stalwart, and acknowledged that many of his fellow Republicans opposed FAP, he encouraged sceptics to put aside their concerns so that the party could do something about welfare.[14] Nelson Rockefeller, who had begun to tread a more conservative path on socioeconomic issues following a decade of progressive governance in New York, also implored the gathering to support the President's effort.[15] In a re-run of the 1964 Republican primary, Barry Goldwater – who had been returned to the Senate in 1968 – voiced his firm opposition to FAP. Even so, in an attempt to foster unity, Goldwater noted that the Democrats' alternative – 'keep insisting on more and more welfare handouts while cutting back on activities which provide jobs for American workmen' – was far worse. All in all, while conservative Republicans were irreconcilable on FAP, the President stood a decent chance of winning the other three Senate factions. Many Republicans, scarred by years of Democratic rule at both ends of Pennsylvania Avenue, had a strong electoral incentive to hold their nose on a programme about which they remained sceptical and loyally back their party leader. Such pragmatism had often defined the Republican response to the War on Poverty since 1964.

To everyone's surprise, with such deliberations ongoing, the President abruptly ended the debate. On 15 August, in addressing the American people, Nixon announced 'a new economic policy for the United States'. 'It's [*sic*] targets,' he outlined, 'are unemployment, inflation, and international speculation.' To tackle these issues, Nixon declared that he wanted tax cuts to stimulate economic growth and announced that he had ordered a $4.7 billion cut in federal spending, as well as instituting wage and price controls in certain industries, to control inflation. Furthermore, the dollar was to come off the gold standard. Most importantly for America's poor, he asked that consideration of FAP be suspended for one year (and revenue sharing similarly for three months).[16] In essence, the announcements meant that, over the course of one speech, as *Congressional Quarterly* observed, 'FAP went from being a "first priority" to a lost priority for Nixon.'[17]

The President's actions – which relied on Keynesian measures, such as tax cuts to stimulate growth and wage and price controls to fight inflation – encouraged conservative fears of Nixon's move to the left.[18] Politically, though, Nixon was doing the opposite; in abandoning FAP and shifting focus to combatting stagnant economic growth, as well as unemployment and inflation, he was moving the nation's socioeconomic discussion in a direction that benefited conservatives opposed to federal antipoverty measures. In Nixon's speech there was no talk of fighting poverty, as the President focused on preserving the earning power of working-class and middle-class Americans. It was a moment that forecast the political weather for the rest of the 1970s. The era of prosperity-fuelled Great Society liberalism was ebbing. Bold gambits at solving American poverty were no longer fashionable. Nixon – the president who had dreamed of presidential greatness through Disraelian-inspired help for the poor – was now moving the country in another direction. In postponing FAP, Nixon had purposely paused his own grand plan for American poverty. It was not, however, his only action that signalled a conservative shift in 1971.

Vetoing the Economic Opportunity Act

Nixon's growing conservatism was further evidenced by his increased determination to do away with the OEO. Stripped of many programmes in Nixon's 1969 reorganisation, the OEO faced more long-term challenges when the President announced his desire for a two-year extension for the OEO's funding with the understanding that his administration would accelerate 'reorganisation' – a word widely known in Congress to mean dismantling. Nixon's desire to see the end of the OEO was likely hastened by an awkward spat between his administration and California governor, Ronald Reagan, over the latter's desire to end an OEO-funded initiative in the Golden State. The Democratic Congress, however, had little desire to blithely follow Nixon's wishes, and despite howls of conservative Republican protest at the ineffectiveness of antipoverty programmes, countered the President's proposals with an increase in antipoverty funding while attempting to block the administration's proposed reorganisation. By the end of the year, progressives and conservatives in the Nixon administration were bitterly divided on whether the president should issue the first ever veto of the War on Poverty. Unsurprisingly, given his ideological shift, Nixon sided with the conservative voices.

While the OEO had survived Nixon's first two years, in the aftermath of the midterm elections it was quick to lose an influential director who had become a successful advocate for its programmes. One of Nixon's last acts of 1970 was to announce a replacement for Donald Rumsfeld, who became a key presidential adviser. The new OEO Director, Frank Carlucci, endured a short and controversial eight-month tenure. In what was dubbed a 'poverty cold war' between the White House and Sacramento, Carlucci and Reagan were at odds over the latter's desire to veto antipoverty funds for California Rural Legal Assistance (CRLA) – an OEO-funded initiative.[19] Under the antipoverty legislation, it was the OEO's prerogative to overrule Reagan, a decision to which Carlucci was inclined. The President, however, was less enthusiastic. Nixon, despite Reagan's guarantee in a January 1971 meeting that California's delegation would be united behind Nixon's renomination in 1972, clearly still feared the ramifications of an angered Reagan. With Nixon also not inclined to put his neck on the line for the OEO, columnists Evans and Novak reported that in a February meeting of the two high-profile Republicans, the President 'blinked in his high-noon staredown over poverty funds' with Reagan and resolved to put pressure on Carlucci to not overturn Reagan's veto.[20]

In the end, a compromise that pleased no one was reached. The OEO would continue to fund CRLA on a short-term basis, pending an investigation done by an independent commission. Nonetheless, within a few months, Reagan began attacking the commission and challenging its independence.[21] Later evidence suggested that CRLA had done little wrong and that Reagan had targeted the organisation to make a political point about his dislike of the War on Poverty.[22] This was little solace to Carlucci as he was quickly shifted to another administration post, with the White House protesting a little too much that it had nothing to do with the Reagan confrontation.[23] Carlucci would be replaced by Phillip Sanchez, whose tenure as OEO director was less controversial. The whole episode reinforced conservative Republican opposition to the OEO and the reluctance of Nixon to spend any political capital in repelling such disgruntlement.

Back in Congress, familiar partisan battle lines were drawn as Nixon's requests in April for a two-year extension to the EOA and more OEO reorganisation led to a long battle over the War on Poverty's future. Since the EOA first passed in 1964, it had been through four renewals – all of them contentious. The 1971 experience would be little different. In offering their criticisms, conservative and stalwart Republicans acknowledged that these were arguments that they had proffered before, but complaints that they believed experience of the antipoverty effort had borne out. In the House, Wilmer Mizell (R-NC), a conservative, excoriated the War on Poverty for overpromising the poor, and declared, 'I rise at this time, as I have on so many occasions in the past, to express my total and vigorous opposition to the continued existence of the Office of Economic Opportunity.' Mizell believed that not only was the OEO not helping the poor, but it was hurting them because 'the fact that as a result of OEO's controversial image, the generous compassion of many Americans has been seriously compromised'.[24] Of course, Mizell was less inclined to acknowledge the fastidious work that Republicans had done to stoke such controversy and distrust since 1964.

Just as predictable as Mizell's attack was the liberal Democratic counterattack that the antipoverty effort had greatly helped the poor. Indeed, one Democrat phrased his support in Republican language, declaring that the OEO had allowed thousands of people to bring themselves 'up by their own bootstraps'.[25] This rhetorical emphasis signalled that Democrats were increasingly on the defensive, aware that in many cases the public believed that the War on Poverty offered a free handout, rather than transitioning poor Americans into productive members of the workforce.

The 1971 renewal battle focused on three key issues: OEO reorganisation, legal services for the poor, and an ambitious new childcare programme. With regard to reorganisation, Nixon proposed that Community Action be transferred to the Office of Community Development in HUD, VISTA be merged with the Peace Corps, and legal services be run by a new, independent corporation. In this situation, the OEO would be left with little more than a scattering of small initiatives relating to Native Americans, migrants and health, as well as its research and development mission,[26] thus, making it easier to scrap the OEO altogether as it would have few constituencies left to defend it.

Democrats were quick to challenge the seemingly uncontroversial naming of 'reorganisation'. 'Why don't you say what you're doing?' California Democratic Rep. Augustus Hawkins asked the administration, 'You're dismantling OEO, stripping it of all its programs, and there won't be any agency to coordinate the programs for the poor.'[27] Democratic supporters of the antipoverty effort were right to be concerned. Nixon advocated a two-year extension as his advisers privately suggested it would be easier to shift programmes out of the OEO through executive action than by asking Congress to neuter the OEO.[28] Having got wind of this White House ruse, liberal Democrats in the Senate amended the renewal bill with a mechanism to prevent the administration from spinning off any OEO programmes to other departments.[29] Republicans – including progressives such as Jacob Javits, who sought to aid the White House – failed in their attempt to reverse such changes.[30] In the final legislation, OEO dismantling was decisively blocked.

Elsewhere, legal services acquired a new salience as a source of controversy. Most elected Republicans had always viewed the War on Poverty as a partisan effort, and many came to focus their ire on legal services as a hub of liberal attorneys who acted, Republicans accused, not on behalf of the poor, but at the behest of the Democratic Party. Indeed, it was no accident that Reagan had focused his White House confrontation on the CRLA, a legal services initiative, as opposed to another Californian CAA. In an attempt to placate Republicans, Democrats agreed to set up an independent legal corporation to continue to provide aid to the poor. Nonetheless, this did not satisfy most Republicans, who believed the corporation would be independent in name only. Nixon was also opposed, and demanded more power to appoint the directors of the corporation.[31] The legal services problem was unresolved in 1971, but was a reminder of the partisan hue that always coloured debates over the War on Poverty.

Finally, the most controversial aspect of EOA's renewal was the new Child Development provision for the poor that Democrats introduced to the legislation. Broadly modelled on Head Start, this ambitious programme would see states, cities and local governments provide a range of services – including day care, medical help, nutritional support – that would be free for very poor children, with the federal government footing 80 per cent of the bill. Attempting to force the President's hand, Democrats reminded Nixon of his first message on poverty, issued in February 1969, in which he had announced that his administration would focus antipoverty efforts on the 'First Five Years of Life'.[32] There was also some progressive Republican support for the measure, with Javits declaring during Senate debate that 'We have no right to pass a war-against-poverty bill at this stage of our national life without this child development title and the concept of child development.'[33]

Most Republicans did not echo such sentiments and firmly opposed the measure. Javits aside, Senate Republicans spent much of the debate in August and September voting to amend or recommit the bill to scrap the child development section. Most GOP concerns centred on the cost of the programme and also a fear that the federal government would be assuming an unhealthy role in a

217

child's life to the detriment of the parents. 'In the context of a Communist society, in which children are regarded as wards of the state and raised in state-controlled communes,' one Republican scolded, 'this scheme might be sensible.'[34] When Republicans failed to strike this provision from the final bill, which emerged from House–Senate Conference in November, many urged a presidential veto.

The prospect of a veto by Nixon aroused passions within his own administration. On the anti-veto side, new OEO Director Sanchez urged the President to consider the damage a veto would do to his carefully constructed public image as not a typical Republican. 'When we came into office many Americans felt that we would be insensitive and unresponsive to the needs of the poor,' Sanchez reminded Nixon, arguing that, 'In the past three years, we have been able to turn around many of these views.'[35] Meanwhile, Elliot Richardson, the moderate HEW secretary, followed the Democratic line of argument, highlighting that Congress was merely following Nixon's own 1969 call to focus on early life. Richardson believed that it would make Nixon look disingenuous if he vetoed EOA, and he also thought conservative claims of communist-like family planning were nonsense, as the programme was voluntary.[36] Echoing these sentiments, a mixture of ten House and Senate Republican progressives signed a joint letter urging the president to affix his signature to an expanded antipoverty effort.[37]

On the other side, Patrick Buchanan – a conservative aide with substantial influence in the Nixon administration – emerged as the key close advocate for vetoing EOA. Buchanan broke his argument into both ideological and nakedly pragmatic reasons. On the ideological side, Buchanan minced few words:

This [Child Development] boondoggle is the brainstorm of the mental health crowd and two individuals from the Commission on Children – whose objectives . . . are nothing less than removing the parent and instituting the state with primary responsibility for raising children. Here is something we can strangle in the crib, with a clearcut veto message.[38]

Buchanan also noted that conservative publications were extensively editorialising in support of a veto. Perhaps, however, the most convincing argument Buchanan advanced to Nixon was that it had little electoral benefit as the Child Development measure had 'no constituency which is ours'.[39] Namely, it would benefit the poor and minorities, whom Nixon did not view as gettable voters.

Nixon sided with Buchanan, and vetoed the legislation. In doing so, he cited three factors: the Child Development programme, the congressional restraints on his ability to reorganise the OEO and defund certain initiatives, and the proposal for an independent legal services corporation, which did not afford him enough power to appoint friendly directors. The bill was 'ill-conceived, unwieldy, unworkable, and exorbitantly expensive', press secretary Ron Zeigler said.[40] Meanwhile, Nixon received thanks from conservative Republicans, including Reagan, for vetoing.[41] The political tides, it appeared, were shifting in a conservative direction. The *New York Times* spoke to one former War on Poverty employee, who summed up the prevailing mood. 'The war against poverty is "no longer fashionable",' the official bemoaned, 'and attitudes about the poor "have never been so hostile."'

Poverty politics in the 1972 election

The 1972 presidential election was not defined by poverty politics. Instead, the conflicting antipoverty messages emerging from the two campaigns served to further cement the narrative that led to a landslide Nixon victory. Most historians and political scientists correctly assess that Sen. George McGovern's candidacy lurched too far left of the American electorate, both on domestic and foreign policy issues.[42] While poverty politics played little role in the autumn campaign – a dull affair with little excitement given Nixon's commanding polling lead – McGovern's bold antipoverty proposal in early 1972 was a key contributor in disqualifying him from the American mainstream. In offering his 'demogrant' – a proposal to guarantee $1,000 for every man, woman and child in the United States – McGovern misread the mood of a voting public that was tiring of Great Society liberalism in an era of emerging financial difficulties. Moreover, McGovern's demogrant played squarely into Nixon's successful strategy – borrowed from LBJ's successful duel with Goldwater eight years earlier – to define his opponent as too extreme to govern the United States.

McGovern's surprise capture of the Democratic nomination made Nixon's abandonment of FAP relatively easy. The South Dakotan had been an early and vigorous adopter of a generous guaranteed income. While in the Senate, he had quickly outbid Nixon's initial $1,600 offer, as well as going beyond the alternatives of most liberal Democrats. McGovern's initial proposal, the Office of Management and Budget (OMB) estimated, would likely have cost $20 billion per annum, and could have gone as high as $40 billion.[43] But, in January 1972, candidate McGovern went even further; promising his demogrant from the federal government.[44] While such a proposal may have held appeal for the 'New Politics' voters whom McGovern cultivated in his march to the nomination, it did not hold the same attraction for most Americans.

McGovern's proposal – with its vast financial outlay and lack of a work incentive – was the culmination of a long shift among many liberal Democrats, many of whom were disillusioned with the perceived ineffectiveness of Johnson's War on Poverty. As Gareth Davies posits, such Democrats abandoned the Johnsonian – and, indeed, mainstream American – view that the poor deserved an opportunity to better themselves, to the New Left view that those in poverty were entitled to money from the federal government. Such a change was unpopular with a majority of voters, who were increasingly resentful at the focus on the poor.[45] Moreover, these views continued to be tinged with race, as the poor remained associated in the public mind with urban African Americans. Such prejudices were only reinforced in March, when a National Welfare Rights Organization protest saw some 30,000 attendees – with a notable turnout from black women and children – arrive in Washington, DC to push Congress to enact generous welfare reform.[46]

In 1970, Nixon had sought to use McGovern's initial outlandish proposal, coupled with conservative Republican opposition to any guaranteed income, to help position FAP as the centrist option. Two years later, however, Nixon chose a different path. McGovern's demogrant helped make the concept of a guaranteed income appear more ridiculous to voters, and allowed Nixon to walk away from FAP without incurring much political damage.[47] In April, at a Camp David meeting, the President instructed his advisers to 'Flush [FAP]'. Reflecting the concerning economic outlook, he told them that they should blame his abandonment of FAP on the budget.[48]

Despite such bravado in secure surroundings, Nixon continued to keep his true intentions hidden from the public. In the realms of domestic policy, in which he hoped to appeal to moderate Democrats while not upsetting conservative Republican activists, Nixon's re-election campaign aimed to make as little news on domestic policy as possible.[49] Indeed, White House aides were acutely aware that the public were unimpressed by Nixon's domestic programme, as voters accurately perceived him as only half-heartedly committed to his own reforms.[50] Buchanan, promoting the views of another crucial part of the President's coalition, worried that even this tepid commitment to liberal welfare reform had alienated 'sullen, bitchy, and angry' conservative activists who had pounded the pavements for Nixon in 1968. In June, Buchanan warned his boss that 'our little old ladies in tennis shoes are not all enamoured of H.R.1'. The White House strategy was therefore to mute their own policy pronouncements, while simultaneously amplifying the controversial economic and cultural implications of McGovern's plans. As Buchanan put it: 'Under George McGovern two dozen and one hippies could get together and set up a commune in Taos, New Mexico, and not do a lick of work all year – and McGovern would send them every year a check for $25,000.'[51]

As part of this strategy, the White House avoided any public abandonment of FAP, which would have stirred an unwanted media debate over Nixon's governing philosophy and diverged focus from McGovern's proposals. As such, when the Senate returned to FAP in June, Nixon was evasive and noncommittal. Agreement among SFC members proved elusive, with the committee divided between pursuing Ribicoff's proposal of a $3,000 guaranteed income floor (rising to $4,000 in three years) with similar work incentives to Nixon's initial plan, and a conservative 'workfare' alternative. Few White House tears were shed when Congress, faced with widely differing plans and an election looming, kicked the welfare can down the road and decided to test all three plans before making a decision.[52] While Congress failed on welfare reform, it did pass SSI and thus federal support, including a guaranteed minimum income, to the elderly, blind and permanently disabled.[53] The failure of FAP and the success of SSI would contribute to a growing trend whereby the number of elderly Americans in poverty significantly declined from the 1970s onward, only for more and more children to fall below the poverty threshold during the same period.[54]

With Nixon having vetoed the EOA's proposed renewal in 1971, Congress also got to work saving Johnson's War on Poverty in 1972. In large part, however, congressional leaders worked to meet Nixon's objections that he had outlined in vetoing the legislation. The controversial Child Development section was quickly forgotten, while an agreement was almost reached on an independent legal services corporation that would have allowed the President to appoint ten of the nineteen board members. Nevertheless, Nixon did not get all of his wishes, as the House–Senate Conference in July appropriated $3 billion for the next two fiscal years – $2 billion more than Nixon had requested. Meanwhile, Congress did not allow Nixon the power to dismantle the OEO as he pleased.[55]

In the end, Nixon signed the EOA extension without fanfare on 20 September – the last possible day on which he could have done so – and the antipoverty effort was temporarily salvaged for another two years. Nixon likely did not want the symbolism of vetoing the War on Poverty six weeks before an election. Nonetheless, in private, he was already plotting an end for both the OEO and an array of antipoverty programmes that the EOA had spawned. Four days prior to signing the bill, he told White House advisers that his number one priority for the future was to keep federal expenditure down. He justified the War on Poverty's continued survival by telling the group that he was a minority president battling a Democratic Congress, and when he was elected the cities were falling apart. Now that he anticipated a landslide re-election, he told the gathering that he would get rid of the OEO, Community Action, Model Cities and food stamps. While he hoped for a Republican Congress to support such measures, he resolved to act independently if the legislative branch remained in Democratic hands.[56]

With Congressional business complete, Nixon and McGovern embarked on an election campaign that, according to the *US News & World Report*, had 'all the suspense, throat-gripping drama and sense of hand-to-hand combat of an international chess match played through the mail'.[57] Such was Nixon's domination, Washington correspondents of foreign publications received word from their editors to reduce their election content.[58] With McGovern already tagged as the candidate of 'amnesty, acid, and abortion' in the Democratic primary, the Nixon campaign was pushing at an open door when it sought to label McGovern as an extremist unqualified to be president. As the autumn campaign began in earnest, McGovern attempted to pivot to the typical Democratic message of portraying himself as the workingman's candidate, while simultaneously portraying Republicans and Nixon as the party of big business. The disciplined Nixon campaign, however, refused to take the bait. Instead, they resolved to keep the focus squarely on McGovern and avoid any defence of Nixon's domestic record.[59]

During the few high-profile campaign events that Nixon held, he used welfare as both a cultural and an economic issue to rally those opposed to the current system.[60] For instance, in late October, Nixon travelled to Uniondale, New York and stoked resentment at welfare recipients. Speaking to a large crowd, Nixon put the issue in biblical language, telling his audience that, 'I would suggest tonight an Eleventh Commandment: No one who is able to work shall find it more profitable to go on welfare than to go to work.' Having inflamed cultural resentment of welfare recipients, he reminded his audience of the economic impact of welfare – namely, that it was their taxes that was paying for the system.[61] Nevertheless, Nixon, running a 'Front Porch' campaign, took this message to very few places.

Come Election Day, Nixon won an extraordinary landslide illustrated by the statistic that, in a two-horse race, McGovern only won 4 per cent of the nation's counties – the lowest in American history.[62] It was, however, a hollow personal victory devoid of a clear domestic mandate. While Johnson had employed a similar strategy to discredit his opponent in 1964 on the way to a land-slide, LBJ's coat-tails had proved extensive and swept in liberal Democratic majorities that would support his Great Society. Nixon was a lonely victor; once again, the Republican brand had failed to capture the electorate's imagination. While Nixon was winning every state except Massachusetts (and the District of Columbia), ticket-splitting voters continued to show their distrust of a GOP that had failed to shed its image of negativism and privilege.[63] Overall, Republicans made net losses of one governor's mansion and two seats in the Senate, and gained a paltry twelve seats in the House. The Democratic Party thus strengthened its vice-like grip on the Senate (56–42), retained a comfortable advantage in the House (242–192), and governed thirty-one of the nation's states to the GOP's nineteen.

The 1972 elections offered few clues for which ideological direction the Republican Party should travel. While Republicans claimed mostly open Senate seats, Democrats knocked off estab-lished incumbents, including Gordon Allot (R-CO), Jack Miller (R-IA), Margaret Chase Smith (R-ME) and J. Caleb Boggs (R-DE) – a mix of stalwarts and moderates. Conservatives could point to the Senate victory of firebrand conservative broadcaster Jesse Helms in North Carolina, and also Pete Domenici in New Mexico. Meanwhile, progressive senators Ed Brooke (R-MA) and Charles Percy (R-IL) won substantial re-election victories. As such, disap-pointment rather than a clear ideological message was the one thing upon which the GOP was united. While not quite back to square one, the Republican Party's challenges remained immense in the face of continued Democratic dominance below the presi-dential level.

Nixon – the party's standard bearer – deserves his share of the blame for the GOP's failure. Arriving in office, he had toyed with an activist agenda to appeal to the white working class and lower middle class that lay at the bedrock of the Democratic Party's coalition. In saving the War on Poverty and proposing the Fam-ily Assistance Plan, Nixon and his aides hoped they could revive Republican fortunes by escaping the party's image as the 'Party of Privilege'. The catch, however was that Nixon's 'commitment to reformism', as Robert Mason notes, 'was uncertain, ambivalent, and apathetic' (and in fact, by 1972, starkly oppositional, even).[64] In the presidential election campaign, the White House's myopic focus on McGovern's unfitness for office, and the unusually large presence of foreign affairs, further diluted Nixon's activist rhetoric. Nixon had also thoroughly neutered the party apparatus and centralised fundraising in the White House through the Committee for the Re-election of the President (CREEP).[65] He continued to have poor relations with congressional Republicans, thus limiting their ability to come together with the White House and pursue a united agenda. As the dust settled, outrage with the President, and especially CREEP, was palpable among Republicans. 'For all the good he did us,' one defeated campaign aide growled, 'Nixon may as well have been running as a Democrat.'[66]

All-out war on the war on poverty, 1973–74

During his short second term in office, Nixon quickly aligned himself with the conservative Republican agenda in his approach to poverty. Gone was the Disraelian facade that Nixon had sought to maintain in the two years prior to the 1972 election. This Nixon was now the Commander-in-Chief seeking to end both the Vietnam War and the War on Poverty in the same year. Moreover, he was relentless in his pursuit of the latter, asking aides to dig up dirt on OEO programmes so that he could have the whole antipoverty enterprise discredited. He also instructed aides that FAP was now policy-non-grata in the White House. In Congress, his shift faced considerable opposition from Democrats, but only a few progressive Republicans. For the most part, congressional Republicans – otherwise disillusioned with a president who treated them with barely concealed disdain – lined up to back his proposals. Although Nixon left office in disgrace, he bestowed a substantial legacy upon the Republican Party. In his pursuit of the War on Poverty's end, Nixon laid the groundwork for the anti-government rhetoric that conservatives would learn to sell as a positive – not negative – message in the years that lay ahead.

In the wake of his landslide re-election, Nixon sought to convince the country that the War on Poverty was an idea which, while born of an altruistic American spirit, had in reality been a

225

'dismal failure'.[67] In March 1973, he told the American people that the 'utopian' programmes of the 1960s were not the way to beat poverty. Instead, 'the real miracles in raising millions out of poverty . . . have been performed by the free-enterprise economy, not by Government anti-poverty programs'.[68] In a separate message, he also declared that the urban crisis was over, citing the absence of rioting during his presidency (although failing to acknowledge that urban conditions were arguably worse than in the 1960s).[69] As a result, Nixon said it was time to get rid of the OEO and, in a message sent to Congress in March, told the legislative body that he would impound funding that had already been appropriated for Community Action.[70] More broadly, Nixon urged the American people to turn away from government – especially the federal government – as the solution to every social problem. Rather than a negative decision brought on by grim economic forecasts, however, Nixon cast this instruction as a positive choice for the American people to make.

A more assertively conservative Nixon administration charged full speed ahead in its attempt to get rid of the OEO. This effort had already begun in earnest when, in January, Nixon replaced OEO director Phillip Sanchez with Howard Phillips, a founding member of the conservative Young Americans for Freedom (YAF). With Nixon's blessing, the combative Phillips – who relished the chance to scrap the antipoverty effort – blocked OEO grants from being spent on existing initiatives. In typical Nixonian style, Phillips enjoyed jousting with the press, later commenting that 'Attila the Hun had better press relations than I did'.[71] The White House also advised OEO staff of an intention to halve the number of employees by June, with most surviving staff moved out of Washington, DC to regional offices – thus effectively ending the OEO as an influencer in the nation's capital.[72]

Keenly aware that the Democratic Congress was unlikely to grant his wishes, Nixon conducted a dedicated public relations campaign to undermine the OEO. He was urged on by Buchanan, who sent the President clippings from an issue of *Philadelphia* magazine with 'graphic, specific, and hard examples of [OEO] waste and corruption', with which Nixon could 'make the case to the American people about these horrendous ongoings'.[73]

Reviewing Buchanan's memo, Nixon instructed Ehrlichman to put 'brighter people on the job' and scatter negative OEO anecdotes around Congress and surrogates, believing that it would do 'far more good than tons of lofty rhetoric which we are spewing out in such volume'. By the end of March, all of the President's spokesmen were requested to use one or two 'horror stories' about the antipoverty effort per speech.[74] The administration that had trodden so carefully in the realm of poverty politics in its first term was now unabashedly seeking the War on Poverty's demise.

Such decisiveness was evident in Nixon's actions with regard to welfare reform, which the President promptly abandoned. Following his re-election, he responded with bluntness when he saw that FAP was still listed on an internal document as an administration objective. 'I was surprised and somewhat disappointed,' Nixon told domestic policy advisors Ehrlichman and Ken Cole, 'to find . . . the reference to family assistance. I don't think I could have made it more clear over the past few months that I am convinced that the Family Assistance Plan no longer is viable.' Showing just how far he had travelled since his days of seeking a new majority based largely on white working-class and lower-middle-class Democrats, he was particularly annoyed at the 'tired old reference to subsidizing the "working poor"'. Instead of pursuing expensive socioeconomic programmes, Nixon advised that his administration should focus on other social issues, such as women's rights and environmentalism.[75] Accordingly, on 1 March, in the same message in which he announced the OEO's dismantling, Nixon told Congress he no longer wanted FAP to pass. He justified this abandonment by stating that welfare was no longer so urgent an issue, as the number of claimants was levelling off after the previous surge witnessed in the 1960s and early 1970s. A guaranteed income for the poor was therefore no longer on the table.

Nixon's rhetoric and actions on antipoverty issues chimed well with conservative Republicans looking to plot a path back to the majority after another round of disappointing results. Sen. Carl Curtis, speaking on the GOP's future in early 1973, said the party had failed because it had not articulated a positive case for the middle class. According to Curtis, the 'American middle class is tired of working to help pay for the "voluntary poor"'. Curtis contested that those citizens that were not ill, aged or victims of great disaster should not receive help from a 'big brother government'. 'The Republican Party should,' in Curtis's view, 'exalt the virtues of hard work, self-reliance, and lack of dependence upon government in Washington.'[76] The *Christian Science Monitor* recognised the increased electoral appeal of such a message, editorialising that 'probably a majority of Americans today are tired of hearing about poverty, resentful of money to attack poverty, and particularly reluctant to do anything special for the black ghettos . . . in the cities'.[77]

The Democratic Congress, however, was in no mood to acquiesce to this disenchantment around poverty programmes, and particularly unwilling to assist a president whom they held with an evolving contempt as Watergate unfolded. In 1973, *Congressional Quarterly* noted, Nixon took a 'beating' from Congress with the Watergate scandal as the 'theme music'. Already angered at Nixon's unwillingness to allow members of his administration to testify in the Watergate hearings, Congress's ire was also piqued by Nixon's impounding of money that had already been appropriated for socioeconomic initiatives, including OEO funding. Congress, attempting to prevent Nixon from seeking to rule by executive decree via impoundment, opposed him more often than it had opposed any president in the previous twenty years.[78]

Nixon's hopes of a compliant Congress were further dented by a continuing poor relationship with congressional Republicans. During 1973, Republicans of all ideologies were growing more annoyed at the administration. In his speech calling for a conservative way forward, Curtis took aim at those around Nixon who 'have yet to extend diplomatic relations to the Congress'.[79] Meanwhile, Nixon exploded at Minority Leaders Ford and Scott, when they urged him to mend fences with Congress. 'Bring them down for cookies?' an incredulous Nixon raved, 'Our Senators are nothing but a bunch of jackasses. . . .We can't count on them. Fuck the Senate!'[80] With Republicans ever more concerned by their President's lack of leadership, they sought to re-establish the Republican Coordinating Committee (RCC) to guide GOP policy.[81] And when new HEW Secretary Caspar Weinberger independently floated the idea of returning to welfare reform without White House knowledge, he met a furious response from backbench Republicans. One conservative Wisconsin Republican went as far to threaten Nixon that, 'I may, as a defense against F.A.P., have to help spend more money on other programs in order to run the deficit up to discourage all out F.A.P. support by you and your administration.'[82]

Essentially, as 1973 went on, Republicans felt increasingly free to direct GOP policy at the expense of an embattled White House. Congressional Republicans were filling a vacuum left by Nixon, whose domestic agenda was reduced to firefighting scandal. From October 1973 – which saw Vice President Spiro Agnew's resignation (soon replaced by Gerald Ford) and Nixon's controversial firings of Attorney General Elliot Richardson and Watergate Special Prosecutor Archibald Cox – there was no further coordinated White House domestic policy. Such an absence of presidential leadership explains why Weinberger was even allowed to float the idea of returning to a version of FAP, when Nixon had fully abandoned the proposal.

With Nixon on the sidelines, and with media speculation once again swirling that the War on Poverty was set to end, the antipoverty effort pulled off another Houdini act. In June 1974, Congress surprisingly saved much of the War on Poverty that it had looked set to scrap. Most emblematic of the turnaround in fortunes was the continued existence of Community Action. At the beginning of the year, the press believed there were fewer than 100 votes in Congress to save a programme whose name was axiomatic with controversy and scandal. Yet, in a surprising twist, a successful campaign was launched by local CAP directors and the new OEO director Alvin Arnett (who had replaced the controversial Howard Phillips) to save a key pillar of Johnson's War on Poverty. The group had hired a public relations firm, headed, ironically, by former Florida Republican congressman – and vehement War on Poverty opponent – William Cramer. Cramer's firm gathered testimonies from thirty-two governors, dozens of mayors, a host of local Chambers of Commerce, and previously poor Americans who had directly benefited from CAAs. They even secured an endorsement from George Wallace, another former War on Poverty opponent. The campaign was so successful that the House of Representatives approved, by a 331–53 margin, the Community

229

Services Act, which essentially saved every existing antipoverty programme, while at the same time abolishing the OEO.[83]

Beyond the public relations effort, there were other reasons why Congress agreed to continue the programmes. First, as Al Quie – still a key Republican voice on antipoverty policy – noted, it was the ideal way to please everyone: 'The people who hate O.E.O. could say, "look we're getting rid of it." The people who like the individual programs could say, "Look, we're keeping them." Very often they were the same people.' Indeed, hitting a note that had occurred throughout the GOP's decade-long response to the War on Poverty, many Republicans praised their own local CAAs, while railing against the federal agency that funded them. John Rhodes, Ford's successor as House Minority Leader, advised the White House that while he was ideologically against Community Action, he could not help Nixon sustain a veto, as his local Phoenix CAA was highly regarded in Arizona.[84]

Also, by 1974, Community Action had simply become less toxic, and even politically convenient, to continue. As one Republican staffer noted, CAAs – which had long been perceived as a headache for local officials – had come to serve as a buffer between the poor's demands and the mayoral office as well as other state and local offices.[85] Thus, governors and mayors urged Community Action's continuance for fear that a whole new set of problems would land in the lap of poorly funded state and local government. This changed perception was also undoubtedly aided by the Nixon administration's efforts at aggressively investigating corruption. By 1974, the most controversial CAAs had been defunded or begun to operate in a manner acceptable to Washington.[86] Ironically, such efforts meant that a programme Nixon intensely disliked looked set to be saved.

Despite this, Nixon's intensified war on the War on Poverty was still successful. Saving Community Action was a Pyrrhic victory for antipoverty advocates. The OEO was gone, with its replacement, the Community Services Administration (CSA), intentionally serving as a pale shadow in terms of political influence and staffing. While existing antipoverty programmes looked set to continue, they were to be scattered across the federal government. Additionally, the federal money tap had

been turned off during the Nixon years. Despite high inflation rates in the early 1970s, funding levels remained similar to
those Nixon inherited in 1969. Beyond policy, ambitious rhetoric about solving, or even reducing, poverty was gone. Indeed,
the word 'poverty' had all but disappeared from the American
political lexicon by the time the 37th President departed in
disgrace. 'We don't even call it a War on Poverty any more,'
reflected CSA spokesperson John Macomber in 1980, 'The
antipoverty campaign has never recovered from Nixon.'[87]

Gerald Ford and the further decline of antipoverty priorities

Nixon's resignation paved the way for a new Republican president – Gerald Ford. During Ford's short two-and-a-half-year
presidency, poverty fell further down the list of politicians' priorities. The new President, an economic conservative operating
in troubled financial times, drove this shift. He faced opposition
from a strengthened Democratic congressional party, buoyed
by remarkable 1974 midterm election gains. While Ford made
an attempt to establish better relations with Congress than his
predecessor, he also vetoed sixty-two bills during his brief tenure, most in an attempt to limit federal spending. Specifically
on antipoverty policy, Ford signed the legislation that officially
ended the OEO, and was contemptuous of the newly created
CSA. Despite such a record, Ford found himself criticised from
the emerging Republican right wing, many members of which
hoped to entice Ronald Reagan to challenge the sitting president for the GOP's nomination. Bright spots for antipoverty
advocates were few and far between, but by the time of Ford's
departure, most poverty programmes still existed in some form.
Ford also signed into law the Earned Income Tax Credit (EITC),
which would become an important tool in fighting poverty over
the following five decades. Overall, however, the direction of
travel was clear: poverty was not only no longer a priority in
American politics – it was barely on the agenda.

If antipoverty workers had initially feared a Nixon presidency,
they could take little solace in looking at his successor's record. Ford

was a Midwestern stalwart who had voted against the original Economic Opportunity Act of 1964, and had, while Minority Leader, directed frequent Republican attempts to reduce the federal effort to end poverty. Historians offer a mixed assessment of the 38th President's modus operandi while in the Oval Office. Some see President Ford as essentially a loyal party figure who lacked a fixed ideology, which thus resulted in a presidency that charted an unclear philosophical path.[88] Others, however, persuasively stress Ford's deep desire to reverse the trend of Great Society liberalism. As Yanek Mieczkowski notes, 'In Ford's view, much of the 1970s disillusionment with government was because Americans grew disgusted with the sheer size and scope of government social programs.'[89]

Ford was ideologically flexible on controversial social issues, such as abortion and women's rights, that were central to the new conservative movement that was becoming more influential in the Republican Party. Nevertheless, he was an old-school balanced-budget, small-government, economic conservative to his core. The new president, raised in a conservative district of Michigan during the Great Depression, was a high achiever throughout his life and thoroughly believed that work ethic was central to overcoming poverty. If work ethic proved not enough for an individual, then Ford believed that state and local government, in combination with the private sector, were plenty enough help without the federal government poking its nose in.[90] While conducting House business, Ford loved to repeat the aphorism, 'a government big enough to do everything for you is a government big enough to take everything away from you'.[91] As President, he still boasted of winning five 'Watchdog of the Treasury' awards during his congressional career.[92] It was little surprise then that the new President obfuscated when asked at his first press conference whether he intended to revive the OEO.[93] A few months later, he used the occasion of his first State of the Union address to bemoan the recent tendency for the federal government to act like an 'indulgent parent'.[94]

Upon taking office, Ford was faced with the mountainous challenge of the fast-approaching midterm elections. With Nixon having sullied the Republican brand, Ford ripped it to shreds by pardoning his predecessor. It was a decision which attracted accusations that Nixon had promised Ford the presidency in exchange for clemency, and it abruptly ended any short honeymoon Ford was enjoying. In fairness to Ford, it is much likelier that he was honourably trying to end what he termed the nation's long nightmare; the new President had little love for the way Nixon had treated him and the rest of the Republican leadership over the previous five years.[95] In addition to this challenge, Ford also faced an economy ravaged by inflation. His attempt to rally the nation to wear Whip Inflation Now (WIN) buttons, and thus provide a slogan for GOP candidates to preach to the electorate around the country, was a gimmick that was widely mocked.[96] With a recently disgraced president, a newly tarnished incumbent, a weak economy and no strong campaign message, Republican disaster loomed.

Disaster duly arrived when voters went to the polls on Election Day and stripped forty House seats and four Senate seats from an already minority Republican cohort. Many conservative incumbents, often those who had publicly stood by Nixon the longest, lost in shock upsets as disillusioned voters stayed at home in an election where only two out of every five Americans voted (low by the standards of the era). Such was the blow, one Republican pollster warned the party that the GOP was in danger of being extinct in two or three decades if present trends continued.[97] Some conservative senators took the prediction to heart, with Jesse Helms among those who considered forming a new conservative party as the prospects for Republicans gaining a majority appeared ever more distant.[98] In addition to the challenge posed by having to deal with a strengthened Democratic Party, Ford now had to revive a beleaguered Republican congressional cohort. Political scientist Christopher Bailey contests that 'The morale of the Republican Party in the Senate at the beginning of the 94th Congress . . . was at its lowest since the New Deal election of 1936.'[99] While Ford made a far greater effort than Nixon to court congressional Republicans, he had little success with the legislative body throughout his short tenure.[100]

While the elections proved a boon for Democrats, the midterm results offered little hope for reviving the War on Poverty. Indeed, many of the 'Watergate babies' – as the press christened the new Democratic cohort – eschewed Johnsonian liberalism and especially the antipoverty effort. Gary Hart, the 'rock star of the 1974 Democratic candidates', was scathing of the War on Poverty during his successful senate race with Peter Dominick in Colorado.[101] In one speech, Hart condemned the 'ballyhooed War on Poverty' as it 'succeeded only in raising the expectations, but not the living conditions, of the poor'.[102] In doing so, he sounded more like his Republican rival than a Democrat. Once elected, such Democrats were more interested in reforming Congress than reviving the antipoverty effort. Even if they had wanted to breathe new life into the War on Poverty, the numbers behind the midterm elections showed an electorate that, while it wanted to punish the Republican Party for Nixon's mess, was growing ever more conservative. Roughly half of voters – presumably turned off by the excesses of the 1960s and worried about present economic conditions – now considered themselves 'conservative', when asked by pollsters.[103] Such numbers offered little incentive for either Ford or congressional Democrats to embark upon a new round of substantial social welfare legislation.

By 1974, the War on Poverty simply did not fit the times. As it had been in the 1930s when the nation was ravaged by depression, and as it was in the 1960s when prosperity propelled the nation to spend freely, the economy was key to this change. Now, however, it was the rampant inflation of the mid-1970s that drove the political winds. 'While government seemed the answer to the Great Depression,' Mieczkowski notes, 'less government appeared the answer to the Great Inflation.'[104] Indeed, inflation played into a key argument that Republicans had made against the War on Poverty in the 1966 midterms – when inflation briefly flared as a political issue in that decade. During the Ford presidency, Republicans could – and did – once again contest that inflation hurt the poor most.[105] The simple logic that an increased price for a carton of milk hurt those on low incomes more than those on higher salaries was an easy argument to make. Thus, when Republicans contested that the cure for inflation was to reduce government spending – including poverty programmes – antipoverty advocates were on the back foot. Continuance of existing programmes in this context would be an achievement in its own right. Of course, this would not have been such a prickly problem if the War on Poverty had achieved bipartisan buy-in prior to the economic challenges of the mid-1970s.

For the rest of the Ford presidency, the War on Poverty was neglected. 'At a time of deep national recession,' the *New York Times*'s William Farrell observed, 'the voice of the nation's chronically poor has been muted in the halls of government by the demands of a multitude of other special interests seeking limited federal dollars.'[106] Noting the appetite for cutting antipoverty initiatives, the *Washington Post* also observed: 'it is the misfortune of poor people that they have no place to hide until this fever passes'.[107] Ford's first budget proposal included a $60 million cut for the already threadbare Community Action budget.[108] In response, led by Carl Perkins, a true Great Society Democrat, the House ignored Ford and passed an increase in Community Action's funding later in the year. Showing the dire straits of the antipoverty effort, Perkins argued that 'we are only speaking about letting community action survive, and I mean actually survive'.[109] Most Republicans voted against the measure and the Ford White House made its opposition known – the funding increase failed to materialise.[110]

Ford's contempt for federal antipoverty efforts was made further apparent by his failure to arrive at a decision over whether the newly created CSA – already dogged by charges of poor management – should be an independent agency or take its place within the existing executive branch.[111] Moreover, in a special message to Congress in February 1976 on the future of the Community Services Act, the White House advocated that it wanted a bill packed with conservative changes. Ford demanded a reduction in the burden on the states to match federal funding, less red tape, a decrease in federal monitoring, and focus on only the very poor.[112] Elsewhere, he called for reductions in other antipoverty measures, such as food stamps.[113]

While the Ford years were marked by his vetoes of spending measures, one important antipoverty measure did emerge from Congress that grew out of the continuous efforts at welfare reform that Nixon had begun in 1969. Russell Long proposed the Earned

Income Credit (EIC) to provide tax credits to the poor. Since it was tied to income tax, it would benefit only the politically uncontroversial working poor. As historian Dennis Ventry notes, it was popular because it was both anti-poverty and anti-welfare, and it was directed at Americans deemed deserving of government help. Still, while EIC – which would soon become the Earned Income Tax Credit (EITC) – would grow arms and legs in future decades, it was a relatively small-scale proposal when it passed as part of the Tax Reduction Act of 1975.[114] It did not represent a renewed focus on poverty. By 1975, antipoverty workers – hoping that a Democrat might win the upcoming presidential election – had already made the decision to 'hunker down until 1976 when maybe things will change'.[115]

Conclusion

The swiftness and significance of Richard Nixon's conservative turn means that it is arguable that the War on Poverty was over by the time he left office. Certainly, by 1974, many involved in the effort felt that government's offensive against poverty had concluded. In the month following Nixon's departure, the *New York Times* published a ten-year anniversary analysis of the antipoverty effort in which the War on Poverty was discussed in the past tense throughout. The article quoted the liberal economist and sociologist Sar A. Levitan, whom the *Times* deemed the antipoverty effort's 'official historian'. 'Why didn't we eliminate poverty?' Levitan asked, regretfully answering his own question, 'We never really tried.'[116] By 1974, most of the War on Poverty's various experimental programmes were scattered across the government with minimal funding. Perhaps more importantly, few politicians dared to dream of ending poverty, and were already beginning to steer clear of the topic altogether. Fashion is an underrated aspect of understanding politics. The War on Poverty was no longer fashionable – just like the hippie preaching peace and love, it was so very sixties, but not at all seventies. This change made it easier for Republicans to intensify calls for the antipoverty effort to end.

Nixon, having been the key Republican in keeping the antipoverty flame alive until 1970, was similarly important in ensuring the torch was promptly extinguished. As he prepared for re-election, his turnaround manifested itself mostly in private, with the exception of his public call to postpone FAP in 1971. From the moment he was re-elected, Nixon's conservative turn became more evident. He turned against both the OEO and his own FAP proposal with an abruptness that shocked those who had been in his company during the first two years of his presidency. Such was the shift that in 1973 a bereft Daniel Patrick Moynihan wrote to Ehrlichman asking Nixon's key domestic adviser whether the President had ever wanted FAP to pass.[117] Away from FAP, Nixon also sought to end his predecessor's antipoverty efforts. Shedding himself of any accommodationist approach to Johnson's War on Poverty, he actively sought horror stories with which to tarnish Community Action and attempted to dismantle the OEO despite Congress's wishes.

With such actions, Nixon was in harmony with conservative Republicans – a bloc which, save for the 1974 midterm debacle, was gaining strength in the party. It was music to this group's ears when Nixon started to outline a compelling rejection of big government. Rather than preaching this in typical negative GOP fashion, Nixon began to outline a positive case in favour of private enterprise, while blaming excessive government for having overreached in the 1960s, thus leading to the economic problems of the 1970s. Gerald Ford largely continued the trend begun by Nixon, in terms of economic policy, albeit without the same ability to fashion a positive conservative message. Before long, it would be Ronald Reagan who would pick up the baton of positive conservatism. In the process, he would finish the job that Nixon started and ensure that the War on Poverty – save for a few poorly funded initiatives – was officially consigned to the history books.

Notes

1. Macomber quoted in William Chaze, 'After 15 Years of "Great Society" Spending', *US News & World Report*, 30 June 1980.
2. Joan Hoff, *Nixon Reconsidered* (New York: Basic Books, 1995); Morgan, *Nixon*; Thomas, *Being Nixon*; Romain Huret, 'Richard Nixon, the Great Society, and Social Reforms: A Lost Opportunity?'

in *A Companion to Richard Nixon*, ed. Melvin Small (Chichester: Wiley Blackwell, 2011); McAndrews, *The Presidents and the Poor*; Mason, *From Hoover to Reagan*.

3. RMN, 'Annual Message to the Congress on the State of the Union', 22 January 1971, TAPP.
4. RMN quoted in Mason, *Richard Nixon and the Quest*, 216.
5. Rae, *Decline and Fall of the Liberal Republicans*, 172.
6. Kabaservice, *Rule and Ruin*, 331.
7. H. R. Haldeman Diaries Collection, 13 July 1970: https://www.nixonlibrary.gov.
8. Burns, *Secret Diary*, 29.
9. RMN quoted in Reichley, *Conservatives in an Age of Change*, 172.
10. Herbert Parmet, *Richard Nixon and His America*, (Boston, MA: Little Brown, 1990), 558.
11. *CQ Almanac 1971*.
12. Ibid.
13. Rep. Jack H. McDonald and Rep. John Byrnes quoted in ibid., 525–6.
14. Bob Dole remarks, RNC Meeting, Denver, 22 July 1971, reel 8, PRP.
15. NAR quoted in ibid.
16. RMN, Address to the Nation Outlining a New Economic Policy: 'The Challenge of Peace', 15 August 1971, TAPP.
17. *CQ Almanac 1971*.
18. Rae, *Decline and Fall of the Liberal Republicans*, 172.
19. Rowland Evans and Robert Novak, 'The Poverty Cold War', *Washington Post*, 1 March 1971.
20. Evans and Novak, 'The Nixon–Reagan Staredown', *Washington Post*, 3 February 1971.
21. Evans and Novak, 'Nixon, Reagan: Collision Seen', *Washington Post*, 12 May 1971.
22. Mark R. Arnold, 'The Good War That Might Have Been', *New York Times*, 29 September 1974.
23. Caroll Kilpatrick, 'Nixon Shifting Poverty Chief: President Will Shift Poverty War Chief', *Washington Post*, 28 July 1971.
24. Mizell quoted in *CQ Almanac 1971*.
25. Daniels in ibid.
26. Ibid.
27. Hawkins quoted in Jack Rosenthal, 'Democrats Charge Nixon Tries to Dismantle Poverty Agency', *New York Times*, 23 March 1971.

28. Frank Carlucci to John D. Ehrlichman, 9 March 1971, box 52 White House Central Files, Welfare Subject File, Poverty Programs, Richard M. Nixon Library.
29. Max Friedersdorf to Ed Harper, 12 August 1971, box 52, WHCF, WE, PP, RMN.
30. Ibid.
31. *CQ Almanac 1972*.
32. Marjorie Hunter, 'House Clears Poverty Bill Despite Nixon Veto Threat', *New York Times*, 8 December 1971.
33. Javits quoted in *CQ Almanac 1971*.
34. Burke quoted in ibid.
35. Phillip V. Sanchez to JDE, 26 November 1971, box 52, WHCF, WE, PP, RMN.
36. Elliot Richardson to JDE, 15 November 1971, box 52, WHCF, WE, PP, RMN.
37. Letter to RMN, 7 February 1971, box 53, WHCF, WE, PP, RMN.
38. Patrick J. Buchanan to JDE, 12 October 1971, box 52, WHCF, WE, PP, RMN.
39. Ibid.
40. Press Conference with Ron Ziegler, 9 February 1971, box 53, WHCF, WE, PP, RMN.
41. Ronald W. Reagan to RMN, 11 December 1971, box 53, WHCF, WE, PP, RMN.
42. Peter Khiss, 'War on Poverty Unfashionable, Ex-Official Tells Jewish Group', *New York Times*, 15 December 1971.
43. Ed Harper to JDE, 28 December 1971, box 53, WHCF, WE, PP, RMN.
44. Parmet, *Richard Nixon and His America*, 559.
45. Davies, *From Opportunity to Entitlement*, 235–8.
46. '30,000, Many of Them Children, Protest Nixon Welfare Policies', *New York Times*, 26 March 1972.
47. Parmet, *Richard Nixon and His America*, 559.
48. RMN quoted in ibid. 559.
49. Editorial, 'The Republicans on the Home Front', *Washington Post*, 28 August 1972.
50. Ed Harper, 'Selling Domestic Programs', box 16, White House Special Files, WHCF Confidential Files, 1969–74, RMN.
51. PJB to H. R. Haldeman, 8 June 1971, box 14, WHSF, Staff Member and Office Files, PJB, 1972 Election Files, RMN.
52. *CQ Almanac 1972*.
53. McAndrews, *The Presidents and the Poor*, 52.

54. US Census Bureau, 'Current Population Survey, 1960 to 2019 Annual Social and Economic Supplements'. Available at https://www.census.gov/content/dam/Census/library/visualizations/2019/demo/p60-266/Figure11.pdf (accessed 4 November 2020).
55. *CQ Almanac 1972*.
56. Burns, *Secret Diary*, 77.
57. *US News & World Report*, 9 October 1972.
58. *US News & World Report*, 23 October 1972.
59. PJB to RMN, 6 August 1972, box 21, Nixon Presidential Returned Materials Collection, WHSF, RMN; Editorial, 'The Republicans on the Home Front', *Washington Post*.
60. HRH Diaries, 14 October 1972.
61. RMN, Remarks in Uniondale, New York, 23 October 1972, TAPP.
62. '1972 Presidential Election Statistics', *Dave Leip's Atlas of U.S. Presidential Elections*. Available at https://uselectionatlas.org/RESULTS (accessed 4 November 2020).
63. Carl Curtis, Speech at Coeur D'Alene, Idaho, 12 February 1973, [CF] SP 5/FG# [Other Government Officials]. 1971-74.-1974, WHSF, Part 1: Confidential Files; Part 2: Subject Files. RMN. Archives Unbound. http://go.gale.com.ezproxy.is.ed.ac.uk/gdsc/i.do?&id=GALE%7CSC5104647672&v=2.1&u=ed_itw&it=r&p=GDSC&sw=w&viewtype=Manuscript.
64. Mason, *Richard Nixon and the Quest*, 236.
65. Klinkner, *The Losing Parties*, 137.
66. Lou Cannon, 'Victory Bittersweet for GOP', *Washington Post*, 9 November 1972.
67. RMN, Radio Address About the State of the Union Message on the Economy, 21 February 1973, TAPP.
68. RMN, State of the Union Message to the Congress on Human Resources, 1 March 1973, TAPP.
69. McAndrews, *The Presidents and the Poor*, 55.
70. *CQ Almanac 1973*.
71. Jules Witcover, 'Present, Former Directors Tell Views on Poverty War', *Washington Post*, 16 March 1973.
72. Lou Cannon, 'Poverty War Critic to Lead OEO Cutback', *Washington Post*, 13 January 1973.
73. PJB to JDE, 15 February 1973, box 53, WHCF, WE, PP, June '70–July '74, RMN.
74. RMN to JDE, 14 March 1973, box 53, WHCF, WE, PP, June '70–July '74, RMN.

75. RMN to JDE and Ken Cole, 28 December 1972, reel 7, President's Speech File, Papers of the Nixon White House.
76. Carl Curtis, Speech at Coeur D'Alene, Idaho, 12 February 1973.
77. Editorial, 'Of Politics and Poverty', *Christian Science Monitor*, 21 March 1973.
78. *CQ Almanac 1973*.
79. Curtis, 12 February 1973.
80. RMN quoted in Kaufman, *Ambition, Pragmatism, and Party*, 158.
81. RNC meeting, Washington, DC, 10 September 1973, reel 11, PRP.
82. Harold V. Froehlich to RMN, 19 December 1973, box 62, WHCF Subject Welfare, Family Security Plans, RMN.
83. Mark R. Arnold, 'The Good War That Might Have Been', *New York Times*, 29 September 1974.
84. Ken Cole to RMN, 17 May 1974, box 53, WHCF, WE, PP, RMN.
85. Arnold, 'The Good War'.
86. William E. Farrell, 'Poverty Programs Lag as Slum Intensifies Federal Aid Demand', *New York Times*, 10 April 1975.
87. Macomber quoted in Chaze, 'After 15 Years of "Great Society" Spending'.
88. Kaufman, *Ambition, Pragmatism, and Party*; Donald T. Critchlow, 'The Rise of Conservative Republicanism: A History of Fits and Starts', in Mason and Morgan, *Seeking a New Majority*, 13–31.
89. Yanek Mieczkowski, *Gerald Ford and the Challenges of the 1970s* (Lexington, KY: University Press of Kentucky, 2005), 74; Cannon, 'Gerald R. Ford', 260–85.
90. Kaufman, *Ambition, Pragmatism, and Party*, xii–xiv.
91. Mieczkowski, *Gerald Ford*, 75.
92. GRF, Remarks in Los Angeles at a Republican Party Fundraising Dinner, 29 October 1975, TAPP.
93. GRF, The President's News Conference, 28 August 1974, TAPP.
94. GRF, Address Before a Joint Session of the Congress Reporting on the State of the Union, 15 January 1975, TAPP.
95. Cannon, 'Gerald R. Ford', 276.
96. Yanek Mieczkowski, 'Gerald R. Ford's Domestic Policy', in *A Companion to Gerald R. Ford and Jimmy Carter*, ed. Scott Kaufman (Chichester: Wiley Blackwell, 2015).
97. Teeter quoted in Mason and Morgan, *Seeking a New Majority*, 5.
98. Christopher J. Bailey, *The Republican Party in the US Senate: 1974–1984: Party Change and Institutional Development* (Manchester: Manchester University Press, 1988), 2.

99. Ibid. 1.
100. Mieczkowski, 'Gerald R. Ford's Domestic Policy'.
101. Rick Perlstein, *The Invisible Bridge: The Fall of Nixon and the Rise of Reagan* (New York: Simon & Schuster, 2014), 317.
102. Hart quoted in ibid. 317.
103. Mason and Morgan, *Seeking a New Majority*, 1–12.
104. Mieczkowski, *Gerald Ford*, 306.
105. See Chapter 7.
106. William E. Farrell, 'Poverty Programs Lag as Slum Intensifies Federal Aid Demand', *New York Times*, 10 April 1975.
107. 'Politics and Poverty '76', *Washington Post*, 3 March 1976.
108. Farrell, 'Poverty Programs'.
109. Perkins quoted in CQ *Almanac 1975*.
110. Ibid.
111. Ibid.; Jack Anderson and Les Whitten, 'Confusion on Poverty Programs', *Washington Post*, 12 August 1976.
112. GRF, Special Message to the Congress Urging Enactment of Proposed Community Services Legislation, 23 February 1976, TAPP.
113. 'Politics and Poverty'.
114. Dennis J. Ventry, 'The Collision of Tax and Welfare Politics: The Political History of the Earned Income Tax Credit, 1969–99', *National Tax Journal*, vol. 53, no. 4 (2000), 983–1026.
115. Farrell, 'Poverty Programs'.
116. Levitan quoted in Arnold, 'The Good War'.
117. Daniel Patrick Moynihan to JDE, box 53, WHCF, WE, PP, RMN.

7

The end? Poverty politics and the
'Reagan Revolution', 1977–81

The press is dying to paint me as now trying to undo the New
Deal. I remind them I voted for F.D.R. 4 times. I'm trying to
undo the 'Great Society'. It was L.B.J.'s war on poverty that led
to our present mess.[1]

Ronald Reagan, diary entry, 28 January 1982

Between 1964 and 1981, Ronald Reagan's steadfast opposition
to the War on Poverty was a rare constant throughout seventeen
tumultuous years in American politics. In October 1964, one
month after Lyndon Johnson's antipoverty effort began, Reagan
launched his political career by mocking Johnson's domestic war
as cynical and unfeasible in equal measure: 'so now we declare
"war on poverty." . . . Now do they honestly expect us to believe
that if we add 1 billion dollars to the 45 billion we're spending,
one more program to the 30-odd we have . . . that poverty is suddenly going to disappear by magic?' When Reagan advanced this
very public critique in 1964, he was an outlier in the GOP. On the
campaign trail, most Republicans were shying away from attacking the War on Poverty, fearful that voters would deem any politician who opposed such an effort as hard-hearted, overly negative
or privileged. Such fears appeared correct when Lyndon Johnson
crushed Barry Goldwater – one of the few Republicans who did
loudly denounce the antipoverty effort – in November and thus
the Republican Party trod with care regarding poverty politics
over the next decade.

By January 1981, when Reagan was sworn in as the 40th
President, his antipathy to federal antipoverty efforts remained

unchanged. Only now, his party and enough of his fellow Americans had come to agree with him. In spending the political capital accrued from his landslide victory over President Jimmy Carter, and facing a weakened Democratic opposition, Reagan corralled near unanimous Republican support in passing the Omnibus Budget and Reconciliation Act (OBRA) of 1981, which instigated sweeping cuts that fell disproportionately on programmes for the poor. While scholars in recent years have preferred to focus on what OBRA did not cut – namely Social Security, Medicare and other universal entitlement programmes – its impact on American politics and policy development should not be underestimated.[2] Within a few months of seizing power, the Republican Party – with some help from conservative southern Democrats – had signalled that the federal government was no longer to be viewed as an instrument to fight poverty, unless the recipients were old or unmistakably unable to work. The War on Poverty, originally envisioned as an effort in which Washington would cure poverty by leaning on the combined might of federal dollars and carefully crafted initiatives, was over.

Reagan was able to achieve this shift for numerous reasons. First, and most notably, by 1981 most Americans were receptive to a change in policy direction. In the late 1970s, a potent cocktail of economic malaise and lingering public resentment at the federal government facilitated voter receptiveness to small government conservatism.[3] Second, the Carter administration, hamstrung by its own contradictions on antipoverty policy, had failed to reinvigorate the War on Poverty despite enjoying substantial Democratic majorities in Congress. Third, when Reagan took office, he did so as the head of a newly confident and largely conservative Republican Party. Most Republicans shared Reagan's cynicism about the War on Poverty and were happy to aid their president in his attempts to undo LBJ's creation. Republican unity held firm during the Reagan Revolution's critical summer. Fourth, when Reagan and many other Republicans embraced supply-side economics, it helped the GOP escape the familiar trap of negativism or privilege. Reagan – a relentless optimist in public settings – was able to reframe cuts to poverty programmes not as a harsh measure on impoverished Americans, but instead a necessary change to stimulate growth and set rich and poor alike on the road to greater prosperity. Lastly, the Reagan White House ran a slick operation that focused relentlessly on a few big-ticket measures – one of which was cutting antipoverty programmes.

Throughout its troubled lifespan, the War on Poverty was always a partisan endeavour. It was a Democratic initiative that won over only a few Republicans. Of all those in the GOP, Reagan was its most consistent opponent. It is therefore simply unsurprising that when acceding to power, Reagan and the Republicans all but ended the War on Poverty.

Prelude to power: Republicans, poverty politics and the Carter presidency

Teleport an observer of American politics from 1965 to 1977, and they could be forgiven for thinking, at first sight, that little had changed. A southern Democrat was in the White House, supported by eye-popping Democratic majorities in both the House and Senate. Congress and the media were alive with talk of grand socioeconomic programmes that might emerge from a Capitol Hill.[4] Meanwhile, the Republican Party was on its knees, attempting to avoid another intraparty civil war, and without a clear path to achieve relevance, let alone take back the White House and Congress. Looking back on the previous year, the closeness of the 1976 presidential race was the Republicans' only real solace. In the summer, a Carter landslide over incumbent Gerald Ford loomed, but ended in a narrow victory of less than two points for the Georgian. At the congressional level, there was no such consolation; the Republican Party gained one net Senate seat and lost one net House seat. Given the uniquely disastrous context in which the 1974 midterm elections took place for the GOP, the lack of any rebound in House was stunning and spoke to a wider issue with the Republican brand.[5] With Democrats in the ascendancy, it was possible that the nation was about to have its fourth round of liberal reform in the twentieth century.

The year 1977, however, was not 1965. Jimmy Carter was no Lyndon Johnson, and a tide of liberal socioeconomic measures never materialised. While Johnson was a creature of Congress, who made a career out of knowing any individual representative or senator's needs and wants, Carter continually alienated even his fellow Democrats on Capitol Hill.[6] And while Johnson grandly proclaimed a War on Poverty as the key to achieving a Great Society, Carter never once mentioned American poverty in his acceptance speech and avoided the issue on the campaign trail.[7] As many scholars have noted, Carter – who had compassionate impulses towards the poor – was, at heart, a fiscal conservative.[8] He would spend his final year in office not crusading against poverty, but trying to balance the budget.

The Carter years, however, were not a completely busted flush for antipoverty advocates in Washington who, with antagonistic Republican executives in the White House during the 1970s, had dreamed of a Democratic president riding to the rescue. Everyone's favourite poverty programme, Head Start, received a sharp increase in funds.[9] Meanwhile, the Earned Income Tax Credit (EITC) became a permanent fixture in US policy, albeit with a small maximum credit of $500 and thus not a particularly potent antipoverty weapon.[10] In 1977, the Economic Opportunity Act (EOA) was also extended for three years in uncontroversial fashion and with some Republican support.[11] Nevertheless, by now, the War on Poverty's foundational legislation was barely worth arguing over. The Office of Economic Opportunity (OEO) – long loathed by Republicans – was gone, and the newly created Community Services Administration (CSA) had little power and received a paltry budget of less than one quarter of the OEO's in its heyday.[12] Instead, the fulcrum of poverty politics centred on more expensive and politically explosive items, most notably welfare. Carter did twice offer large welfare reform proposals – known on each occasion as the Program for Better Jobs and Income (PBJI). Both proposals had echoes of Nixon's Family Assistance Plan: because they included a form of guaranteed income coupled with work requirements, and because they were killed off in Congress, mostly by conservative Democrats and Republicans who remained hostile to a guaranteed income of any kind.[13] Elsewhere, Democrats pursued and passed the Humphrey–Hawkins Full Employment Act in 1978, which eschewed poverty programmes in favour of attempting to commit the government to guaranteeing a job for every American. Nonetheless, the bill Carter ultimately signed was 'neutered' and had little impact on poverty.[14] Overall then, the Carter presidency neither advanced nor retrenched antipoverty efforts. After a loss of focus on poverty during the latter half of Nixon's presidency and throughout the Ford years, stasis was all the Democrats could muster.

Even a president skilled in the arts of congressional politics would have faced strong headwinds in advancing significant antipoverty initiatives in the late 1970s. In 1977, the United States had only recently emerged from a sharp recession and the economy remained shaky throughout Carter's term in office before slipping back into recession in 1980. The causes of the economic challenges were numerous – oil shocks, rising global manufacturing competition, and a legacy of overspending on the Vietnam War and (Republicans argued) the Great Society – to name a few. The main symptom was initially inflation, the rate of which grew to double digits by 1979. By 1980, when the US economy entered recession, inflation was then accompanied by rising unemployment. Fundamentally, 'stagflation', as it was termed, challenged the assumption of unending American prosperity that had underpinned the politics of the previous two decades.

The implications for poverty politics were profound. With Americans already sceptical of their leaders in Washington following the twin calamities of Vietnam and Watergate, the economic downturn, which threatened to create a new generation of Americans who were poorer than their parents, only compounded voters' distrust of the federal government. By the end of the decade, only one in four Americans trusted the federal government to do the right thing most of the time. By contrast, when the War on Poverty was launched in 1964, this figure stood closer to three quarters of Americans.[15] For the public to remain supportive of a government-led antipoverty effort, they needed to actually believe the federal government was competent enough to prosecute such an endeavour. Yet, when polled in 1978 and 1980, most respondents – at least 60 per cent in both instances – believed that federal antipoverty efforts either had not helped or had even made things worse.[16] The American public also appeared to have less empathy with the poor, particularly the African American poor, whom most Americans perceived as the main beneficiaries of poverty programmes. The rising cynicism of the decade – which contrasted with the idealism of the 1960s – meant that more and more white Americans simply viewed the black poor as an 'interest group' (a term now frequently used as a pejorative by politicians across the political spectrum) that was successfully milking Uncle Sam.[17]

The economic downturn also meant that any attempt to reinvigorate the War on Poverty demanded sacrifice (in the form of tax hikes) from well-off Americans – something that, even in the prosperous 1960s, LBJ never asked of the American people. He had sought to grow the size of the pie, rather than ask others to take a smaller slice. A tax cut, not a tax raise, had preceded the 1964 Economic Opportunity Act. By the late 1970s, however, an increasing number of middle-class Americans were in febrile mood about taxation. Inflation gave rise to 'bracket creep', whereby middle-class Americans typically began to pay tax rates that were designed for the upper classes. Tax revolts followed. In 1978, Californian Howard Jarvis started, in Kevin Phillips's words, a 'small national prairie fire' when Jarvis's activism culminated in the passage of Proposition 13, which amended the Golden State constitution to restrict property taxes and gave rise to similar uprisings across the country.[18]

Aside from bracket creep, inflation posed another challenge to Great Society liberalism. As Republicans had long argued when opposing increased antipoverty spending, inflation had a disproportionate effect on the poor. Those with minimal incomes were hardest hit when their wages could not keep pace with the rising prices of basic necessities on the supermarket shelves. The GOP anti-inflation argument had gained traction in the prosperous 1960s, when inflation stood at 3.5 per cent in 1966 during their successful midterm election comeback. By 1979, inflation surged to an alarming 13.3 per cent.[19] Even aides in the Carter White House were convinced that liberalism's penchant for greater government spending might hurt the poorest most. As such, most spending proposals that Carter offered had anti-inflationary measures attached, which alienated liberals who wanted to use Democratic control of the White House and Congress to spend big on social problems.[20] Such confusion among the Democrats redounded to Republican benefit. When Carter's mixed messaging failed to get anything of significance passed in his first congressional session, the new Senate Minority Leader, Howard Baker (R-TN), gleefully noted that 'we have a Democratic president singing a Republican song'.[21]

For Republicans, who, when Carter was inaugurated, seemed as far away from power as they ever had been, the public's loss of faith in government and the severe economic challenges offered a political opportunity that the GOP succeeded in grabbing. The GOP's turnaround was as impressive as it was sudden. While Watergate had temporarily sullied the Republican brand, it had not stemmed the growth in conservatism, which had continued to proliferate in both the GOP and the nation. The party's new Sunbelt leadership in Congress – Baker and House Minority Leader John Rhodes (R-AZ) – symbolised the shifting geography and ideology of the GOP. By the late 1970s, the Republican heart lay not in George Romney's industrial Midwest or Nelson Rockefeller's Northeast, but in Barry Goldwater's Arizona and nearby Southern California, the hardscrabble Mountain West and – increasingly – the South. The former regions had sent many moderates and progressives to Congress, imbued with a Republicanism that offered smarter (or simply cheaper) alternatives to Democratic social programmes. The latter sent conservatives to Congress on the proviso that they reverse the growth in the federal government, particularly to limit income redistribution through curtailing taxation and liberal social programmes.[22] The end result was that when the Republicans did re-emerge into power, they were a more cohesively conservative Sunbelt-orientated party, particularly on socioeconomic issues.

While most Republicans had been at least quietly hostile to the War on Poverty since its inception, the more uniformly conservative approach to socioeconomic policy only hardened this opposition. Moreover, in the late 1970s, intellectual heft emerged to support conservative hostility to antipoverty spending. American corporations, who had largely sat out partisan battles in the 1960s, were now firmly in the Republican corner and funding think tanks that confirmed the conservative doctrine that unleashing private enterprise, not federal benevolence, was the solution to poverty.[23] These works, most notably Martin Anderson's *Welfare* (1978) and later George Gilder's *Wealth and Poverty* (1981), deemed the War on Poverty both a moral and a political failure. These authors claimed that, rather than solve poverty, the antipoverty effort had produced a 'New Leisure Class' that lived off government aid.[24] Thus, conservatives contended, federal spending on the poor should be greatly reduced both for the benefit of the nation's finances and to allow the poor to rediscover the work ethic and spur them to achieve the American Dream.[25]

Perhaps the most significant change to take hold in the late 1970s was that Republican politicians advanced small-government critiques of liberalism with more confidence. Fewer Republicans feared that in arguing for smaller government and spending cuts they would be perceived as reinforcing the GOP's traditional stereotypes of negativism and privilege. By the late 1970s, more and more Republicans began talking explicitly about conservative socioeconomic ideas. They even took the message to previously hostile – and Democratic – audiences. For instance, in 1978, Reps. Marvin Edwards (R-OK) and Phil Crane (R-IL), visited the soul of American industry – Youngstown, Ohio – and enjoyed a receptive blue-collar audience for the Republican small-government vision.[26] Partly, this boldness in message was because the new breed of conservative Republicans were true believers in smaller government, but it was also because the changed economic context posed challenges to liberalism and allowed for a more assertive conservativism.

With the midterm elections looming, a compelling Republican alternative to the War on Poverty finally emerged: supply-side economics. This economic approach argued for – among other fiscal measures – reducing income taxes across all income brackets. Supply-siders theorised that if sweeping tax cuts were implemented, then upper- and middle-class Americans would be free to invest more money, start or expand businesses, create jobs, and thus grow the whole economy. Such growth would then 'trickle down' to lower income Americans, through increased employment opportunity and also having less tax to pay themselves, thus benefiting all of society. The most evangelical supply-siders even contested that the reduction in tax rates would not be accompanied by a fall in federal revenues, but would actually see the government collect more taxation.[27] This was underpinned by economist Arthur Laffer's 'Laffer curve', which theorised that 'low tax rates would produce a reflow of revenue to government' as individuals would be encouraged to work harder, save more and contribute more taxes.[28] Most economists, including many Republican-leaning scholars, would later discredit this element of supply-side thinking, but at the time it appeared to offer a panacea for the sluggish American economy: economic growth, poverty reduction, less taxation, all while balancing the budget.[29]

For the Republican Party, supply-side economics was as crucial in their electoral ascendance as any other factor. For so long, Republicans had failed to escape the Democratic charge that, on socioeconomic issues, they were the negative party, that while Democrats would spend to help the people, Republicans – panicked about maintaining a balanced budget – were the crusty, tut-tutting bank managers saying 'no' to every flashy new programme. Supply-side economics meant Republicans could now promise working-class Americans tax cuts, economic growth and, thanks to the promise of increased tax revenues, a continuation of the country's most beloved social programmes. Party roles were thus reversed. When Democrats incredulously mocked supply-side ideas as fantastical, they were cast in the role of the naysayers, standing in the way of a glitzy Republican idea to help working people.

In the late 1970s, not all Republicans advocated supply-side economics – congressional Republicans were roughly divided on its merits, with many believing that the theory was magical thinking that would send the deficit skyrocketing.[30] Nonetheless, some of the most visible faces of Republicanism spread the gospel of supply-side thinking with fervour. In Congress, former football player Rep. Jack Kemp (R-NY) was the most prevalent preacher, introducing a broad tax-cutting bill repeatedly in Congress from 1977 onwards (often joined by Sen. William Roth [R-DE], and thus 'Kemp-Roth' became a shorthand for discussing supply-side ideas).[31] Kemp was an atypical Republican, who represented Buffalo, New York – the city of both his beloved Buffalo Bills and a substantial African American population. Throughout his career, he advocated for Republicans to do far more in terms of civil rights, to avoid 'dog whistle' racist politics, and also for the government to help those in poverty. Rather than big spending programmes, however, Kemp – who toyed with a run for president in 1980 before forgoing and endorsing Reagan – saw tax cuts and targeted business incentives (known often as either 'Empowerment Zones' or 'Enterprise Zones') as key to helping the black community.[32]

Supply-side economics was significant for antipoverty politics because it appeared to offer a conservative solution to the economic problems of 1970s, without seeming cruel to the poor. From his syndicated perch, Ronald Reagan championed Kemp's supply-side advocacy. In late 1977, he wrote proudly that because of Republican supply-siders, the two parties were in the midst of a role reversal, with the Republicans finally embracing positive change and the Democrats, who opposed tax cuts, now the 'aginners' of American politics.[33] For the Republicans, it offered an escape hatch from the negativism that had dogged the party's approach to socioeconomic issues for so long. During the 1978 campaign, more Republicans were vocal about their desire to roll back government, with many candidates also running on a supply-side platform.[34]

The 1978 midterms, in which conservative Republicans enjoyed success, signalled that something was afoot among the American electorate. Republicans won a net three Senate seats and fifteen House seats, while clawing back control of seven state legislatures. This is despite the fact that the election was well timed for the Democrats: Carter had recently brokered the lauded Camp David Agreement between Israel and Egypt, and the economic conditions in November 1978 were about as good as they ever were during Carter's troubled tenure. Republicans – hollowed out from two disastrous elections at state and local level – also lacked decent candidates for many winnable seats.[35] Nonetheless, the night still belonged to the GOP. Among the notable arrivals were senators William Armstrong (R-CO), Thad Cochran (R-MS) and Gordon Humphrey (R-NH), who joined fellow conservatives Jesse Helms and John Tower, each of whom survived tricky re-election battles. In the House, future household names Newt Gingrich (R-GA) and Dick Cheney (R-WY) arrived as part of a new generation of assertive conservatives. Meanwhile the loss of progressive Republican Ed Brooke – still the only serving black senator since Reconstruction – to Paul Tsongas (D-MA) was a further portent of the declining strength of progressives and moderates in the GOP. As such, the Republican caucus on Capitol Hill shifted rightward. Once in office, Republicans worked – often successfully – to stymie further liberal efforts at spending.[36] As Carter's problems mounted, Republicans lay in wait for the 1980 presidential elections to catapult themselves into power.

Republicans, for a change

Ronald Reagan, who first sought the presidency in 1968, spent much of the 1970s in the national spotlight with a continued eye on the White House. And when he was in the spotlight, he used his national platform to advocate less government and a more conservative approach to socioeconomic issues. In the early 1970s, as governor of the nation's most populous state, he made news for having high-profile spats with the Nixon White House over his opposition to the Family Assistance Plan and when he sought to axe antipoverty initiatives in California that Nixon's OEO Director wanted to continue. When it came time to run in 1980, Reagan often leaned on his tenure in California – the seventh biggest economy in the world in its own right – as evidence that he had the experience to become America's chief executive.[37] Reflecting on Reagan's gubernatorial record, his 1980 campaign noted proudly that Reagan had taken 'a strong stand against federal "anti-poverty" projects' and 'used his power to veto more such projects than any other governor'. Moreover, the campaign boasted that Reagan had instituted a string of welfare reforms to curb the growth in Californians claiming government cheques.[38]

During his governorship and throughout his political career, Reagan stressed that he believed government should support the 'truly needy' but he doubted that there were many such Americans left. In 1974, term limited and soon to depart Sacramento, he used a commencement address at California Polytechnic State

University to question whether poverty really existed in the United States: '95% of the families in this country have an adequate minimum daily intake of nutrients, and I think part of the 5% who don't are on a diet. 99% of the homes in America have gas or electric appliances; 96% of them have TV.' Questioning the contemporary definition of poverty, Reagan claimed that if judged by the current measure, then 90 per cent of Americans were in poverty during his childhood in the 1920s and 1930s.[39] In this sense, he was a remarkably consistent politician. He had advanced similar arguments – and even used the joke about those lacking nutrition being on a diet – during the 1964 speech on behalf of Goldwater that launched Reagan's political career.[40]

Reagan, sensing the rising conservative tide in the GOP and the soft support for incumbent Gerald Ford, challenged the sitting president in 1976. Reagan's primary challenge went all the way to the convention before Ford's use of White House power and patronage helped the sitting president finally secure victory. During his campaign, Reagan made federal social welfare programmes the 'centerpiece' domestic issue.[41] In August 1975, as he geared up to run, he declared that 'if through some set of circumstances welfare did disappear tomorrow, no one would miss a meal'.[42] In January 1976, as the all-important New Hampshire primary loomed, he began regaling audiences with his tale of the Chicago 'welfare queen'. The story was about a black woman (whom Reagan never named), Linda Taylor. Taylor, whom journalist Josh Levin has recently unveiled as a convicted fraudster who assumed eighty aliases and likely committed murder, was scamming the welfare system for tens of thousands of dollars.[43] Reagan used Taylor as an avatar of a welfare system that was stuffed full of fraud and serving ablebodied people who did not need the money and who refused to work. As Levin notes, 'The "welfare queen" became a convenient villain, a woman everyone could hate. She was a lazy black con artist, unashamed of cadging the money that honest folks worked so hard to earn.'[44] In 1976, Reagan's remedy for reforming the system was to devolve control of federal social welfare programmes to the states and localities that, he contested, could administer such initiatives best.

Nonetheless, in 1976, social welfare reform likely proved Reagan's undoing. Journalists pressed Reagan on how New Hampshire – a state with no income tax – would pay for the programmes that helped the poor if they were transferred from federal to state and local level. Under pressure, Reagan confessed that yes, if his vision were put into place, New Hampshirites would have to raise their own taxes if they wanted to maintain various social welfare programmes.[45] This revelation put Reagan on the back foot; he lost New Hampshire and each of the other first five states, only regaining momentum when Ford had accrued a lead that Reagan was never quite able to overcome. Still, his recovery in later primaries suggested that while he might have to finesse his argument in future, Reagan was the heir apparent for the GOP. This was only confirmed when Reagan overshadowed Ford at the Republican National Convention with a speech that wowed the delegates and showed the vast affection that rank-and-file Republicans had for Reagan.[46]

During the Carter years, Reagan continued to position himself for the GOP nomination – and he also continued to take aim at federal poverty programmes. In his syndicated columns and radio talks, Reagan frequently advocated for the GOP to stay the conservative course. Following the 1976 election, Ford's former Press Secretary, Jerald terHorst, opined in the *Los Angeles Times* that Republicans needed to act more progressively on socioeconomic issues; to show more compassion for the 'little guy, white and black' and thus shirk off the perception of the GOP as 'callous, cruel, and insensitive'.[47] Reagan mocked terHorst for sounding like a liberal Democrat. In a follow-up column, Reagan noted polling that showed conservative attitudes to government were rising among Americans, and told Republicans to 'go where the ducks are' in pursuing this growing vote.[48] When Republicans then made gains in 1978, he attributed it to the public's more explicitly conservative attitudes on taxes and spending, and laid bare the Democratic Party's challenge during a time of economic malaise:

For Democratic politicians long used to harvesting votes by dispensing nearly unlimited amounts of middle-class tax dollars, the new reality is going to be hard to get used to. No one has yet explained satisfactorily how a politician can be a 'fiscal conservative' and a liberal about paternalistic social programs at the same time. No wonder there were some sweaty Democratic brows the other night.[49]

Reagan urged Republicans to support the Kemp–Roth tax cuts, which he believed offered a clear and popular message that spoke the 'language of incentives, optimism and continued growth (the only way America's "haves" got to where they are)'.[50]

And as he was gearing up to declare his candidacy in 1979, Reagan returned to one of his favourite topics: corruption and waste in the War on Poverty. Devoting two radio broadcasts solely to the topic of 'Antipoverty Abuses', Reagan cited recent separate investigations into both the CSA and the Volunteers in Service to America (VISTA). Regarding the former, he quoted *Reader's Digest*, which claimed to have found at the CSA, 'an ugly trail of mismanagement, corruption, waste, and misconduct', adding that 'tens of millions of dollars earmarked for the needy have been stolen or frittered away'.[51] Reagan said his 'favorite' example of this corruption was that the head of one Community Action Agency drove a Mercedes-Benz that cost the group almost $6,000 to lease per annum. 'With friends like this [sic],' Reagan scorned, 'the poor don't need enemies.'[52] He also recounted that a recent congressional investigation by Rep. Bob Michel (R-IL) showed VISTA volunteers becoming actively involved in political campaigns. Concluding that 'the war on poverty looks as if it has turned into a war on the poor', Reagan challenged Carter to fire Sam Brown, head of the agency that oversaw VISTA.[53] While Carter unsurprisingly ignored Reagan's calls, the Georgian could not ignore the Gipper for long.

With Carter looking vulnerable, many Republicans jumped at the chance to challenge the incumbent, but in spite of the packed field, the nominating contest was always Reagan's to lose. Reagan simply had built up the most affection, the most contacts, possessed the relevant experience, and above all, his ideological views represented the core of the GOP. 'The Republicans named the aspirant,' political scientist Gerald Pomper observed, 'with the most widespread support among party members and the one who represented best the ideological bent of the party.'[54] Despite a spirited challenge from former CIA director, RNC chair and congressman, George H. W. Bush, Reagan won forty-one states and the nomination comfortably before – in a show of strength – selecting his closest rival as his running mate. Aside from Bush's oft-replayed comment during the primary campaign that supply-side thinking was 'Voodoo Economics', Reagan sustained little damage and was quickly able to turn the focus onto Jimmy Carter's record.

As the economy worsened and the national drama of the Iran hostage crisis continued to play out on the nightly news, things went from bad to worse for the incumbent president. Carter spent the primary season facing down a relentless – albeit flawed – challenge from Sen. Ted Kennedy (D-MA). Representing disillusioned liberal Democrats, Kennedy took his contest with Carter all the way to the convention, before lending only a tepid endorsement to the president. Even Rep. John Anderson's (R-IL) decision to bolt the Republicans and run as an independent presidential candidate concerned Carter more than it did Reagan. Carter worried (probably correctly) that disaffected Republican or swing voters who viewed Reagan as extreme and unfit for the presidency would now cast their ballot for Anderson rather than Carter.[55] Anderson, a moderate Republican who had placed third in the GOP nominating contest, formed the National Unity Party and selected a Democratic running mate. The National Unity Party's platform positioned itself between the two parties on socioeconomic issues – more liberal than the Republicans and more conservative than the Democrats. Anderson, however, who considered himself an economic conservative, was mainly motivated to bolt the GOP over differences on cultural issues – namely the Equal Rights Amendment and a woman's right to have an abortion.[56] Thus his decision to leave did not expose a deep chasm in the GOP's approach to poverty.

The Carter campaign envisaged the general election as a rerun of the 1964 presidential contest, with the incumbent Democratic president portraying the conservative Republican challenger as an extremist on both domestic and foreign issues. If successful, the public would go into the voting booths believing that Ronald Reagan was likely to start a war – perhaps one that involved nuclear weaponry – and to take away Social Security and Medicare from hardworking Americans.[57] In 1964, the Republican Party – exposed as

257

hopelessly divided at their chaotic convention – had ably assisted the impression that the GOP candidate was an extremist. In 1980, Anderson's lonely departure aside, there was no such issue. Instead, Republicans were in a united and hopeful mood when they met in July to anoint Reagan as nominee in Detroit. Despite lingering personal resentment from 1976, former President Ford heartily endorsed his erstwhile foe. In his speech, Ford criticised antipoverty programmes, and offered an alternative Republican – and Reagan-esque – vision: 'We have forged a giant government out of compassion for the needy. Now we can trim that government out of compassion for the taxpayers.'[58] He then cut a television ad, in which Ford – a respected former president – assured Americans that Reagan was the safe and correct choice.[59] When it came to Reagan's turn to speak at the convention, he warned against the peril of federal benevolence: 'government is never more dangerous than when our desire to have it help us blinds us to its great power to harm us'. Thus, in a speech that mentioned 'government' more than thirty times, Reagan framed the election as a contrasting choice between the liberal Democratic embrace of social programmes to solve the nation's ills and his promise to reduce taxes, reduce spending and unleash American free enterprise.[60]

The Republican mood was bolstered by something else: the GOP brand was no longer so toxic. Nothing highlighted this shift more than the Republicans' embrace of their own name. Rather than downplay partisan labels, the GOP election slogan, 'Republicans, For a Change', emphasised it. While Nixon and Ford had run away from their party in a bid to secure Democratic support, Reagan ran happily and enthusiastically as the 'Republican' candidate. Bolstered by a revitalised party apparatus headed by RNC chair William Brock, formerly a senator from Tennessee, an ambitious conservative and prolific fundraiser, the Republicans acted as a party that knew their moment had arrived.[61] During the autumn campaign, this image of Republican unity was secured by a joint appearance between the presidential candidate and almost all congressional candidates on the steps of the Capitol. Republicans also did not hide their governing agenda. Releasing a 'solemn covenant with the American people', the GOP pledged to cut taxes, reduce the federal budget, increase military weaponry and promote business investment.[62] The RNC hosted 'party of the people' events

258

and spent significant money to recast the formerly privileged and negative image of the GOP.[63] Republicans, rather than attempting to borrow votes from working-class Democratic voters during election time, were now actively trying to convert such voters to become permanent Republicans.

Reagan's own presidential campaign had two specific goals: to moderate the candidate's image and to emphasise the contrast in leadership qualities with the faltering Carter. Regarding the former, they stumbled out of the gate. On 3 August, Reagan – having overruled many dissenting advisers – launched his campaign with a none-too-subtle appeal to states' rights in Neshoba County, Mississippi, known nationally for the murders of three civil rights workers during Freedom Summer in 1964. Intriguingly, Reagan's infamous declaration – 'I believe in states' rights' – came in the middle of a section in which he excoriated federal welfare programmes for keeping the poor in poverty and boasted of his reforming record in California.[64] Reagan's audience at the country fair enthusiastically welcomed his criticism of welfare and support for states' rights, but the speech was less well received nationally.[65] Instead, it seemed Reagan was confirming the Democratic accusations that he was an extremist who was unfit to lead modern America. Nevertheless, only days after his Dixie trip, Reagan was seen addressing the National Urban League and speaking to poor black residents in the Bronx, New York. Such events, Richard Wirthlin, the campaign's pollster, reasoned, might not win black voters, who would almost certainly vote Democratic, but would placate moderate white voters who did not think of themselves as racist.[66]

Reagan's speech to the annual convention of the National Urban League was a forthright acknowledgement of the negative perception which conservatives – and indeed, Republicans in general – struggled to shake on the issue of poverty: that they lacked compassion for the poor and racial minorities. Comparing his own appearance to John F. Kennedy's famous speech in front of a Protestant audience in 1960, Reagan said:

> For too many people, conservative has come to mean anti poor, anti black, and anti disadvantaged. Perhaps some of you question whether a conservative really feels sympathy and compassion for victims of social and economic misfortune, and of racial discrimination.

Rather, Reagan argued, 'What I want for America is, I think, pretty much what the overwhelming majority of black Americans also want.' Nonetheless, Reagan's prescriptions (deregulation, spending not to be increased but localised, and tax incentives) differed from those preferred by his audience, most of whom likely saw the benefit in federal antipoverty programmes.[67] When Reagan visited the destitute Charlotte Street area of the Bronx the following day, he told the crowd that there were no federal programmes for the poor that could wave a 'wand' and revitalise an area. In response, he was heckled by residents shouting: 'you ain't gonna do nothing'.[68] Still, given that Carter had stood in the same spot in 1977 and promised federal spending that would transform the area, many voters might have concluded that Reagan was on the right side of the argument.

Come October, Reagan's attempt to portray himself as a stronger leader than Carter was only half working. Voters were thoroughly dissatisfied with the incumbent, but they were still unsure that Reagan was any better. At one point, Carter – who spent campaign appearances railing against Reagan's extremism and unfitness for office – appeared close to drawing level in polling after having trailed heavily over the summer.[69] When the candidates met for their solitary debate, which took place only one week before Election Day, the stakes were tremendously high for both candidates.

In terms of domestic policy, the debate revolved around the proper role for the federal government: should it interfere on the side of both middle-class and disadvantaged Americans or was its very presence in socioeconomic affairs driving up inflation, harming working Americans and creating a permanent underclass? Reagan had been honing his message on the issue for nearly two decades. Carter, who had often confusingly advocated both government spending and fiscal conservatism, far less so. This 'battle about social policy', political scientist Ira Katznelson correctly writes, was 'fought by combatants of unequal conviction'.[70] In the opening section of the debate, Carter tiptoed towards a typical Democratic criticism of Republicans, telling the record-breaking 80.6 million Americans watching at home that Reagan's solutions to economic problems were 'a heartless kind of approach to the working families of our country, which is typical of many Republican leaders of the past, but, I think, has been accentuated under Governor Reagan'.[71] Yet, Carter, rather than promising government-led solutions as most Democrats would have done, pivoted immediately to attacking Reagan for raising taxes while California governor – a charge that Reagan easily rebutted. The tone was set. Reagan genially batted away any suggestion he would pare back Social Security, refused to name any programmes that he would cut to balance the budget, and offered his tax cuts as the key to an economic recovery that would help all Americans, rich and poor. Carter, the incumbent during a horrid economy and a politician who did not believe in New Deal/Great Society remedies to such problems, offered often incoherent responses.[72]

One week later, millions of Americans decided to vote Republican, for a change. The 1980 election was a remarkable result for both Reagan personally and the Republican Party more broadly. Reagan's landslide victory over Carter was so sweeping that NBC broke with tradition and called the election when millions of Americans in the Western time zones were still voting. While Reagan only won 50.9 per cent of the vote, his electoral college margin of 489 to 49 suggested that the American people had decisively chosen new leadership. Equally important, Republicans – and mostly conservative Republicans – were winning up and down the ballot. The GOP gained a remarkable twelve Senate seats and seized control of that chamber for the first time since 1955. Meanwhile, the party netted thirty-four additional House seats. Without the enduring loyalty that many southerners continued to feel to their local (often conservative) incumbent Democrats, the lower chamber would almost certainly have fallen into Republican control.

Many scholars have assessed the election result to be a consequence of Carter's unpopularity rather than an endorsement of Republicans and Reagan.[73] This is only half true. While Carter's travails were important, Iwan Morgan observes, 'Americans could have had little doubt about the direction in which [Reagan] intended to lead the nation.'[74] The result was also a 'party victory' for Republicans. 'For the first time in fifty years,' Pomper noted shortly after the contest, 'a President has been elected who admits that he is a Republican.' Even more specifically, it was a victory for conservative Republicanism. The most symbolic Republican victory came in the New York Senate race – a seat that the GOP already held. Jacob Javits, the foremost progressive Republican senator for two decades, and the GOP's most vociferous supporter of the War on Poverty – was defeated in his primary by conservative challenger Al D'Amato (who then went on to win the general election). Among the new crop of GOP Senate freshmen, only two were not endorsed by the conservative group, Americans for Constitutional Action (ACA).[75] Importantly, conservative Republicans achieved this success by not shying away from their conservative positions on socioeconomic issues. The War on Poverty's days appeared numbered. With its greatest opponent in the White House and Republicans now controlling the Senate, the Democratic House stood as the antipoverty effort's last line of defence.

The end? The War on Poverty and the Reagan revolution

Franklin Roosevelt's First Hundred Days took the first steps in creating an American welfare state that put the federal government in the business of providing aid to poorer Americans. Almost fifty years later, Ronald Reagan's Second Hundred Days retrenched the welfare state and proscribed a heavy dose of free market enterprise as an alternative cure for poverty. While Roosevelt's emergency measures were forged in the excitement of spring, Reaganomics (the term applied to Reagan's 1981 budget measures) was a summer affair – marked by the passage of the misleadingly mundane-sounding Omnibus Budget and Reconciliation Act (OBRA) and the Economic Recovery Tax Act (ERTA). Roosevelt's New Deal tapestry was haphazard and pragmatic. Reagan's legislation, even though it contained necessary compromises, embodied an ideology the 40th President had nurtured for over two decades. From the moment Reagan was elected, his White House worked studiously towards enacting the three pillars of their boss's vision: cutting taxes, cutting domestic spending (especially means-tested programmes that targeted the poor) and increasing military spending.[76] Reagan was able to achieve his landmark legislation by keeping congressional Republicans unified and building public support for his ideas to the extent that many southern Democrats felt unable to resist the new president for fear of voter backlash. Nonetheless, in achieving his legislative goals, Reagan was quickly on the defensive. As the economy worsened and more Americans fell into poverty, the enduring image of the Gipper as a heartless president who cared little for the poor took hold. With his first year in office drawing to a close, the debate over poverty – and how to fight it – was back in the headlines.

Reagan's team began planning how to execute the redirection of American socioeconomic policy long before the voters entered the polling booths in November. As early as April 1980, the Reagan transition team brought in hundreds of largely conservative thinkers and created task forces to draft policy and strategy.[77] When the administration's recruitment drive began, conservatives were hired and moderates were ignored. There would be no similar figure to Nixon's Daniel Patrick Moynihan arguing for a progressive alternative in the Reagan White House.[78] Instead, the West Wing was quickly adorned with pictures of Calvin Coolidge by aides who celebrated the former president's declaration that the 'chief business of the American people is business'.[79] With inauguration approaching, the administration agreed that a key mission was 'To reduce substantially the need for dependency on federal social, health and public assistance programs.'[80] The early Reagan White House was a focused operation with clear ambitions in domestic policy.

Once in office, Reagan used the bully pulpit to sell his vision to the American people. During his inaugural address, Reagan, echoing the conservative view of the War on Poverty's effect on the poor, demanded that 'Government can and must provide opportunity, not smother it; foster productivity, not stifle it.'[81] Less than a month later, he stood before Congress – and, by proxy, the nation – and pitched his Program for Economic Recovery. During the speech, he asked Congress for $49.1 billion in cuts for the following year's budget. In asking for the cuts, Reagan sought to disabuse elected representatives of the 'exaggerated and inaccurate stories' that such cuts would take away support for the poor's basic needs. Instead, he pledged that the United States would continue to care for the deserving poor, whom Reagan defined as 'those who through no fault of their own, must depend on the rest of us – the poverty stricken, the disabled, the elderly'. 'All those with true need,' Reagan pledged, 'can rest assured that the social safety net of programs they rely on are exempt from any cuts.'[82]

On 3 March, Reagan then sat down with Walter Cronkite. Cronkite, who would retire three days later from his role as *CBS Evening News* anchor, for which he was renowned as 'America's Most Trusted Man', challenged Reagan that potential cuts to Aid to Families with Dependent Children (AFDC) would 'create considerable hardship' for poorer – particularly urban – Americans. Reagan, however, casually swatted aside 'Uncle Walter', assuring Cronkite that such concerns resulted from liberal bureaucrats scaremongering in a bid to preserve their own jobs.[83] In private settings, Reagan continually repeated the story of the Chicago welfare queen to nervous Republicans representatives asking why such change was drastically needed. He recited the anecdote so often that its frequency became a running joke among his aides.[84]

Despite Reagan's bravado and his campaign team's assertion that he had won a mandate for change, the House remained in Democratic hands. The new President's tax and spending proposals were a high-stakes power game that teetered back and forth. Bill Brock, now Reagan's trade ambassador, warned Democrats that any attempt at frustrating the President's budget proposals would see them lose at the polls. He also threatened opposing legislators that 'We have raw power and the ultimate weapon is the veto power.'[85] In Congress, Rep. Vin Weber (R-MI), a freshman conservative, forced the CSA to investigate a Florida Community Action Agency (CAA) that Weber accused of lobbying against Reagan's welfare proposals. The CSA – destined for the axe as part of Reagan's plans – was then forced to send notice to all CAAs that they must cease any public attempts at arguing against cuts.[86] Republicans, sensing their moment, were unwilling to let the opportunity pass by without achieving significant change in the nation's approach to socioeconomic problems.

Counterattacking, Democrats repeated the same charge that they had used since the 1930s – that the Republicans were merely a heartless, privileged party, with no sense of compassion for the poor. Speaker Thomas 'Tip' O'Neill (D-MA), appearing on ABC's *Issues and Answers*, told Americans that the new President had 'no concern, no regard, no care for the little man of America . . . Because of his lifestyle, he never meets those people.' Meanwhile, he deemed those advisers surrounding Reagan as 'very, very self-ish people' who had made themselves wealthy but now wanted to pull the ladders of opportunity up behind them.[87] An even harsher line of argument emanated from Mohammed Coner, the CAA head who had so annoyed Weber. 'President Reagan don't give a damn if you breathe if you're poor,' Coner told a largely black audience. '[Poverty programs] that have lifted poor black people out of the muck of this country will be cut.'[88] Unfortunately for Democrats, their arguments were not cutting through, with one Democrat admitting in April that 'We've been waiting for the Reagan program to be rejected by the people, and that hasn't happened.'[89]

Reagan was able to overcome entrenched Democratic opposition for multiple reasons. First, his own personal popularity undoubtedly helped. Throughout the battle for OBRA and ERTA, Reagan enjoyed artificially inflated job approval ratings as the country rallied behind him after his near assassination by John Hinckley Jr on 30 March. Many Americans warmed to Reagan's phlegmatic and jocular response to the tragedy while he was recovering in hospital. When Reagan returned to action in April, he skilfully used the moment to appear in front of an emotional Congress and urge passage of his tax and spending proposals.[90] During the crucial summer in which the 'battle of the budget' took place, the White House revelled in Reagan's 67 per cent approval rating, with only 22 per cent expressing opposition to the president.[91] Such high ratings made it hard for Congress to oppose the President without risking the wrath of public opinion.

Reagan's personal popularity and his singular focus on his economic reforms were supplemented by the fact that elected Republicans were united behind their leader. Most GOP votes were not hard to corral from a more uniformly conservative delegation than had existed in the 1960s and 1970s. For instance, by 1981, 80 per cent of House Republicans were members of the conservative Republican Study Committee.[92] While some conservatives were anxious that the tax-cutting measures in Reaganomics might rapidly increase the deficit, most were thoroughly behind cutting antipoverty programmes and welfare spending – two of the big-ticket items in Reagan's budget. As such, the White House had most of the Republican votes that were needed without having to expend too much effort.

The one threat to Republican unity emerged in the form of a group of House Republicans who dubbed themselves the 'Gypsy Moths'. Hailing from Northeastern and Midwestern manufacturing areas dubbed the 'Frostbelt', some two dozen House GOP members organised into a power bloc when they realised that the White House was spending more time negotiating details of the budget with conservative southern Democrats – nicknamed 'Boll Weevils' – than they were with concerned Republicans. Gypsy Moths, often located in swing metropolitan districts, were most worried by Reagan's proposals as they felt that the cuts were falling disproportionately on their 'urban' (often a coded term in the 1980s for 'poor black') constituents.[93] Gypsy Moths also believed that the budget benefited the Sunbelt – now the centre of gravity in the GOP – at the expense of the old industrial North, which was currently enduring the worst of the economic recession. In April, Rep. Charles Dougherty (R-PA) expressed concern about voting for Reagan's budget proposals as he feared that Reagan was 'abandoning urban America' at a time when four new city wards in Philadelphia were about to be added to his swing district.[94]

During the budget showdown, the White House assuaged the Gypsy Moths through showering them with White House attention and restoring some small items to the budget. In response to Dougherty's concerns, the White House stressed that the best way to rebuild urban America was through a healthy economy and emphasised to Dougherty that any defections on Reagan's proposals would only help the Democrats.[95] While Dougherty did not vote for the final budget package, he did support the administration in two other key votes. In such situations, Reagan was often personally involved, meeting with members individually and deploying the telephone as a weapon, reminiscent of Lyndon Johnson during the heyday of the Great Society.[96] He also made small concessions to Gypsy Moths when necessary. Regarding one antipoverty measure, he had his budget director David Stockman – a true small-government conservative who was determined to slash spending – restore an experimental programme that sent military contracts to poorer districts.[97]

Republican cohesion was continually nurtured by the White House and congressional leadership. Elected Republicans were given explicit instructions on how to campaign for Reagan's proposals. When Congress recessed in April, all House and Senate Republicans were sent home with instructions on how to use this 'great opportunity to build support for the President's economic program'. Among the advice was that they should give speeches in favour of the proposals, drop by local news media to advocate for Reagan's plan, and cut radio soundbites promoting Reaganomics.[98] When Republicans returned to Capitol Hill, new House Minority Leader Bob Michel gathered his troops and encouraged them to unify in support of the President and repudiate Tip O'Neill's attempts at stifling Reagan's budget proposals.[99] Such sentiments won the day – on the crucial budget votes in 1981, Republican defections numbered 0, 2 and 1.[100] Even when a Republican defected, Reagan skilfully played his role as party leader. After agonising over the final OBRA vote, freshman Rep. Claudine Schneider (R-RI) joined Dougherty as the only other Republican in opposition, as she could not justify the cuts that would be made to social programmes that affected her constituents. The next day, the President personally called Schneider to tell her that he understood her decision, adding that if any Republicans expressed hostility about her vote, 'have them see me'.[101]

Southern Democrats were next in the White House's firing line. In 1980, many conservative southern Democrats had carried their district while Reagan was romping to victory at the top of the ticket. By the summer, the President was polling 70 per cent support in the South. The White House was determined to use this leverage to force such 'boll weevil' Democrats to defect from the Speaker's attempts at defeating Reaganomics in the House. The White House deployed a range of techniques – codenamed 'Southern Blitz', and coordinated by Lyn Nofziger in the political office – to apply pressure to recalcitrant members of the opposition. One such congressman, Rep. Butler Derrick (D-SC), a moderate conservative, was targeted relentlessly. The White House orchestrated pressure from Derrick's campaign contributors and Political Action Committees (PACs), as well as inciting a letter-writing campaign from influential people in Derrick's district. They also dispatched Republican bigwigs to South Carolina to grab local media attention. With the stick applied, the White House then offered the carrot – beguiling Derrick with personal presidential attention. Crucially, Derrick was quietly informed that the White House would not back a Republican challenger in his district. The strategy worked, Derrick sided with the White House, and he cruised to re-election with no Republican opponent.[102] Over the course of the budget fights, twenty-six other House Democrats joined Derrick, and proved crucial in making Reaganomics a reality.[103] Reflecting on the achievement, congressional liaison aide Max Friedersdorf rejoiced that 'Together . . . the House Republicans and the 27 Democrats are a helluva base!' *Congressional Quarterly* observed that this conservative coalition was the 'bedrock of the Reagan Revolution' and its success rate in 1981 was the highest ever recorded.[104]

Reagan also knew which fights on domestic policy to abandon. Despite a brief misstep, the Gipper continued the Republican tradition of pragmatic opposition to liberal social programmes. In May, while the budget was still being negotiated, the White House floated the idea of trimming Social Security benefits. Democrats were jubilant. While they were unable to stir the public in opposition to cuts that targeted the poor, the possibility of any changes to Social Security hit a nerve among voters. Soon thereafter, special elections held in Maryland, Ohio and Mississippi went the Democrats' way. The National Republican Congressional Committee (NRCC) found that the key issue in the contests was fears among voters over Social Security changes. It gave the Democrats a 'bread-and-butter issue,' columnists Rowland Evans and Robert Novak argued in the *Washington Post*, 'to appeal to the masses beyond social workers and welfare recipients'.[105] When the winnable Mississippi race fell to the Democrat in August, Nofziger warned his colleagues, 'It should not take a stroke of strategic genius to note that Republicans are being killed on [Social Security].'[106] Accordingly, Reagan quickly pivoted away from Social Security and accused Democrats of 'misinformation' and 'demagoguing' on the issue.[107] The episode served as a reminder in the White House that the administration was on safer political ground in cutting the War on Poverty than in suggesting changes to universal programmes that tangibly benefited all Americans.

Undoubtedly, poverty programmes remained easier targets as a result of their continued association with the black urban poor. Nonetheless, the White House and Republicans insisted that spending cuts would benefit this group in the long run. Conservative Republicans, bolstered by the publication of Gilder's *Wealth and Poverty* in early 1981, argued that the War on Poverty had trapped the urban poor in a cycle of dependency that discouraged work.[108] During the budget debates, conservative Sen. Orrin Hatch (R-UT) went as far as equating welfare to black bondage. 'This is a new slavery worse than the old,' Hatch misguidedly suggested. 'I cannot imagine a worse humiliation than to be freed, given civil rights, and then told: "Don't worry, the government will look after you."'[109] Hatch was not the only Republican to share this view. Some black Republicans – a small minority of African Americans by the 1980s – echoed the Senator. W. Gregory Wims, an official in Reagan's agriculture department (and later NAACP membership chairperson), wrote in the *Lincoln Review* that 'Anti-poverty programs have assumed the position of parents toward the recipients . . . Welfare is very clearly a form of bondage like slavery.'[110] During a speech to Texas Republicans in late 1981, Reagan claimed that many black Americans felt like Sims. He spoke of a letter he had received from an elderly Louisiana lady. According to Reagan, 'She was black, but she said, "Thank you for doing away with the war on poverty." She said, "Thank you for letting us once again try our own muscle and not become helpless dependents."'[111]

Nonetheless, most black Americans did not agree with Reagan on welfare, nor did they trust the Reagan White House in general. In 1980, more than any other group, they had decisively rejected Reagan, with only 14 per cent lending him their vote.[112] Reagan's actions in office only cemented this antipathy: his budget cuts, lack of black political appointees and opposition to extending civil rights protections further alienated black Americans. Reagan biographer Lou Cannon notes that when speaking to the NAACP in June 1981 the president received one of the 'coolest receptions of his presidency' from an audience who believed Reagan's budget proposals were a 'new kind of bondage'.[113] By the end of his first year in office, Elizabeth Dole – the head of the White House's Office of Public Liaison – bemoaned that a 'dangerous stereotype' had taken hold 'of a President who is unsympathetic to the plight of the poor and the needy, and a threat to gains in civil rights over the past twenty years'.[114] For Reagan, though, there was never any likelihood that he could win round a substantial number of black voters and thus their opposition was not key in his bid to reverse antipoverty policy.

The Reagan Revolution's key date was 13 August 1981, when the President signed ERTA and OBRA into law. Taken together, the two pieces of legislation changed the direction of American socioeconomic policy and politics. ERTA was the nation's biggest ever tax cut, reducing individual income tax rates by 23 per cent over the next three years, while the top tax rate for the wealthiest Americans went from 70 per cent to 50 per cent. OBRA, however, had clearer implications for poverty policy. Of the $140 billion in spending cuts that OBRA prescribed over three years, 70 per cent was drawn from means-tested programmes that helped either poor or low-income Americans.[115] Despite Reagan's claims that his proposals sided with those perceived as the deserving poor, it was 'the working poor – families that had some job income but still were near the poverty level', who, according to *Congressional Quarterly*, 'suffered serious losses'.[116] From 1 October, 400,000 working families lost all welfare assistance, while 300,000 endured partial cuts. Meanwhile, one million fewer received food stamps and three million would no longer receive a free school lunch. Finally, funding was cut for health care to the poor (Medicaid) and fewer students would be guaranteed federal loans to attend higher education.[117]

With OBRA's passage, many Johnson-era initiatives that were begun by the Economic Opportunity Act were either abolished or turned into block grants with reduced funding. Most notably, OBRA abolished the CSA and thus the last vestige of a poverty agency within the federal government. The CSA was replaced by a Community Services Block Grant to the states with fewer federal dictates over what the money should be spent on. The funds appropriated for the grant were even smaller than the threadbare amount that had been earmarked for the CSA. Reagan's embrace of block grants, the conservative Heritage Foundation happily observed, represented 'a major attempt to reverse the Twentieth Century's flow of power to Washington'.[118] Elsewhere, other anti-poverty initiatives, such as Legal Services and VISTA, retained their identity, but with reduced funding. Job training programmes also suffered severe cuts. Only Head Start and Foster Grandparents (Nancy Reagan's favourite initiative) received a funding boost.[119] Moreover, the simultaneous passage of ERTA suggested that these spending reductions were permanent. In selling his tax cuts to the American public, Reagan had declared that the money not taken from Americans in tax 'won't be available to the Congress to spend, and that, in my view, is what this whole controversy comes down to'.[120] Despite the fact that polling showed that most Americans believed Reagan's budget was unfair to the poor, his public appeal was met with widespread support.[121] By August, it appeared that a jubilant Reagan had won his war on the War on Poverty.

An enduring shift?

While it seemed that Reagan had delivered the knockout punch to his congressional foes over the summer, the second round of the bout between the President and the Democratic House proved a more even contest. Only one month after a beaming Reagan had signed his landmark legislation, economic indicators turned sour. Census Bureau figures showed that the number of Americans in poverty was increasing, while analysts projected much higher budget deficits than expected. From the serenity of August, journalists now painted a picture of a White House in disarray. With economic challenges as the mood music, Evans and Novak noted that suddenly Washington was struck down by 'so much confusion and a lack of confidence'. They reported that even budget-conscious Republicans were nervous – some of whom had severe doubts about supply-side economics and were interested in restricting the ERTA tax cuts before they kicked in.[122]

271

Rather than accede to this new reality, Reagan and his allies determined to plough ahead with plans for further cuts. On 24 September, Reagan addressed the nation, seeking to stiffen American spines and assure the public that Reaganomics would work in the long run by stimulating growth and widening the tax base.[123] During the speech, he also proposed a further $13 billion in spending cuts. Nonetheless, Reagan's charm offensive was not as compelling as it had been in the summer. To many Americans and to Gypsy Moth Republicans, Reagan's deeper cuts seemed cruel rather than necessary at a time when the nation was becoming aware of the increased poverty spurred by the worst recession since the 1930s.

It did not help Reagan's cause that the media, which had largely ignored poverty for the previous decade, now trained their focus on the issue. The three main television networks, which between them had featured only fourteen stories about poverty during the whole of 1980, dramatically increased their output. Some of this coverage reflected common concerns of the 1960s and 1970s – white fears of a growing urban black 'underclass' characterised by single parent families, permanent poverty and criminality. The publication of Ken Auletta's *The Underclass* (1981) reinforced such fears of an unruly and uncontrollable section of society.[124] In addition to this focus, however, was a new – previously ignored – media trope: white poverty. As Martin Gilens's research shows, in 1968, black Americans were the focus of 90 per cent of poverty-related stories on the three main networks, and still over 70 per cent in 1972. In the early 1980s, with Americans of all races losing their jobs, this dropped to 50 per cent and more stories featured impoverished whites.[125] With white poverty back in focus, the prospect of a public backlash to further cuts to antipoverty programmes undoubtedly increased. Nonetheless, on 2 October, Reagan doubled down on his philosophy, with the White House proclaiming 'American Enterprise Day'. 'Free enterprise,' the President affirmed, is the true 'enemy of poverty.'[126]

With his popularity sagging, however, Reagan's words carried less weight and suggested that his victory over the War on Poverty might well have been only a temporary affair. Even some in his own party began openly rebelling over his new proposals. In

November, the Gypsy Moths rejected a White House plan to enact further cuts on social welfare spending and joined with Democrats to pass an appropriations bill which cut military funds instead.[127] Over in the Senate, Republican dissension was also growing. Mark Hatfield (R-OR), the moderate chair of the Appropriations Committee, warned the President that he wanted defence cuts prioritised over any further intrusions into domestic budgets.[128] Tensions came to a head when a House coalition of Democrats and Gypsy Moths passed a resolution to fund the government with less than one quarter of the cuts that Reagan had requested.[129] The President promptly vetoed the measure, and a prolonged government shutdown was only narrowly avoided. By early December, Congress agreed to $4 billion in further cuts. While Reagan declared victory, it also only represented less than one third of what he had requested. Moreover, he was only able to secure Gypsy Moth support by promising the moderate Republicans more funding for health, education and fuel assistance for the poor.[130] Republican unity thus just about survived. The political sands, however, appeared to be shifting from under the President's feet. Democrats, once fearful of losing their House majority in 1982, now licked their lips at the prospect of winning back the Senate. The domestic policy of Reagan and Republicans, they charged, lacked 'fairness'.

Conclusion

Reagan's deep antipathy for the War on Poverty stood alongside his contempt for communism as one of the two animating forces of his political career. So much so, that America's 40th President was determined to see that the federal antipoverty effort joined the Soviet Union on the 'ash heap of history'. In 1981, he and his party significantly curtailed the War on Poverty in one of the twentieth century's rare bursts of reform. In terms of domestic policy, only 1933–35 and 1964–65 compare to 1981. As Baker beamed in December, 'this Congress has made more fundamental changes in the public policy of this nation than any Congress in decades'.[131] Reagan and the Republicans – together with some support from southern Democrats – enacted spending cuts that mostly fell on the poor. By also passing tax cuts, they ensured that any future politician who wanted to revive a government-led assault on poverty would find that there was less funding available for such an endeavour. James Tobin, 1981's Nobel laureate in economics, observed that taken together OBRA and ERTA represented a 'historic reversal of direction' in the government's attempt at achieving equality of opportunity.[132] While Reagan left elements of the social safety net in place, free enterprise – long lauded by Republicans as America's greatest weapon in fighting poverty – was now expected to do the hard work in uplifting the nation's poor.

By the end of his first year in office, Reagan's presidency – and by extension the endurance of his 'revolution' – hung in the balance. Importantly, in selling supply-side economics as the cure to both rich and poor, Reagan had been able to refashion a previously stale, fuddy-duddy, anti-government message into a positive, upbeat appeal. This approach, at least initially, allowed Republicans to sidestep the typical charge of negativism and privilege. Additionally, the popularity of Reagan's budget with voters, and the White House's determination to use that as leverage, was enough to ensure that sceptical moderate Republicans and conservative southern Democrats played their part in the Reagan Revolution. Paradoxically, Reagan's success in cutting antipoverty programmes revived media scrutiny and public interest in how government was caring for the poor. Reaganomics, combined with a worsening economy, succeeded in putting poverty policy back in the spotlight. The endurance of the changes ushered in by the Reagan Revolution were now very much reliant on an economic recovery.

Notes

1. Ronald W. Reagan, *The Reagan Diaries*, ed. Douglas Brinkley (New York: HarperCollins, 2007), 65.
2. Davies, *See Government Grow*; Zelizer, *The Fierce Urgency of Now*.
3. William G. Mayer, *The Changing American Mind: How and Why American Public Opinion Changed between 1960 and 1988* (Ann Arbor, MI: University of Michigan Press, 1992).
4. *CQ Almanac 1978*, vol. xxxiv (1978).
5. In 1977, polling showed one fifth of voters identified Republicans, as opposed to one half for Democrats. Cited in Mason, *From Hoover to Reagan*, 247.

6. Timothy Stanley, 'Carter's Domestic Dilemmas, 1977–1978', in *A Companion to Gerald R. Ford and Jimmy Carter*, ed. Scott Kaufmann (Chichester: Wiley Blackwell, 2015), 335–49.

7. Jimmy Carter, Address Accepting the Presidential Nomination at the Democratic National Convention, New York, 15 July 1976, TAPP.

8. Stanley, 'Carter's Domestic Dilemmas'; McAndrews, *The Presidents and the Poor*, 96–7.

9. Rose, 'Head Start: Growing beyond the War on Poverty', 177.

10. Ventry, 'The Collision of Tax and Welfare Politics'.

11. Vote on H.R. 7577, Govtrack.us: https://www.govtrack.us/congress/votes/95-1978/h1235.

12. Chaze, 'After 15 Years of "Great Society" Spending'.

13. Crafton, 'The Incremental Revolution', 39.

14. Patrick Andelic, '"The Old Economic Rules No Longer Apply": The National Planning Idea and the Humphrey–Hawkins Full Employment Act, 1974–1978', *Journal of Policy History*, vol. 31, no. 1 (2019), 89.

15. John Samples, *The Struggle to Limit Government: A Modern Political History* (Washington, DC: Cato Institute, 2010), 66.

16. Kathleen A. Frankovic, 'Public Opinion Trends', in *The Election of 1980: Reports and Interpretations*, ed. Marlene Pomper (Chatham, NJ: Chatham House, 1981), 114.

17. Samples, *The Struggle to Limit Government*, 65; Carter's own memoirs included one discussion of welfare issues in which the former president railed against a 'special interests feast', Jimmy Carter, *Keeping Faith: Memoirs of a President* (Fayetteville, AK: University of Arkansas Press, 1982), 84.

18. Kevin P. Phillips, *The Politics of Rich and Poor: Wealth and the American Electorate in the Reagan Aftermath* (New York: Random House, 1990).

19. Historical Inflation Rate, US Bureau of Labor Statistics: https://www.bls.gov/cpi/data.htm.

20. McAndrews, *The Presidents and the Poor*, 94.

21. Baker quoted in *CQ Almanac 1978*, 9.

22. McGirr, *Suburban Warriors*, 192.

23. Jason Stahl, *Right Moves: The Conservative Think Tank in American Political Culture since 1945* (Chapel Hill, NC: University of North Carolina Press, 2016).

24. Martin Anderson, *Welfare: The Political Economy of Welfare Reform in the United States* (Stanford, CA: Hoover Institution

Press, 1978); George Gilder, *Wealth and Poverty* (New York: Basic Books, 1981).

25. Roger A. Freeman, *The Wayward Welfare State* (Stanford, CA: Hoover Institute, 1981), 209–12.
26. Mason, *From Hoover to Reagan*, 251.
27. Donald L. Koopman, *Hostile Takeover: The House Republican party, 1980–1995* (Rowman & Littlefield: Lanham, MD, 1996), 69–84.
28. Iwan Morgan, 'Taxation as Republican Issue in the Era of Stagflation', in Mason and Morgan, *Seeking a New Majority*, 183.
29. Lewis Gould, *The Republicans: A History of the Grand Old Party* (New York: Oxford University Press, 2014), 278.
30. Kabaservice, *Rule and Ruin*, 350–1.
31. 'Rep. Jack Kemp', Govtrack: https://www.govtrack.us.
32. Morton Kondracke and Fred Barnes, *Jack Kemp: The Bleeding Heart Conservative Who Changed America* (New York: Sentinel, 2015).
33. RWR, 'Party Roles', 11 January 1977, box 12, 1980 Campaign Papers, 1965–1980, Ronald W. Reagan Library.
34. Mason, *From Hoover to Reagan*, 251.
35. RWR, 'Election Night, 1978', 16 January 1978, box 12, 1980 Campaign Papers, 1965–1980, RWR.
36. *CQ Almanac 1979*, 34.
37. RWR, 'Presidential Debate in Cleveland', 28 October 1980, TAPP.
38. 'The Reagan Record, 1967–74', 1980 Campaign Papers, 1965–1980, Series 1: Hannaford / CA HQ: Ronald Reagan Files, box 10.
39. RWR, California Polytechnic State University, San Luis Obispo, CA, 15 June 1974, 1980 Campaign Papers, 1965–1980, Series 1: Hannaford / CA HQ: Ronald Reagan Files, box 10.
40. RWR, 'A Time for Choosing', 27 October 1964, Reagan Library.
41. Jules Witcover, *Marathon: The Pursuit of the Presidency, 1972–1976* (New York: Viking Press, 1977), 387–8.
42. RWR quoted in Witcover, *Marathon*, 98.
43. Josh Levin, 'The Welfare Queen', *Slate*, 19 December 2013.
44. Levin, 'The Welfare Queen'.
45. Witcover, *Marathon*, 378–9.
46. RWR, Remarks at Republican National Convention Speech, 19 August 1976, Reagan Library.
47. J. F. terHorst, 'Sinking of GOP is No Accident', *Los Angeles Times*, 16 November 1976.
48. RWR, 'The Election', box 10, 1980 Campaign Papers, RWR.
49. RWR, 'Election Night, 1978'.
50. RWR, 'Party Roles'.

51. RWR, 'Antipoverty Abuses – Part One', 1 January 1979, box 12, 1980 Campaign Papers, RWR.
52. Ibid.
53. Ibid.
54. Gerald Pomper, 'The Nominating Contests', *Election of 1980*, 2.
55. Gerald Pomper, 'The Presidential Election', *Election of 1980*, 84.
56. Jim Mason, *No Holding Back* (Lanham, MD: Rowman & Littlefield, 2011), 352–5.
57. Pomper, 'The Presidential Election', 77.
58. GRF quoted in Ira Katznelson, 'A Radical Departure: Social Welfare and the Election', in *The Hidden Election: Politics and Economics in the 1980 Presidential Campaign*, ed. Thomas Ferguson and Joel Rogers (New York: Pantheon Books, 1981), 316.
59. 'Pres. Ford', *Living Room Candidate*, Museum of the Moving Image.
60. RWR, Republican National Convention Acceptance Speech, 17 July 1980, Reagan Library.
61. Klinkner, *The Losing Parties*, 133–49.
62. Pomper, 'The Presidential Election', 91.
63. Klinkner, *The Losing Parties*, 146–9.
64. RWR, Remarks at Neshoba County Fair, 3 August 1980.
65. Editorial, 'Chilling words in Neshoba County', *Washington Post*, 11 August 1980.
66. Rick Perlstein, *Reaganland: America's Right Turn, 1976–1980* (New York: Simon & Schuster, 2020), 829–30.
67. Lou Cannon, 'Reagan Makes Appeal for Black Votes', *Washington Post*, 6 August 1980.
68. 'Reagan, in South Bronx, Says Carter Broke Vow', *New York Times*, 6 August 1980, A16.
69. John Sides, 'What Really Happened in the 1980 Presidential Campaign', *Monkey Cage*, 9 August 2012. Available at https://themonkeycage.org/2012/08/what-really-happened-in-the-1980-presidential-campaign/ (accessed 6 November 2020).
70. Katznelson, 'A Radical Departure', 313.
71. 'Highest Rated Presidential Debates 1960 to Present', Nielsen, 6 October 2008. Available at https://www.nielsen.com/us/en/insights/article/2008/top-ten-presidential-debates-1960-to-present/ (accessed 6 November 2020).
72. 'Presidential Debate in Cleveland', 28 October 1980, TAPP.
73. For example, see Pomper et al. in *The Election of 1980*.
74. Iwan Morgan, *Reagan: American Icon* (London: I. B. Tauris, 2016) [Kindle].

75. Charles E. Jacob, 'The Congressional Elections', in *The Election of 1980*, 130.
76. These legislative priorities were combined with deregulation and monetarist fiscal policies.
77. James P. Piffner, 'The Paradox of President Reagan's Leadership', *Presidential Studies Quarterly*, vol. 43, no. 1 (2013), 81–6.
78. Ibid.
79. Phillips, *Rich and Poor*, 65–6.
80. Meeting Regarding a Welfare Reform Program for the Reagan Administration, Blair House, Washington DC, 6 January 1981, box 38, White House Staff Files, Ed Meese Files, RWR.
81. RWR, Inaugural Address, 20 January 1981, TAPP.
82. RWR, Address Before a Joint Session of the Congress on the Program for Economic Recovery, 18 February 1981, TAPP.
83. Excerpts from an Interview with Walter Cronkite of CBS News, 3 March 1981, TAPP.
84. Lou Cannon, *President Reagan: Role of a Lifetime* (New York: Simon & Schuster, 1991), 518.
85. Spencer Rich and Hobart Rowan, 'Ax Poised for Poverty Agency and Anti-Smoking Program', *Washington Post*, 5 March 1981.
86. Vin Weber, News Release, 1 May 1981, box 1, Lee Atwater Files, Series 1, Subject, 1981–82, RWR.
87. O'Neill quoted in Patrick Andelic, *Donkey Work: Congressional Democrats in Conservative America* (Lawrence, KS: University Press of Kansas, 2019), 134.
88. Charles Bermpohl, 'Blacks Urged to Assail Proposed Welfare Cuts', *The Florida Times-Union*, 1 May 1981.
89. Rowland Evans and Robert Novak, 'Evans and Novak Political Report Newsletter', 29 April 1981, box 1, Margaret Tutwiler Files, Series I COS Correspondence, RWR.
90. RWR, Address Before a Joint Session of the Congress on the Program for Economic Recovery, 28 April 1981, TAPP.
91. Lyn Nofziger to James Baker III, 14 July 1981, box 3, MT Files, Series I COS Correspondence.
92. Rae, *Decline and Fall of the Liberal Republicans*, 172.
93. Ibid, 185–6.
94. Max Friedersdorf to JBIII, 21 April 1981, box 2, MT, series I, RWR.
95. Ibid.
96. EN, 1 July 1981, MT, series 1, box 1.
97. Rae, *Decline and Fall of the Liberal Republicans*, 174–86.
98. Max Friedersdorf, Recess Letter to Hill Republicans, 8 April 1981, box 2, MT, series 1, RWR.

99. Robert Michel quoted in Meg Jacobs and Julian Zelizer, *Conservatives in Power: The Reagan Years, 1981–1989* (Boston, MA: Bedford/St Martin's, 2011), 95–6.
100. Rae, *Decline and Fall of the Liberal Republicans*, 183.
101. David Broder, '"Vulnerable" Republicans Making the Most of a Difficult Situation', *Washington Post*, 27 July 1981.
102. Evans and Novak, 'How the Budget was Won', 'Evans and Novak Political Report Newsletter', 1981.
103. Max Friedersdorf to Kenneth Duberstein, 5 August 1981, box 2, MT, series 1, RWR.
104. *CQ Almanac 1981*, vol. xxxvii.
105. Evans and Novak, 19 May 1981.
106. Lyn Nofiziger, 'Mississippi 4', 6 August 1981, box 3, MT, series 1, RWR.
107. RWR, Address to the Nation on the Program for Economic Recovery, 24 September 1981, TAPP.
108. Gilder, *Wealth and Poverty.*
109. Orrin Hatch quoted in Americans Against Welfare Dependency Position Paper, Summer 1981, box 9, White House Staff Files, Robert B. Carleson Files, RWR.
110. W. Gregory Wims, 'Blacks and Conservatism Closer Than We Think', *Lincoln Review*, October 1981.
111. RWR, Remarks at a 'Salute to a Stronger America' Republican Fundraising Dinner in Houston, Texas, 13 November 1981, TAPP.
112. 'How Groups Voted in 1980', Roper Center. Available at https://ropercenter.cornell.edu/how-groups-voted-1980 (accessed 6 November 2020).
113. Cannon, *President Reagan*, 521.
114. Elizabeth Dole quoted in Jacobs and Zelizer, *Conservatives in Power*, 105–8.
115. *CQ Almanac 1981*.
116. Ibid.
117. Morgan, *Reagan.*
118. Heritage Foundation, 'Block Grants and Federalism: Decentralizing Decisions', 6 May 1981, box 4, Martin Anderson Files, series 1, subject file, RWR.
119. *CQ Almanac 1981*.
120. RWR, Address to the Nation on Federal Tax Reduction Legislation, 27 July 1981, TAPP.
121. Steven V. Roberts, 'G.O.P. "Gypsy Moths" Test Their Wings', *New York Times*, 26 July 1981.
122. Evans and Novak, 15 September 1981.

123. RWR, 24 September 1981.
124. Patterson, *America's Struggle*, 216–17.
125. Martin Gilens, *Why Americans Hate Welfare: Race, Media, and the Politics of Antipoverty Policy* (Chicago, IL: The University of Chicago Press, 1999).
126. RWR, Proclamation 4866 – American Enterprise Day, 2 October 1981, TAPP.
127. Evans and Novak, 13 October 1981.
128. Hatfield quoted in Ibid.
129. Ibid.
130. Martin Tolchin, 'How the Federal Budget Was Shaved by $4 Billion', *New York Times*, 13 December 1981.
131. Baker quoted in Helen Dewar, 'Dominated by Reagan, Senate Makes Much History in a Hurry', *Washington Post*, 17 December 1981.
132. Tobin quoted in Ann Crittenden, 'Economic Scene: Rich and Poor in U.S. Today', *New York Times*, 16 December 1981.

Epilogue: Poverty won? Republicans and poverty, 1982–2018

> My friends, some years ago, the Federal Government declared
> war on poverty, and poverty won. [Laughter][1]
>
> Ronald Reagan, State of the Union address,
> 25 January 1988

On 26 March 1982 ground was finally broken in Washington,
DC for the Vietnam Veterans Memorial Wall. Nine years after
American withdrawal, it appeared that the nation was finally
ready to honour those personnel who had fought and died in the
United States' failed war in Southeast Asia. Exactly one month
earlier, and only a few blocks away in the Mayflower Hotel,
Ronald Reagan attempted to cast the War on Poverty as another
war that Americans had lost and from which it was time to move
on. Speaking to a friendly audience at the Conservative Political
Action Conference (CPAC), Reagan lambasted his Democratic
opponents who were labelling his 1981 antipoverty cuts 'unfair'.
While he conceded some of his left-leaning foes possessed genuine concern for the poor, Reagan told the approving CPAC delegates that many liberals had 'a vested interest in the permanent
welfare constituency'. 'No one should have a vested interest in
poverty or dependency,' the President chided Democrats, 'these
tragedies must never be looked at as a source of votes for politicians.' Looking ahead, Reagan confidently predicted that when
his economic recovery arrived it would be 'for all Americans –
working people, the truly needy, rich and poor'.[2] As far as the
Gipper was concerned, the War on Poverty was over and it was
time to let free enterprise get to work.

281

The problem for Reagan, however, was that the economic recovery remained elusive. More Americans were falling into poverty, and – with midterm elections fast approaching – his 1981 cuts were now seen by many voters as emblematic of a heartless president.[3] During 1982, Democrats spent the year hammering home the 'Fairness Issue', portraying the Reagan administration as uncaring towards the most vulnerable in society at a time when the nation was enduring economic pain and high unemployment. Democrats, hoping to exploit the 'Gender Gap' (whereby men had voted for Reagan and Republicans at a significantly higher rate than women), also pointed out that Reagan's cuts were falling disproportionately on women, thus leading to a 'feminization of poverty'.[4] In 1982, poverty, not economic growth and American renewal, was back in the headlines and the Reagan Revolution was on the defensive.[5] Put simply, the electorate was growing sympathetic to Democratic characterisations of Reagan – whose Everyman image and focus on economic growth had served him well during 1981 – as just another member of the 'Party of Privilege'.

This shift enabled congressional Democrats to push back against Reagan's agenda. Led by a revived Speaker Tip O'Neill, who had been outfoxed by Reagan the previous year, Democrats proved adept at blocking Reagan's proposals for deeper spending cuts, and even managed to reverse some of the 1981 cuts.[6] Democrats were helped by the fact that many stalwart and moderate Republicans were anxious that the GOP had gone too far, too soon, in enacting the Reagan Revolution. Senate Finance Committee Chair Bob Dole (R-KS) was particularly worried that Reaganomics was leading the federal government towards huge budget deficits, and squeamish about the fact that most of Reagan's cuts were falling on the poor.[7] Following tense negotiations throughout 1982, Congress and the White House agreed on a deal whereby Reagan agreed to raise taxes on the proviso that for every tax dollar raised, three dollars in spending cuts would be enacted by Congress. Nonetheless, Congress – after passing the Tax Equity and Fiscal Responsibility Act (TEFRA), which was dubbed the biggest tax hike in American history – simply ignored their spending commitments.[8] Instead, a coalition of Democrats and Republicans comfortably passed a supplemental appropriations bill in September over the President's veto. While the bill did not restore most of the previous year's anti-poverty cuts, some provisions were made for additional job training, health care for the poor and unemployment insurance.[9] Perhaps Reagan's triumph over the War on Poverty was a fleeting one.

Inside the Reagan administration, there were fears that the political gains made by conservative Republicans over the previous few years might quickly be lost. 'We are being savaged by the fairness issue,' one political aide noted, 'Our moral and, correspondingly, our political base has been badly eroded.'[10] More worryingly for Reagan – and the Republicans facing re-election in November – the President's approval ratings reflected this erosion, spending the year sliding towards 40 per cent.[11]

With the 1982 midterms looming, Reagan hit the campaign trail and attempted to rewrite the narrative that his Administration was heartless towards the nation's poor. Counterattacking, Reagan frequently returned to his charge that the War on Poverty had failed to help the poor, while simultaneously enriching middle-class bureaucrats. In his curtailing of poverty programmes, he was not acting heartlessly, the President claimed. Instead, he was putting a failed, corrupt and costly endeavour out of its misery. During the campaign, Reagan, who often communicated most effectively in anecdotal form, also debuted a new antipoverty fable. In his telling, while he was California governor, he had been sent a proposal for a poverty programme that 'was going to put 17 people to work helping keep the parks clean in a little rural county in California'. Which, initially, Reagan claimed, seemed like a praiseworthy endeavour, 'But over half the budget was going for 11 administrators to see that the 17 got to work on time. And I thought that was a little out of balance, so I vetoed the program.'[12] He repeated the story to various audiences, often to incredulous laughter from the audience.

In September, Reagan's speech to the National Black Republican Council Dinner offered a high-profile defence of his anti-poverty policies. Earlier in the year, the administration had found that Reagan's support among black voters was down to single digits – 8 per cent.[13] During his address, Reagan argued that poverty – including black poverty – had been in steep decline until the

Great Society got in the way of American enterprise. According to Reagan, by 1980 the average black family would have had $3,000 more spending power without the Great Society's inflationary programmes that also encouraged dependency amongst the poor. Relying on another anecdote to make his point, Reagan claimed:

> [Great Society programmes] reminded me of that old story about the fellow riding the motorcycle on a chilled, cold, winter day. The wind coming through the buttonholes in the front of the jacket was chilling him. So finally he stopped, turned the jacket around, and put it on backward. Well, that protected him from the wind, but it kind of hindered his arm motion. And he hit a patch of ice and skidded into a tree. When the police got there, and they elbowed their way through the crowd, and they said, 'What happened?' They said, 'We don't know.' They said, 'By the time we got his head turned around straight, he was dead.'

Instead of harming the poor, as Democrats were claiming, Reagan argued that his measures to control inflation were giving the poor more spending power and restoring self-sufficiency.[14]

Reagan's stout defence of his record ultimately did little to forestall Republican losses in November. With the economy in the worst recession since the 1930s and the Cold War resurgent, Republicans faced a tough electoral climate. It did not help when Democrats uncovered a Republican fundraising letter, enquiring whether GOP donors would support making Social Security voluntary. The letter helped Democrats ensure that the 'Fairness Issue' was not just relevant to the poor and unemployed, but to a much broader swathe of the electorate.[15] Having previously held high hopes of taking control of the House, Republicans lost twenty-six seats in the lower chamber, while they held steady in the Senate. The most substantial losses were among 'Gypsy Moth' moderate Republicans, thus ensuring that the Republican House caucus shifted rightward once again.[16] Overall, the GOP's losses suggested that the Reagan Revolution was now stalled. Had Reagan's victory over the War on Poverty been total or would a revived Democratic majority swept in on 'Fairness' seek to revamp the antipoverty effort? Much relied on when – or if – Reagan's much vaunted economic recovery arrived.

Happily for Reagan – and Republicans more broadly – the economic recovery appeared quickly and in style. With unemployment peaking in December 1982, economic indicators took off in early 1983 and the United States experienced uninterrupted economic growth for the next six years. As Iwan Morgan notes, the economic expansion, which averaged a remarkable 4.3 per cent growth per annum, 'was more than twice the average length of post-1945 expansionary cycles'.[17] Reagan was quick to claim the credit for the economic boom and thus a clear justification for his policies – including his deep spending cuts for poverty programmes. Indeed, the President quickly began joking about the War on Poverty as if it was a relic of a misguided past. Speaking to a Republican fundraiser in Kentucky, Reagan premiered the gag that he would later use in his final State of the Union address in 1988. The President received a hearty laugh from his GOP crowd when he recalled the War on Poverty, which 'poverty won'.[18] In one sense, Reagan was right to gloat, he had achieved his political goal: there was no going back to the Great Society's antipoverty policies. The following year's presidential election, in which Reagan coasted to re-election over unrepentant Great Society liberal Democrat Walter Mondale, served to confirm a national shift in attitudes towards antipoverty efforts. Rather than promise the poor more spending, Reagan simply declared that it was already 'Morning in America'.[19]

Nonetheless, while Reagan's recovery did allow for more working-class and middle-class Americans to climb the economic ladder, the rising tide did not quite lift all boats. There were clear winners and losers in the new economy.[20] Congressional Democrats, journalists and activists drew attention to the rise of homelessness in Reagan's America.[21] Meanwhile, continued concerns about a permanent underclass, not basking in the America's 'morning' dawn, remained.[22] Such concerns were eloquently voiced at the 1984 Democratic National Convention when New York governor Mario Cuomo critiqued Reagan's oft-repeated characterisation of the United States as a 'shining city upon a hill'. 'The hard truth,' Cuomo claimed, 'is that not everyone is sharing in this city's splendor and glory.' Citing the struggling poor, Cuomo directly addressed Reagan: 'Mr. President you ought to know that this nation is more a "Tale of Two Cities" than it is just a "Shining City on a Hill.""[23] Still, the sweeping rhetoric only masked the fact that liberals in the Democratic Party had few new ideas on how to solve poverty. In the 1980s, as historian Patrick Andelic notes, Democrats were adept at defending popular liberal achievements like Social Security and Medicare, but they struggled to articulate a new compelling socioeconomic agenda to counteract Reaganomics.[24] The post-1983 economic recovery put Democrats in a further bind and ensured that, for all Cuomo's eloquence, there was no serious liberal offensive to refight the War on Poverty.

For the rest of Reagan's presidency, Congress passed some small and uncontroversial antipoverty measures in bipartisan fashion. Most notably, the Earned Income Tax Credit (EITC) was expanded in 1986 as part of Reagan's second round of tax reforms. Including an EITC expansion helped offset charges that the new tax changes, which included a reduction in the top tax rate from 50 per cent to 38.5 per cent, were merely a giveaway to wealthy Americans. During the 1980s, congressional Republicans happily supported the EITC as it enjoyed broad public support due its association with work.[25] Alongside the EITC, Head Start continued to receive bipartisan support among lawmakers, even as more studies emerged questioning its long-term benefits.[26] Still, these were small measures that hardly affected the general trend towards less government involvement in alleviating poverty.

Regarding black poverty, which was still intimately associated with the War on Poverty, Republicans initially flirted with social justice initiatives before eventually choosing 'law and order' for the black urban poor. By the mid-1980s, Republicans – and many Democrats – were in full agreement that the black communities had systemic issues, such as poverty, crime and single-parent families.[27] In 1984, Rep. Jack Kemp (R-NY) proposed 'Empowerment Zones', a conservative social justice solution, which would provide tax incentives for businesses to locate and provide jobs in poor urban areas. Nonetheless, despite being nominally in favour of Empowerment Zones, the Reagan administration offered only lukewarm support and Kemp's legislation failed in Congress. Ironically, in a rehash of Republican criticisms of the War on Poverty, Democrats claimed Empowerment Zones were an election-year gimmick and stalled the effort.[28] By the time Reagan left office, spending on the cities had plummeted.[29]

Concurrent with the failure to pass Empowerment Zones, Republicans and Democrats combined to begin the War on Drugs in earnest. The landmark Anti-Drug Abuse Act of 1986, which disproportionately sentenced those who used crack cocaine (often poor urban blacks and Latinos) over those who used powder cocaine (usually middle-class suburban whites), was passed with near unanimous margins.[30] This legislation, combined with other draconian 1980s drug statutes, contributed significantly to placing poor urban black Americans in jail, to the extent that, thirty years later, African Americans – 13.2 per cent of the population – would constitute 37.8 per cent of the prison population.[31] Historian Elizabeth Hinton deems the Reagan-era War on Drugs, 'the culmination of a bipartisan consensus to disinvest in welfare programs and expand crime control'. While it is more accurate to attribute the disinvestment in welfare to Reagan and conservatives, Hinton is correct in calling Reagan's presidency a 'turning point with respect to the contours of poverty and institutionalized racism in America'.[32] African American Rapper Tupac Shakur summed up the directional shift succinctly, decrying in his 1992 song 'Changes', 'Instead of war on poverty, they got a war on drugs so the police can bother me.'[33]

Post-Reagan, a more uniformly conservative GOP continued to agree with the former President's view that the War on Poverty was a colossal mistake that merely contributed to degrading welfare dependency at the expense of the hardworking taxpayer. 'Since 1980,' historian Tim Thurber notes, 'the GOP has routinely blasted federal efforts to help the poor, particularly the black poor, as ineffective at best, counterproductive at worst, and an unjust transfer of wealth from the deserving to the unworthy.'[34] Republican prescriptions for fighting poverty in the twenty-first century have failed to go beyond affirming the need for volunteerism, turning current federal programmes over to the states and, most importantly, creating good jobs. In truth, however, Republicans rarely talk about tackling poverty, and therefore it is unsurprising that while over fifty years have passed since the War on Poverty's launch, the GOP's remedies remain largely the same.

287

Promising a 'kinder, gentler nation' than Reagan's, President George H. W. Bush launched his 'thousand points of light' initiative that, reminiscent of George Romney's approach in the 1960s, placed emphasis on volunteerism as the solution to poverty. Nevertheless, Bush failed to offer any substantive policy and combined his 'thousand points of light' vision with an attack on Johnson's Great Society. In 1991, as LBJ had in 1964, Bush delivered the commencement address to students at the University of Michigan in Ann Arbor, during which the Republican told students that, 'If we've learned anything in the past quarter century, it is that we cannot federalize virtue.'[35] Bush also rejected various proposals of his Housing and Urban Department Secretary Kemp, who urged the president to launch a conservative War on Poverty.[36] In Bush's most substantive antipoverty speech, he concluded with a familiar Republican refrain: 'We all know where opportunity really begins . . . it begins with a job.'[37]

In the 1990s, Republicans enjoyed political success with a message that stressed personal endeavour among the poor rather than greater government initiatives. Despite Bush's defeat by Democratic challenger Bill Clinton in 1992, Republicans finally recaptured the House majority two years later – ending what commentators had dubbed the 'Permanent Democratic Congress'.[38] Republicans were led to their first House majority since 1949 by conservative rabble rouser, Newt Gingrich. In bidding to retake the House, Gingrich stressed that 'Our generation must replace the welfare state with the opportunity society.'[39] During the 1994 elections, Republicans released a 'Contract with America' that featured a list of Republican legislative items that would receive an up-or-down vote in a GOP Congress. Among the items featured were standard Republican appeals for tax cuts, strict crime measures, and a renewed emphasis on traditional American families.[40] As expected, there were no antipoverty measures.

On welfare specifically, Republicans promised the Personal Responsibility Act, which would kick welfare recipients off Aid to Families with Dependent Children (AFDC) after two years on the programme and restrict access to single pregnant women. Ultimately, the Gingrich-led Republican Congress pushed President Clinton into signing welfare reform in 1996, which among other conservative measures scrapped AFDC and replaced it with the aptly named Temporary Assistance to Needy Families (TANF). The Clinton White House, despite a booming economy, was so concerned with the prevailing political climate on antipoverty measures that they avoided discussing any such proposals.[41] The President only dared speak about the issue towards the end of his second term once he no longer had to face voters. Indeed, with a new election on the horizon, emboldened Republicans even proposed cutting the popular EITC.[42] Such Republican efforts threatened to revive the 'Party of Privilege' moniker even amongst an electorate that was hostile to government spending on the poor.

On this issue, President George W. Bush showed a sensitivity to the perception that Republicans were hostile to the poor.[43] In his run for the presidency, Bush II declared himself a 'compassionate conservative' and chastised congressional Republicans who had proposed cutting the EITC.[44] As historian Lawrence McAndrews notes, though, compassionate conservatism 'would often seem like a philosophy in search of a policy'.[45] While Bush expanded federal efforts in universal areas such as health care (Medicare Part D) and education (No Child Left Behind), for the poor specifically he offered little but rhetoric. Partly, this was because Republicans in Congress had little appetite for the small faith-based initiatives that Bush did propose, but it was also clearly not a priority for the President. While Bush desired a different public image, he still held fast to the Republican belief that government approaches to poverty had failed. 'Many Americans,' Bush reflected, 'were injured by the helping hand.'[46] In expanding both Medicare and federal aid to education while shunning more antipoverty initiatives, the younger Bush offered yet more proof of how Republicans continued to pragmatically support Great Society era legislation, but with the War on Poverty a notable exclusion.

What seems undeniable is that Republicans have won this argument politically: the majority of Americans no longer appear to believe that the federal government should be engaged in a War on Poverty. Historian Michael Katz calls poverty a 'third rail' issue – one which politicians dare not touch – and noted that, by 2011, despite the poverty rate rising to 15 per cent, poverty 'received almost no mention by presidential candidates and most other politicians'.[47] Indeed, a casual observer of the 2012 presidential election – which was keenly contested on socioeconomic grounds – would have heard both major party candidates relentlessly focus their empathy and promises on the 'middle class'. The impoverished were largely left out of the discussion except when Republican candidate, Mitt Romney, made an ill-advised remark at a private function where he asserted that 47 per cent of Americans would never vote for him as they were dependent on government help. Romney's revealing comment showed the longevity of Republican dogma that Democrats merely encourage dependency on government to secure votes at election time. His comment backfired and received considerable negative media attention – aiding Barack Obama's narrative that focused on income inequality as a tentative move towards a discussion of poverty.[48] Nonetheless, Obama, who had declared 'Let's be the generation that ends poverty in America', when he announced his run for the presidency, left office having achieved almost no substantial antipoverty measures, excepting Medicaid's expansion as part of health care reform.[49]

In 2014, the War on Poverty's 50th anniversary saw conservative congressional Republicans, perhaps concerned that Romney's candidacy had revived the Party of Privilege image, make a lot of noise about a renewed attack on poverty, but offer very little substance.[50] Rep. Paul Ryan (R-WI), soon-to-be House Speaker, blamed Johnson-era 'bureaucratic, top-down anti-poverty programs' for 'wrecking families and communities'.[51] Ryan – a Kemp protégé – offered only a vague proposal of an 'Opportunity Grant' for poor families. The proposal, however, quickly disappeared and showed the lack of desire in the party for a Republican alternative on poverty.[52] An exasperated Obama, who had been stifled by Republican Congresses since 2011, declared: 'Republicans don't care about that issue.'[53] In his declaration, Obama merely revealed what most Democrats have long believed about their GOP counterparts.

At the time of writing, Donald Trump's ascension to the presidency has done little to reverse the trajectory of GOP antipoverty policy. When the Trump administration declared in 2018 that the War on Poverty had been largely won, they did so to justify further restrictive access to benefits by the poor.[54] Despite being an atypical Republican, at least in style, Trump has thus far acted as a conventional Republican regarding socioeconomic issues.

Reflecting on the modern GOP's approach to poverty, historian and former Republican staffer, Bruce Bartlett, wrote of Republicans that 'They want to care, but they're so imprisoned by their ideology that they can't offer anything meaningful.'[55] Of course, many Republicans would reject the idea of any 'imprisonment'. Many sincerely believe that their ideology – faith in free enterprise over government programmes – is the correct course to lift Americans out of poverty. In their eyes, they need only point to Lyndon Johnson's antipoverty effort as sufficient proof that poverty is not a problem that the federal government can solve. Nonetheless, it is also true that this ideology means that Republicans have nothing – beyond vague promises of prosperity – to offer the poor. Instead, as the *Washington Post*'s liberal columnist Dana Millbank correctly asserted, Republicans are far happier fighting 'the War on the War on Poverty'.[56]

Recent historians have been persuasive in arguing that, contrary to a common perception that an ascendant conservatism replaced and rolled back the Great Society's achievements, the Johnson years actually 'bequeathed an era' of federal government expansion.[57] Even under Republican presidents, Great Society era programmes such as Medicare and aid to education have continued to grow at a startling rate since the departure of Lyndon Johnson from 1600 Pennsylvania Avenue. It is, however, harder to argue that the War on Poverty bequeathed an era of action on poverty. Indeed, many liberal Democrats appear to no longer have the optimism – or the hubris – to believe that the federal government can make a real dent in poverty. If they do hold this belief, then they keep quiet about it during campaigns. Head Start has survived, and VISTA remains under another name, but the impetus to do battle with poverty that was briefly experienced in the 1960s, and even sustained during the early Nixon years, has left American politics. Thus, Republicans – the vast majority of whom opposed the War on Poverty from the moment it was announced – have been successful in persuading the American people that the heart of Johnson's Great Society was a mistake. Ronald Reagan's list of victors in the War on Poverty could justifiably be expanded to include his own party.

Notes

1. Ronald W. Reagan, State of the Union Address, 25 January 1988, TAPP.
2. RWR, Remarks at a Conservative Political Action Conference Dinner, Mayflower Hotel, 26 February 1982, TAPP.
3. 'Historical Poverty Tables: People and Families – 1959 to 2018', US Census Bureau.
4. Patterson, *America's Struggle*, 218.
5. Ben J. Wattenberg, 'Playing Games with Poverty', *Washington Post*, 3 March 1982.
6. Andelic, *Donkey Work*, 128.
7. Morgan, *Reagan*.
8. Ibid.
9. 'H.R. 6863 (97th): Supplemental Appropriations Act, 1982', Govtrack: https://www.govtrack.us.
10. Memo, Mike Horowiz to David Stockman and Ed Harper, 'The Fairness Issue and the Administration's Fortunes', 19 July 1982, box 7, Susan Lauffer Files, Ronald W. Reagan Library.
11. 'Presidential Approval Ratings – Gallup Historical Statistics and Trends', Gallup: https://news.gallup.com/.
12. RWR, 'Interview with Skip Weber of the Iowa Daily Press Association in Des Moines', 9 February 1982, TAPP.
13. Memo, Elizabeth H. Dole to James Baker III, 'Black Strategy', 24 February 1982 in Jacobs and Zelizer, *Conservatives in Power*, 105–8.
14. RWR, Remarks at a National Black Republican Council Dinner, 15 September 1982, TAPP.
15. Morgan, *Reagan*.
16. Kabaservice, *Rule and Ruin*, 364–5.
17. Morgan, *Reagan*.
18. RWR, Remarks at a Fundraising Luncheon for Gubernatorial Candidate Jim Bunning in Louisville, Kentucky, 7 October 1983, TAPP.
19. Gil Troy, *Morning in America: How Ronald Reagan Invented the 1980s* (Princeton, NJ: Princeton University Press, 2007).
20. Phillips, *Rich and Poor*.
21. Haynes Johnson, *Sleepwalking through History: America in the Reagan Years* (New York: Norton, 1991).

22. Patterson, *America's Struggle*, 216–17.
23. Mario Cuomo, 1984 Democratic National Convention Keynote Speech, 16 July 1984, C-SPAN: https://www.c-span.org.
24. Andelic, *Donkey Work*, 128.
25. Ventry, 'The Collision of Tax and Welfare Politics'.
26. Rose, 'Head Start: Growing beyond the War on Poverty', 178–81.
27. Charles Murray's *Losing Ground* echoed the recent conservative criticisms of the War on Poverty that it had encouraged dependency and hampered rather than helped the poor. Nonetheless, Murray claimed that social welfare policies since 1964 had further disincentivised marriage and a solid family unit in largely black urban areas; *Losing Ground: American Social Polity, 1950–1980* (New York: Basic Books, 1984).
28. McAndrews, *The Presidents and the Poor*, 112–13.
29. Ibid. 118.
30. 'H.R.5484 – Anti-Drug Abuse Act of 1986', Congress.gov: https://www.congress.gov.
31. Peter Wagner and Bernadette Rabuy, 'Mass Incarceration: The Whole Pie 2017', Prison Policy Initiative, 14 March 2017: www.prisonpolicy.org; 'Inmate Race', Federal Bureau of Prisons, 29 July 2017: www.bop.gov.
32. Hinton, *From the War on Poverty to the War on Crime*, 307.
33. Tupac Shakur, 'Changes' (1992).
34. Thurber, *Republicans and Race*, 378.
35. George H. W. Bush, Remarks at the University of Michigan Commencement Ceremony in Ann Arbor, 4 May 1991, TAPP.
36. Jason DeParle, 'How Jack Kemp Lost the War on Poverty', *New York Times*, 28 February 1993.
37. GHWB, Remarks at a Meeting of the American Society of Association Executives, 27 February 1991.
38. Steve Kornacki, *The Red and the Blue: The 1990s and the Birth of Political Tribalism* (New York: HarperCollins, 2018), 33–4.
39. Gingrich quoted in ibid. 249.
40. The Republican 'Contract with America' (1994).
41. McAndrews, *The Presidents and the Poor*, 161–85.
42. Kornacki, *The Red and the Blue*, 397–8.
43. Ibid. 417.
44. Ibid. 397–8.
45. McAndrews, *The Presidents and the Poor*, 186.
46. George W. Bush, Remarks on the Welfare Reform Agenda, 26 February 2002, TAPP.

47. Michael B. Katz, *The Undeserving Poor: America's Enduring Confrontation with Poverty* (New York: Oxford University Press, 2013), x.
48. Chris Cillizza, 'Why Mitt Romney's "47 percent" Comment Was so Bad', *Washington Post*, 4 March 2013.
49. Barack H. Obama, Remarks Announcing Candidacy for President in Springfield, Illinois, 10 February 2007, TAPP.
50. Mike Lee, 'Bring Them In – Remarks to the Heritage Foundation's Anti-Poverty Forum', 13 November 2013: http://www.lee.senate. gov; Francine Kiefer, 'What Would a Republican "War on Poverty" Look Like, circa 2016?' *Christian Science Monitor*, 8 January 2014.
51. Paul Ryan quoted in Lori Montgomery, 'Paul Ryan, GOP's Budget Architect, Sets His Sights on Fighting Poverty and Winning Minds', *Washington Post*, 18 November 2013.
52. Paul Ryan, 'Expanding Opportunity in America', remarks at American Enterprise Institute, Washington, DC, 24 July 2014.
53. BHO quoted in McAndrews, *The Presidents and the Poor*, 245.
54. David Boyer, 'White House Says U.S. Has Won War on Poverty, Calls for More Work Rules for Welfare Recipients', *Washington Times*, 12 July 2018.
55. Bruce Bartlett quoted in Montgomery, 'Paul Ryan, GOP's Budget Architect'.
56. Dana Millbank, 'The GOP's War on the War on Poverty', *Washington Post*, 8 January 2014.
57. Davies, *See Government Grow*, 287.

Bibliography

Primary sources

UNPUBLISHED DOCUMENTARY SOURCES

A. Frank Smith, Jr. Library Center, Southwestern University, George-
town, TX
    John G. Tower Papers
        Austin Office
            1966 Tower Senatorial Campaign
        Campaign/Political
            Elections
            Tower Senate Club
        Press Office
            Speeches 1961–84
            VIP Correspondence 1961–84

Albert and Shirley Small Special Collections Library, University of Virginia, Charlottesville, VA
    Hugh D. Scott Papers, 1925–77
        Additional
        Speeches

Bentley Historical Library, University of Michigan, Ann Arbor, MI
    George W. Romney Papers, 1939–73
        Governor's Papers

Frank Melville, Jr. Memorial Library, Stony Brook, NY
    Jacob K. Javits Papers
        Press Files

Gerald R. Ford Presidential Library, Ann Arbor, MI
    Gerald R. Ford Congressional Papers
        Correspondence File
        Legislative File
    Melvin R. Laird Congressional Papers
        Baroody Subject File
    Robert T. Hartmann Papers
    Robert L. Peabody Research Interview Notes, 1964–67

Library of Congress, Washington, DC: Manuscript Division
    Edward W. Brooke Papers
        Attorney General Office Files
        Senatorial Papers
            Correspondence File
            Legislative File
            Press and Public Relations File, 1966–78
        Speeches and Writings File, 1961–80
        Campaign Materials, 1960–78
        Political File, 1963–78

Lyndon B. Johnson Presidential Library, Austin, TX
    Papers of Lyndon Baines Johnson, 1963–69
        Office Files of Ceil Bellinger
        Office Files of George Reedy
        Office Files of Frederick Panzer
        Office Files of Robert Hardesty
    Records of the Democratic National Committtee
    Research
    White House Central File
        Legislative Background
            Civil Rights Act of 1964
            War on Poverty
        Name File
            Barry Goldwater
            Charles Percy
            Gerald Ford
            John Lindsay
            Nelson Rockefeller
            Richard Nixon
            Ronald Reagan
        Reports on Pending Legislation

Richard M. Nixon Presidential Library, Yorba Linda, CA
    Presidential Papers
        Central Files
            Welfare Subject File
        Special Files
            Staff Member and Office Files
        Pre-Presidential Papers
            Special Files
        Wilderness Years Collection
            Correspondence
            1964 Campaign

Rockefeller Archive Center [RAC], Sleepy Hollow, NY
    Rockefeller Family Archives
        Nelson A. Rockefeller Personal Papers
            Papers of Ann C. Whitman
            George L. Hinman Files, 1959–70
            Oscar M. Reubhausen Files, 1967–70
        Nelson A. Rockefeller Gubernatorial Papers
        Papers of Winthrop Rockefeller

Ronald W. Reagan Presidential Library, Simi Valley, CA
    Governor's Papers, 1967–75
        1966 Campaign
        Research Unit
    1980 Campaign Papers, 1965–80
    White House Staff and Office Inventories, 1981–89

PUBLISHED DOCUMENTARY SOURCES

Congressional Record
http://congressional.proquest.com/

C-SPAN
https://www.c-span.org

Dave Leip's Atlas of US Presidential Elections
https://uselectionatlas.org/RESULTS

Dirksen Center
www.dirksencenter.org
> Dirksen Center Special Projects
>> Joint Senate–House Republican Leadership Minutes, 1961–68
>> The 1960s: A Multi-media View from Capitol Hill

Donald Rumsfeld Papers
https://papers.rumsfeld.com/

GovTrack.us
www.govtrack.us/

Living Room Candidate (Museum of the Moving Image)
www.livingroomcandidate.org/

Moynihan, Daniel Patrick, 'The Negro Family: The Case for National Action', March 1965, Office of Policy Planning and Research, United States Department of Labor.

Papers of the Nixon White House [microform]

Papers of the Republican Party [PRP] [microform], ed. Paul L. Kesaris (Frederick, MD: University Publications of America, 1986)

Political Activities of the Johnson White House, 1963–1969 [PAJWH] [microform], ed. Paul L. Kesaris (Frederick, MD: University Publications of America, 1987)

Presidential Recordings of Lyndon B. Johnson: Digital Edition, ed. David G. Coleman, Kent B. Germany, Guian A. McKee and Marc J. Selverstone (Charlottesville, VA: University of Virginia Press, 2010) War on Poverty series
http://presidentialrecordings.rotunda.upress.virginia.edu/

The American Presidency Project [TAPP]
www.presidency.ucsb.edu/

The Governor's Commission on the Los Angeles Riots, 'Violence in the City – An End or a Beginning?' 2 December 1965

The Republican 'Contract with America' (1994)

United States. Kerner Commission, *Report of the National Advisory Commission on Civil Disorders* (Washington, DC: US Government Printing Office, 1968)

MEDIA SOURCES

Chicago Tribune
Christian Science Monitor
CQ Almanac
FiveThirtyEight
Life
New York Herald Tribune
New York Times
Wall Street Journal
Washington Post
The Reporter
US News & World Report

STATISTICAL SOURCES

Bureau of Labor Statistics: www.bls.gov
Center for American Progress: www.americanprogress.org
Federal Bureau of Prisons: www.bop.gov
Pew Research Center: www.pewresearch.org/
Prison Policy Initiative: www.prisonpolicy.org
US Census Bureau: www.census.gov

Secondary sources

Andelic, Patrick, *Donkey Work: Congressional Democrats in Conservative America* (Lawrence, KS: University Press of Kansas, 2019).
Andelic, Patrick, '"The Old Economic Rules No Longer Apply": The National Planning Idea and the Humphrey-Hawkins Full Employment Act, 1974–1978', *Journal of Policy History*, vol. 31, no. 1 (2019), 72–100.
Anderson, Martin, *Welfare: The Political Economy of Welfare Reform in the United States* (Stanford, CA: Hoover Institution Press, 1978).
Andrew, John A., *Lyndon Johnson and the Great Society* (Chicago, IL: Ivan R. Dee, 1998).
Andrews, Kenneth T., 'Social Movements and Policy Implementation: The Mississippi Civil Rights Movement and the War on Poverty, 1965 to 1971', *American Sociological Review*, vol. 66 (1971), 71–95.

Anon., 'The Family Assistance Plan: A Chronology', *Social Service Review*, vol. 46, no.4 (1972), 603–8.

Ashmore, Harry, *Hearts and Minds: The Anatomy of Racism from Roosevelt to Reagan* (New York: McGraw-Hill, 1982).

Bailey, Christopher J., *The Republican Party in the US Senate: 1974–1984: Party Change and Institutional Development* (Manchester: Manchester University Press, 1988).

Bauman, Robert, *Race and the War on Poverty: From Watts to East L.A.* (Norman, OK: University of Oklahoma Press, 2008).

Bowen, Michael, *The Roots of Modern Conservatism: Dewey, Taft, and the Battle for the Soul of the Republican Party* (Chapel Hill, NC: University of North Carolina Press, 2011).

Brennan, Mary, *Turning Right in the Sixties: The Conservative Capture Of the GOP* (Chapel Hill, NC: University of North Carolina Press, 1995).

Brown, Michael K., *Race, Money and the American Welfare State* (Ithaca, NY: Cornell University Press, 1999).

Bullion, John L., *LBJ and the Transformation of American Politics* (New York: Pearson Longman, 2008).

Burns, Arthur, *Inside the Nixon Administration: The Secret Diary of Arthur Burns* (Lawrence, KS: University Press of Kansas, 2010).

Busch, Andrew E., *Horses in Midstream: U.S. Midterm Elections and Their Consequences, 1894–1998* (Pittsburgh, PA: University of Pittsburgh Press, 1999).

Button, James W., *Black Violence: Political Impact of the 1960s Riots* (Princeton, NJ: Princeton University Press, 1978).

Califano, Joseph A., *The Triumph and Tragedy of Lyndon Johnson: The White House Years* (New York: Simon & Schuster, 1991).

Cannato, Vincent J., *The Ungovernable City: John Lindsay and His Struggle to Save New York* (New York: Basic Books, 2001).

Cannon, James, 'Gerald R. Ford: Minority Leader of the House of Representatives, 1965–1973', in *Masters of the House: Congressional Leadership Over Two Centuries*, ed. Roger H. Davidson, Susan V. Hammond and Raymond Smock (Boulder, CO: Westview Press, 1998), 260–85.

Cannon, Lou, *Governor Reagan: His Rise to Power* (New York: Perseus, 2003).

Cannon, Lou, *President Reagan: Role of a Lifetime* (New York: Simon & Schuster, 1991).

Carmines, Edward G. and Stimson, James A., *Issue Evolution: Race and the Transformation of American Politics* (Princeton, NJ: Princeton University Press, 1989).

Caro, Robert A., *The Years of Lyndon Johnson: The Passage of Power* (New York: Knopf, 2012).

Carter, Dan T., *From George Wallace to Newt Gingrich: Race in The Conservative Counterrevolution, 1963–1994* (Baton Rouge, LA: Louisiana State University Press, 1996).

Carter, Jimmy, *Keeping Faith: Memoirs of a President* (Fayetteville, AK: University of Arkansas Press, 1982).

Cazenave, Noel A., *Impossible Democracy: The Unlikely Success of the War on Poverty Community Action Programs* (Albany, NY: State University of New York Press, 2007).

Clayson, William, '"The Barrios and the Ghettos Have Organized!" Community Action, Political Acrimony, and the War on Poverty in San Antonio', *Journal of Urban History*, vol. 28, no. 2 (2002), 158–83.

Clifford, Scott, 'Compassionate Democrats and Tough Republicans: How Ideology Shapes Partisan Stereotypes', *Political Behavior* (March 2019).

Conkin, Paul, *Big Daddy from the Pedernales: Lyndon Baines Johnson* (Boston, MA: Twayne Macmillan, 1986).

Conlan, Timothy, *From New Federalism to Devolution: Twenty-five Years of Intergovernmental Reform*, 2nd edition (Washington, DC: Brookings Institution, 1998).

Converse, Philip E., *The Dynamics of Party Support* (Los Angeles: SAGE, 1976),

Crafton, William, 'The Incremental Revolution: Ronald Reagan and Welfare Reform in the 1970s', *Journal of Policy History*, vol. 26, no. 1 (2014), 27–47.

Crespino, Joseph, *Strom Thurmond's America* (New York: Hill & Wang, 2012).

Critichlow, Donald, *Phyllis Schlafly and Grassroots Conservatism: A Woman's Crusade* (Princeton, NJ: Princeton University Press, 2005).

Critchlow, Donald, *The Conservative Ascendancy: How the GOP Right Made Political History* (Cambridge, MA: Harvard University Press, 2007).

Dallek, Matthew, *The Right Moment: Ronald Reagan's First Victory and the Decisive Turning Point in American Politics* (New York: Simon & Schuster, 2000).

Dallek, Robert, *Lyndon B. Johnson: Portrait of a President* (New York: Oxford University Press, 2004).

Darman, Jonathan, *Landslide: LBJ, Reagan, and New America* (New York: Random House, 2014).

Davidson, Roger H., 'The War on Poverty: Experiment in Federalism', *Annals of the American Academy of Political and Social Science*, vol. 385 (1969), 1–13.

Davies, Gareth, *From Opportunity to Entitlement: The Transformation and Decline of Great Society Liberalism* (Lawrence, KS: University Press of Kansas, 1996).

Davies, Gareth, *See Government Grow: Education Politics from Johnson to Reagan* (Lawrence, KS: University Press of Kansas, 2007).

De Jong, Greta, 'Staying in Place: Black Migration, the Civil Rights Movement, and the War on Poverty in the Rural South', *The Journal of African American History*, vol. 90, no. 4 (2005), 387–409.

Derthick, Martha, 'Crossing Thresholds: Federalism in the 1960s', in *Integrating the Sixties: The Origins, Structures, and Legitimacy of Public Policy in a Turbulent Decade*, ed. Brian Balogh (University Park, PA: Pennsylvania State University Press, 1996), 64–80.

Edsall Thomas Byrnes with Edsall, Mary D., *Chain Reaction: The Impact of Race, Rights, and Taxes on American Politics* (New York: Norton, 1992).

Ehrlichman, John D., *Witness to Power: The Nixon Years* (New York: Simon & Schuster, 1982).

Erskine, Hazel, 'The Polls: Demonstrations and Race Riots', *Public Opinion Quarterly*, vol. 31, no. 4 (1967–68), 655–77.

Esty, Amos, 'North Carolina Republicans and the Conservative Revolution, 1964–1968', *North Carolina Historical Review*, vol. 82, no. 1 (2005), 1–32.

Evans, Rowland and Novak, Robert D., *Lyndon B. Johnson: The Exercise of Power* (London: Allen & Unwin, 1966).

Fairlie, Robert W. and Sundstrom, William A., 'The Racial Unemployment Gap in Long-run Perspective', *The American Economic Review*, vol. 87, no. 2 (May 1997), 306–10.

Farrington, Joshua D., *Black Republicans and the Transformation of the GOP* (Philadelphia, PA: University of Pennsylvania Press, 2016).

Feldman, Glenn, ED., *Painting Dixie Red: When, Where, Why, and How the South Became Republican* (Gainesville, FL: University Press of Florida, 2011).

Flamm, Michael, *Law and Order: Street Crime, Civil Unrest, and the Crisis of Liberalism in the 1960s* (New York: Columbia University Press, 2005).

Ford, Gerald R., *A Time to Heal: The Autobiography of Gerald R. Ford* (New York: Harper & Row, 1979).

Freeman, Roger A., *The Wayward Welfare State* (Stanford, CA: Hoover Institute, 1981).

Gilder, George, *Wealth and Poverty* (New York: Basic Books, 1981).

Gilens, Martin, *Why Americans Hate Welfare: Race, Media, and the Politics of Antipoverty Policy* (Chicago, IL: University of Chicago Press, 1999).

Glickman, Norman J., Lynn Jr, Laurence E. and Wilson, Robert H., 'Understanding Lyndon Johnson's Neglected Legacies', in *LBJ's Neglected Legacy: How Lyndon Johnson Reshaped Domestic Policy and Government*, ed. Robert H. Wilson, Norman J. Glickman and Laurence E. Lynn Jr (Austin, TX: University of Texas Press, 2015), 3–20.

Goldberg, Robert Allan, *Barry Goldwater* (New Haven, CT: Yale University Press, 1995).

Goldman, Eric F., *The Tragedy of Lyndon Johnson* (London: Macdonald, 1969).

Goodwin, Doris Kearns, *Lyndon Johnson and the American Dream* (New York: Harper & Row, 1976).

Goodwin, Richard N., *Remembering America: A Voice from the Sixties* (Boston, MA: Little, Brown, 1988).

Gould, Lewis L., *The Republicans: A History of the Grand Old Party* (New York: Oxford University Press, 2003).

Hamby, Alonzo, *Liberalism and Its Challengers, FDR to Reagan* (New York: Oxford University Press, 1985).

Harrington, Michael, *The Other America: Poverty in the United States* (New York: Macmillan, 1962).

Haveman, Robert H., 'The War on Poverty and the Poor and Nonpoor', *Political Science Quarterly*, vol. 102, no. 1 (1987), 65–78.

Heclo, Hugh, 'Sixties Civics', in *The Great Society and the High Tide of Liberalism*, ed. Sidney M. Milkis and Jerome M. Mileur (Amherst, MA: University of Massachusetts Press, 2005), 53–82.

Heineman, Kenneth J., 'Model City: The War on Poverty, Race Relations, and Catholic Social Activism in 1960s Pittsburgh', *The Historian*, vol. 65 (2003), 867–900.

Hess, Stephen and Broder, David, *The Republican Establishment: The Present and Future of the G.O.P.* (New York: Harper & Row, 1967).

Hinton, Elizabeth, *From the War on Poverty to the War on Crime: The Making of Mass Incarceration in America* (Cambridge, MA: Harvard University Press, 2016).

Hodgson, Godfrey, *The world Turned Right Side Up: A History of the Conservative Ascendancy in America* (New York: Houghton Mifflin, 1996).

Hoff, Joan, *Nixon Reconsidered* (New York: Basic Books, 1995).

Hopkins, Michael J., 'The Influence of Lyndon Johnson on the Origins and Politics of the War on Poverty: A Study of Presidential Strengths and Weaknesses', PhD dissertation, California State University, 2003.

Hulsey, Byron, *Everett Dirksen and His Presidents: How a Senate Giant Shaped American Politics* (Lawrence, KS: University Press of Kansas, 2000).

Huret, Romain, 'Richard Nixon, the Great Society, and Social Reforms: A Lost Opportunity?' in *A Companion to Richard M. Nixon*, ed. Melvin Small (Malden, MA: Wiley Blackwell, 2011), 202–11.

Jacobs, Meg and Zelizer, Julian, *Conservatives in Power: The Reagan Years, 1981–1989* (Boston, MA: Bedford/St. Martin's, 2011).

Javits, Jacob, *Order of Battle* (New York: Atheneum Books, 1964).

Johns, Andrew L., *Vietnam's Second Front: Domestic Politics, the Republican Party, and the War* (Lexington, KY: University Press of Kentucky, 2010).

Johnson, Haynes, *Sleepwalking through History: America in the Reagan Years* (New York: Norton, 1991).

Johnson, Robert David, *All the Way with LBJ: the 1964 Presidential Election* (New York: Cambridge University Press, 2009).

Kabaservice, Geoffrey, *Rule and Ruin: The Downfall of Moderation and the Destruction of the Republican Party, from Eisenhower to the Tea Party* (New York: Oxford University Press, 2012).

Katz, Michael B., *The Undeserving Poor: America's Enduring Confrontation with Poverty* (New York: Oxford University Press, 2013).

Katznelson, Ira, 'A Radical Departure: Social Welfare and the Election', in *The Hidden Election: Politics and Economics in the 1980 Presidential Campaign*, ed. Thomas Ferguson and Joel Rogers (New York: Pantheon Books, 1981), 313–40.

Katznelson, Ira, 'Was the Great Society a Lost Opportunity?' in *The Rise and Fall of the New Deal Order, 1930–1980*, ed. Steve Fraser and Gary Gerstle (Princeton, NJ: Princeton University Press, 1989), 185–211.

Kaufman, Scott, *Ambition, Pragmatism, and Party: A Political Biography of Gerald R. Ford* (Lawrence, KS: University Press of Kansas, 2017).

Kearney, Melissa S. and Harris, Benjamin H., 'Ten Economic Facts about Crime and Incarceration in the United States', Brookings Institution, 1 May 2014.

Keough, Brian, 'Politics as Usual or Political Change: The War on Poverty's Community Action Program in Albany, New York, 1959–1967', *Afro-Americans in New York Life and History*, vol. 36, no. 2 (2012), 37–65.

Klinkner, Philip A., *The Losing Parties: Out-Party National Committees, 1956–1993* (New Haven, CT: Yale University Press, 1994).

Kondracke, Morton and Barnes, Fred, *Jack Kemp: The Bleeding Heart Conservative Who Changed America* (New York: Sentinel, 2015).

Koopman, Donald L., *Hostile Takeover: The House Republican party, 1980–1995* (Lanham, MD: Rowman & Littlefield, 1996).

Kornacki, Steve, *The Red and the Blue: The 1990s and the Birth of Political Tribalism* (New York: HarperCollins, 2018).

Kotlowski, Dean J., *Nixon's Civil Rights: Politics, Principle, and Policy* (Cambridge, MA: Harvard University Press, 2001).

Laird, Melvin, ed., *Republican Papers* (Garden City, NY: Anchor Books, 1968).

Lassiter, Matthew B., *The Silent Majority: Suburban Politics in the Sunbelt South* (Princeton, NJ: Princeton University Press, 2006).

Leach, Richard H., 'The Federal Role in the War on Poverty Program', *Law and Contemporary Problems*, vol. 31, no. 1 (1966), 18–38.

Mason, Jim, *No Holding Back* (Lanham, MD: Rowman & Littlefield, 2011).

Mason, Robert, *Richard Nixon and the Quest for a New Majority* (Chapel Hill, NC: University of North Carolina Press, 2004).

Mason, Robert, *The Republican Party and American Politics from Hoover to Reagan* (New York: Cambridge University Press, 2012).

Mason, Robert and Morgan, Iwan, eds, *Seeking a New Majority: The Republican Party and American Politics, 1960–1980* (Nashville, TN: Vanderbilt University Press, 2013).

Matusow, Allen, J., *The Unraveling of America: A History of Liberalism in the 1960s* (New York: Harper & Row, 1984).

Mayer, William G., *The Changing American Mind: How and Why American Public Opinion Changed between 1960 and 1988* (Ann Arbor, MI: University of Michigan Press, 1992).

McAndrews, Lawrence J., *The Presidents and the Poor* (Lawrence, KS: University Press of Kansas, 2018).

McGirr, Lisa, *Suburban Warriors: The Origins of the New American Right* (Princeton, NJ: Princeton University Press, 2001).

McPherson, Harry, *A Political Education: A Washington Memoir* (Austin, TX: University of Texas Press, 1995).

Meeker, Martin, 'The Queerly Disadvantaged and the Making of San Francisco's War on Poverty, 1964–1967', *Pacific Historical Review*, vol. 81, no. 1 (2012), 21–59.

Melnick, R. Shep, *Between the Lines: Interpreting Welfare Rights* (Washington, DC: Brookings Institution, 1994).

Middendorf II, J. William, *A Glorious Disaster: Barry Goldwater's Presidential Campaign and the Origins of the Conservative Movement* (New York: Basic Books, 2006).

Mieczkowski, Yanek, *Gerald Ford and the Challenges of the 1970s* (Lexington, KY: University Press of Kentucky, 2005).

Mieczkowski, Yanek, 'Gerald R. Ford's Domestic Policy', in *A Companion to Gerald R. Ford and Jimmy Carter*, ed. Scott Kaufman (Chichester: Wiley Blackwell, 2015).

Mjagkij, Nina, ed. *Organizing Black America: An Encyclopaedia of African American Associations* (New York: Garland, 2001).

Moley, Raymond, *The Republican Opportunity in 1964* (New York: Duell, Sloan and Pearce, 1964)

Morgan, Iwan, *Nixon* (New York: Oxford University Press, 2002).

Morgan, Iwan, *Reagan: American Icon* (London: I. B. Tauris, 2016).

Moynihan, Daniel P., *The Politics of a Guaranteed Income: The Nixon Administration and the Family Assistance Plan* (New York: Vintage Books, 1973).

Murray, Charles, *Losing Ground: American Social Polity, 1950–1980* (New York: Basic, 1984).

Murray, Charles, 'The Two Wars against Poverty: Economic Growth and the Great Society', *Public Interest*, vol. 69 (1982), 3–17.

Nixon, Richard, *In the Arena: A Memoir of Victory, Defeat and Renewal* (New York: HarperCollins, 1990).

Norton Smith, Richard, *On His Own Terms: A Life of Nelson Rockefeller* (New York: Random House, 2014).

Osborne, Cynthia, 'LBJ's Legacy in Contemporary Social Welfare Policy: Have We Come Full Circle?', in *LBJ's Neglected Legacy: How Lyndon Johnson Reshaped Domestic Policy and Government*, ed. Robert H. Wilson, Norman J. Glickman and Laurence E. Lynn Jr (Austin, TX: University of Texas Press, 2015), 259–80.

Parmet, Herbert, *Richard Nixon and His America* (Boston, MA: Little Brown, 1990).

Patterson, James T., 'American Politics: The Bursts of Reform, 1930s–1970s', in *Paths to the Present: Interpretative Essays on American History since 1930*, ed. James T. Patterson (Minneapolis, MN: Burgess Publishing, 1975), 57–101.

Patterson, James T., *America's Struggle against Poverty, 1900–1980* (Cambridge, MA: Harvard University Press, 1994).

Patterson, James T., *Grand Expectations: The United States, 1945–1974* (New York: Oxford University Press, 1996).

Patterson, James T., *The Eve of Destruction: How 1965 Transformed America* (New York: Basic Books, 2012).

Perlstein, Rick, *Before the Storm: Barry Goldwater and the Unmaking of the American Consensus* (New York: Hill & Wang, 2001).

Perlstein, Rick, *Nixonland: The Rise of a President and the Fracturing of America* (New York: Scribner, 2008).

Perlstein, Rick, *Reaganland: America's Right Turn, 1976–1980* (New York: Simon & Schuster, 2020), 829–30.

Perlstein, Rick, *The Invisible Bridge: The Fall of Nixon and the Rise of Reagan* (New York: Simon & Schuster, 2014).

Phelps, Wesley G., 'A Grassroots War on Poverty: Community Action and Urban Politics in Houston, 1964–1976', PhD dissertation, Rice University, 2000.

Phillips, Kevin P., *The Emerging Republican Majority* (New Rochelle, NY: Arlington House, 1969).

Phillips, Kevin P. *The Politics of Rich and Poor: Wealth and the American Electorate in the Reagan Aftermath* (New York: Random House, 1990).

Phillips-Fein, Kim, *Invisible Hands: The Making of the Conservative Movement from the New Deal to Reagan* (New York: Norton, 2009).

Piffner, James P., 'The Paradox of President Reagan's Leadership', *Presidential Studies Quarterly*, vol. 43, no. 1 (2013), 81–100.

Piven, Frances Fox and Cloward, Richard A., 'The Politics of the Great Society', in *The Great Society and the High Tide of Liberalism*, ed. Sidney M. Milkis and Jerome M. Mileur (Amherst, MA: University of Massachusetts Press, 2005), 253–69.

Quadagno, Jill, *The Color of Welfare: How Racism Undermined the War on Poverty* (New York: Oxford University Press, 1994).

Rae, Nicol, *The Decline and Fall of the Liberal Republicans: From 1952 to the Present* (New York: Oxford University Press, 1989).

Reagan, Ronald W., *The Reagan Diaries*, ed. Douglas Brinkley (New York: HarperCollins, 2007).

Reedy, George, *The Twilight of the Presidency: From Johnson to Reagan* (New York: First Mentor, 1987).

Reichley, A. James, *Conservatives in an Age of Change: The Nixon and Ford Administrations* (Washington, DC: Brookings Institution, 1981).

Reinhard, David W., *The Republican Right since 1945* (Lexington, KY: University Press of Kentucky, 1983).

Richardson, Heather Cox, *To Make Men Free: A History of the Republican Party* (New York: Basic Books, 2014).

Rigueur, Leah Wright, *The Loneliness of the Black Republican: Pragmatic Politics and the Pursuit of Power* (Princeton, NJ: Princeton University Press, 2014).

Roper, Kem, 'From the "War on Poverty" to Reagan's "New Right," What's in a Name? The Symbolic Significance of the "Welfare Queen" in Politics and Public Discourse', PhD dissertation, University of Louisville, 2012.

Rose, Elizabeth, 'Head Start: Growing Beyond the War on Poverty', *LBJ's Neglected Legacy: How Lyndon Johnson Reshaped Domestic Policy and Government*, ed. Robert H. Wilson, Norman J. Glickman, Laurence E. Lynn Jr (Austin, TX: University of Texas Press, 2015), 153–86.

Rose, Harriett DeAnn, 'Dallas, Poverty, and Race: Community Action Programs in the War on Poverty', PhD dissertation, University of North Texas, 2008.

Rumsfeld, Donald, *Known and Unknown: A Memoir* (New York: Sentinel, 2011).

Samples, John, *The Struggle to Limit Government: A Modern Political History* (Washington, DC: Cato Institute, 2010).

Scammon, Richard M., and Wattenberg, Ben J., *The Real Majority* (New York: Coward-McCann Inc., 1970).

Schapsmeier, Edward L. and Schapsmeier, Frederick H., 'Serving under Seven Presidents: Les Arends and His Forty Years in Congress', *Illinois Historical Journal*, vol. 85, no. 2 (Summer 1992), 105–18.

Schmitt, Edward R., 'The War on Poverty', in *A Companion to Lyndon B. Johnson*, ed. Mitchell B. Lerner (Malden, MA: Wiley Blackwell, 2012), 93–110.

Scott, Hugh D., *Come to the Party* (Englewood Cliffs, NJ: Prentice Hall, 1968).

Shafer, Byron E. and Claggett, William J. M., *The Two Majorities: The Issue Context of Modern American Politics* (Baltimore, MD: Johns Hopkins University Press, 1995).

Shesol, Jeff, *Mutual Contempt: Lyndon Johnson, Robert Kennedy, and the Feud That Defined a Decade* (New York: Norton, 1998).

Small, Melvin, 'The Election of 1968', in *A Companion to Richard M. Nixon*, ed. Melvin Small (Malden, MA: Wiley Blackwell, 2011), 143–63.

Smith, Mark A., *The Right Talk: How Conservatives Transformed the Great Society into the Economic Society* (Princeton, NJ: Princeton University Press, 2007).

Spitzer, Scott J., 'Nixon's New Deal: Welfare Reform for the Silent Majority', *Presidential Studies Quarterly*, vol. 42, no. 3 (2012), 455–81.

Stahl, Jason, *Right Moves: The Conservative Think Tank in American Political Culture since 1945* (Chapel Hill, NC: University of North Carolina Press, 2016).

Stanley, Timothy J., 'Carter's Domestic Dilemmas, 1977–1978', in *A Companion to Gerald R. Ford and Jimmy Carter*, ed. Scott Kaufmann (Chichester: Wiley Blackwell, 2015), 335–49.

Stern, Mark, *Calculating Visions: Kennedy, Johnson, and Civil Rights* (New Brunswick, NJ: Rutgers University Press, 1992).

Stockman, David A., *The Triumph of Politics: Why the Reagan Revolution Failed* (New York: Harper & Row, 1986).

Sugrue, Thomas J., *The Origins of the Urban Crisis: Race and Inequality in Postwar Detroit* (Princeton, NJ: Princeton University Press, 1996).

Sundquist, James L., *Politics and Policy: The Eisenhower, Kennedy, and Johnson Years* (Washington, DC: Brookings Institution, 1968).

Thomas, Evan, *Being Nixon: A Man Divided* (New York: Random House, 2015).

Thurber, Timothy, 'Goldwaterism Triumphant? Race and the Republican Party, 1965–1968', *Journal of the Historical Society*, 7 (2007), 349–84.

Thurber, Timothy, *Republicans and Race: The GOP's Frayed Relationship with African Americans, 1945–1974* (Lawrence, KS: University Press of Kansas, 2013).

Tower, John G., *Consequences: A Personal and Political Memoir* (New York: Little, Brown, 1991).

Troy, Gil, *Morning in America: How Ronald Reagan Invented the 1980s* (Princeton, NJ: Princeton University Press, 2007).

Turner, Julius, *Party and Constituency: Pressures on Congress*, rev. Edward V. Schneier Jr (Baltimore, MA: Johns Hopkins University Press, 1970).

Updegrove, Mark K., *Indomitable Will: LBJ in the Presidency* (New York: Crown Publishers, 2012).

Various, *Seeking a New Majority: The Republican Party and American Politics, 1960–1980*, ed. Robert Mason and Iwan Morgan (Nashville, TN: Vanderbilt University Press, 2013).

Various, *The Election of 1980: Reports and Interpretations*, ed. Marlene Pomper (Chatham, NJ: Chatham House, 1981).

Ventry, Dennis J., 'The Collision of Tax and Welfare Politics: The Political History of the Earned Income Tax Credit, 1969–99', *National Tax Journal*, vol. 53, no. 4 (2000), 983–1026.

Von Bothmer, Bernard, *Framing the Sixties: The Use and Abuse of a Decade from Ronald Reagan to George W. Bush* (Amherst, MA: University of Massachusetts Press, 2010).

Wallison, Peter J., *Ronald Reagan: The Power of Conviction and the Success of His Presidency* (Boulder, CO: Westview Press, 2003).

Ward, John L., *The Arkansas Rockefeller* (Baton Rouge, LA: Louisiana State University Press, 1978).

Watson, Marvin W., *Chief of Staff: Lyndon Johnson and His Presidency* (New York: Thomas Dunne Books, 2004).

Weidenbaum, Murray, *Rendezvous with Reality: The American Economy after Reagan* (New York: Basic Books, 1988).

Weisbrod, Burton A., *The Economics of Poverty* (Englewood Cliffs, NJ: Prentice-Hall, 1965).

Weisman, Steven R., *Daniel Patrick Moynihan: A Portrait in Letters of an American Visionary* (New York: Perseus, 2010).

White, Theodore, *The Making of the President, 1968* (New York: Atheneum Books, 1969).

Williams, Daniel K., *God's Own Party: The Making of the Christian Right* (New York: Oxford University Press, 2010).

Wills, Garry, *Nixon Agonistes: The Crisis of the Self-made Man* (Boston, MA: Mariner, 2002).

Wilson, James Q., 'American Politics, Then and Now', *Commentary*, vol. 62, no. 2 (1979), 39–46.

Witcover, Jules, *Marathon: The Pursuit of the Presidency, 1972–1976* (New York: Viking Press, 1977).

Witcover, Jules, *The Resurrection of Richard Nixon* (New York: G. P. Putnam's Sons, 1970).

Woodsworth, Michael, 'The Forgotten Fight: Waging War on Poverty in New York City', PhD dissertation, Columbia University, 2013.

Zelizer, Julian E., *On Capitol Hill: The Struggle to Reform Congress and Its Consequences, 1948–2000* (New York: Cambridge University Press, 2004).

Zelizer, Julian E., *The Fierce Urgency of Now: Lyndon Johnson, Congress and the Battle for the Great Society* (New York: Penguin, 2015).

Index

Finney, John, 150
Fino, Paul, 67–8, 102, 104, 107,
    125, 139, 160
Flamm, Michael, 41–3, 153
Fleeson, Doris, 136
Follow Through, 177
food stamps, 179, 211, 222,
    270
Ford, Gerald R.
  1966 campaign and, 76, 79,
    81–3, 104
  1968 campaign and, 155, 160
  1974 campaign and, 233
  1976 campaign and, 245, 254
  1980 campaign and, 258
  and 'law and order', 114
  and Family Assistance Plan,
    184, 190, 192
  and Great Society, 76, 94
  and Model Cities, 106–7
  and race, 79
  and rent supplements, 101, 104
  and urban crisis, 97, 106–7,
    112, 115–16
  as House Minority Leader,
    56–7, 59, 101, 104, 106–7,
    109–16, 173, 184, 187,
    192, 211
  as Republican Party leader, 258
  on conservative coalition,
    115–16
  on inflation, 81–3
  presidency of, 231–7
  relationship with Nixon
    White House, 173, 187, 211,
    228, 233
  War on Poverty and, 28, 76,
    81–3, 101, 106–7, 112,
    115–16, 208, 231–7

Foster Grandparents, 175, 271
Fraser, Donald, 107
Freedom Budget, 110, 118
Frelinghuysen, Peter, 24–5,
    34, 59
Friedersdorf, Max, 268

Gallup, 55, 72, 114, 136,
    146, 170
Gender Gap, 282
Gilder, George, 250, 269
Gilens, Martin, 272
Gilette, Howard, 146
Gingrich, Newt, 253,
    288
Goldman, Eric, 45
Goldwater, Barry
  1964 campaign and, 14–15,
    23, 38–46, 154
  1964 campaign and, 36
  and conservatives, 22
  and extremism, 15, 38, 40
  and Family Assistance Plan,
    212
  and health care, 40
  and 'law and order', 42
  and race, 30–2
  and Southern support, 98
  and War on Poverty, 13, 23,
    25–6, 28, 38–40
  impact on Republican Party
    of, 30–2, 43, 55, 76, 86, 98,
    114, 243, 249
  legacy of, 147
  Republican opposition to, 24
Goodell, Charles, 34, 56–7,
    59, 61–6, 69, 86, 139, 153,
    158, 191
Graham, Billy, 179

EU representative:
Easy Access System Europe
Mustamäe tee 50, 10621 Tallinn, Estonia
Gpsr.requests@easproject.com

www.ingramcontent.com/pod-product-compliance
Lightning Source LLC
Chambersburg PA
CBHW050628280326
41932CB00015B/2562